Pagans and Philosophers

CW01082056

Pagans and Philosophers

THE PROBLEM OF PAGANISM FROM
AUGUSTINE TO LEIBNIZ

John Marenbon

PRINCETON UNIVERSITY PRESS

Princeton and Oxford

Copyright © 2015 by Princeton University Press
Published by Princeton University Press, 41 William Street, Princeton, New Jersey 08540
In the United Kingdom: Princeton University Press, 6 Oxford Street, Woodstock, Oxfordshire
OX20 1TR

press.princeton.edu

All Rights Reserved

First paperback printing, 2017

Paper ISBN: 978-0-691-17608-6

The Library of Congress has cataloged the cloth edition as follows:

Marenbon, John.
Pagans and philosophers : the problem of paganism from Augustine to Leibniz /
John Marenbon.
      pages   cm
Includes bibliographical references and index.
ISBN 978–0-691–14255–5 (hardcover : alk. paper) 1. Paganism—History. 2. Philosophy—
History. 3. Philosophy and religion. I. Title.
BL432.M37 2015
261.2'2—dc23
        2014011053

British Library Cataloging-in-Publication Data is available

This book has been composed in Sabon

Printed on acid-free paper. ∞

Printed in the United States of America

To the Memory of Jeremy Maule

Contents

Preface

THERE IS A STORY BEHIND MY DEDICATION, AND IT TELLS A GREAT DEAL not only of how this book came to be written, but also about its goals. Jeremy Maule, who died fifteen years ago in his mid-forties, was my colleague when my job was to teach English literature to undergraduates at Trinity College. Although the actual writing of this book was almost all done in the past year or so, its origins go back to that time. 'Paganism' had been chosen as an optional set topic for the Medieval English Paper. Since much of my own work was on Boethius and Abelard, the subject fascinated me. But my job was to give not lectures but individual supervisions to Trinity undergraduates: I encouraged them to choose 'Paganism', but when they came to talk about their essays, there was so much background for me to supply that the sessions turned into a monologue. I looked to see if there was any general book on the area, and there was none. So I wrote to the English Faculty, suggesting I might give a set of lectures on the topic, since none was planned. But my offer was indignantly refused. It was at this point that Jeremy, who was responsible for organizing the teaching at Trinity, stepped in, with the suggestion that I should teach about paganism in the form of college lectures—a form of Cambridge teaching unheard of for decades. I gave them for two years, and then the faculty relented and invited me to make the lectures part of its teaching, until the special topic was changed.

Over the years my views on almost every text discussed have changed, and the range of material I covered in those lectures is only a small part of what I consider in this book. Yet they have shaped its content and aims in three ways. First, by being asked to think about the topic of (simply) Paganism in medieval writing, I quickly saw that there was an important theme of which recognized topics such as pagan virtues and the salvation of pagans are just the disparate parts: I realized that there was a Problem of Paganism, even before I coined the name for it. Second, because the Medieval English Paper stretched up to 1550, from the start I included in my scope not just the pagans of Greece and Rome, but contemporary pagans, such as the Native Americans. Third, and perhaps most important of all, I was forced to bring together two sides of my work which I had always kept apart: my research and writing on medieval philosophy, and my teaching on medieval literature. I had always known that the philosophers and theologians helped to illuminate the poets, but I came to realize that, on a subject such as paganism, writers such as Dante, Chaucer and Langland also made a philosophical contribution in their own right. For the past ten years, I have been able to devote myself to medieval philosophy, and it is from that perspective that I have written this book. But, thanks to its origins, in writing the book I have discovered a grain in the marble that, without such serendipity, would have remained hidden: a broader conception of medieval philosophy than I could have imagined. And it is particularly fitting that such a project should go back to Jeremy's initial encouragement, since he was someone whose extraordinary knowledge, surpassed only by his boundless curiosity, was unfettered by disciplinary constraints.

I am also grateful to Zygmunt Baranski, Delphine Faivre (Carron) and Aurélien Robert for generously letting me see their work before publication, and to George Corbett, from whose writing and conversations about Dante I have learned much. I am especially grateful to Peter von Moos. Not only did he let me see and use his important study of the salvation of pagans and the edition of a treatise on the salvation of Aristotle with which it is being published; he also read the whole of my manuscript after it was submitted to the publisher and gave me very valuable critical comments, as did the two anonymous readers commissioned by the publisher. I hope that I have managed to improve the book thanks to their advice.

The Centre for Medieval Studies at the University of Toronto and the Pontifical Institute for Mediaeval Studies there arranged for me to be a visiting fellow in the autumn of 2010, and gave me the chance to deliver public lectures and organize a series of seminars on the Problem of Paganism: I am grateful to all who attended and discussed my ideas, and especially to John Magee, who made the stay possible and so enjoyable. Ian Malcolm at Princeton University Press, more recently Al Bertrand and Hannah Paul, and most recently (for the production of the book) Debbie Tegarden have all given me both every possible encouragement and support, and I have been greatly assisted by the patient work of my copy editor, Joseph Dahm. My greatest debts of all are to Trinity College, which has given me the means, place and time to write this book, and to Sheila and Maximus, who have not only put up with it and me, but even sometimes let slip that, unlike anything else I have written, my 'pagans' might actually be quite interesting.

Cambridge, 5 March 2013

A Note on References and Citations

WHERE A WORK IS VERY WIDELY KNOWN AND AVAILABLE IN MANY EDITIONS and translations, as in the case of some ancient and patristic writings, and those of Aquinas*, reference is made to the internal divisions of the text. Where appropriate, reference to other patristic works is made to Migne's *Patrologia Latina* (PL), *Patrologia Graeca* (PG) or, if available, the *Corpus Christianorum, series latina* (CCSL). Otherwise, references are made to internal divisions (where appropriate) and to particular editions, using the author-date system. Quotations from the Bible are given according to the Douai translation. Otherwise, all translations are my own.

*All of Aquinas's works in Latin are conveniently available at http://www .corpusthomisticum.org. Usually, the editions provided are the best ones, but sometimes not. This website also provides a list of the best editions of each work.

Pagans and Philosophers

Introduction

The Problem of Paganism

Readers who are puzzled by the phrase 'the Problem of Paganism' should not think that it is famous Problem that has somehow slipped through the net of their reading. It is a newly invented label, and the central contention of this book is that it serves an important purpose.[1] It picks out a set of closely connected issues about pagan virtue, knowledge of God and salvation—issues which reveal a central tension within the culture of Western Europe in the period from c. 200 to c. 1700, the 'Long Middle Ages'.[2] More often than not they are sidelined or hidden, but they are given sustained attention by a number of the most remarkable thinkers and writers of the period.

[1]I have introduced the idea of 'the Problem of Paganism' into some of my previous writings: Marenbon 2004b, 2009b, 2012a, 2012d. But there are some slight variations in how I have used the term. Since it is a term of my own devising, there are, of course, no existing studies on 'the Problem of Paganism', except for these. But individual aspects of the problem in particular authors, especially those from the sixteenth and seventeenth centuries, have been much studied and I have profited enormously from much of this work, which is cited in my footnotes. There are also some studies which cover wider areas of my ground, under various different labels. Cary Nederman's work (Nederman 2000) on medieval toleration brings together a number of the same authors. Capéran 1934 and Harent 1922 offer fine studies of one strand of the problem, the salvation of pagans. Harent's essay, though learned and detailed, has ultimately doctrinal, rather than historical aims. Capéran's treatment of the eleventh to fifteenth centuries is somewhat thin, but his 150 pages on the sixteenth and seventeenth centuries are very rich. Sullivan 2002 gives a more popularizing, but clear account; Frezza 1962 is insubstantial. Von Moos, in his introduction and commentary to a late fifteenth-century work on the salvation of Aristotle (von Moos 2013a), gives a rich and detailed discussion of various aspects of the problem, along with a general introduction. (von Moos 2013b provides a briefer account, in French, of some of the material.) Von Moos has also written suggestively on another aspect of the problem in his comments on a 'praeter-spiritual' tradition of thinking in John of Salisbury, Boethius, Abelard, Engelbert of Admont and others: see von Moos 1988b, 491–94; 2012. There have also been studies of pagan virtue. Some are linked to Middle English literature (Hahn 1974; Vitto 1989; Minnis 1982). Grady 2005 pursues a particularly interesting line of discussion, arguing that the encounter with a virtuous pagan had become a topos in late medieval English poetry and can be analysed formally. Others are linked to Dante (Colish 1996—a wide-ranging discussion; and see chapter 10 for studies more narrowly linked to Dante) and seventeenth-century French literature (Herdt 2008; Moriarty 2011— particularly valuable because of its detailed study of the theological background). Grellard (2014)—important for the theme of invincible ignorance—appeared after my book was finished.
[2]On the 'Long Middle Ages', see below, p. 5.

A POET, A HEROINE, A PHILOSOPHER AND A CANNIBAL

Four figures, who will reappear later, will help not just to explain the questions involved in the Problem of Paganism, but also this book's scope and method. The first three illustrate, in turn, the three main aspects of the problem: the salvation of pagans, pagan virtue and pagan knowledge. The first of them appears in the opening pages of the most famous of all medieval poems, Dante's *Commedia divina*, written early in the fourteenth century. The poet, lost and threatened, encounters what he quickly finds is the shade of Virgil, the ancient poet whom he reveres above all others, his *maestro*. Virgil will be his learned and understanding guide through his visit to Hell and part of Purgatory, though no further. For, as the reader quickly learns, despite his supreme eloquence, his virtue and his goodness, Virgil is himself in Hell, albeit its most comfortable corner. He is damned because he was pagan and so lacked Christian faith.

The second, Lucretia, lived at Rome in far earlier days, and she is presented in the pages of an author who looked back on Roman history at the moment when Christianity had almost, but not completely, displaced the old pagan religion. Lucretia, as every Roman knew, set an example of heroic virtue when, after being raped by king's son, she ensured that the crime would be punished and then, to preserve her honour, killed herself. In his *City of God*, however, Augustine describes her as someone led by pride into committing the crime of suicide. Her virtue, like that of other pagan heroines and heroes, turns out to be a sham.

The third is Aristotle: not, however, the solid reality of the Greek philosopher, but the image of Aristotle—what he stood for in the eyes of the thirteenth-century Arts Master, Boethius of Dacia. Boethius thought that Aristotle had a comprehensive and coherent view of the universe, and he dedicated his professional life to expounding it. But he also knew that some of these doctrines, such as the view that the universe had no beginning, were incompatible with his Christian faith. Boethius tackled this problem by trying to confine pagan, Aristotelian wisdom to its own sphere, where it could be considered in its own terms—a type of limited relativism.

The fourth figure is from the pages of Montaigne's *Essais*, first published in 1580. He is evoked in a strange and violent scene. Everyone is naked, and they are not Europeans but Native Americans. He is tied to a cord, held by members of a crowd that surrounds him, brandishing clubs and swords with which, he knows, he is about to be killed. Then they will roast him on the fire that has been prepared and eat him. He knows too that he need only beg his captors for mercy and he will be set free—but nothing is further from his mind. Rather, he has spent the weeks since he was taken prisoner taunting his captors that when they eat him, they will be eating their own ancestors and families, since he has feasted on them so many times.

At the centre of the Problem of Paganism, as the case of Dante's Virgil brings out better than perhaps any other example, is a discrepancy between the status of some pagans as moral, intellectual and cultural heroes and the fact that they were pagans. The question of salvation puts the discrepancy most sharply in focus. Why, since Dante makes it clear that Virgil was not just the greatest of poets, but also a good and wise man, is he not in Heaven? The theological doctrines that are taken by Dante to exclude him do not seem to square with God's goodness and justice. Either the doctrines must be altered or negotiated, as they often were—many medieval writers considered that people like Virgil had been saved—or it must be explained how, despite appearances, they do not make God unjust.

Augustine's treatment of Lucretia is one extreme way of handling the problem of pagan virtue, by insisting that, without Christian belief, there can be no true virtue: she is just one of a whole series of pagan heroes and heroines whose virtues are shown to be merely apparent. Some sixteenth- and seventeenth-century writers followed or even exaggerated this line of thought, but in general medieval thinkers did not accept Augustine's position, although they did follow him in distinguishing between the virtues of a Christian and those of pagans. The result was, in some cases, to mark out an area of virtuous human behaviour, to be regarded in its own terms, apart from specifically Christian virtue.

Such an attitude to pagan virtue parallels Boethius of Dacia's approach to pagan knowledge. But Boethius's limited relativism was an important, but minority strategy. Most thinkers in the Long Middle Ages refused to separate revealed and natural knowledge so sharply. Some, like Aquinas, strove to see the unity of pagan and Christian wisdom; others emphasized the mistakes and deficiencies in the views of even so wise a pagan as Aristotle. But Aristotle is the central figure in just one strand of the problem of pagan knowledge, which is problematic for the same ultimate reason as pagan virtue: because of the exclusiveness of Christian claims. Just as, at least according to some elements in Christian doctrine, only those who believe in Christ can be virtuous, so the full truth about God is that which Christianity alone teaches. There is, though, an important difference. Where with regard to virtue, especially once salvation came into question, doctrinal requirements tended to encourage a sharp division between Christians and those who were not, there was much more room to think of knowledge of the true God as coming by degrees, so that non-Christians can have a more or less partial grasp of it. This explains not only why so many thinkers avoided Boethius of Dacia's division of spheres, but also how the problem of pagan knowledge is not confined to obviously wise pagans such as Aristotle. The same underlying questions about knowledge posed about the prodigiously intelligent and cultivated, long-dead philosopher could be posed too about ordinary, unsophisticated and perhaps uneducated living pagans. How true is their conception of God, and what is the explanation, in each case, for the extent to which pagans grasp the truth and by which they fall short of it?

Thinking about such contemporary pagans forms an important strand in the Problem of Paganism, not just in the period after Columbus, but from the thirteenth century onwards (and even before then), and questions about pagan virtue and pagan salvation, as well as knowledge, are involved. Montaigne's cannibal suggests some of the special difficulties of this side of the problem, and how it links with studying the origins of anthropology and ethnography.

Although they raise different issues, the four figures have one important feature in common, which indicates the character of the discussions in this book. None of them is a real person, though none is entirely imaginary. Dante's Virgil is not Virgil, nor Augustine's Lucretia Lucretia, nor Boethius of Dacia's Aristotle Aristotle, nor Montaigne's cannibal any one of the Tupí Indians. The Problem of Paganism is a matter not of how Christians interacted with pagans, but rather of how they thought about them. Contacts with contemporary pagans, especially from the thirteenth century onwards, certainly affected how the problem was conceived and addressed, but their interest, for the present project, is in the conceptions they produced or changed, or the new questions they generated, rather than in what in fact took place.

There is another common feature of these four illustrations that is equally revealing about the following chapters—that they are indeed *illustrations*, involving figures, rather than concepts and their subdivisions, or a set of positions or arguments. Although most of this book will be occupied by looking at concepts (such as faith, natural law, virtue, reason), at the positions taken by different writers on, for instance, pagan virtue or the salvation of pagans and at the arguments made for and against them, it is not merely a matter of presentation to begin with four concrete figures. The Problem of Paganism presents itself frequently in terms of particular imagined pagans, whether they hark back to a known individual or a type, or they are purely imaginary. This is why, although this is a book about medieval *philosophy*, among the authors examined are poets, literary, imaginative writers and authors or inventors of travel stories, as well as specialist philosophers and philosopher-theologians.

Scope

The different backgrounds of the four figures point to the range of those who will be regarded in what follows as pagans: anyone, at any period, who is not a Christian, a Jew or a Muslim. This categorization is not, of course, intended as one that could be defended nowadays, when, although many would place in one group the 'Abrahamic Religions' (Judaism, Christianity and Islam), few would be happy to lump together all other faiths under the same, negative-sounding label. But it does correspond to how beliefs were classified by educated Christians in Western Europe in the Middle Ages and later. In the classification given in the thirteen century by Aquinas, 'pagans' or 'gentiles' were a distinctive subgroup of the wider class of unbelievers (*infideles*) that also included Jews and heretics.[3] It is true that the difference between pagans and Muslims was less clear cut than that between pagans and Jews or heretical Christians. Less well-informed writers and much popular opinion represented Muslims as idolaters and polytheists and grouped them along with the pagans. But the educated recognized that Islam is a monotheistic religion and tended to regard it as a type of distorted Christianity, so that the Muslims were heretics rather than pagans.[4] Paganism, as understood in this book, following the medieval example, is wider, however, than the connotations of the term today would suggest. Many pagans—including those most relevant to the Problem of Paganism—discussed by medieval writers were, though not Christians, Jews or Muslims, considered to have been or to be worshippers of a single, immaterial God.

The four figures just discussed span most but not all of the period considered in the book. After a look at the ancient background, it starts with the early Christian Greek tradition and extends to close with Leibniz, who died in the early eighteenth century. It runs therefore from c. 200 (with some glances back to the century and a half before) to c. 1700. Usually, these years are divided into four different eras: Late Antiquity, the Middle Ages, the Renaissance, the Early Modern Period. But there are arguments—and one of the most important of this book's conclusions is to strengthen them—that in the history of philosophy it is more illuminating to think of these fifteen centuries as a single period, the Long Middle Ages.[5]

---

[3] I generally translate the word *infidelis* as 'unbeliever', a word that avoids the archaism of 'infidel' and the clumsiness of 'non-faithful'. But 'unbeliever' should be taken merely as a token for the technical meaning of *infidelis* as explained here.

[4] See Daniel 1993; Gauthier 1993, 110; and Tolan 2002; and for an important exception, below pp. 109–13.

[5] For a more general justification for using the Long Middle Ages as a period in the history of philosophy, see Marenbon 2011b; 2012c, 6–7.

In order not to make the book too unwieldy, however, the material at the beginning and the end of the tradition has been treated in less detail. The Problem of Paganism was very important for those Church Fathers who lived in a culture and society that was still mostly or partly pagan. Its treatment by Greek thinkers such as Justin Martyr, Clement of Alexandria and Origen, and Latin ones such Ambrose and Jerome deserves a book to itself. But the particular form of the Problem of Paganism in the Latin tradition right up to Leibniz was set by Augustine, and so there is good reason for him to be the first thinker studied here in some depth, with only the briefest sketch of his predecessors. In the sixteenth and seventeenth centuries, the Problem of Paganism, far from dwindling (as would be expected by those who think of this period as a time when medieval categories and concerns were replaced by a new science and philosophy), became a more central intellectual preoccupation than ever before. To treat this period comprehensively would be far beyond the scope of this single volume. The strategy here has been, rather, to select some of the most significant texts and developments in the three areas of pagan knowledge, virtue and salvation, in order to show how they are part of this continuous tradition of thought about paganism, stretching back through the Middle Ages. Many important names and areas have had to be left aside.[6]

Although the Middle Ages presented here is Long, it is not, at least in an important respect, broad, since it is confined to Western European Latin and vernacular material. The Greek Christian, Islamic and Jewish traditions all have, to some extent, their own versions of the Problem of Paganism, and a comparative study could be fascinating. But, because the shape of the Problem of Paganism depends on precise theological doctrines, it would need to be reformulated for each branch (even between Greek Christian doctrine and that of the Latin world, decisively influenced by Augustine, there are sharp differences). Moreover, the problem seems to be especially rich in the Latin world, for two reasons. First, although ancient *philosophy* was transmitted to all four cultures, only the Latin and Greek traditions also inherited ancient *literature*. In Byzantium, however, such was the suspicion of 'Hellenism' (the revival of a pagan past) that the Problem of Paganism was usually suppressed, although occasionally it emerged, even in extreme form (as in the case

---

[6]For example, there is nothing on Erasmus, Gassendi, Locke, Spinoza or the so-called Cambridge Platonists, all of whom are important for the subject, nor is there an attempt to look at poets, in the way that Chaucer and Dante were examined in the previous section. Although some Protestant writers, such de Léry and Bayle, are discussed, the Catholic tradition is favoured in the treatment of the sixteenth and seventeenth centuries, because the strong influence of Augustine on many Protestant authors made it comparatively easy for them to resolve the Problem of Paganism, to their own satisfaction, in an Augustinian way.

of Gemisthos Plethon). In Western Europe, where such worries were less pervasive, one main reason why the Problem of Paganism became a special concern for some thinkers was that concerns about the theological and philosophical problems posed by paganism combined with, and were often fired by, an admiration for the classical world as presented through its literature. The list of writers in the Latin tradition who were specially engaged by the Problem of Paganism bears out the point: many of them—Augustine, Boethius, Abelard, John of Salisbury, Vincent of Beauvais, John of Wales, Dante, Boccaccio, Robert Holcot, Chaucer, Valla, Moore, Montaigne, La Mothe le Vayer—were, in their different ways, steeped in the Roman classics. Second, although Islamic travellers and explorers wrote accounts of strange peoples and their beliefs, there is nothing in the other branches to compare with the two very different Western European encounters with contemporary pagans at the end of the period studied here: with the natives of America (ranging from isolated island tribes to the people of the great Aztec and Inca Empires) and with the Chinese.

An Approach

The following chapters aim to show readers now how writers in the Long Middle Ages saw and tackled the complex of issues about pagan virtue, knowledge and salvation labelled here the Problem of Paganism. They will therefore be considering ideas, positions and arguments developed within cultural and intellectual contexts very different from today's. There are many different possible approaches. At one extreme, there is the antiquarian approach, which aims to keep as close as possible to the medieval and Early Modern texts, following their vocabulary and method of presentation, avoiding anachronism at all costs. Its practitioners are rather like explorers who, coming across the ruins of an ancient city, record every detail with minute precision and then consider that their work has been done. At the other extreme, there is the narrowly philosophical approach, which takes just whatever ideas and arguments seem, or can be re-read or adapted to be, of value within contemporary philosophical discussion. Its exponents resemble explorers who take from the ancient city's rubble whatever they can use for their own purposes. The approach taken here falls between these two extremes. It sets out to make the views and differences of medieval and Early Modern writers comprehensible to readers today by translating them into terms which people today can understand, explaining the context in which they arose, their aims and presuppositions. The explorer, in this case, would be one who, from the traces which remained, attempted to describe not only how the city looked when it stood intact and proud, but also the life which once went on within its walls.

An important part of the context which needs to be supplied is theological. The Problem of Paganism was given shape by a set of strict, though in part changing Christian doctrinal requirements. The last part of this introduction gives a sketch of their outlines, which is filled in and adjusted as necessary in the following chapters. It might seem that, by contrast, broader notions, such as religion or monotheism, need no explanation or translation, because they are still current. But such terms can be false friends, since they were understood very differently in the Long Middle Ages.

One of the most striking features of the Problem of Paganism is that, for thinkers in the Long Middle Ages, the virtuous and wise pagans they consider, especially from antiquity, are usually envisaged as being believers in the one God. Our contemporary concept of monotheism seems to provide a way to think about this aspect of their views, especially since there is a current controversy over, apparently, this very point. Until recently, the view of some ancient pagans as monotheists would have seemed a medieval anachronism, since it was generally held that even the philosophers were polytheist in religion. But this assessment has been challenged. Plenty of ancient philosophers, from pre-Socratics such as Xenophanes, Anaxagoras and Antisthenes onwards, talked of a single, supreme principle: Aristotle recognized an unmoved mover, Intellect (*nous*) engaged in thinking itself, an 'eternal, living, most good' being; whilst the Stoics, though materialists, looked to an immanent god, which organized the universe rationally.[7] Where classical scholars traditionally separated such philosophical views from their judgements about ancient Greek and Roman religion, the revisionists argue that this distinction is artificial, and add that there is also evidence for monotheistic pagan worship.[8]

Yet this contemporary controversy in fact blurs understanding of the how thinkers in the Long Middle Ages thought about pagans and God. The question of whether or not a religion is monotheistic belongs the repertoire of Comparative Religion. It arises from a scientific approach, in which different religious practices and beliefs are scrutinized for their likenesses and dissimilarities. Monotheism in this sense was a concept

---

[7] See Jaeger 1947; Liebeschuetz 1979; Gerson 1990. For Aristotle, see *Metaphysics* XII, 1072–75.

[8] See Athanassiadi and Frede 1999 for the revisionist case, for which the editors' introduction (1–20) and Frede's own essay, 'Monotheism and Pagan Philosophy in Later Antiquity', provide a manifesto. The position has been criticized: see Edwards 2004 and 2010, and Frede 2010 for some replies. For a summary of the debate, see the editors' introduction to Mitchell and Van Nuffelen 2010.

alien both to the ancient world itself and the Long Middle Ages, even to those sixteenth- and seventeenth-century writers who engaged in a serious and informed comparative study of religious beliefs.[9] They regarded themselves, not as monotheists—as holding a religious belief which belongs to a certain category, Monotheism, which might take many different forms—but as believing in and worshipping the one, true God. All evidence about beliefs and practices of worship other than their own had to be understood in the light of God's existence, and his creation and providential disposition of the universe. They did not, therefore, try to place the beliefs of pagan philosophers within a neutral scheme of classification, into which they could also fit their own religious conceptions. Rather, they asked themselves to what extent these pagans had comprehended the one, true God. For this reason, they also reacted differently from scholars today to evidence—less clear to them, but still unmistakable—that many of the ancient pagans who recognized a single supreme God also accepted and worshipped many lesser gods. In the contemporary debate, the question is whether 'monotheism' should be defined broadly enough to include such people. For writers in the Long Middle Ages, the problem was rather to explain, in a way which made sense in terms of divine justice and providence, how those who had grasped to some extent the truth about the supreme deity could still fall into the error of having false gods.

Whilst some contemporary notions which seem to be useful prove dangerous, others, which might appear quite inappropriate, turn out to be exactly what are required in making the necessary translation. The most important of all these is the idea of relativism. Relativism is usually considered a particularly modern, or even post-modern, notion, with as its earliest great epigones nineteenth-century figures such as Nietzsche. But it will emerge from the following chapters that, throughout the Long Middle Ages, there was an important tendency towards ways of thinking that are properly characterized as relativist, although almost never unqualifiedly so; on some occasions, indeed, their relativism is explicitly and reflectively discussed.

WHAT THIS BOOK IS SUPPOSED TO BE AND DO

Is this book a study in intellectual history, or does it belong to the history of theology or literature, or even that, more loosely defined, of 'mentalities'? In some ways, it is all of these and none of them. But what it seeks

[9]On the appropriateness or not for scholars today to use 'monotheism' in connection with the ancient world, see Van Nuffelen 2010 and Cerutti 2010.

to be above all, is a book about the history of *philosophy*. There are two reasons, however, why this aim might seem to be an impossible one, in view of its subject and a considerable part of its contents. First, the whole theme seems to be a theological one, since the Problem of Paganism is set up by various Christian doctrines, biblical passages and patristic authorities. Yet these elements, which are internal to Christianity, give particular form to a more general problem, from whatever religious or non-religious standpoint: how can we understand, and how should we judge beliefs and values different from our own? Although, then, the Problem of Paganism is *not* itself a living problem (even for the most resolutely old-fashioned religious believer), it is a form of a general philosophical problem which is very much alive. This kinship opens up the possibility that treatments of the Problem of Paganism can be understood philosophically: not indeed by those philosophers who are interested only in what they can use for present-day discussions, but by those who are willing to think themselves into contexts that offer them no such immediate, first-level benefits, and yet are not utterly detached from our own intellectual predicament.

The second reason for questioning this book's claim to be concerned with philosophy is that a number of the texts it discusses are not, in the main, devoted to presenting and discussing arguments. Perhaps, indeed, in a narrow sense, the history of philosophy ought to be concerned only with such writing. In a wider sense, however, the history of philosophy should accept within its purview texts which examine philosophical themes in a mixed mode, combining argument with narrative or description. The central core of the material examined in the following chapters comes from philosophical or theological works and is argumentative in the traditional philosophical manner. The less purely argumentative texts are closely related to this core, and the different types of writing are often linked by shared motifs, such as the story of Pope Gregory and Trajan, found in scholastic theological treatises, learned disquisitions, hagiography and vernacular poetry. Moreover, the Long Middle Ages are rich in writing (from Boethius's *Consolation of Philosophy* and Abelard's *Collationes* to More's *Utopia* and Montaigne's *Essays*) that combines philosophical sophistication with a literary form which requires far more of interpreters than simply to understand an argument. One of the subsidiary aims of this book is to reclaim such texts for philosophy.

Its main aim, however, is the one announced in the first paragraph: to show that the Problem of Paganism, which it introduces for the first time, is a valuable concept for understanding philosophy in the Long Middle Ages. It can show it only by doing it. If readers finish the book convinced that the very different types of material discussed, from twelve centuries and many countries, fit together to show how thinkers in a coherent period addressed a single, though many-stranded underlying problem, it will have succeeded. It does not, of course, seek to be comprehensive, since its purpose is to open up a new subject, not to complete and dispose of it. Nor will it offer any neat conclusions of the kind through which some intellectual historians like to understand the past, but rather a negative one which might, ultimately, be more instructive.

Some Theological Premises

The Problem of Paganism, as already mentioned, depends on particular, precise theological doctrines. Contrary to the popular stereotype of Christian doctrine as a fixed, authoritative body of teaching, it was constantly changing and under dispute throughout the whole Long Middle Ages, as the following chapters will make clear. But it is useful to start with a framework—a sketch of the theological issues surrounding pagan knowledge (of God), virtue and salvation which made paganism a problem.

There are four characteristics of God which few if any medieval Christians disputed. First, he is one, and nothing else is a god. Second, although he is one, he is also a Trinity of Father, Son and Holy Spirit. Third, he became incarnate in the person of the Son. Fourth, he is not simply a first, natural cause or principle, but a personal God, who acts voluntarily. Each of these features, except the first, posed problems for pagan knowledge, so that Christian writers were forced either to maintain that even apparently very wise pagans were fundamentally ignorant about God, or else to find ways of attributing to pagans beliefs which, to an observer nowadays, it seems unlikely they held. The first feature, too, *ought* to have caused problems, because it is doubtful whether many pagans believed in God exclusively in the manner of Christians (and Jews and Muslims). But writers in the Long Middle Ages were remarkably ready to discover exclusive belief in the one true God in pagans both long dead and contemporary. Many, especially before the thirteenth century, also found knowledge of the Trinity among pagan thinkers. Such knowledge, some argued, could be reached simply by reasoning (although most writers from the thirteenth century onwards rejected this view).[10] Knowledge of the Incarnation, however, could not be derived from reasoning. But it

[10] For the classic later medieval position, see, e.g., Aquinas, *Summa Theologiae* I, q. 32, a. 1. Some writers, especially those engaged in proselytizing, such as Ramon Llull, disagreed.

had been made available by the Gospel, and there was a widespread view that the Gospel had been preached to all peoples (a view shaken, but not entirely displaced, by the discoveries of new lands in the late fifteenth and sixteenth centuries). Before Christ, the Incarnation could be known only through prophecy. The Old Testament was usually read as foretelling the coming of Christ, and there were also supposed to have been ancient Roman prophecies of Christ through the Sibyls. But it was recognized that few ancients other than the Jews showed signs of knowing about Christ's future birth. Problems were also raised with regard to some other areas of knowledge about God. Many fourteenth-century theologians insisted that even the wisest pagan philosophers did not know that God acts as a voluntary contingent agent, not a necessary natural cause. Many of their predecessors and successors, however, found no such gap in pagan knowledge.

Knowledge of the true God was intimately connected to conceptions of virtue, and both knowledge and virtue to the possibility of salvation. Although Augustine's view of pagan virtue as almost an oxymoron was, as already noted, extreme, there were powerful doctrinal reasons for not simply accepting that pagans could be morally good in exactly the same way as Christians. All Christians until quite recently accepted the idea of Original Sin: that, whilst Adam was created capable of leading a morally upright life, by sinning he lessened the ability of his progeny to do so. The view advanced by Pelagius that it was still possible, unaided, to act well consistently, but just very difficult, was recognized by everyone in the Latin tradition as heretical, although many saw fallen humanity as less completely corrupt than it was held to be by Augustine and Augustinians such as Gregory of Rimini, Luther and Jansenius, and some of Pelagius's writings did in fact circulate pseudonymously and had considerable influence. To be virtuous and lead a good moral life required, therefore, God's special assistance or 'grace', and there was general agreement that God's generally gracious disposition of all things was not enough: each individual needed to receive God's grace and retain it, or else in some sense fail to live well.[11] There were various divisions of types of grace, and differing

---

[11] The theology of grace is exceedingly complicated; elements of it will be touched on in the following chapters. One important distinction which came to be made was between *gratia gratis data*, a gift of grace which could be made even to someone in a state of sin, and *gratia gratum faciens*, that which makes a person in a state of grace and so acceptable to God and to be saved if he or she dies in this state. Another was the distinction between merit in the strict sense, *de condigno*, which could be earned only by those in a state of grace, and merit *de congruo*, which according to some thinkers attached to good actions performed out of a state of grace and provided a reason for God to infuse grace and so enable the agent to merit in the strict sense. A good introduction to this area is provided by McGrath 2005.

conceptions of these divisions, but typically it was seen in relation to a Christian's life. Baptism was, in Christian times, the remedy for Original Sin and brought Christian infants into a life of grace in which, with God aiding them in this way, they might in principle avoid any serious sins. To be in a state of grace means that a person acts out of a disposition of charity, and charity was considered to be the third of a trio of supernatural, infused virtues—that is to say, virtues which are not acquired through habituation or effort, but are put into people by God. The first two of these 'theological' virtues are faith and hope: faith in God and in Christ, the Redeemer, leads to the hope of salvation and that, in turn, to a state of charity, in which a person acts from love of God. Without some sort of belief in the Incarnation, there can be no faith in the Redeemer, and so, if pagans knew nothing of the Incarnation—as it seemed was true for many of them—then the path seemed to be blocked to the morally good life, which is made possible only by the gracious help needed to overcome Original Sin.

Even from this sketch, however, there seems to be enough of a gap between the excellent grace-directed life of a Christian, and a wicked, immoral, vice-ridden existence, to suggest that there could be pagan virtue which is genuine, but falls short of Christian perfection. Many thinkers developed such a notion, but they then were faced by a much less easily soluble problem about salvation. Christian doctrine recognizes just two ultimate destinies for humans in the world to come: eternal suffering (of varying degrees) in Hell, or eternal happiness (of varying levels) in Heaven.[12] In the twelfth and thirteenth centuries, Latin thinkers fully developed the idea of Purgatory, where sinners not destined for Hell would be punished and purified, but Purgatory was no one's final destination. All theologians agreed that, at the Final Judgement, when immortal souls will be reunited with their spiritualized bodies, Purgatory will cease to exist and all humans will be among the damned or the saved. It was also accepted in Latin theology that the judgement to bliss (perhaps after purging) or to damnation made at a person's death is final and irreversible.[13]

[12] The souls of unbaptized children who die before they are old enough to sin were thought by some theologians not to receive eternal punishment, but to spend eternity in limbo (the edge of Hell), where they neither suffer nor are happy. A few writers, most notably Dante, suggested that virtuous pagans too might be in limbo or somewhere similar.

[13] The Jewish prophets, patriarchs and many other Old Testament Jews, who were destined for salvation, were usually thought not to have gone to Heaven until after the Crucifixion, and so to have waited in another limbo (the so-called *limbo patrum*). Some Greek theologians, but not the Latin tradition, thought that, on his descent to Hell, Christ preached there, giving pagans the chance to believe in him and reverse the sentence of damnation. There were apparent exceptions to the irreversibility of damnation in the Latin

If virtuous pagans, then, are not saved, they will be condemned to eternal punishment, and yet it is hard to see how such a judgement—endless punishment as the reward for those who have lived good lives—could be made by a just God.

An Augustinian, who denies that any pagans live good moral lives, does not face this dilemma. It might seem that those who accepted some form of pagan virtue in principle could also avoid it, by supposing that, although pagans could act virtuously in many ways, there are definite sins linked to paganism which justify the damnation of pagans. Many pagans were idolaters: they worshipped things other than the one God, such as natural objects or images. Idolatry was considered to be a sin, since even without revelation humans were thought able to know that God alone is to be worshipped. Moreover, *infidelitas* ('unbelief' as it will be translated here) could be positive or negative.[14] Positive unbelief is not pure ignorance of the faith, but involves the refusal to accept it. Such unbelief, unlike simple ignorance of Christ (negative unbelief), was considered sinful. In so far as the Gospel was thought to have been universally disseminated, therefore, pagans living after the time of Christ are likely to be guilty of the sin of positive unbelief.

None the less, some pagans, most notably the philosophers of ancient Greece and Rome, seemed not to be idolaters; those who lived before Christ, and not among the Jews, appeared to be genuinely ignorant about the coming Incarnation, and it was usually admitted that, in theory at least (and after 1500, by many, in fact also), that someone living after the Gospel had been preached might never have heard about it. But Christian doctrine seemed to stand in the way of allowing that any such virtuous pagans should, despite their good lives, be saved from damnation. The obstacle was not in itself lack of baptism, although this reason was often given, simplistically, to explain why non-Christians were damned.[15] Baptism was not required until it was instituted with the coming of Christ, and it was widely thought that, before then, prayers, sacrifices and, for the Jews alone, circumcision acted as remedies for Original Sin. Moreover, it was accepted from early on that there were circumstances in Christian times when someone could be considered to be baptized without a literal

---

tradition, especially the case of the soul of Trajan, freed from Heaven by Pope Gregory's prayers (discussed extensively below). But here it was said that he was never definitively sent to Hell.

[14]There is a particularly clear discussion of negative and positive unbelief in Aquinas's *Summa Theologiae* IIaIIe, q. 10, a. 1.

[15]The classic supporting biblical verse is John iii, 5: 'Unless a man be born again of water and the Holy Ghost, he cannot enter into the kingdom of God'.

baptism by water having taken place.[16] Rather, the problem was that only those in a state of grace could be saved, and to be in such a state required the supernatural virtue of charity, which in its turn required faith (as well as hope). If, then, it was accepted that there could be a virtuous pagan, such a person seemed to be condemned to damnation simply for not having heard about Christ, prophetically or through the Gospel.

---

[16] See Dublanchy 1923, col. 2238–44 for the patristic sources of this doctrine, which was formalized in the twelfth century. The Council of Trent (session 6, 13 January 1547, chapter 4; Denzinger 1976, no. 1524/796) gives a carefully balanced view of what had been widely accepted for centuries: baptism *or the wish for it* (*aut eius voto*) is necessary 'after the promulgation of the Gospel'; cf. Sesboüé 2004, 125–26.

PART I

The Problem Takes Shape

CHAPTER 1

Prelude: Before Augustine

THE TERMS OF THE PROBLEM OF PAGANISM, AS IT WOULD BE DISCUSSED in the West until the end of the seventeenth century, were set above all by two late ancient writers, Augustine and Boethius, the subjects of the two chapters following. This chapter provides a prelude. It begins by looking at the earliest Christian reaction to ancient paganism, in the New Testament texts which became points of reference in later discussions, before offering a glimpse of how the problem was addressed by Christians in the ancient world, before Augustine transformed it for the Latin tradition.

THE PROBLEM OF PAGANISM IN THE NEW TESTAMENT

Elements of the Problem of Paganism are found from very early in the Christian tradition: not in the Gospels, set in their firmly Jewish environment, but in the Acts of the Apostles and in Paul's letter to the Romans. Luke's account, in the Acts, of Paul's time in Athens has the apostle appalled by the idolatry of the inhabitants, scoffed at by Epicurean and Stoic philosophers (xvii, 18), but willing to concede a share of wisdom to the Athenians by identifying the unknown God to whom they had dedicated an altar with the true God he was preaching: 'what therefore you worship, without knowing it, that I preach to you'.[1] When Paul preached the resurrection of the dead, Luke writes (xvii, 32–34), some mocked him, some wanted to hear more, and 'certain men adhering to him, did believe', including an Areopagite (a member of the court which sat there) called Dionysius. (Sometime in the fifth century, a Christian writer heavily

---

[1] Acts xvii, 23. Here and elsewhere, biblical texts are from the Rheims-Douai translation in the Challoner revision (1749–50). This translation is close to the Vulgate Latin, the text used almost exclusively in the Latin world during most of the Long Middle Ages.

influenced by Neoplatonism supplied this Areopagite with a set of writings, which were intensively studied in the Middle Ages.)[2]

Paul's own attitude, as expressed in his letter to the Romans, was both more complex and less friendly to pagans than what Luke attributed to him:

> For the invisible things of him, from the creation of the world, are clearly seen, being understood by the things that are made; his eternal power also, and divinity: so that they are inexcusable. Because that, when they knew God, they have not glorified him as God, or given thanks; but became vain in their thoughts, and their foolish heart was darkened. For professing themselves to be wise, they became fools. And they changed the glory of the incorruptible God into the likeness of the image of a corruptible man, and of birds, and of fourfooted beasts, and of creeping things. Wherefore God gave them up to the desires of their heart, unto uncleanness, to dishonour their own bodies among themselves. Who changed the truth of God into a lie; and worshipped and served the creature rather than the Creator, who is blessed for ever. Amen. (Romans i, 20–25)

Paul regards the pagans as corrupt and idolatrous, and he wants to condemn them. But he has in mind the unspoken objection that, if they had no knowledge of the true God and his law, they could not be blamed, and so he suggests that the pagans did know God through his visible creation but did not properly glorify him and became vain and immoral. In the same vein, in the next chapter he talks of Gentiles who lack revealed law but have 'the law written in their hearts'.[3] This passage therefore, despite its hostile tone, could—and would—be used to give biblical authority to the idea that wise pagans knew the true God through his creation.[4]

Paul influenced not only views about pagans' virtue and wisdom, but also the discussion about their salvation. Indeed, it was he—and the way he would be read by Augustine—who made it a problem. Christian doctrine might well have developed in such a way that the salvation of just pagans, at least in the period before Christ, was a matter of course, had it not been for Paul's emphasis on justification by faith in Christ, and on the gratuitousness of God's choice of whom to save. As reconstructed by scholars today, Paul's concern was to lessen the importance of the Jewish Law as part of his efforts to convert non-Jews. But his repeated

---

[2] See below, p. 43.

[3] Romans ii, 14–15: 'For when the Gentiles, who have not the law, do by nature those things that are of the law; these having not the law are a law to themselves: Who shew the work of the law written in their hearts, their conscience bearing witness to them, and their thoughts between themselves accusing, or also defending one another'.

[4] See, for example, Abelard, *Theologia Christiana* I.34, II.6.

statements that we can be justified only by faith in Christ made it seem difficult or impossible to explain how anyone who did not believe in Christ—such as a virtuous pagan, even a monotheistic one—could be saved.[5] And the rhetoric of Romans ix, which proclaims God's freedom, as creator, to show mercy to one person, and harden the heart of another, to cast away a human as a potter might a vessel of clay, seemed to explain how such seeming injustice befits the divinity.

THE PROBLEM OF PAGANISM IN THE EARLY CHURCH: A SKETCH

Paul's letters date from the middle of the first century, the Acts from ten to twenty years later. When, in the early second century, converts started to include men with a philosophical and literary education, they developed a much more unambiguously positive view of the wisdom of pagan philosophers, though one which—understandably in the polemical context—was none the less designed to show its inferiority to the Christianity which they preached. Justin, who was martyred in 160, presented Christianity as the true philosophy. Basing himself on an idea which probably owed more to Jewish than Greek tradition, he explained that through the seed of the *logos* (the Word) naturally implanted in them, the pagan philosophers had gained a partial grasp of the truth; it was available fully to the Christians through the *logos* itself, Christ.[6] Justin also explained parallels between Plato and other Greek philosophers and Christian teaching by the idea, which Jewish thinkers had already proposed, that the pagan thinkers had read Moses.[7]

Clement of Alexandria (c. 150–c. 215) developed Justin's approach to pagan philosophy. Guided by the reason implanted in us, we are able, he thought, to pick out what is good in the various traditions—Platonism, Aristotelianism, Stoicism and Epicureanism.[8] This philosophy offers some, but incomplete, knowledge of the true God (VI.5), and—as Clement stresses—much of it is taken from the 'barbarians', non-Greeks, most especially the Jews (V.14; VI.3). Clement also has an ingenious way,

---

[5]The central passages are Romans iii, esp. 22–26 and Galatians iii. But readers of Paul's epistles could also find a different view in I Timothy ii, 4: 'Who will have all men to be saved, and to come to the knowledge of the truth'. For a nuanced discussion, with reference to a wide range of Pauline texts, see Dunn 1998, 371–85.

[6]See especially *Apology* II, 13.2.3–6 (Justin 2006, 363–64); cf. Munier's introduction to this edition, pp. 56–67 and Edwards 2009.

[7]*Apology* I.59; Justin 2006, 282–84. The first Jewish thinker to make this suggestion was Aristobulus, in the second century BC; Philo (d. AD 40–50) also followed this line: see Justin 2006, 245n3.

[8]*Stromata* I.7.

already adumbrated by Justin, of resolving the problem of how just pagans who lived before Christ's time could be saved. In his first epistle, Peter talks of Christ going, after his Crucifixion, to the prison (Hell) where all humans who had died until then were held and preaching to them (1 Peter iii, 19–20). On Clement's reading, this preaching in Hell gave those who died before Christian times the same chance to believe in Christ and so be saved by faith as those able to hear the Christian message in their lifetimes (VI.6). Although this idea was widely adopted by Greek thinkers, Augustine would reject it, and it never formed part of the Latin discussion.[9]

The tradition of 'apologetic' writing begun by Justin and Clement (and other writers, less friendly to classical culture, such as Athenagoras and Tatian) was continued in the third century by Tertullian, Minucius Felix, Origen and Eusebius, and by Arnobius and Lactantius in the fourth. It was directly concerned to confront paganism, whether with the philosophical learning and depth of Origen writing against the pagan Platonist Celsus, or the elegance of Minucius Felix's Platonic dialogue, or in the more embattled tones of Athenagoras and Tertullian. More generally, all the more educated and thoughtful Church Fathers, such as Basil and Gregory of Nyssa among the Greeks, Ambrose and Jerome among the Latins, had to think about the relationship between the pagan philosophy or literature they knew well and the Christian teaching they were giving. Unlike the works of Justin and Clement of Alexandria, which were not generally known until the sixteenth century (when they were often cited to counter Augustine's severe views on pagan virtue and salvation), much of this other material was widely read in the Middle Ages. But even widely read and highly respected Latin Fathers, such as Ambrose and Jerome, had little voice once the distinctive form of the Problem of Paganism was formulated by Augustine and, though much less obviously, moulded by the influence of Boethius.

[9] See Trumbower 2001.

CHAPTER 2

Augustine

ON 24 AUGUST 410, THE GOTHIC LEADER ALARIC AND HIS ARMY ENTERED Rome and sacked it. Palaces were looted and burned, prisoners taken, women raped, bodies left to rot in the streets.[1] Although the Goths withdrew after just three days, the fall of the Eternal City shocked educated Romans throughout the empire.

Why had such a disaster taken place? The discussion centred on the place of Christianity and the abandonment of the policy of toleration towards paganism, culminating in the Emperor Theodosius's ban on pagan cults in 391 and his order for the destruction of the great temple of Serapis in Alexandria. This focus may seem surprising, since the Goths who ransacked Rome were Christians, though adherents of what the Catholic Church regarded as the Arian heresy, which denied the divinity of Christ. But it was argued by the few remaining pagans that the Goths had been able to enter Rome because the public worship of the gods had been abandoned, and so the city no longer enjoyed their protection.

By this time most Romans were Christians, including the members of the senatorial aristocracy who had once been the guardians of paganism. Yet their Christianity was often superficial.[2] Worried that their weak faith would be challenged by the pagan argument, Augustine set out to reply to it, and in doing so produced his most ambitious work, a Christian rethinking, not just of the history of Rome, but of the relationship between God and the course of human history. Written in the safety of North Africa (where, however, the influx of refugees kept the events in Italy vividly present), the *City of God* (CG), begun probably in 412 but not finished until about fourteen years later, is not merely an intellectual masterpiece; it is a foundational book for the Problem of Paganism.[3]

---

[1] For the sack and the events leading up to it, see Demougeot 1951, 376–485; Courcelle 1964, 50–56; Matthews 1975, 284–91; Heather 1991, 208–18.

[2] Earlier scholars represented the senatorial aristocracy as a stronghold of paganism. Cameron (2011) has argued impressively against this view, and against the persistence of paganism up until this time, but he accepts (2011, 689) that there were still some pagans who blamed the ban on pagan sacrifice for the sack of Rome, and concludes (2011, 793) that the *City of God* was written for an audience of 'Christians, many of them recent converts . . . whose motives and sincerity alike were suspect'.

[3] On the dating, see O'Daly 1999, 34–35.

Although the problem has somewhat different contours for him from those it would take on in the Middle Ages, from the time of Abelard onwards, when pagan antiquity was no longer even a moribund reality, in the *City of God* and other works Augustine looks closely at three of the main strands of the problem—wisdom, salvation and virtue—and takes positions which set the agenda for almost all subsequent discussion.

The vicissitudes of Augustine's own life had put him in the position to play this foundational role. Son of (probably) a pagan father and a Christian mother, his education as a rhetorician instilled in him the values of classical Roman civilization, but he shared a widespread discontent with them. In his *Confessions* (397–401), he tells of his long search for a set of firm beliefs. For a time, he became a follower of Manichaeism, a dualist religion which he may have regarded as a type of Christianity. Then he transferred his intellectual allegiance to Platonism, before finally, in his early thirties (386), in an experience of conversion which he presents as both miraculous and transformational, he committed himself fully to Christianity, the religion he had known from birth, and gave up his secular ambitions.[4] None of the writings from before his conversion survives, but chronological study of his works shows that, in a sense, the process of Christianization continued. At first, Augustine wrote in a manner close to that of a philosopher in the Platonic mould, but he came to take on specifically Christian subjects and sources, especially the Bible. By the time he came to write the *City of God*, in the last two decades of his life, he seems to look out from the stronghold of Christian teaching to the pagan culture which had formed him as something alien, but his own intellectual and spiritual journey never ceases to complicate this perspective.

PAGAN WISDOM

Augustine's response to the pagans' arguments about the fall of Rome led him to rewrite Roman history.[5] He shows with a wealth of historical evidence that the pagan gods were never the protectors of Rome their upholders claimed. The story of Rome is one of disasters and bloodshed, which the public worship of the gods did nothing to prevent (II.3; III). The only difference between the most recent calamity, the Gothic sack of Rome, and those of the past tells in favour of Christianity: the Goths respected the churches as places of sanctuary, in a way which no invader

---

[4] For the problems in assessing this conversion, see below, pp. 26–27.

[5] On Augustine's judgement of Roman history and culture, see Maier 1955, 84–116, 195–98. For the overall structure and themes of the *City of God*, see Guy 1961 and Madec 1994, 189–213.

had treated pagan temples (I.1–2). On a second level, Augustine argues that it is wrong to think that God acts simply by rewarding those he has chosen, let alone some particular nation or empire, with worldly prosperity. Nations and empires flourish and decline as God wills, but often God's design is inscrutable. God may, indeed, repay good behaviour with success, as he did in the case of the Rome of Cato, where a few men, at least, showed high moral qualities in their devotion to public life (V.12, 15). But he sends affliction equally to the good and wicked, partly to emphasize that it is in the hereafter that reward and punishment will be given, partly because even good people are too attached to worldly things, and partly because the same adversities will be used differently by the wicked, whom they punish, and the good, whom they chasten and improve (I.8–10). Augustine rejects, then, any historiography that sees the Roman Empire in either pagan or Christian triumphal terms. It had been tempting for Augustine's Christian predecessors, who witnessed the empire convert more and more fully to Christianity, to discern in its flourishing the workings of God's plan. For Augustine, too, divine providence controls the Roman Empire, but not in any easily discernible way. Yet he does not believe that God's providence is hidden. On a third level, Augustine answers the pagans by replacing a secular (though sometimes Christianized) historiography with a theology of history. The first ten books of the *City of God* discuss Rome, its gods and its history. The final twelve trace out the plan of sacred history, from the creation to the last judgement. The City of God—not a physical city but the community of those who are, or will be, in Heaven—has a clear history and future. They are set out, not in the books of Roman history, but in the Bible. The past which Christians should make their own is not that of Roman triumph and Roman virtue—which, in any case, are illusory—but that of the Old Testament and its fulfilment in Christ.

Given this outlook, it might be expected that Augustine would think that pagans, even the philosophers, were merely victims and purveyors of false beliefs, not sources of knowledge. He did indeed dismiss the claims of any sort of polytheism, even Varro's sophisticated presentation of it, to be taken seriously. But his approach to the dominant pagan philosophical school was very different: personally engaged, nuanced and, though with qualifications, highly appreciative.

During the first two centuries of Christianity, the leading school of philosophy in the Roman Empire had been Stoicism. Its adherents might, in some sense, be considered worshippers of one God, and there was room for some of the earliest Christian thinkers to see Greek philosophy as a preparation for their own doctrine. But the type of philosophy which became dominant from the third century onwards had a relationship with Christianity at once closer and yet far more conflicted.

Plotinus (c. 204–70) presented himself as an interpreter of Plato's philosophy, but the ideas he advanced, often labelled 'Neoplatonism', owed much also to Aristotle, earlier followers of Plato and Plotinus's own philosophical genius. Like Plato, Plotinus believed that the world we perceive with our senses must be explained by what we can grasp only with our intellects. He distinguished three levels of explanation: the One, because the ultimate source of things must be entirely unitary; then Intellect, in which he places Plato's Ideas; and finally Soul, which accounts for movement and life in the universe. These three levels of explanation are not, however, constructs, but hierarchically ordered realities—indeed, they are alone what is truly real. There is (and was always for Christian readers) a temptation to see in these so-called hypostases Plotinus's God, which thereby turns out to be, not merely immaterial and ineffable, but also triune. Yet many interpreters would say that there is nothing in Plotinus's universe very similar to God in the Christian sense. Moreover, unlike Plotinus himself, his followers, Porphyry (c. 232–c. 305) and Iamblichus (c. 240–c. 325), considered pagan religious practices indispensable for the philosopher's intellectual ascent, and they linked Platonism with defence of the classical gods and opposition to Christianity.

Despite its congenial elements, the Platonism of Plotinus and Porphyry would, therefore, have presented much which a Christian of Augustine's time would have found rebarbative. Yet Augustine's overall view of Platonism was surprisingly generous.[6] Although their grasp of the truth was deficient and linked to the wrong attitude, Augustine believed that, so far as they went, the best of the Platonists were right in their beliefs about God. He could hold this view because he tended to exaggerate their belief in strictly one God, who fulfils much the same role as the Christian God.

One reason for this unexpectedly high estimate of the Platonists' knowledge is provided by an aspect of his biography already mentioned. He had first read the 'books of the Platonists'—thought to be translations of texts by Plotinus and Porphyry—in 386, when he was a professor of rhetoric in Milan, the imperial capital.[7] According to the *Confessions*, these books taught him what, until then, he had not understood about God: that he is entirely incorporeal, eternal and good, and that evil is not

---

[6] On Augustine and Platonism, see especially Dörrie 1971; Madec 1962, 1981 and 1994, 51–69; O'Connell 1984; O'Meara 1959; along with the response by Hadot 1960. Both Dörrie and Madec consider Augustine's attitude to Platonism somewhat less complex than it is here argued to be: for Madec Augustine's Platonism is, even from the beginning, firmly rooted in a visceral attachment to Christianity; for Dörrie it is a stance, adopted to encourage educated pagans to convert.

[7] There has been much controversy about the identity of the 'books of the Platonists', well summarized by O'Donnell in Augustine 1992, II, 421–24; and see Courcelle 1968 157–59.

an existing thing at all (VII.x.16–xvii.23). In this way, Augustine explains, his reading of the pagan Platonists played an important part in bringing about his conversion. Historians have not fully agreed on the accuracy of Augustine's retrospective account, or how exactly to interpret it. Was Augustine far more than nominally a Christian at the time he read the Platonists' books, and was he also influenced by a Christian Platonism, through the preaching of Ambrose, Bishop of Milan? Or, by contrast, was his attachment to pagan Platonism longer and closer than he reveals as an autobiographer?[8] Whatever the answer, it seems clear that Augustine read the Platonic texts he encountered as talking about one God, even though by his time Platonism was strongly associated with polytheistic worship, and in Porphyry, if not Plotinus, there was much which, at least ostensibly, favoured polytheism. Augustine was aware of the polytheistic elements in the books of the Platonists, the 'idols of the Egyptians', but he was not misled by them and he was able, like the Israelites stealing Pharaoh's gold, to take from them just the truths which they had put to wrong use.[9] He might easily have decided that all pagan Platonism was itself inextricably tied to polytheism, but he seems, rather, to have concluded that there was strictly monotheistic, proto-Christian gold to be found in the pagan writings, hidden but not essentially corrupted.

This central idea shapes two of the three main themes which, from his earliest comments on Platonism, in the works written immediately after his conversion, to his latest, remain constant. First, Augustine holds that there is a body of important truths about God, valuable for Christians, which is taught by the Platonists. Second, he considers that the best Platonists did not seriously and consistently believe in the polytheism they apparently indulged. But there is also a third theme, in a different key: the Platonists' lack of humility.

The first theme is very obvious. For instance, in *Against the Academics* (387) Augustine is willing (at least as an interim measure, pending further enquiry) to accept so far as 'human wisdom' is concerned, what the Platonists hold, as 'not going against our [i.e., Christian] sacred doctrines'.[10] A few years later, writing *On True Religion* (389–91), Augustine (III.3) portrays Plato's central teaching as a call to abandon a life of sensory pleasures and to learn how to contemplate God's eternity and thereby merit eternal life. He accepts this teaching. If, he goes on (III.7), Plato and his followers were to come to life again, 'they would make a few

[8] For a summary of the controversy (with bibliography), see Madec 1994, 51–69. More recently, Dobell (2009) has re-examined the question and produced serious arguments to show that the intellectual journey from Platonism to a full understanding of the Incarnation went on for years after Augustine's spiritual and moral conversion.
[9] *Confessions* II.ix.15.
[10] *Against the Academics* XX.43.

adjustments to their language and doctrines and become Christians, as many Platonists of recent times have done'. In the *Confessions*, Augustine brings out even more strikingly than before the extent to which the teachings of Plato and his followers coincide with Christianity by (VII. ix.13–14) quoting the opening of the Gospel of John, which tells how God made all things in the Word, and saying that he read this in the 'books of the Platonists'—'not indeed in these words, but entirely the same thing is put forward there with a multitude of arguments'.

In the *City of God*, after declaring that 'no other philosophers are nearer to us' than Plato and his followers, Augustine goes on (VIII.6–8) to show how their teaching about God was right in each main part of philosophy—physics, logic and ethics. There is no difference, he says later (X.1), between us and the Platonists about God as the source of all happiness, for angels as well as human beings. The closeness between Plato and Christian doctrine is so great that it makes it plausible to Augustine that Plato should have known something of the Old Testament, even though direct contact with a translation did not seem to him chronologically possible (VIII.11). He also argues (X.23) that Porphyry's understanding of the hypostases suggests that, unlike the other Platonists, he knew not just of the first and second persons of the Trinity, but also of the Holy Spirit, and that Porphyry had an idea of grace (X.29). And, near the end of the *City of God* (XXII.27), he suggests that, by putting together what Plato and Porphyry said, the truth about the final resurrection could be reached.

The second theme is stated clearly, though briefly, in *On True Religion*, where (III.2) Augustine admits that the philosophers went along with polytheism, but suggests that they did not really believe in it. Writing against Faustus, the Manichee (397–98), Augustine suggests that some of the pagan philosophers did not share the people's worship of idols and demons but did not dare to try to stop it (XIII.15). In the sermon *Against the Pagans*, the theme emerges through the figure of Pythagoras, who did *not* call on the pagan gods to help him in his intellectual quest (§36).

In the *City of God*, the theme is developed especially in discussing Porphyry. Porphyry might seem an unlikely subject for it, since he was well known for his polytheism and, indeed, for his virulent anti-Christianity. But Porphyry did certainly have reservations about theurgy and, unlike later Platonists, believed that it helped the soul only in the lower stages of its intellectual quest. Such hesitations about the links between pagan worship and philosophy are able to provide the basis for wider doubts about Porphyry's commitment to polytheism, because the conflict between Platonists and Christians in this area is a different and subtler one than the modern reader might expect. Augustine does not think that the pagan gods and lesser gods or daemons are simply figments of the imagination. He accepts that they are real. Sometimes, he thinks, what the pagans are referring to—when it is clear that the beings in question are good—are angels (IX.23). For the most part, though, they are referring to beings which, although the pagans may not be aware of it, are evil demons, intent on corrupting humans; Augustine identifies them with the angels who fell with Lucifer.[11] The pagan Platonists do not err, then, by thinking that what they call gods and demons exist. Their mistake, as Augustine repeatedly explains through the length of books IX and X, is to think that they these beings can act as mediators between man and God if they are worshipped; an error particularly obvious in the practice of theurgy. Such worship is wrongly directed if the beings in question are really angels, because the angels desire all worship to be given to God alone (X.7); and it is even worse directed, when the beings worshipped are evil demons. There is much in Porphyry's work, Augustine recognizes, which seems to mark him as a demon worshipper and theurgist. But did Porphyry really think that the demons were intermediaries? And did he in fact favour theurgy?

Augustine quickly raises the doubt: 'Porphyry promises a sort of quasi-purification of the soul through theurgy, but hesitantly and speaking as if he were ashamed of what he is saying. But he denies that this practice enables anyone to return to God. So you can see him shifting, from one remark to another, between wicked, over-inquisitive sacrilegiousness and the teachings of philosophy' (X.9). Augustine makes particular use of a letter to an Egyptian priest, Anebo, where Porphyry does take a rather hostile view of theurgy and considers whether the demons are not evil and deceitful. Here his fault was to have been too tentative—'it was hard', Augustine remarks sarcastically (X.11), 'for so great a philosopher to acknowledge the existence of the whole demonic fellowship and openly attack it. But any Christian old lady immediately recognizes and detests it'. Where in this letter Porphyry appears to enquire about various Egyptian religious practices, Augustine suggests that perhaps he has adopted the stance of a someone who wants to learn in order to undermine his correspondent's views and lead him away from them (X.11). Elsewhere (X.26) Augustine describes the theurgists as friends of whom Porphyry is ashamed, and as people he is unwilling to offend. Porphyry hands over to them the vast mass of people who are unable to follows the rigours of Platonic philosophy but, Augustine suggests, he has no use for them himself (X.27). Porphyry is presented, then, as prevaricating and uncaring about the multitude, but not a polytheist. As for Plato himself (who receives much less direct attention than Porphyry), his insistence that the gods are all good and that the representations of them in Greek

[11] *Letter* 102.18; cf. Mandouze 1958, 213.

poetry are lies makes him an ally of Augustine's in his attacks on demon worship (VIII.13–14, 18, 21). If the identification made by Augustine (though not in connection with Plato himself) between good gods and angels is applied, then Plato emerges as a strict and unhesitant believer in the one God.

How is this attitude to Plato and Porphyry to be reconciled with the fact that Augustine's favourite text when discussing pagan thinkers is Paul's comment on natural theology in his letter to the Romans (i, 20–25), discussed above—words he turns to remorselessly, quoting them, alluding to them, commenting on them?[12] According to Paul, the Gentiles who discovered God turned away from him because of pride and became polytheist idolaters. Paul's letter provides conveniently for the case of the sophisticated pagans, for whom the gods stood for parts of the world, since it mentions, not just straightforward polytheists, but also those who worship 'the creature rather than the creator'. Nothing in Paul's comment, however, fits those philosophers who, for Augustine, seem to have been believers in the one God. Usually, Augustine deals with this potential contradiction by using Paul's comment to describe the behaviour of pagan thinkers in general, without linking it specifically to those he would hesitate to call polytheists. Sometimes, in *The City of God*, a reminiscence of Paul's words is linked to a qualification, which makes it clear that some of the philosophers, although not open opponents of polytheism, did not themselves worship more than one God.[13] In the sermon *Against the Pagans* (§36), Augustine tackles the problem more directly.[14] Pythagoras and those like him, who do not seek help in purifying their souls from the pagan gods or from anything else, but rely on philosophy alone, must be considered, says Augustine, among those who, in Paul's words, 'turned God's truth into a lie'—a phrase usually applied to out and out idol worshippers. For such philosophers' confidence in their own powers is pride: 'whoever presumes on himself, presumes on human beings', and every human, Augustine says, is a liar. Even, then, those philosophers who rejected pagan gods and recognized the true God have erred, not by choosing the wrong sort of mediation, but by rejecting all mediation, even the true mediator, through pride.

This is the third of Augustine's themes.[15] It occurs almost whenever he discusses pagan philosophy. Humans, Augustine believes, cannot reach God without a mediator, and that mediation was provided by the Incarnation. It is not enough, then, that the philosophers knew of the Son as

[12] See Madec 1962. Madec does not notice the way in which Augustine differs from Paul over the pagans' polytheism.
[13] X.3; cf. X.1.
[14] See also *On the Trinity* IV.15.20.
[15] Attention is drawn to it by Madec 1962; 1994, 51–69 and Rémy 1979, esp. I, 136–50.

God. They needed, but refused to accept his Incarnation. Augustine links their refusal directly to their pride—either their excessive confidence in their own powers, or, more commonly, a rejection of the humility needed in order to accept the apparent debasement of God implied by his death on the cross. 'They did not wish to hold to Christ's humility . . . for them, Christ's cross was a dirty thing'.[16] As a result, the philosophers were left stranded, unable to reach the destination they had glimpsed: 'what does it profit someone proud and who, for this reason, blushes at the wood of Christ's cross, to see from far off his country beyond the sea?'[17] This theme structures Augustine's autobiographical treatment of the relationship between Platonism and Christianity in the *Confessions*. From the moment Augustine receives the pagan Platonists' books from 'a man of enormous pride' (VII.ix.13), the reader is not allowed to forget the association between pagan pride and Augustine's own refusal, at this stage in his spiritual life, to recognize Christ as anything more than a very wise man. Each truth about God and his Son which those books taught him, and which Augustine pointedly summarizes by quoting from the opening of John's Gospel, is complemented by a deficiency, a truth about the Incarnation and Christ's life on earth which the Gospel contains, but not 'those books' (VII.ix.13–14). 'Those pages do not contain . . . the tears of confession, your sacrifice, a contrite and humble heart, the salvation of the people' (VII.ix.21). The final phrase brings up another element in Augustine's picture of pagan philosophical pride. The philosophers had been shamelessly elitist. They had not even imagined that they could win the mass of people from polytheism and idolatry and offer them a way to salvation—and Porphyry even recommends for the multitude the polytheistic ceremonies he rejects for himself.[18] Yet the mediation of Christ *does* offer a way for all to salvation: 'this is the universal way for the salvation of the soul', as Augustine repeats refrain-like through the concluding pages of his account of Platonism in the *City of God*.

In short, when he considers Platonism, Augustine changes the emphasis of Paul's comment on natural theology, putting ideas of a reversion to polytheism into the background, and making a direct connection between pagan pride and the negative error of failing to see the incarnate Christ as the true mediator. On examination, then, Platonism does not escape Augustine's condemnation of Roman civilization, and its downfall, pride, is a vice closely related to Rome's prevailing characteristic, the desire for glory.

[16] *Sermons on John*, tr. II, 4.
[17] *On the Trinity* IV.15.20; more famous is the slightly different metaphor used in the *Confessions* VII.21; and cf. *CG* X.29 and Rémy 1979, 131–36.
[18] See *On True Religion* III.3; *CG* X.32.

The Salvation of Pagans

As will be clear from the discussion above, Augustine—following Paul's insistence that justification is by faith—thought that people could be saved only by recognizing and accepting the incarnate Christ as their mediator. Pagans of his own day or a little earlier (like Porphyry and Plotinus) made, or could be plausibly taken to have made, a conscious decision to reject Christ. The preaching of his Gospel had certainly reached them, and many of those who lived where and when they did had become Christians. Augustine does not seem to have held out any hope for their salvation. They are dead, and lost, though their followers are still living and might be converted (*CG* X, 29). But what of the generations who preceded the coming of Christ, or who—before, and in, and after Augustine's time—lived or would live where the Gospel had not yet been preached? Augustine's attitude to them was simple, if slightly paradoxical. They too could only be saved by faith, explicit faith, in the incarnate Christ—but such faith was *not* an impossibility.

Augustine spells out his approach most fully and clearly in his *Letter* 102 in answer to a line of argument said (II.8) to be put forward by Porphyry.[19] Why did Christ wait for so long before becoming incarnate and so offering people the possibility of salvation? He answers by asserting that 'from the beginning of the human race, whoever believed in him and in some way understood him and lived piously and justly according to his commands, whenever and wherever they might be, were without doubt saved by him' (II.12). Augustine goes on to make it clear that there were indeed 'ancient people' who believed and were saved. Their ceremonies may have been different, and the object of their faith lay in the future rather than the past, but their faith was the same as Christians' faith in Augustine's time. The main group of pre-Christian Christians Augustine has in mind are the Jews, whose prophecies of Christ illustrate his point. But he is explicit that the Jews were not alone: 'For since a number of people are mentioned in the Hebrew Bible, from the time of Abraham onwards, who were not of his stock, nor of the people of Israel, nor foreigners who became part of the people of Israel, and yet who participated in this sacrament [i.e., of prophesying Christ's coming], why may we not believe that there were other men and women in other races in other parts of the world, although they are not mentioned in the Bible for us to read about?' (II.15). He is equally explicit in the sermon *Against the Pagans* (§38) and no less definite in the *City of God*, although here (XVIII.47)

---

[19]See Rémy 1979, 697–705 for an analysis. Augustine thought—almost certainly wrongly—that this Porphyry was the same as the 'famous' Porphyry about whom he frequently wrote—cf. *Retractions* II.31.

he sets out his evidence more cautiously. He brings up the particular example of Job, whom the Bible considers more just than anyone of his time—the third generation of Israel—but who was neither a Jew nor a convert to Judaism. This one instance, Augustine suggests, was intended by God to show that there were non-Jews, before the coming of Christ, who were pleasing to God and would be saved by—as he stresses—belief in the incarnate Christ, whose future coming was foretold to these good people of ancient times.

In the sermon *Against the Pagans*, Augustine sets out the conditions under which someone living before Christ would be given the revelation needed in order to be saved. What they required was humility (§38): 'for those—whoever sought him humbly—the humble mediator was not lacking . . . so that, persevering in their humility, they might merit purification through him, the humble mediator'. In letter 102, he even declared, 'In this way, the salvation of this religion—the only true religion through which true salvation is truly promised—was never lacking for anyone who was worthy, and those for whom it was lacking were not worthy' (II.15). On the face of it, Augustine seems to be suggesting that it was open to anyone at anytime to be saved, since whoever was worthy would be given the necessary revelation. That is to say, people were always able to earn their salvation by being good enough. (The sermon would seem to have the same implication, with the added explanation that humility was an essential part of the goodness). This is exactly how the passage was read by the supporters of Pelagius, Augustine's opponents in his last years. They wanted to ensure that people's unaided efforts to live well played a role in securing their salvation. Augustine insisted, against them, on the dependence of humans for salvation on God's unfathomable and unmerited grace. But here, in *Letter* 102, they pointed out that Augustine himself seemed to speak like a Pelagian. Augustine disagreed, explaining that he had not said that the people in question were able to come to belief through their unaided wills. Salvation was, indeed, 'never lacking for anyone who was worthy'. But 'if it should be discussed and questioned from what anyone is worthy, there is no shortage of those who will say, "By human free will". But I say: "By divine grace and predestination"'.[20] To some extent Augustine may be retrospectively reinterpreting what he had earlier written. But if he had really ever believed that salvation was genuinely open to all from the beginning of the world, he would be left having to explain *why* so many people in centuries past were so unworthy that they were not able to earn the revelation necessary for salvation. Given that Augustine

[20] *On the Predestination of the Saints* IX.17–X.19 (quoted passage from X.19); cf. *Retractions* II.31. The objection is put to Augustine in *Letter* 226.3. See Rémy 1979, 704.

never gave reason to think that more than a handful of ancient pagans were really Christians (due to a special revelation), he needed the notion of absolute dependence on unearned grace to square his theory about the universal availability of salvation with what he took to be the facts. A phrase from Letter 164 (§4) brings out very clearly how Augustine thinks that the rights and wrongs of salvation cannot be judged in ordinary human terms. He is referring to the ancient poets, orators and philosophers, who scorned the pagan gods, practised frugality and sobriety, and risked their lives for their country, who are all, he believes, eternally in Hell. 'There is something in-built in our minds by which these virtues so please us that we would wish the people who had them, alone or with the rest, to be freed from punishment', he remarks, and then adds the rider, 'were human sense not one thing, and the creator's justice another'.

THE FALSE VIRTUES OF THE PAGANS

As this passage from *Letter* 164 indicates, Augustine's unsparing critique of Roman claims and ideals left him little room to appreciate the Roman virtues. In his view, the ruling trait of the celebrated Romans was a desire for praise and glory. This desire did, he recognizes, help to restrain the Romans from moral corruption and encourage behaviour which merited the earthly rewards God gave it, by allowing the Romans to rule over a vast empire. Yet Augustine does not accept that any behaviour motivated in this way is really virtuous (*CG* V.12–20). He analyses some of the best-known examples of virtuous Roman behaviour in such a way as to show that they too were motivated by concern for reputation. Lucretia's suicide after her rape by Tarquin was not, as other Christian writers took it, an example of devotion to chastity, but the result of her 'excessive desire for honour': she was ashamed that people might think, though wrongly, that she was to some extent an accomplice in Tarquin's act (*CG* I.19).[21] Even Cato's suicide, after Caesar's victory, is put down, not to high-mindedness, but a sort of pride—an unwillingness to let Caesar win praise by sparing him (*CG* I.23).

These psychological analyses of individual, famous candidates for pagan virtue are underwritten by a theory which explains why, in principle, no pagan can be truly virtuous. The theory involves two strands of thought, neither of them set out in one place or step by step, which come together to support the same conclusion. One strand concerns what virtues are; the other is about who can have virtues and how.

[21] See Maier 1955, 87 and n. 12 for other Christian authors who use the story.

The first strand of thought pits Augustine's understanding of the nature of virtue against both the ancient philosophers' conduct and their own theoretical view. Augustine defines virtue (CG XV.22) as 'the order of love'. He sees this love as manifested in actions, but it is not enough to perform certain sorts of actions in order to be virtuous. The love must be rightly directed; that is to say, the actions must be referred to the right end. As Augustine puts it explicitly in *Against Julianus* (IV.2; written 420–1), 'Virtues should be distinguished from vices not by their functions (*officia*) but by their ends (*fines*). The function is what is to be done; the end that for which it is to be done. When therefore a person does something where he does not appear to sin, if he does not do it on account of that for which he should do it, he is shown to sin'. Augustine has no doubt at all about the end to which love should be directed and actions, if they are to be virtuous, referred: it is God. Although we can rightly love human beings, it is only when we regard them as the image of God and so we are directing our love to God through them.[22]

Pagans, Augustine argues, do not direct their actions towards God, because they do not worship him, but rather worship a multiplicity of false gods. So, for example, he reaches his celebrated conclusion (CG XIX.21) that the Romans never had the true virtue of justice. Justice, he says, citing the Ciceronian definition, is the virtue 'which gives to each his own'. 'What sort of justice', he then asks, 'does a man have who takes the man away from God and subjects him to unclean demons?' Since Augustine was willing to allow that some of the Platonists did believe in the true God, it might seem that they could be genuinely virtuous, since they could refer their actions to the right end. But he would not accept this conclusion: for the philosophers to refer their actions to God, it is not enough for them just to know the true God, whilst continuing to worship false gods. Although he does not make the point explicitly, Augustine indicates it by going from his explanation of why Roman justice was not the true virtue to a discussion (CG XIX.22–3) of how Porphyry sacrificed to demons, even though the scriptures of the God of the Hebrews, whom he acknowledged, proclaim that anyone who sacrifices to other gods will be eradicated. Porphyry is an example of a (in some respects) wise pagan, but by no means of a virtuous one.

Augustine does not leave this line of thinking here, however. There is a deeper, theoretical disagreement between the pagan conception of virtue and his one. For Augustine, the virtues themselves are simply means to an end. Here he differs sharply from the ancient schools on which

[22]The fullest discussion of this theory is in Book I of *On Christian Doctrine*, begun in 413; see esp. chaps. 5 and 22. The idea is repeated often in the later works; see, e.g., CG XV.22.

he concentrates his discussion, Stoics, Aristotelians and the Old Academy, as presented by Varro. The difference may be masked at first sight by the fact that Augustine and the philosophers share the view that the ultimate aim for each human is to be happy (*beatus* in Augustine's vocabulary). But they do so simply because to call a human happy means for them all just that he or she has reached the ultimate aim. 'Happiness' is a mere place holder; the substantive question is the identity of 'that which, when someone attains it, he or she is happy'—the Highest Good for humans. For the philosophers, having the virtues is all or part of the Highest Good, what makes a person happy. The virtues are intrinsically valuable; indeed, for the Stoics they alone are intrinsically valuable. For Augustine, by contrast, the virtues are means to a Highest Good which is distinct from them. They are needed to help us fight against vices: temperance to restrain our lusts, courage because we need patience in the face of the ills of earthly life, justice because we need constantly to work to subordinate the soul to God and the body to the soul, and prudence to distinguish good from the evils that surround us (*CG* XIX.4). The virtues are aids, though imperfect ones, by means of which we hope to gain salvation. Salvation (or heavenly peace)[23] is our Highest Good, since it brings happiness, which is not found on earth, in Heaven, where there is no longer need for virtues. The pagan philosophers are wrong, then, not only in thinking that happiness can be gained in this life—a view Augustine dismisses with vehement irony,[24] but also in holding that the virtues intrinsically provide some, or for the Stoics all, of this happiness. And this intellectual error about the nature of virtue is closely connected, he suggests, with a moral error, since the result of cultivating virtues for their own sake is a vice—pride: 'For although the virtues are thought by some to be true and worthy when they are referred to themselves and not sought for anything else, rather in this case they are proud and puffed up, and so should be judged not to be virtues but vices' (*CG* XIX.25).

The other strand in Augustine's thinking, about who can have the virtues and how, is simpler, although it involves one of his most characteristic and controversial ideas. A prerequisite for any good action, Augustine believes, is that the agent has charity: 'whatever someone thinks he does well, he in no way does well if he does it without charity'.[25] But charity requires faith.[26] This doctrine makes being Christian a necessary condition

---

[23] Cf. *CG* XIX.11 and the discussion of peace below, pp. 39–41.

[24] For Stoics, the sage is happy just because he is virtuous. The other schools held that some material goods were also necessary for a happy life. For the critique, see *CG* XIX.4.

[25] *On Grace and Free Will* 18.37.

[26] Augustine holds, in an inchoate form, what would become the doctrine of the theological virtues: faith, hope (which presupposes faith) and charity (which presupposes both faith and hope). His clearest presentation is in *Enchiridion* 3 (*CCSL* 46, 49–114).

for performing good actions, and so for having any of the virtues. It is closely tied to Augustine's views about ordering and directing love to the right object. Charity is simply rightly directed love (e.g., *CG* XIV.7). It is not, then, merely that, as just explained, pagan philosophers in fact did not direct themselves to the right end; lacking faith, they *could* not do so. When, therefore, Augustine is presented with the case of non-Christians who perform what seem to be good actions and so seem to be virtuous, he is adamant that their actions are not really good. Take the case even of a 'gentile who does not live on the basis of faith' who 'clothes the naked, saves those in peril, tends the wounds of the sick, uses his wealth to help the worthy people he cherishes and will not bear false witness, even under torture'. These are good works, but, Augustine asks, does he do them well or badly? If he does them badly, then he sins in doing them. But to claim otherwise and say he does them well would imply that good fruit comes from a bad tree, and that is impossible.[27]

The reason why the tree is bad, Augustine goes on to explain, lies in the man's will. Here Augustine links his views about pagans with his wider thinking on the Fall and grace. By the time Augustine was writing the later books of the *City of God*, he believed that, by sinning, Adam had destroyed the power of the human will to act well, unless restored and then aided by God's grace. Moreover, his conflict with Pelagius and partial followers of Pelagius, such as Julian of Eclanum, had strengthened his views about the gratuity of grace. All humans, by inheriting Adam's sin, belong to the *massa damnationis*. God takes no notice of the differences between one person and another (*acceptio personarum*) in making his inscrutable choice to give one grace, and deny it to another.[28] It is for this reason that Augustine spoke of two cities: the City of God has as its citizens all those chosen by God who will go to Heaven, whilst the rest of humanity belong to the earthly city (*CG* XI.1). Although in the world the two cities are intermingled, only the citizens of the City of God—who consist of Christians, though by no means all of them, some pre-Christian Jews and a few people from all races who, before Christ, were granted a special Christian revelation—can act virtuously.

Augustine's thought about pagan virtue fits precisely, therefore, with his ideas about the salvation of pagans. But it faces a special problem. Augustine's views on salvation make God seem very severe and some would say even unjust. Augustine can insist, however, that this stern vision is what the Bible implies and humans cannot understand divine justice. If, however, he is insisting that all pagans are equally without virtue, then

---

[27] *Against Julianus* IV.3.30 (*PL* 44, 754).

[28] See, for instance, *CG* XXI.12. The theme is developed in many late works; the clearest exposition is still that given in Merlin 1934.

how can he distinguish morally—as he must if he is to present any sort of moral theory—between those pagans who clothe the naked or keep to the truth under torture and those who lie, steal and murder?[29]

Augustine is aware of this problem. There are a number of passages in his later works where, in a way seemingly at odds with his dismissal of pagan virtue, he apparently acknowledges that pagans sometimes act well. For example, one of Augustine's ways of reading Paul's words about the Gentiles who have the 'law written in their hearts' accepts that there are some who do not 'worship the true God truly and justly' who performed deeds about which we have read, know or heard, 'which not only according to the rule of justice can we not censure, but which we rather deservedly and rightly praise, even though, were it examined for what end they were done, there would scarcely be found those which would merit the due praise and defence of justice'.[30] And even when Augustine is insisting that the pagans will be damned and that they are not acting according to the right end, he allows that 'according to a certain custom of this life' they are called good, and that they 'quasi-observe what is ordained in the law', honouring their parents and abstaining from murder, theft, adultery and bearing false witness.[31] He allows, in the *City of God* (V.13), that when people restrain their vicious passions simply through desire for human praise and glory, they are less shameful, even though certainly not saints. The incorruptible Fabricius lacked true virtues, but, says Augustine, he deviated from them less than someone such as the traitor Catiline (and so will be punished less in the afterlife).[32] For Regulus, the Roman general who returned to face death from his Carthaginian captors in order to keep his word, Augustine has almost nothing but praise, and he can only recommend Christians to follow and surpass him.[33] Altogether there were Romans, he believes (*CG* V.15)

---

[29] Terence Irwin (2007, 423–33) gives a careful and philosophically sophisticated discussion of Augustine's attitude to pagan virtue. He contends that Augustine's criterion for virtue is merely moderately strict, requiring a correct, but not wholly correct, conception of the final end, and that, according to Augustine, some pagan philosophers did have a partly correct conception of the ultimate end and so could be virtuous. It is questionable, though, whether for Augustine loving virtues for their own sake shows even a partly correct conception of the end.

[30] *On the Spirit and the Letter* XXVII.48; CSEL 60, 202:4–11. For the passage, see above and cf. Irwin 2007, 415.

[31] Cf. *Sermons on the Gospel of St John* 45.2; CCSL 36, 389:8–16; cited by Wang 1938, 116 (but as evidence of Augustine's harshening line because of the Pelagian controversy). See also the passage from *Letter* 164 discussed above in connection with the salvation of pagans.

[32] *Against Julianus* IV.25; PL 44, 751.

[33] *CG* I.15, 24; II.23; V.18; cf. Maier 1955, 87–89; but for a rare critical comment *CG* III.18.

who acted selflessly for the common good, adhering to the law and not yielding to sensual desires. They followed something 'like the true path' (*tamquam vera via*), were it not directed towards honour, empire and glory (and, because they achieved honour, empire and glory, they cannot complain that they have not been justly rewarded, even though they are damned).

Augustine, then, seems to be saying that pagans can indeed have virtues—but they are *false* virtues. They are false because they are not directed towards God, and they do not lead towards salvation, but in purely earthly terms they are just like virtues. From what has been said so far, however, it might seem as if, by qualifying them as 'purely earthly', they are being dismissed entirely; that they are being called 'false' in the way that counterfeit bank notes are false. But in the *City of God* (XIX) Augustine develops an idea which, in a certain way, bridges the gap between the two cities and even between true and false virtues—the idea of peace. Peace (*pax*) functions as an alternative to happiness (*beatitudo*) as the end to which humans strive. 'Peace', Augustine says, can be used to describe eternal life in Heaven, which he considers to be our ultimate good. In this sense, it has the same reference as 'happiness'. But 'peace' is a broader term than happiness, and it functions differently from it. In Augustine's view, it is simply wrong to claim that people can be happy during their earthly lives.[34] Whatever is not the true happiness of Heaven is not happiness at all. 'Peace' follows a different rationale in its usage. As well as heavenly peace, there is earthly peace. 'Peace' in this earthly sense has a very wide range of reference. Augustine uses it to name the state all humans and even wild animals seek, even when they seek it by war or violence (CG XIX.12). He defines various different sorts of peace (CG XIX.13):

> The peace of the body . . . is the ordered tempering of its parts, the peace of the irrational soul the ordered putting to rest (*requies*) of its appetites, the peace of the rational soul the ordered matching of cognition and action, the peace of the body and soul the ordered life and the health of the living thing, the peace between mortal man and God ordered obedience in faith under the eternal law, the peace of men ordered harmony, the peace of the household the ordered harmony of those who live together in commanding and obeying, the peace of the city the ordered harmony of the citizens in commanding and obeying, the peace of the celestial city the most ordered and most harmonious

---

[34] See, e.g., *CG* XIX.4: 'Let us therefore not believe that we have already gained happiness to which we wish to come in victory, so long as we are in internal war' (the 'internal war' is the conflict with our bad desires which, it is made clear, continues throughout our lives).

fellowship of enjoying God and one another in God, the peace of all things the tranquillity of order. Order is the disposition of similar and dissimilar things which gives to each its place.

In this list, Augustine deliberately mixes types of peace which all humans—and, indeed, all things—can attain with those (between God and man, and that of the celestial city) available only to those chosen by God for salvation. 'Peace' can be applied in so many ways because, as he explains at the end of the paragraph, things have peace when they are ordered. The definition of order given at the end of the paragraph is verbally similar to the Ciceronian definition of justice Augustine uses ('justice is the virtue which gives to each his own'), but in fact it describes a very different structure. Justice relates objects to those to whom the objects are due; order (and so peace) simply relates objects to each other. If an agent is mistaken about the ultimate end of all actions, which is God, he or she will in any act be failing to give to each his own, since it is God's own to be recognized as the supreme end. In consequence, the agent will not be just.[35] By contrast, not only can there be peace without recognition of the supreme end (indeed, for inanimate things without any recognition of ends at all); peace can also be brought about—as in the peace of the family or the city—without a correct grasp of the supreme end: it just requires that the elements (the family members, the citizens) are correctly placed in relation to one another.[36]

The false virtues which Augustine recognizes in some pagans are the qualities which lead to earthly peace (witness the long-lasting and mostly peaceful Roman Empire, founded on these false virtues). Although he does not develop a full theory, he connects them directly with this peace: 'When, if we live rightly, we mortals have the sort of peace that can be had here in mortal things, virtue uses its goods rightly; and when we do not have it, virtue also uses well the evils which man suffers. But it is true virtue when it refers all the goods which it uses well, and all the good and bad things it makes good use of, and itself, to that end where there will be such and so much peace that there could be none better nor greater' (CG XIX.10). The 'virtue' to which Augustine refers in the first sentence must be false virtue, since it is contrasted, in the next sentence, with true virtue which refers everything to God. But even this false virtue is able to use good things well, to achieve earthly peace, and to use bad things well when peace is absent. The false virtues of pagans can, therefore, be valued as contributing towards something which is valuable in itself: the earthly peace, which is used by the citizens of the heavenly city (CG

---

[35] See above on Augustine's discussion of why Romans lacked the true virtue of justice.
[36] This passage is discussed in Ruokanen 1993, 30–31 and in Geerlings 1997, 228–31, but is understood very differently.

XIX.26). They are not like fake money, which is useless once the forgery is exposed, but like a fake diamond necklace, which will help its wearer to be the belle of the ball, but not to make her rich.

Historians of political thought have argued powerfully that, especially in the *City of God*, Augustine gives a large measure of autonomy to human political life. Just because its values and aims are not those of the heavenly city, they need to be considered in their own terms.[37] The same tendency can be seen in his treatment of pagan virtues, or rather, in his terms, pagan false virtues. Whereas his answer to the problem about pagan salvation is to deny its possibility, except to those who were really hidden Christians, and to the problem of pagan wisdom to trace how far some ancient philosophers came towards reaching the truth, he treats pagan virtue by a sort of relativization. Pagan virtues can be discussed in their own terms, as false virtues: the classification of virtues remains the same (indeed, Augustine shamelessly takes over his classification of true virtues from the pagan philosophical tradition), and so are the sorts of acts that characterize them. But their end is different, and for that reason they are false and, ultimately, valueless. Although Augustine's severe judgements on both pagan salvation and virtue would inspire many in the coming centuries (often to an attitude even more extreme than his own), this element of grudging relativism would also have its followers.

---

[37] See especially Markus 1970, 72–104 and Ruokanen 1993; but cf. Lee 2011 and the references there.

CHAPTER 3

Boethius

A striking contrast to Augustine's answer to the Problem of Paganism is provided by Boethius, an author nearly as widely read through the Long Middle Ages and whose *Consolation of Philosophy*—the work principally in question here—was translated into the gamut of medieval vernaculars, from Old High German to Hebrew.[1] But the *Consolation* does not *obviously* put forward an answer, or even state the Problem of Paganism, and on the reading followed by many specialists, Boethius was not concerned with it at all. To see why their judgement is wrong, the *Consolation* needs to be considered as a complex literary work that can be properly understood only when placed in its author's unusual cultural context.

BOETHIUS'S CONTEXT

Boethius was born in (probably) 476, a little more than a century after Augustine. In some ways, Augustine's classical world had by now disappeared. North Africa had been conquered by the Vandals. In Italy, where Boethius lived, the last Western Roman emperor had been deposed by the Goth Odoacer, who in turn was removed by Theoderic the Ostrogoth. Theoderic had in theory been sent by the Eastern emperor and governed under his aegis, but in practice he regarded himself as the ruler. The vestigial paganism, which had influenced Augustine's early life and with which he had later to contend, had disappeared. The senatorial aristocracy to which Boethius belonged was by now uniformly Christian, as were the people of Rome, and even Theoderic and his Gothic soldiers, although they followed the Arian heresy (Christ is subordinate to the Father, who alone is truly God). In other ways, however, Boethius was far closer to the classical Roman and Greek past than Augustine, a provincial parvenu, had ever been. Not only did Boethius grow up and live in Rome—still a capital culturally though not politically. He belonged to one of the

---

[1] For the vernacular translations and influence of the *Consolation*, see Kaylor and Phillips 2012.

grandest Roman families and had been adopted into another of them: as such, he received an education in the Latin classics and—going beyond what was usual, even in his class—in not only Greek, but also Greek philosophy. His wealth and contacts meant that he had access to a range of Greek manuscripts so that, although almost certainly did not attend the Platonic school of Athens or Alexandria, he became familiar with much of their syllabus.[2]

It was in these Platonic schools that the few remaining philosophical adherents of ancient paganism were still to be found. The School of Athens survived until it was closed by Justinian in 529, shortly after Boethius's death; the School of Alexandria, which took a more accommodating line to Christianity, right up until the town fell to the Muslims in 641. The delicacy with which Boethius was able to negotiate the relations between his Christianity and the philosophical tradition he inherited depended on his remoteness from its contemporary pagan exponents. In the East, Christian philosophers preferred to follow a less ambiguous strategy. For instance, John Philoponus studied in Alexandria under Boethius's pagan contemporary, Ammonius. In his early works he based himself on his teacher, but much of his mature writing is a critique, on powerfully argued philosophical grounds, of aspects of Aristotelianism incompatible with Christianity. Or, to take an even more striking example, during Boethius's lifetime, a Christian author, perhaps a Syrian monk, deeply familiar with Proclus and the Platonic tradition, wrote a set of prayerful, mystical yet philosophically informed and suggestive texts. Their themes are explicitly Christian—the Trinity, the orders of angels, the ranks of the Church, and their language is rich in biblical echoes. But the hierarchical ordering of creation and the sophisticated negative theology they present are adapted from the pagan Neoplatonists, though with important changes. The author guaranteed his own anonymity and the fame of his writings by issuing them as the work of Dionysius, the Areopagite converted by St Paul (see above, pp. 19–20). By picking Dionysius, as opposed to any other early Christian, the writer was responding in a bold and direct way to the Problem of Paganism. Before he was converted by Paul, Dionysius had been a learned pagan; the late ancient writer, anachronistically, sees him as a Platonist of his own days. After his conversion, the writer indicates, Dionysius could keep most of the structure of his pagan philosophical universe, and express it in Christian terms. Platonism and Christianity can be syncretized, by accepting and baptizing pagan wisdom.[3]

[2] On the social and intellectual context of Boethius's life, see Moorhead 2009 and Chadwick 1981.

[3] Although the author does not conceptualize the question in terms of 'the Problem of Paganism', an approach to pseudo-Dionysius on these lines, and in greater depth, has been

Boethius's approach to the problem would be far less direct, and in part the result of the shape of his life. Most of it was spent, as was common for men of his class, in learned leisure. Boethius had a special interest in making Greek philosophical culture available to Latin speakers. He formulated an ambitious plan to translate into Latin, and provide with commentaries, all the works of Plato and Aristotle—though he never went beyond Aristotle's logic, for which he showed an especial fascination.[4] At the same time, although not a priest, Boethius wrote on Christian subjects. These short treatises were gathered together as his five *opuscula sacra*. The first, on the Trinity, and the fifth, on the union between God and Man in Christ, share a common method. Very probably written to contribute to the doctrinal controversies of the time, the two treatises are striking because of the way they use Aristotelian physics, metaphysics and logic to probe theological problems. Boethius believes that he can show that two heretical formulations about the relationship between God and Man in Christ (he is two natures and two persons; he is one nature and one person) are incoherent in terms of natural philosophy. The true doctrine, that he is one person and two natures, divine and human, is argued to be cogent from a philosophical point of view, but requiring a step in argument beyond what would be acceptable except when talking about God. Similarly, Boethius shows how, up to a certain point, we can make logical sense of the idea that God is three and one, and he charts the point at which the philosophical analysis can no longer compass this mystery.[5] The third treatise, explaining how all things are good simply in virtue of existing, anticipates the *Consolation* by being written so that it could equally well be from the pen of a pagan Platonist as from that of a Christian. By contrast, the fourth treatise is a simple account of orthodox Christian faith which concentrates on the narrative of sacred history. The unlikeness of this little work to anything else of Boethius's has led some to regard it as inauthentic, but most are now convinced by the case for its genuineness.[6] Indeed, a fragment has been found, quite possibly part of an original preface to the fourth treatise removed by Boethius's earliest editors because they found it too daring. It can be interpreted as seeing faith as the highest of our cognitive faculties, which grasps the truth more purely than they do.[7] This

developed in Stang 2012, who also gives full references to earlier discussions of these issues by Louth, Schäfer and others.

[4] On Boethius as a logician, see Ebbesen 1990, 2009; and Marenbon 2003, 17–42.

[5] For a more detailed exposition of this view, see Marenbon 2003, 70–87. The theological background to the *Opuscula* is explored in Chadwick 1981, 180–202, 211–22. There is a commentary (so far just to Treatises II, III and IV): Galonnier 2007.

[6] See Chadwick 1981; Galonnier 2007, 38–409.

[7] See Troncarelli 2000.

interpretation fits very well with the idea that philosophical reasoning can grasp divine things *up to a certain point*: it is there that faith must take over the task.

THE CONSOLATION OF PHILOSOPHY

In 522, Boethius gave up his scholarly life in Rome to become the chief minister of Theoderic in his capital, Ravenna. Court intrigue, Boethius's high principles and, perhaps, his links with Greece and the Byzantine Emperor soon led to his downfall. He was imprisoned on charges which included treason and sentenced to death.[8] It was during these final months or years that he wrote the most famous of his works, the *Consolation of Philosophy*. Unlike his previous works, written in elegant Latin but with little literary artifice, the *Consolation* is an elaborately contrived piece of writing as well a philosophical text.[9] The setting is Boethius's own prisoner's cell. At the beginning of the text, as he laments his change of fortune in Ovidian verse, there appears to Boethius the prisoner a woman 'with burning eyes that saw more clearly than the run of humans', young and vigorous and yet so old that she seemed to belong to another era, sometimes of normal height, sometimes 'seeming to touch heaven with her head'. She is dressed in a seamless garment, which has been torn (I.1.5) by those trying to snatch away parts of it—a simile, it is explained, for the different schools which break up the unity of true philosophy. This figure shoos away the poetic muses who had been allowing him, the prisoner to wallow in his misery and, when he has recovered from his astonishment, the prisoner recognizes (I.3.2) 'Philosophy in whose house I had spent time since I was a young'. The work is a dialogue between Boethius the Prisoner and this figure of Philosophy, in which sections of argumentative prose are broken up by verse passages, reflecting on or developing the argument. Generically, it is therefore what is called a 'prosimetrum' or 'Menippean satire'. In ancient literature the genre of a piece sets up certain expectations about, not just the structure of a work, but its contents and aims, and so the fact that Boethius chose this form for the *Consolation* may be important in interpreting it.

The argument of the dialogue begins from the prisoner's own situation. Boethius represents himself as having forgotten the lessons of

---

[8] On Boethius's trial and condemnation, see Morton 1982 and Moorhead 1992, 219–26.

[9] There is extensive discussion of the work's genre and relation to Latin literary tradition in Relihan 2007 and Shanzer 2009b. Gruber 2006 gives a thorough commentary, directed especially to questions of literary background.

philosophy, dazed by his sudden fall from power and prosperity, and as
believing from his own experience that God takes no care of humans,
allowing the good to be oppressed while the wicked prosper. Philosophy
disagrees. She begins by convincing the prisoner that the goods he has
lost, such as riches and status, are not true goods. At this stage she allows that there are true goods which people can gain in their lives, such
as sufficiency and respect, but the prisoner still has these.[10] She goes on,
however, to develop a monolithic conception of the good, which is identified with the Highest Good, which is God. She argues that only by seeking this good alone, and not by pursuing any other goods separately, can
we achieve happiness. Taking up the prisoner's complaint that the wicked
prosper, Philosophy claims, in terms borrowed from Plato's *Gorgias*, that,
on the contrary, the wicked suffer because of their very wickedness, and
the good are rewarded merely by being good. God is seen here and in
other passages as purely a final cause, who does need to intervene in the
running the universe: simply because he is the aim to which all things are
directed, the universe orders itself justly. But she also proposes in other
passages a different view, in which God is seen as an arranger as well as
a final cause, distributing prosperity and adversity with the ultimate best
interests of people in mind, whether in punishing the wicked, favour-
ing the virtuous or testing and improving them through hardship. This
theme is further developed by a discussion of chance and providence.
Chance events, Philosophy explains, are those which occur when two
chains of cause and effect coincide, but they, as all other events, are part
of the overall pattern of cause and effect disposed by God. The human
will, however, is still held to be free in its decisions and so morally ac-
countable.[11] But the prisoner sees a different threat to this freedom. God
knows all things, past, present and future. How is such knowledge of the
future compatible with the claim that the future is open, since a human
being can choose to will or not to will this or that act? The last, and by
far the philosophically densest, part of the work ends with the Prisoner's
elaboration of this problem, and Philosophy's intricate solution, which
involves the special relationship between an eternal God's way of knowing and the flow of time.[12]

    As in the case of the third theological treatise, there is nothing on
the surface of the *Consolation* which points to a Christian author. The

[10] See Marenbon 2003, 105.
[11] This summary of the (not entirely harmonious) arguments proposed in the *Consolation* is based on the much more detailed exposition in Marenbon 2003, 96–124.
[12] There have been many analyses of this section, philosophically the richest, of the *Consolation*: see Marenbon 2003, 125–45; Sharples 2009 (a very fine and balanced assessment
of the interpretative debate); and Marenbon 2013b (corrects and amplifies my earlier discussion and gives a new reading of the argument).

prisoner converses with, and is convinced by, Philosophy—and not by a personification of Faith or Revelation. Philosophy works by means of rational argument from supposedly evident premises. Her arguments lead, indeed, to God, but it is a God which would not be obviously unacceptable to a pagan Platonist of Boethius's day. Yet there is certainly no trace of polytheism, and the metaphysical scheme lacks the multiple levels of emanation which Iamblichus and Proclus populated with the Graeco-Roman pantheon. Probed more deeply, this complete neutrality turns out to be qualified, though not seriously, on both sides. The language reveals Christian vocabulary and turns of phrase, as well as some biblical reminiscences. The most significant of them is (III.12.22) when Philosophy says, in the same words as the biblical Wisdom (viii, 1) that 'it is the highest good that rules all things strongly and disposes them sweetly'. Not only is the phrase a very direct echo of Scripture, but the prisoner replies by saying that he is delighted, not only by the conclusions Philosophy has reached but 'the very words' she has used.[13] On the other side, there are perhaps some ideas put forward by Philosophy which would not be acceptable to Christians, at least in poem ('metrum') nine of book III, a solemn prayer to God, in which she summarizes the *Timaeus*. Medieval readers—as will become apparent—were certainly troubled by the references here to the World Soul and to the doctrine of reincarnation. But it is not clear whether Boethius himself would have regarded even this passage as unacceptable for Christians.[14]

INTERPRETATIONS OF THE CONSOLATION

Why did Boethius choose to leave anything openly Christian out of this highly personal work, which he knew would be a final testament? Specialists on Boethius accept that they need to answer this question, but they usually do so in such a way as to suggest that the Problem of Paganism did not concern him. Most interpreters can be classed as Hellenizers, Christianizers or Syncretists.[15]

---

[13]The still very useful edition by Fortescue (Boethius 1925) contains (204–6) an index of biblical traces, reprinted in Bieler's Corpus Christianorum edition (*CCSL* 94) of the *Consolatio*; and a list partly based on it is given in Shanzer 2009a, 75–78, but none besides the reference to Wisdom viii, 1 is close. See De Vogel 1972, 12–17 for an assessment.

[14]The prisoner himself accepts the Platonic doctrine of recollection (III.12.1; V m.3, lines 22–31—this metrum is put into the prisoner's mouth) and, if he is considered to take it literally, he would also commit himself to reincarnation; yet such a view would not in his time have been obviously heterodox for Christians.

[15]This follows the division in Marenbon 2003, 156, but substitutes 'Syncretists' for 'Augustinists', since this wider category is able to include Shanzer and Troncarelli.

The Hellenizers regard the *Consolation* as a work of pagan, or at least non-Christian philosophy. They point to the fact that Boethius introduces Philosophy as the authoritative figure, sticks entirely to philosophical arguments and says nothing explicitly Christian; scriptural allusions and Christian language are seen as the unintended result of ingrained habit.[16] Perhaps, faced by death, Boethius abandoned Christianity.[17] Or perhaps, as some more recent scholars have argued, although Boethius was clearly a Christian, he was either only superficially one, or else he made an absolute separation between his writing as a philosopher and his Christian beliefs.[18]

The Christianizers argue, by contrast, that the *Consolation* was designed as a clearly Christian work. A simple version of this view lays emphasis on the Christian language and allusions, and on the ease with which Philosophy can be assimilated to the biblical figure of Wisdom.[19] A more sophisticated version looks to the degree to which the younger Augustine, although a committed Christian writer, followed Platonic teaching. According to this view, Boethius would have found no tension, nor expected his readers to detect any, in the extent to which, though a Christian, he thinks and writes in the terms of Platonic philosophy.[20] This type of reading might therefore be described as Syncretist, though with a Christianizing bent. A purer Syncretist reading sees Boethius as deliberately trying to write a work based on the common ground between 'the matter of philosophy and that of religion'.[21]

The Hellenizing view is somewhat implausible. The *Consolation* presents itself, by its setting and the fact that the only human character is Boethius himself, as a personal work, written by a man facing death. It is hard to see how he could simply put his Christianity to one side when writing in such a way, and even harder to admit that the Christianity of the writer of the *opuscula* was merely superficial. Moreover, Boethius's

---

[16]The nineteenth-century hypothesis that the *opuscula sacra* were written by a different Boethius from the (supposedly pagan) author of the *Consolation* was disproved by a fragment from Cassiodorus (the *Anecdoton Holderi*; published in Usener 1877); cf. Galonnier 1997, 40–58.

[17]Momigliano 1955, 213.

[18]See Courcelle 1967 for separation; Galonnier 2007—Boethius's Christianity is a formality, and theology is seen by him as the servant of philosophy. Shanzer (2009b, 244) entertains the idea of 'apostasy or failure of faith' on Boethius's part, but opts rather for syncretism (see below).

[19]Klingner 1966.

[20]Chadwick 1981, 249.

[21]See Shanzer 2009b, 244–45; cf. 2009b, 73. Her view contrasts with Chadwick's, since she believes that he is thinking 'outside the Christian framework'. Troncarelli (2000) also thinks of Boethius as a syncretist, as did Fortescue (Boethius 1925, xlviii), who, however, like Chadwick, emphasizes his Christianity.

control of his language is exceptionally fine, and it is most unlikely that, if he wished to set Christianity aside, he would have let so much Christian and biblical language into his text. The prisoner's explicit acknowledgement and welcoming of the words Philosophy borrows from the biblical book of Wisdom is particularly hard to explain on this view.

There is a sense in which, by contrast, the Christianizing interpretation is indeed probably right. The earliest readers saw the *Consolation* in this way, and Boethius almost certainly would have expected most of them to do so. But the question remains whether Boethius wrote the *Consolation* in a way that would suggest to some readers—the more careful, most reflective and best educated ones—a more complex interpretation. The reasons why the question needs at least to be posed are that, on its own, the Christianizing view leaves unexplained why Boethius should have chosen to disguise the obvious Christian message he is supposedly putting by removing all explicit Christian references from the work; and, further, why he chose the particular, elaborate and unusual form for the work—a prosimetrum in which the Christian Boethius debates with a personification of ancient, pagan philosophy. The fact that the one explicit biblical quotation is from the book of Wisdom underlines this point. Wisdom, identified by this allusion with the Highest Good, is at once a biblical figure, from the Judaeo-Christian world, but of a sort which is accessible outside this tradition—and so to Philosophy.[22]

These reservations about the Christianizing view seem to favour the Syncretizers. They are certainly correct that Boethius writes in a manner acceptable both to pagan Platonists and to Christians. But did he, by the form in which he wrote the *Consolation*, intend also to raise questions about how pagan philosophy and Christian belief are related?

One view, not yet considered, holds that Boethius raised these questions in such a way as to undermine the appearance of harmony in the work between philosophy and revealed religion: the *Consolation*, it holds, is a satirical work. To the alert reader, it carries a message which is the very opposite of what its title and plan suggest—much in the way that a satirical eulogy aims to lambast the pretended recipient of praise. The main advocate of this interpretation is Joel Relihan.[23] According to Relihan, Boethius's central point is that, although Philosophy promises consolation, she does not end by providing any. The work charts the failure of Philosophy to meet the prisoner's challenges and, through the Christian hints and allusions, suggests that his way to happiness is not

---

[22] Shanzer presents the allusion in this way convincingly (2009a). So taken, it fits the dialogic interpretation advanced here as much as it does her own syncretistic one.

[23] In Relihan 1993, the author advances his interpretation of the *Consolation* (187–94) in the context of a general study of Menippean satire; Relihan 2007 nuances and enriches the same general line of interpretation, with more close attention to Boethius's text.

to follow her but through humble prayer to God. Relihan uses two main types of evidence to support his view. First, there is the genre of the work. Prosimetrum or Menippean satire is, as he explains, associated with the ridiculing of pretention, especially pretention to wisdom. The form of the *Consolation*, therefore, alerts the reader to the possibility that Philosophy's claims to guide Boethius to his true home are not all she holds them up to be. This expectation, he argues, is fulfilled by various disappointments and absences in the text. Although described as a 'Consolation', there is no treatment of death or the soul. Philosophy tells the prisoner that he has forgotten who he really is and she will help him to remember; but she never gives an answer to the question. Philosophy promises to lead the prisoner to his homeland, but she does not, in the sense that there is 'no vision of heavenly harmonies . . . no apocalypse. . . .'[24] Boethius the prisoner learns the difficult lesson that, rather than look upwards, he must turn his gaze downwards, to the earth where he lives. There is no easy, philosophical route to a supernal realm, and the way to reach God is through humble prayer—and it is on this note that the work ends, with Philosophy urging Boethius to 'offer humble prayers to the heavens' (V.6.47).

Relihan has noticed some important features of the text and of Boethius's literary choices, but it is hard to accept this satirical reading, because it treats the argumentation, which makes up most of the *Consolation*, as mere padding, fruitless verbiage to show that Philosophy cannot reach her goals. Yet in general Philosophy is made to argue carefully and in many ways powerfully, even if she does not achieve overall coherence. If Boethius had merely been wishing to assert his faith, by showing the inadequacy of philosophizing, why would he have laboured so hard to philosophize? In especial, on Relihan's interpretation it is almost impossible to understand why Boethius chose to include the long and sophisticated argument about divine prescience and contingency at the end of the work. This piece of reasoning is the most impressive and original which Boethius ever devised. The author seems clearly to think that it has solved the problem under discussion and shown that God can foreknow contingent events and, given the premises and understanding of necessity and possibility accepted by both parties, the argument is remarkably successful. If it were the author's intention to show how Philosophy disappoints, why choose to add this section—which could easily have been omitted—in which she successfully reassures the prisoner about an important intellectual concern?

A more modest way to suggest that the *Consolation* demands a complex reading is to see it, not as a satire, but as a genuine dialogue. Like

[24]Relihan 2007, 5.

Relihan's interpretation, this reading finds internal and formal cues which suggest that, for the alert reader, the *Consolation* does not unproblematically syncretize (in the manner of pseudo-Dionysius), but it leaves Boethius with his loyalties to both his religion and philosophy intact. Of course, no one denies that the *Consolation* is a dialogue. But, Relihan apart, interpreters tend to take Philosophy as speaking entirely in the author's voice, proposing correct and adequate answers to problems and objections placed in Boethius the prisoner's mouth. The dialogue is taken purely as a matter of presentation. Yet would not careful readers, at least, have been struck by the fact the *Consolation* is a work by a Christian author, who appears as the main character, and yet the authoritative figure who consoles him is not a Christian, but a pagan? Philosophy looks back in her comments to a tradition of ancient, pagan philosophy and its great exponents. Plato, Aristotle, Socrates and Seneca are her followers, but she mentions no Christians among them (except, of course, for the prisoner Boethius himself). Although, as is only to be expected in an author steeped in Christian as well as pagan literature, there is some Christian language throughout the text, the most Christian-sounding moments come in the prisoner's interventions.[25] Seeing the *Consolation* as a genuine dialogue means not losing sight of the fact that the authoritative figure is a pagan and the man she consoles a Christian, and that, for Christian readers, this juxtaposition must raise some questions.

Rather than, like Relihan, dismiss Philosophy's reasoning as unsuccessful, it may be better to conclude that it is well-managed and, so far as the individual strands of argument go, successful—but the author Boethius deliberately leaves his carefully contrived arguments in tension. Are there individual good things, such as friendship, which even a disastrous change of fortune such as Boethius's cannot destroy and have genuine value? Or is it the case, rather, as the monolithic conception of goodness put forward later implies, that nothing except the Highest Good, which is God, has any true value? Do the wicked punish themselves and the good gain their own reward simply through being virtuous, or does a provident God intervene to plan out humans' destinies according to his inscrutable wisdom and justice? Even the author Boethius's greatest philosophical achievement, Philosophy's highly wrought argument about divine prescience in book 5, although itself impressive, is juxtaposed with her inability to explain coherently how this liberty is compatible also with the fact that God does not just know our actions in advance but ordains them and all things.

[25] Cf. Marenbon 2003, 157–58. De Vogel (1972, 4–6) discusses the strongly Christian language in which Boethius sets out in V.3 the consequences if humans are governed entirely by necessity.

Boethius, so the dialogic reading suggests, wants to suggest by such tensions and gaps that there is a level of knowledge to which Philosophy cannot rise. Despite her supernatural appearance when she enters, Philosophy is not a goddess, but has to work within the limited sphere of human reasoning.[26] She herself is well aware of these limitations. Talking about divine providence, she quotes (IV.6.53) Homer's line, 'But it is hard to explain all these things as if I were a God', and a few lines before she introduces (IV.6.38) a Greek quotation, perhaps from the Chaldean Oracles, by saying, 'For as someone even more excellent than I ‹says›'.[27] One of the developments in pagan Neoplatonism after Plotinus was an increasing lack of confidence in the powers of humans to reach the highest levels of understanding purely through their powers of reasoning. Boethius the author is doing no more, then, than attributing to the pagan philosophical tradition a diffidence about its own capabilities which its exponents themselves shared.

BOETHIUS AND THE PROBLEM OF PAGANISM

If Boethius intended his best readers to read the *Consolation* simply, either as a philosophical discussion separated from Christian belief, or as a Christian work using the language of philosophy, then the text does not address the Problem of Paganism. If it is designed as a syncretic work, compatible with Christianity but deliberately without any of its distinctive doctrines, then it side-steps or brackets the problem. If the work is read as a satire, then it does put forward a view about pagan knowledge and its limitations, but it is a very simple one. It suggests that there seems to be a Problem of Paganism, because of the claims to genuine knowledge made by pagan philosophy, but that in fact these claims are false.

Read as a genuine dialogue, however, the *Consolation* offers a distinct and far more interesting answer to the side of the Problem of Paganism concerned with pagan knowledge of God. It suggests that Philosophy can go a long way towards the truth, but there comes a point where it fails. It can devise excellent individual arguments, but cannot put them into a coherent whole, whilst in some areas, such as the compatibility between human freedom and divine preordination (as opposed to prescience), it fails almost entirely. Philosophy is not, however, depicted as being full of pride, based on an overestimation of its abilities. Boethius draws on the

[26]I suggested (Marenbon 2003, 162) that the initial vision-like appearance of Philosophy may have been set up deliberately so that Philosophy herself can deflate it; Shanzer (2009b, 232) disagrees that there is any deflation, since an epiphany was the most obvious way to introduce a personification such as Philosophy.

[27]Cf. Relihan 2007, 133.

trend in late ancient philosophy to limit the scope of discursive thought so as to make it clear that the philosophers themselves are aware of the limitations of their reasoning—a strikingly anti-Augustinian judgement. If this is the implied position in the *Consolation*, then Boethius is being very consistent with the stance he had already adopted in two of the theological treatises, where he took philosophical reasoning as far as he could, before indicating where reasoning about God has to diverge from thinking about his creation. In the *Consolation*, too, Boethius the prisoner, a Christian, follows Philosophy's path. So far as that path leads, it is the Christian's path too. It is only at the point, dimly indicated beyond the *Consolation*'s horizon, where human understanding fails that the two paths diverge, and only the Christian takes the right one.[28]

---

[28] In Marenbon 2004b, I discussed Boethius and the Problem of Paganism, but before I had fully formulated my general view of the nature of the problem (which I thought then arose only after Boethius's time).

PART II

From Alcuin to Langland

CHAPTER 4

The Early Middle Ages and the Christianization of Europe

THE FIRST THINKER AFTER BOETHIUS TO MAKE THE PROBLEM OF PAGAN-ism a central concern was Peter Abelard, who was born at the end of the eleventh century, and is the subject of the next chapter. But, whatever the unfortunate label of 'Dark Ages' might suggest, the neglect was not the result of any lack of interest in classical antiquity within an exclusively and securely Christian world.[1] Rather, it was due to the ease with which the ancient pagan culture was adopted and adapted to fit into a Christian world (without in many cases being actually Christianized).

MAKING PAGANISM AT HOME WITH CHRISTIANITY: AN UNPROBLEMATIC APPROACH TO THE PROBLEM

In writing which was not strictly theological or philosophical, early medieval scholars used ancient models and language freely within a Christian context: Carolingian scholars such as Einhard, who modelled his *Life* of Charlemagne on Suetonius, or classicizing poets, like Alcuin, Theodulf and Walahfrid Strabo, took the compatibility of pagan culture and Christian belief so much for granted that, in their poetry, the Problem of Paganism did not arise; and the same is true for their predecessors in the sixth and seventh centuries (Venantius Fortunatus, for example, and the Anglo-Saxon, Aldhelm) as for some tenth- and eleventh-century writing. This broad, unproblematic acceptance of classical culture set what would remain the mainstream view throughout the Middle Ages. The worries which made the Problem of Paganism so important for some writers from the time of Abelard onwards came from three main areas of intellectual life: discussions of Christian doctrine, from ancient philosophy and from contacts with contemporary pagans. Before the twelfth century, however, the study of Christian doctrine was unsystematic, so that the

---

[1] On the inappropriateness of the label 'Dark Ages' and the intellectual vitality of early medieval thought, see Marenbon 1988, 45–110, as corrected in Marenbon 2007b, 70–81, 114–29), and, for ninth- and tenth-century culture more generally, McKitterick 1994.

issues explored in depth were usually those which had become the subject of controversy: image worship (in response to Byzantine iconoclasm), Trinitarian relations, predestination, the Eucharist—none of which related to questions about paganism. None the less, as the final pages of this section will show, the Problem of Paganism was occasionally touched on, though unproblematically, in early medieval doctrinal discussions, especially as theology became more systematic in the generation before Abelard's. Most of this chapter, however, will consider the problem in the early Middle Ages in so far as it was raised by the other two areas: in this section, in relation to the reading of ancient philosophy; in the following section, in connection with contemporary pagans.

The range of ancient philosophical material available in the Latin West during this period was very limited. The most carefully studied texts were logical works by Aristotle, Boethius and Porphyry, and Boethius's commentaries on them. In this field, the fact that Aristotle and Porphyry were pagans was irrelevant. Moreover, Alcuin—looking back to Augustine—began a medieval tradition of linking an understanding of logic to a correct grasp of Christian theology, especially regarding the Trinity; and study of Boethius's *opuscula sacra* by succeeding generations strengthened this link. There was also a trio of Platonic texts in circulation: Plato's own *Timaeus*, in Calcidius's partial translation, Boethius's *Consolation of Philosophy* and Macrobius's Commentary on Cicero's *Dream of Scipio*. In the period before 1100, however, the *Timaeus* was no more than sparsely glossed, and the comments do not take up issues, but offer explanations or parallels.[2] There was a fuller tradition of glosses to Macrobius, but they concerned mostly astronomy and geography, or added extra information from other sources.[3] By contrast, there was a rich tradition of early medieval commentary on the *Consolation*, stretching back to Boethius's near contemporary, Cassiodorus, through Charlemagne's teacher and advisor Alcuin, to ninth- and tenth-century masters. Boethius, arguably, had engaged with the Problem of Paganism through the dialogue structure of the *Consolation*. But none of his early medieval readers was aware of this strand in his thinking. What is left, then, is a text with a Platonic flavour written by a Christian author and read by Christian readers. It was in consequence very easy for these readers to make the text so at home in a Christian setting that the Problem of Paganism all but disappeared.

Cassiodorus' edition of the *Consolation* probably contained miniatures which identified Philosophy with the biblical figure of Wisdom.[4]

---

[2] See Somfai 1998, 2002.
[3] White 1981; Caiazzo 2002, 52–57.
[4] See Troncarelli 1981; 2005, 27–96.

Alcuin too suggested this identification. In the preface to his *Grammatica*, Alcuin uses Boethius's phrases to describe how people search for happiness but are misled into pursuing individual, transitory goods. But this search is seen as one for wisdom, and wisdom is characterized in biblical terms, and linked to Solomon's temple, its columns representing both the seven liberal arts, and the seven gifts of the Holy Spirit.[5] In both cases, then, the *Consolation* is brought within a biblical (Old Testament rather than New Testament) frame of reference, with just a touch of specifically Christian doctrine (the gifts of the Holy Spirit), which is not presented as an interpretation of Boethius's text. Or consider some of the ninth- and tenth-century glosses to the beginning of the work. Philosophy is seen as Wisdom and those who have torn her clothes are 'heretics who cut up true doctrine through their heresy'.[6] She looks into Scripture more deeply than humans, or she is even seen as the 'Wisdom of God', Christ himself.[7] Only this final comment actually Christianizes. Or, in a passage discussing fate (IV.6.13), Boethius's reference 'by divine spirits' is explained as 'with the spirit of wisdom', and a gloss in another manuscript refers to a line in Isaiah (xi, 22) about the 'spirit of wisdom and understanding', whilst yet other glossed manuscripts identify the spirits as Cherubim and Seraphim.[8] Or, finally, consider the Old English version of the *Consolation*, which is very far from being a literal translation. The translator adds definite references to the Christian doctrinal world—God the Creator, the afterlife, martyrdom, but, as the work's recent editor explains (in a section none the less titled 'Christianisation') 'there are only two explicitly Christian references in the whole work', and the biblical allusions are not identified as such, nor are any of the Church Fathers cited by name, by contrast with Plato, Aristotle and Cicero.[9] Altogether, in the gloss tradition explicit Christianization is unusual, just like the opposite

[5] Alcuin 1863, cols. 849–54; see Brunhölzl 1965; Courcelle 1967, 33–47; and Marenbon 1994, 172–73.

[6] Silk 1935, Appendix, secs. 16, 44 (Wisdom), sec. 42 (heretics)—material usually attributed to Remigius of Auxerre. For the tradition of glosses, an up-to-date survey is provided by Love 2012. The latest research suggests that it is wrong to think in terms of discrete commentaries, each written by a different author: glosses were teaching material, which circulated freely and were adapted and amalgamated by different teachers. Courcelle 1967—a study which, for all the inadequacies which have been revealed, has still not been replaced—presents the material rather in terms of individual authors: the subtle and sophisticated Anonymous of St Gall, the pedantic and confused Remigius of Auxerre and others. Love 2012 gives grounds for rejecting this approach, following a line which, for the *Consolation*, was pioneered by Fabio Troncarelli—see Troncarelli 1987; 2005.

[7] Cf. Courcelle 1967, 275–76, referring to Anonymous of St Gall.

[8] The information about the interpretation of this passage is taken from Love 2012, 109–10, referring to Anonymous of St Gall manuscripts and other ones.

[9] Boethius 2009, 66–68.

extreme—the marking out of some ideas as unacceptable because un-Christian: 'here Boethius speaks more as a philosopher than a Christian' (*magis philosophice quam catholice*), as one gloss on the passage about fate puts it.[10] Bovo of Corvey (d. 916) stands out because his attitude is entirely this condemnatory one. He explains that Boethius is the author of 'an outstanding book' on the Trinity and of one against Nestorius and Eutyches (the first and last of the theological treatises), but that in the *Consolation* he had decided 'not to say anything about Christian doctrine, but only to open to his readers the teachings of the philosophers, especially the Platonists'.[11] Using Macrobius, he gives an unusually clear and careful explanation of book III, metrum 9, but he considers (or professes to) that the value of his exegesis lies just in exposing its dangerous falsehoods.

This metrum is indeed the most concentratedly pagan section of the *Consolation,* although even here many recent scholars have found ideas and phrases which betray a Christian author. Most of the early medieval glossators, however, were content neither to condemn, nor explicitly to Christianize, except at occasional moments, but rather to neutralize passages such as the one about the World Soul, which taken literally might seem to go against Christian teaching: it is read as being about individual souls, or about the sun.[12] Similarly, lines which could be taken to talk about reincarnation are given a moral interpretation.[13]

The making comfortable within a Christian world, neutralization and occasional explicit Christianization characteristic of the gloss tradition leaves it apart from the Problem of Paganism. These interpretative techniques are ways of handling first-order influence: the ideas, concepts and words which writers of one age take from those of the past. But the Problem of Paganism is connected with second-order influence, which considers how writers of an age think about the past writers they are using.[14] The one commentator from this period who does exceptionally make a definite second-order point about the Problem of Paganism is Adalbold of Utrecht. Glossing the opening of book III, metrum 9, 'O you who govern the world with perpetual reason', he explains that Boethius, because of his Christian faith, was able to see what Plato and Hermes Trismegistus had been blind to—'that the world is ruled by perpetual

[10] Love 2012, 109. The same manuscripts also have a gloss which links Boethius to the biblical tradition of the 'spirit of Wisdom'.
[11] Huygens 1954, 385:51–53.
[12] See Stewart 1916, 33 (attributed to Remigius); Troncarelli 1981, 182–83 (glosses from MS Vatican lat 3363); and see the interpretations given in MS Einsiedeln 179 (Anonymous of St Gall tradition), as edited and discussed in Dronke 2008, 51–53.
[13] Stewart 1916, 34.
[14] Cf. Marenbon 2012a, 6–7.

reason', because 'he understood that it is not just made, but also governed, through the wisdom of God, that is through the Son of God'.[15]
Adalbold considers that Plato and Hermes did grasp the notion of divine
reason, although they had different names for it. His claim, then, seems to
be that, by understanding it in Christian terms as the Son, Boethius could
see, as his pagan predecessors could not, that it is responsible for the continued governance of the world, as well as its initial construction. Adalbold is thus commenting on the extent, but limitation, of pagan wisdom.

Where, in connection with other texts or questions, the Problem of Paganism came to the surface in early medieval writing, it tended to receive
the same sort of reassuring treatment as found in most of the Boethius
commentaries. One such instance occurs in a text by a writer already
mentioned, Alcuin.[16] The setting is unexpected—a treatise on rhetoric,
based on Cicero's *On Invention*. Since Cicero's treatise ends with a section about the four cardinal virtues, it is not at all surprising that Alcuin's
discussion should also take this turn (indeed, the treatise is normally
called *On Rhetoric and the Virtues*). But Alcuin chooses to discuss explicitly the relation between these virtues, described by pagan philosophers,
and Christianity. It was no novelty to use the virtues distinguished by the
pagan philosophers for the moral education of Christians. More than
two centuries earlier (between 570 and 579), Martin, Bishop of Braga,
had epitomized what is almost certainly a lost work by Seneca on the
four virtues with such fidelity that most of its medieval readers would
attribute it to Seneca himself; in his introductory letter, Martin explains
that he is keeping to precepts that can be grasped by humans naturally,
without Holy Scripture, because he is writing for the laity. In his treatise,
written in dialogue form, with the emperor, Charlemagne, himself as the
interlocutor, Alcuin explores more thoroughly the issue that is raised,
implicitly, by this remark. Following but elaborating on Cicero (II.52), he
explains that 'there are some things so excellent and so noble, that they
should not be sought for any other advantage but should be loved and
pursued for their own worth alone'.[17] These things are virtue, knowledge,
truth—and Alcuin adds to Cicero's list 'good love'. Alcuin agrees with
the emperor's suggestion that it is the Christian religion which especially
commends these, and when he is asked what the philosophers have to do
with them, he answers that 'they understood them in human nature and
cultivated them with the greatest zeal'. What, then, Charlemagne understandably asks, is the difference between such a philosopher and a Christian? 'Faith and baptism', replies Alcuin. 'But', commands Charlemagne,

[15] Huygens 1954, 410:18–20.
[16] I have discussed this topic in Marenbon 2011a, 233–35.
[17] Halm 1863, 548:14–16.

'continue with the philosophical definitions of the virtues'—and his teacher duly obliges, on the basis of Cicero's text. Charlemagne then returns to the question about pagan virtues and Christians. 'It makes me wonder at us Christians', he says: 'why, if those philosophers maintained these virtues just because of their worth or for the sake of praise for their lives, we many times turn away from them in perverse error, although now the reward of eternal glory is promised by Truth Itself, Jesus Christ, to those who follow them in faith and charity'.[18] Alcuin is then asked by Charlemagne to show how 'these excellent virtues are to be understood and observed in our Christian religion'. Alcuin explains that wisdom is that by which God is understood and feared and his future judgement is believed, whilst justice, courage and temperance are all argued to be identical with charity. The end for which the virtues should be followed is 'so as to love God and one's neighbour'.

The identity of the virtues with charity and the requirement that they be directed towards God and the image of God in humans are characteristically Augustinian ideas, and in this final section of his work Alcuin borrows themes and passages from Augustine.[19] Yet he ends up by giving a very different view of the pagan virtues. It is not merely that Alcuin goes out of his way to praise the philosophers (even the remark that they followed the virtues to win praise, as well as for their intrinsic worth, does not appear to be intended critically). There is no suggestion in Alcuin's account that the philosophers' virtues are false. The virtues cultivated by the pagan philosophers are real ones, which Christians too need to observe, though in a special way. For Augustine, there is an opposition between the correct understanding of the virtues, as means, with God as their end, and the philosophers' pursuit of them for their own sake. Alcuin does indeed follow Augustine's view that love of God and neighbour are the ends of the virtues, but he does not seem to think it incompatible with the idea—which he takes from Cicero, but elaborates in his own words—that wisdom and the virtues are so excellent and noble that they should be sought for their own sake. Indeed, by adding 'good love' to Cicero's list, he at once Augustinizes it but also undermines Augustine's position according to which good love (that is, love for God), but *not* the virtues, is intrinsically valuable.

Alcuin is not deliberately or consciously opposing Augustine. Rather, he understands him selectively, and in doing so replaces Augustine's stark

[18] Halm 1863, 549:28–32.

[19] See Mähl 1969, 109–16. In his *De virtutibus et vitiis* (PL 101, 613–38), Alcuin does not treat the virtues which pagans can have separately as he does here, and his definitions of the virtues (chap. 35; 637B–38A) immediately add Christian interpretations to them. See Bejczy (2011, 34–37), who gives less weight to Alcuin's un-Augustinian revaluation of pagan virtue than I do here.

division between Christian excellence and false pagan virtue with a harmonizing account. And there is a sign that this accommodating attitude to pagan excellence was not confined just to this work. A short dedicatory poem survives which Alcuin wrote to accompany a manuscript of two texts which he sent as a gift to Charlemagne: the works in question are the (supposed) *Letters* between Alexander and King of the Brahmans, and the (supposed) *Letters* between St Paul and Seneca.[20] They are both texts which suggest the closeness between ancient pagans and Christianity. From the exchange between the Indian philosopher-king and Alexander, it can be gathered that the Brahmans knew of the coming of Christ before the Incarnation and that they lived lives of exemplary austerity;[21] Alcuin says that their way of life 'is wondrous' and the reader is asked see their faith in his mind's eye. From the letters between him and Paul, Seneca is made to appear, at the least, strongly sympathetic to Christianity, and on their basis Jerome (in a passage copied as a prologue in most manuscripts) placed him with the *sancti*.[22]

Another example of an early medieval conciliatory approach to the Problem of Paganism is the first airing in the Latin tradition of the story of Pope Gregory and Trajan. Unusually for the period, it arises within the context of doctrinal discussion, although of a very unsophisticated kind. The story is told in the earliest life of Pope Gregory the Great, an artless composition, written early in the eighth century by a monk of Whitby who knew neither the standard rules for writing a hagiography nor much about the details of Gregory's life.[23] The writer explains how 'the soul of the Emperor Trajan was comforted or baptized (*refrigeratam vel baptizatam*) by the tears of Pope Gregory': 'One day Gregory was crossing the forum, which they say Trajan built with wonderful workmanship. As he was looking at it, he discovered that Trajan, a pagan, had done a deed so charitable that it seemed as if it could be more that of a Christian than a pagan'. He then goes on to tell how Trajan interrupted a military expedition in order to see that a widow whose son was killed was paid compensation by his murderers. The incident reminds Gregory of the biblical injunction to 'judge for the fatherless, defend the widow' (Isaiah i, 17), 'And so through him he had Christ speaking within himself. He did not know what to carry out in order to comfort his soul, and entering St Peter's he wept floods of tears, as he often did, until he merited that it was divinely revealed to him that he had been granted what he wished

[20] Carmen 81, lines 1–6; Dümmler 1881, 300.

[21] On these letters, their origins and their later influence, see chapter 7.

[22] *De viris illustribus* 12. For this fictional correspondence, see Barlow 1938 (edition and testimonia); Fürst et al. 2006 (reprints text and gives further introductory material).

[23] There is a useful discussion of the earliest versions of the Gregory-Trajan story in Whatley 1984b, 27–31.

(*sibi divinitus fuisse exauditum*), since he had never presumed that for any other pagan'.[24] Although the text is vague, the implication seems to be that Trajan, who as a pagan living after the preaching of Christianity had been placed in Hell, was saved as a result of Gregory's intervention. *Refrigerium* could refer to heavenly happiness or just a mitigation of punishment, but the writer adds that Trajan was 'baptized' by Gregory's intervention, and he comments: 'Let no one be surprised that we say "baptized". For no one will ever see God without baptism, and the third sort of baptism is of tears'.[25] Unfortunately, the monk of Whitby was even less of a theologian than he was a hagiographer or historian. In addition to straightforward baptism by water, the Church Fathers recognized baptism of blood (those who died for their Christian faith before they had the chance to be physically baptized) and baptism of fire (those who firmly desire baptism, but die before they can receive it). Baptism of tears seems to be this writer's own invention. Moreover, it was established doctrine that none of the souls in Hell could ever be released, and that Christians should not pray for them. Gregory the Great himself was one of its most forthright proponents.[26] Writers over the next eight hundred years were left with the task of sorting out the mess they had been left by the Whitby monk's doctrinal incompetence, since they were unwilling to reject the story of Gregory and Trajan as a complete fabrication.

Even more influential was another, more theologically competent example of the early medieval accommodative attitude, also concerning pagan salvation, which dates from just before the time of Abelard. The pagans in question are biblical ones. Before Abraham gave a distinct identity to the Jews, the patriarchs of Genesis were pagans, living according to natural law, rather than revelation. Although the Fall should, in strict theological terms, mark an absolute transformation of humanity, from its initial blessed and innocent state to a corrupt and sinful one, the early chapters of Genesis, with their stories of patriarchs who lived for hundreds of years, can be read as an account of an era which, if not golden—the Bible also tells of Cain's murder of Abel, and the Flood— had some strikingly upright individuals, such as Abel, Melchisedech and Noah. This reading received support from a source which was surprisingly available: Augustine's opponent, Pelagius. As already noted, Pelagius had rejected the view that humans were instantly corrupted by the Fall: rather, the habit of sinning became so widespread that it was difficult to resist, but still possible, so he maintained, to resist it without special help from God. The victory of Augustine's doctrine of grace over this

---

[24] Chap. 29; Colgrave 1985, 126–28.
[25] Chap. 29, Colgrave 1985, 126.
[26] See his *Dialogues* IV.44 (*PL* 77, 404CD).

position was complete, and no works were transmitted under Pelagius's own name. But some of his writings did survive pseudonymously, including a letter to Demetriades, misattributed to (his enemy) Jerome, which puts forward very clearly a view of Abel, Enoch, Melchisedech, Lot and Abraham as being specially just and close to God.[27]

Against such a background, the first systematic theologians of the Middle Ages, especially William of Champeaux, but also Anselm of Laon, and their pupils, working at the turn of the twelfth century, put forward a scheme of three periods of history, each distinguished by a different law. There was the period of Natural Law, stretching from the time of Adam at least to that of Abraham, who first received the special commandment of circumcision from God, if not to that of Moses. During this period, there was no written law, but people were able to follow the innate precepts of natural law, such as love of God and neighbour, and not killing or stealing.[28] There followed the period of the Old Law, lasting until the preaching of the Gospel and the institution of the New Law. These theologians generally accepted, as William of Champeaux put it explicitly, 'that it is established that some have been saved under natural law, under written law (the Old Testament) and under the Gospel'.[29] For each period, there was a different way in which Original Sin could be removed. Under the Old Law, the way was the 'sacrament', as it was described, of circumcision; baptism, of course, under the New Law, and under natural law 'sacrifices which, along with the accompanying inner feelings (*cum affectu mentis*) purged all things'.[30]

Although the three laws were attached to successive chronological periods, it was recognized that the Old Law applied only to the Jews, so that members of other races, such as Job, could go on living according to natural law and be saved by it long after the time of Abraham or Moses.[31] By contrast, baptism is a universal injunction, and so no one could be freed from sin in time of the New Law except by it. With regard to the knowledge of God and Christ under natural law, William of Champeaux based himself on Paul's statement (Hebrews xi, 6): 'But without faith it is impossible to please God. For he that cometh to God, must believe that

---

[27] (Ps.-) Jerome, Letter 1, 4–5; *PL* 30, 19D–20C.

[28] On this concept of natural law and the patristic and ancient tradition behind it, see Marenbon 1992, 609–10.

[29] *Sentence* 261:36–37; Lottin 1959, 212. Anselm of Laon (*Sentence* 50; Lottin 1959, 48) makes it clear, however, that they would not actually go to Heaven until after the Crucifixion.

[30] William of Champeaux, *Sentence* 261:45–46; Lottin 1959, 212; cf. Marenbon 1992, 610n8.

[31] Anselm, *Sentence* 49; Lottin 1959, 48; William, *Sentence* 261:51–52; Lottin 1959, 212.

he is, and is a rewarder to them that seek him'. This statement provides a rather low threshold for what is to count as faith: belief in God as a repayer of good and evil. Relying on this Pauline minimum, William declared, 'It should be said that those who were saved before the coming of Christ believed that there is a just and pious judge who would repay the good with good things and the evil with bad things. There were also some who believed that someone would come from God who would redeem the people, but they did not know how he would do so. And there were a very few to whom the manner of the Redemption was known'.[32] It is wrong to describe this as a theory of *implicit* faith (though one would be developed from it). In William's view, the Pauline minimum is enough, both under natural law and the Old Law, to allow a person to be saved.[33]

William was concerned exclusively with biblical figures, but at least one writer of the time, very probably Ralph, Anselm of Laon's brother, extended the same way of thinking to 'the ancient philosophers or anyone else': 'for if they had believed that God exists and that this thing is a rewarder and judge, they would have been saved, since it is clear that some lived well'. The writer goes on to say that this belief, the Pauline Minimum, was 'nothing other' than believing in the coming of Christ, without knowing how they would be rewarded by God, and that from it they would be compelled to a belief in the survival of the soul and resurrection of the body.[34] He seems, though, to be talking about what might have happened but did not: he is arguing, not for the actual salvation of the pagan philosophers, but in the spirit of Paul in Romans that they lost the opportunity they were given (and so have been justly damned).

CHRISTIANIZING EUROPE AND THE PROBLEM OF PAGANISM

Although scholars like Anselm and William could take it for granted that they lived in a Christendom that stretched far further than they were ever likely to travel, Christian Europe came about only as the result of a long process, which had not yet been completed in their time. There were two overlapping processes: the Christianization (of the original inhabitants) of the Roman Empire—a process glimpsed above in the accounts of the early Fathers, Augustine, pseudo-Dionysius and the last pagan Greek philosophers; and what might be called the Christianization of medieval

---

[32] *Sentence* 261:38–42; Lottin 1959, 212.

[33] It was therefore misleading for me (Marenbon 1992, 611; 1997a, 328) to describe William's remarks as putting forward what would later be described as a theory of implicit faith. For implicit faith, see below, pp. 168–72.

[34] Lottin 1959, 188 (Text 235: immediately after a *sententia* explicitly attributed to Ralph and so very probably also by him).

Europe, which took place in three main stages. First, there was the acceptance of Catholic Christianity by the barbarians who, starting with the Visigoths in 376, followed by the Ostrogoths, Vandals, Burgundians and Franks, had entered the Roman Empire and started to settle and establish kingdoms there. This phase was complete by the end of the sixth century, by when the second stage had already begun: the evangelization, beginning in the fifth century and continuing to the end of the ninth, of areas which had never been Romanized or where Christianity had disappeared—Ireland, Britain, Saxony, Frisia, Bavaria and Denmark. The third stage was the Christianization of the outlying northern and eastern areas, a process full of reversals, which was officially complete only in 1386 when Lithuania, a flourishing pagan kingdom for the previous century, adopted the Catholic Church.[35]

In the first phase, there was in fact little direct contact with *paganism*, because the various tribes were already, or rapidly, converted to Christianity, although usually, to a Christianity which followed the Arian heresy. They were gradually brought to Catholic orthodoxy by the end of the sixth century. Although national histories would be written for three of these peoples—Jordanes's *Getica* (sixth century—on the Goths), Gregory of Tours's *History of the Franks* (late sixth century) and Paul the Deacon's *History of the Lombards* (late eighth century)—they contain very little at all about paganism.

The case was different in the second stage of Christianization. The Anglo Saxons were, at least in the main, pagan until the evangelization begun by Gregory the Great's missionary, Augustine of Canterbury. There is accordingly a little more discussion of paganism in Bede's *Ecclesiastical History of the English People* (c.731), including the famous comparison (II.13) made by a pagan nobleman of the life of humans to the brief flight of a swallow, from the wintry night outside, through the warmth and light of a feasting hall and out again into the darkness. We know nothing, he adds, of what came before or may come after our life—an ignorance of the life to come which, unusually and perhaps with the native pagan tradition in mind, Bede attributes in his exegetical works to the 'philosophers and other masters of the Gentiles'.[36] But Bede's overwhelming interest is in *conversion*, and the same is true of the ninth-century accounts of the missionaries who brought Christianity to the remaining pagan parts of Germany, such as Willibald's *Life* of Boniface, the *Life* of Wulfram, Altfrid's *Life* of Liudger and Rimbert's *Life* of Anskar, the first

[35] For a general account, see Christiansen 1980.
[36] In his commentary on Parables (*CCSL* 119B; II.19, line 34), he refers to *philosophi caeterique gentium* magistri, saying that they 'can promise no certain happiness in the future'; in his commentary on Tobias (*CCSL* 119B; 7, lines 8–9) he talks of the learned people of ancient times who 'said nothing certain about eternal things'; cf. Plummer 1896, 100.

evangelist of Scandinavia. The descriptions of pagan customs are not detailed, and there is no suggestion that any of these peoples were regarded as wise or virtuous.

By contrast, from the third stage of European Christianization, stretching far beyond the bounds of the early Middle Ages, there are a number of important texts for the Problem of Paganism, either because they show the beginnings of an ethnographic approach to the question of pagan knowledge of God, or because they touch on pagan virtuousness, or because they involve Christian authors imagining themselves into a pagan setting.

Helmold of Bosau's *Chronica Slavorum* (1163–72) contains a fairly detailed, though pejorative, description of the religion of the Slavs, including the names of its gods, its dualistic character and the human sacrifices it involved.[37] Herbord's *Dialogue* on the life of Saint Otto (1158–60), who preached Christianity to the Pomeranians, contains a description of a pagan temple and its decorations, and of a sacred black horse, too holy for anyone to ride on and able to prophesy military success or failure.[38] Adam of Bremen's *History of the Archbishops of Hamburg-Bremen*, written in the 1060s and 1070s, has been called the first medieval 'systematic ethnography' of a region, because of the final book, which describes the Scandinavian world, including its practices of worship.[39] Adam's most famous description of paganism is his account of the temple to the Norse Gods at Uppsala, and the sacrifices of animals and humans carried out there,[40] although it seems that not only has Adam taken some of his details for the pagan practices from classical Latin sources,[41] but also that there was in fact no pagan temple at Uppsala. (According to one recent scholar, Adam does not even intend his description to be taken literally: the pagans are for him, a staunch supporter of the empire, allegorically, the Christians who have followed the anti-imperial reforming pope, Gregory VII!)[42] The most detailed ethnographic account of North European paganism, from nearly three centuries later, also turns out to be compromised. Peter of Dusburg's *Chronica terrae prussiae*, written in 1326, is a record of the campaigns by the Knights of the Teutonic Order which succeeded in subjugating and evangelizing many of the pagan Baltic peoples from the early thirteenth century onwards. Peter fully shared the Teutonic

[37] Chap. 52; Helmold of Bosau 1963, 196–98; see also chap. 84 (288–90) on the destruction of a pagan sacred grove.

[38] II.32–33; Herbord 1974, 122–26. The horse made its prophecy by stepping over undisturbed spears that had been laid on the floor.

[39] Timothy Reuter, in his preface to Adam of Bremen 2002.

[40] IV.26–28; Buchner and Trillmich 1961, 470–72.

[41] Garipzanov 2011b, 25–28.

[42] Janson 2000.

Knights' warlike, indeed brutal, approach to their crusade, although he was apparently an accurate reporter of the campaign.[43] In one section, however, he pauses to give a fairly lengthy account of the beliefs and worship of his pagan enemies.[44] He identifies a chief priest, Criwe, whom he describes as a 'Pope' and who is said to exercise power over all the pagans of the region, sacrificing a third of all their booty to the gods. The fact that Peter places this Pope in a town called 'Romuwe', after Rome, might raise suspicions, and the leading historian of medieval Lithuania has argued that Criwe—who plays no part in the narrative—is the chronicler's invention, a moral exemplum aimed at those of the Teutonic Knights who were wavering in their support for the real Pope.[45] There remains, however, Peter's account of the pagan practices, which he not only describes but attempts to understand. The Prussians, he says, 'believed in the resurrection of the flesh, but not, however, in the way they should have done: they thought that, if someone was noble or base, rich or poor, powerful or weak in this life, so he would be after the resurrection in the life to come'. Consequently, as he explains, when a nobleman died, along with his corpse were burned arms, servants and handmaidens, clothes, hunting birds and dogs. 'They believed that the things which had been burned would be resurrected with them and serve them as before'. The Prussians worshipped every sort of creature: the sun, the moon, birds, beasts—even the toad. The reason why, Peter explains, is that they had no knowledge of God, and this, in turn, was because they could neither understand him through reason, because they were not intellectually capable, nor read about him, because there was no writing in their culture.[46]

Somewhat surprisingly, given the missionary or warlike context of most of the texts, there are rare moments at which some authors present the pagans, not as embodiments of savagery and evil, but as virtuous. Adam of Bremen describes the Prussians as 'the most human of human beings', remarking on their willingness to help those in danger on the seas or being attacked by pirates and their scorn for silver, gold and furs—all this despite their aggressive paganism, on which he remarks, 'Many things could be said about these peoples in praise of their way of life, if but they had the Christian faith, whose preachers they persecute without limit'.[47] This description clearly appealed to Helmold of Bosau, who copied it verbatim into his *Chronica*.[48] Even more striking is the depiction, in Cosmas of Prague's *Chronicle of the Czechs* (1119–25) of the earliest,

---

[43] See Matuzova 2001.

[44] III.5; Peter of Dusburg 2012, 88–94.

[45] Rowell 1994, 38–40, 125–28.

[46] III.5; Peter of Dusburg 2012, 88.

[47] IV.18 (Buchner and Trillmich 1961, 454–56; the quotation is at 456:9–10).

[48] Chap. 1; Helmold of Bosau 1963, 36:12–29.

pagan inhabitants of the region as showing all the virtues of the Golden Age; he even compares their communal way of life to that of monks.[49]

It is within the half reality of the imagination that writers most engage with the paganism of the edges of Europe. They do so, though in a restricted way, even in historical writing, especially that reaching back to a more or less distant, and pre-Christian past. To the national histories written early in the Middle Ages, others were added in the twelfth and thirteenth centuries. In some, such as Geoffrey of Monmouth on the British, and Giraldus Cambrensis on Welsh and Irish, paganism, perhaps deliberately, remains incidental, just as it did in twelfth-century romances set in pagan Graeco-Roman antiquity.[50] In Hungary, where pagans, as well as Muslims and Jews, were a presence throughout the Middle Ages, the earliest surviving chronicle (by the Anonymous Notary, c. 1200) takes a different approach. It is entirely concerned with pagan times. Although they are not a major element, the Christian author carefully includes fitting details of pagan life, such as horse sacrifice, within his narrative, noting that these are the pagan custom.[51] *Heimskringla*, the history of the kings of Norway, written in the early thirteenth century by (probably) Snorri Sturluson, is open about the paganism of his ancestors, recounting how the ruler and magician Odin (Óthin) establishes priests for sacrificial offerings and the rite of burning the dead, promising that in the afterlife they would have the use of whatever was burned with them. Saxo Grammaticus's *History of the Danes* (finished by c. 1220) addresses the question of paganism even more directly, though in passing, by saying that Odin was *believed*—though wrongly—to be a god, and telling how he took advantage of this apparent divine status.[52] Saxo returns to the idea later on, saying that Odin and a number of other magicians pretended to be Gods: people in Norway, Sweden, Denmark and beyond were taken in and worshipped them rather than the true God.[53] Although, then, paganism is acknowledged in these works of Nordic history, it is quickly explained away.

In writing that makes fewer claims to be history the way is open for an imagined paganism to play a larger role. In the strange *Cosmographia*

[49] I.3; Cosmas of Prague 1923, 8 (see lines 18–20 for comparison with monastic life); cf. Bak 2011, 179, who does not, however, notice the monastic reference. (At almost the same time, Peter Abelard was comparing to the monastic life what he took to be the communal life of the ancient Greek philosophers: see below, pp. 85–86.)

[50] See below, p. 224.

[51] Silagi 1991—see 62:10–11 and 72:18 for horse sacrifice; cf. Veszprémy (2011), who thinks (188) that the author might have been drawing on oral tradition or surviving pagan practice. On the pagan Cumans in medieval Hungary, see Berend 2001, 244–66.

[52] Book I.7.1; Saxo Grammaticus 1931, 25:1–8.

[53] Book VI.5.3; Saxo Grammaticus 1931, 152:3–11.

of Aethicus Ister, written in about 730, which gives in often deliberately obscure Latin an account of Heaven, Hell and, mainly, the geography and inhabitants especially of the North, it is claimed that the author— who pretends to be Jerome—is presenting or summarizing the writing of a pagan Scythian 'philosopher'. The paganism is, however, something of a veneer, since the author's concern in the less purely geographical parts of the book is not so much to imagine a pagan world as to use the freedom of his pagan mouthpiece to reimagine the Christian vision of the universe—so that, in the thirteenth century, Roger Bacon would be able to cite 'Aethicus' as evidence for the harmony between pagan philosophy and Christian thought.[54] *Beowulf*, the greatest of Old English poems, is notoriously difficult to date (conjectures range between the early eighth century and c. 1000, when it was written down in the one surviving man-uscript), but scholars now agree that it is a poem written by a Christian author but given a pagan setting. The story is set centuries earlier and, although Grendel and his mother, the two monsters who will be slain by Beowulf, are explained in biblical terms as the progeny of Cain, the human characters belong to a pagan world and Hrothgar, the king, and his followers are portrayed, near the beginning of the poem (lines 175– 80) sacrificing to their gods (and reproached for it by the narrator). There is, however, little emphasis in what follows on the characters' pagan-ism, and so it remains open whether it is a central theme which is being treated subtly, or a detail which the Christian author prefers to ignore.[55]

In some Icelandic literature, however, imagined paganism is a more central presence. The Prose Edda—thought to be by Snorri Sturlason, from the 1220s—was intended as a manual of Norse poetics. Its longest section (*Gylfaginning*—'The Duping of Gylfi') is a dialogue explaining Nordic mythology. It is placed within an elaborate framework, involv-ing a prehistoric king, Gylfi, Odin and ultimately the biblical story of creation and an explanation of how, having lost the knowledge of God, humans reasoned out the existence of a supreme ruler from the ordering of the world and heavens.[56] But the framework does not intrude on the presentation of the pagan beliefs. Even more remarkable is the Elder (or Poetic) Edda, the collection of Icelandic poetry in the *Codex Regius*, writ-ten in about 1270. The poems differ greatly in style, content and, prob-ably, origin. But scholars now would agree that there are many which, despite their pagan theological content, were written in Christian times.

---

[54] See Aethicus Ister 2011, especially the editor's introduction, for the date, context (per-haps Bobbio) and character of this work.

[55] A good introduction to scholarly debate on the date and background of *Beowulf* is given in Orchard 2003. Robinson (1991) offers an interpretation which emphasizes the deliberate construction of a pagan setting.

[56] On the background, see Dronke and Dronke 1977.

Indeed, it can be argued that the grandest of the mythological poems, *Voluspá*, which tells of the origins, destruction and rebirth of the gods, has a strong and deliberate Christian colouring.[57] Here Christian authors have chosen to inhabit the pagan world of their past. In a way which has its parallels in very different writers of the Long Middle Ages (for instance, Boethius of Dacia trying to mark out an area for pure Aristotelian reasoning; Chaucer reconstructing the world of pagan Thebes),[58] a pagan vision is given the space to be taken seriously, even though it is recognized to be false.

[57] See the edition and commentary in Dronke 1997, esp. 93–98.
[58] See below, pp. 145–47, 224–28.

CHAPTER 5

Abelard

PETER ABELARD WAS THE FIRST THINKER, SINCE AUGUSTINE AND BO-
ethius, for whom the Problem of Paganism was a central concern. Two of
his works, in particular, are among the most remarkable of all medieval
treatments of the area. In book 2 of his *Theologia Christiana*, written
probably in the mid-1120, Abelard gives a golden picture of the wise and
virtuous men and women of ancient Greece and Rome, the philosophers
especially. Not only does he attribute to them knowledge of the true God.
He also argues that the virtues of these pre-Christians were genuine, and
that many of them have been saved. Probably just a few years later, Abelard wrote his *Collationes*, a dialogue, into which he introduces, as the
central figure, an ancient philosopher *redivivus*, unambiguously outside
Jewish and Christian revelation.[1] But for Abelard the Problem of Paganism extends beyond these texts where it is the main theme, since it is
bound up with the aims of the whole theological project which occupied
the second of the two stages of his career, in the 1120s and 1130s, after
he had been castrated and became a monk.[2] Abelard wanted to present
Christian doctrine both as rationally coherent and morally satisfying. By
showing that, at least in part through reason, the ancient philosophers
came to a good understanding of the true God, he strengthened the for-
mer contention, whilst the latter demanded that such obviously virtuous
people should be rewarded in Heaven.

Abelard's first theological work, written c. 1121, was the *Theologia
Summi Boni*. Abelard aimed, using his skill at logical analysis, to show
how the persons of the Trinity differ from one another although they
are one God. But he devoted book 1 to testimonies for the Trinity, not

---

[1] On the dating of the *Collationes*, see Peter Abelard 2001, xxvii–xxxii; and cf. Marenbon 2013a, 23–24. Abelard's major works are cited according to the following editions:
Collationes: Peter Abelard 2001; *Scito teipsum*: Peter Abelard 1971; *Sententie*: Peter Abelard 2006; *Theologia Christiana (TChr)*: Peter Abelard 1969; *Theologia Scholarium (TSch)*:
Peter Abelard 1987; *Theologia Summi Boni (TSB)*: Peter Abelard 1987.

[2] Abelard was castrated because, it seems, the guardian of Heloise, his wife in a secret
marriage, thought that he wanted to abandon her and force her to become a nun. On the
background to Abelard's life and works, see Clanchy 1997 (a biography), Marenbon 1997a
(a general study), Marenbon 2013a, chap. 1 (a survey of the works).

just from the Old Testament (it was a commonplace of Christian biblical exegesis that the Old Testament prophets knew God's triunity), but also, much more remarkably, from the ancient pagan philosophers. When the treatise was condemned as heretical at the Council of Soissons (1121), Abelard's reaction was to rewrite it as the *Theologia Christiana*, a much longer work, which does not retract but rather emphasizes and develops his more controversial views. Book 2, his eulogy of the philosophers, was an entirely new composition, written to counter the criticism of his use of the ancient philosophers as witnesses to the Trinity: 'they condemn the philosophers for being outside the faith since they were Gentiles, and as a result they deny them any authority with regard to faith, since they are damned' (*TChr* II.14).

The first impression from the *Theologia Christiana*, the *Collationes* and many of his other works is that Abelard is a sort of counter-Augustine in his attitude to pagans, despite the extensive use he makes of Augustine's works in discussing this theme. Where Augustine rejects pagan salvation and pagan virtues out of hand, Abelard appears to be arguing strongly for both of them. But this judgement is true only in part. On examination, Abelard's views turn out to be not entirely consistent, both less and more audacious than they seem initially. Their relation to Augustine's position is much more complex than simple opposition. It is easiest to disentangle the various threads by starting with Abelard's view on pagans' knowledge of God, before looking at his treatment of the salvation of pagans and then the question of their virtues.[3]

THE PAGAN PHILOSOPHERS AND THEIR KNOWLEDGE OF GOD

Abelard holds consistently that most of the ancient philosophers believed that there is one God.[4] He considers that they taught the truth, as recognized by Christians, about the immortality of the soul, heavenly reward and punishment and God's ordering of the universe (*TChr* II.26–42); and also that a number of ancient philosophers wrote, in a veiled fashion, about the Trinity, or at least about one or more of its persons, and he sets out his evidence for this judgement in the first book of each version of the *Theologia*.

The first of the ancient philosophers cited by Abelard is Hermes Trismegistus, a strange figure, who had an important role in the

---

[3] Studies of Abelard's treatment of the ancient philosophers include Gregory 1974; Jolivet 1980; and Valente 2011 (especially on philosophy as a way of life), 2013.

[4] In all three versions of the *Theologia* (*TSB* I.31; *TChr* I.57; *TSch* I.97) and the *Sententie* (sec. 90/90a), he supports the claim with a quote from Cicero's popular rhetorical work, *De inventione* (I.29/46): 'Those who engage in philosophy do not believe there are gods'.

historiography of philosophy up until the seventeenth century. The cult
of Hermes Trismegistus grew up in Egypt during the early Roman Empire, apparently fusing the Graeco-Roman god Mercury/Hermes with
the Egyptian god Thoth. To Hermes Trismegistus, who was thought to
have been a contemporary of Moses, was attributed a large range of
writings, in part treatises on magic, in part works of popular philosophy influenced by Platonism and Stoicism and generally monotheistic in
outlook. Some of the Church Fathers discussed the Hermetic writings.
Lactantius treated him respectfully, but in the *City of God* (VIII.23–24,
26; cf. XVIII.39) Augustine attacks him for idolatry. Abelard ignores,
however, Augustine's critical views, but uses material from Lactantius
quoted in the *City of God* and in a treatise wrongly attributed to Augustine to present Trismegistus as a venerable ancient philosopher who
wrote about the Son of God.[5] Hermes is just the first in a whole series of
ancient philosophers presented by Abelard: Pythagoras and Seneca, who
talk about the Holy Spirit, and outstandingly Plato and his followers,
such as Macrobius, who discussed all three person of the Trinity. Abelard
also names a few non-philosophers among the ancient pagans who spoke
or wrote of the Trinity: the Cumaean Sibyl, widely thought in the Middle
Ages to have prophesied the coming of Christ,[6] and the poet Virgil,[7] who
in his fourth eclogue refers to her and talks of the birth of a child who
will bring a new age; Nebuchadnezzar (because he sees, in addition to
the three men he had cast into the fire, a fourth 'who looks like the son
of God');[8] and the Brahmans (*Bragmanni*), known from the tradition of
Alexander literature.[9] There is also Job, whom Abelard often considers
along with the ancient philosophers, since the Bible makes is clear he was
not a Jew, although he was generally accepted as being among the Old
Testament saints.[10]

[5] See Dronke 1990, 223–27 and Lucentini 2007, esp. 72–83. Abelard cites Lactantius
(*TSum* I.61; *TChr* I.127; *TSch* I.190), but he has obviously taken the quotation from Au-
gustine (*CG* XVIII.23); the quotation which he uses to show that Hermes recognized the
Word of God is taken from Quodvultdeus's Sermon 10 'Against the Five Heresies'—itself
based on Lactantius—attributed by Abelard to Augustine: *TSum* I.35; *TChr* I.61; and *TSch*
I.115.

[6] *TSB* I.60; *TChr* I.126–27; *TSch* I.189–90.

[7] *TChr* I.128–29; *TSch* I.191–92.

[8] *TSum* I.62; *TChr* I.130; *TChr* I.194. Cf. Daniel iii, 92: 'Behold I see four men loose, and
walking in the midst of the fire, and there is no hurt in them, and the form of the fourth is
like the Son of God'.

[9] *TChr* I.131–33; *TSch* I.195–97. On the Brahmans, see below, chapter 7.

[10] See, e.g., *TSB* I.65, where Abelard cites Job xix, 25–26: 'For I know that my Redeemer
liveth, and in the last day I shall rise out of the earth. And I shall be clothed again with my
skin, and in my flesh I will see my God', remarking that here Job testifies more openly to the
resurrection of the body than all the prophets.

There was nothing new in arguing that some ancients, especially the philosophers, and particularly among them the Platonists, knew about the Trinity. Many of the Church Fathers, above all Augustine—as Abelard is keen to stress—held this view.[11] Indeed, Abelard says that those who criticize him for bringing in the testimony of the philosophers will have to include 'the holy doctors' in their condemnation and adds, 'I did not take the testimonies collected above from their writings, which I have never seen, but rather from the books of St Augustine'.[12] In addition, there was already a tradition among exegetes of Platonic texts of reading the texts in a way that made them fit more comfortably into a Christian context.[13] Abelard's decision to bring all these pagan testimonies together, to put them in parallel with the biblical evidence, emphasizing their explicitly Christian content was an innovation, however; as was his entirely sympathetic treatment, not just of Plato, but of Hermes Trismegistus, despite Augustine's attacks;[14] and so was the insistence with which he gives a Trinitarian reading to the Platonic texts and defends its orthodoxy as unique, as the comparison in the next chapter will show. Abelard therefore stands at the beginning of a medieval Latin strand of what, in the sixteenth and seventeenth centuries, when this way of thinking, looking back, especially, to early Jewish and Christian Greek writers, would flourish, was called the Ancient Theology (*prisca theologia*).[15] Abelard's view, however, as will become clear, is more complicated than that of most of those who would follow this line, because he envisages both a revelation to the ancient philosophers and also a genuine knowledge of the triune God gained by their power of reason.

Abelard has a strangely ambiguous attitude to the beliefs of the many ancient Greeks and Romans who were neither philosophers nor, like the Sibyls, had prophetic powers. On the one side, he presents the philosophers in parallel with the Old Testament prophets, and he suggests that they had more success than their biblical counterparts in making their message be believed. The Lord, he says, announced the central points (*tenor*) of the faith to the Jews through the Prophets, and to the Gentiles through the philosophers and poets (*uates*). This is why they were (in

[11] See above on Augustine.

[12] *TChr* II.12. This is, though, an exaggeration, since Abelard looks in detail at the text of Plato's *Timaeus* (in Calcidius's translation) and Macrobius's commentary on the *Dream of Scipio*. In *TSch* II.12 Abelard modifies this comment slightly, saying that he knows only a few of the philosophers' writings and referring to the 'holy fathers' generally rather than to Augustine alone.

[13] See above, chapter 4.

[14] Compare *TSB* 1.35, *TChr* I.61–67, *TSch* I.115–22 with Augustine, *De civitate Dei* VIII.23–24.

[15] See chapter 12. For an introduction to this theme, see Walker 1972.

Paul's word) 'inexcusable', if they failed to listen to them. But *some* of the Jews, and *many* of the Gentiles did indeed follow the faith of the Holy Trinity.[16] On the other side, in the *Theologia Scholarium*, the latest of his discussions of the question, while still making this point, Abelard puts forward elsewhere the idea, which he takes from Augustine, that the philosophers differed in their faith from the people and the priests, and indeed were opposed to them, but out of fear participated in the public ceremonies of polytheism and kept their own faith private.[17]

There is even greater tension between Abelard's different statements about how the philosophers' and other pagans' statements on the Trinity related to their own beliefs, and how they gained these beliefs. One line Abelard takes, on Jerome's authority, is a merely defensive one, which distinguishes the value of the teaching from the state of mind and beliefs of the teacher. Testimonies to the truth can be used, even if they come from unbelievers or heretics, in the same way as a non-believer is able to baptize in the name of the Trinity. Indeed, in so far as witnesses are enemies of a truth they witness and praise, they are more reliable, because they cannot be suspected of partiality. And in so far as a prophecy is miraculous—as, for example, in the case of Balaam's ass—it should be taken as all the truer, because it is not at all a matter of human understanding and entirely the work of the Holy Spirit. Abelard develops this approach in especial detail in book 2 of the *Theologia Christiana*, immediately before he launches into his lengthy and eulogistic description of the ancient philosophers and their civilization; he keeps the whole of this exposition in the *Theologia Scholarium*, while cutting out the paean to ancient Greece and Rome almost entirely.[18] And he repeats the same ideas on other occasions,[19] and also speculates explicitly that Virgil may not himself have understood the prophecy 'which the Sibyl or the Holy Spirit was speaking in him',[20] and about part of the philosophers' teaching on the World Soul (their name, he believes, for the Holy Spirit), he says that it was rather God speaking through them 'and they perhaps were ignorant of it'.[21]

This line is at odds, however, with how Abelard more frequently presents the position. He explains that the Platonists deliberately veiled their discussion of the Holy Spirit in metaphor.[22] But how could they deliberately conceal this teaching unless they already understood it? Abelard

[16] *TSB* I.63. The passage is taken over exactly into *TChr* I.136 and *TSch* I.201.
[17] *TSch* I.110–13.
[18] *TChr* II.1–11; TSch II.1–11.
[19] For example, *TSB* I.33–34; *TChr* I.59–60; *TSch* I.105–6; *Sententiae* sec. 99.
[20] *TChr* I.128; *TSch* I.191.
[21] *TChr* I.84; *TSch* I.141.
[22] See *TSB* I.38; *TChr* I.98; *TSch* I.158 and see chapter 6.

even goes on to say that unless what Plato says about the World Soul is to be taken metaphorically—as teaching about the Holy Spirit—then we shall be forced to take 'Plato, the greatest of philosophers, as the greatest of fools'.[23] And, in the *Theologia Scholarium* (I.124), he quotes Claudianus Mamertus to bear out that 'Plato did not only teach the faith of the Holy Trinity but showed clearly that it was so'—a strange remark if Plato himself did not believe it. At the other extreme from regarding the philosophers as unworthy and perhaps uncomprehending instruments of revelation is the view he expresses, at the start of the justification which precedes the account of the philosophers' testimony to the Trinity in the *Theologia Christiana* and the *Theologia Scholarium*, that they were led to their views both by 'the very reason of philosophy' (*ipsa philosophiae ratio*) and also as a reward for their ascetic way of life.[24] There are two different ideas here, though both are flattering to the ancient philosophers. According to both views the philosophers themselves believe the Trinitarian doctrines expressed by their writings, but by the first, they have reached these truths through philosophical reasoning; by the second— absent in the earliest version, the *Theologia Summi Boni*[25]—they gain the understanding through revelation, but they are chosen for the revelation because of their contempt for worldly goods. It was fitting, says Abelard, that God should 'mark out in them, through the gift of more abundant grace, how the person who lives soberly and withdraws himself from the attractions of the world in contempt is more pleasing to him' than one who gives himself up to pleasures.[26]

The first of these ideas fits in with two important themes in Abelards's thinking. One of them is brought out both in *Theologia Christiana* book 2 and, even more strikingly, in a short work christened by its recent editor *Soliloquium*. In dialogue with himself—the two speakers are called 'A(baelardus) P(etrus)' and 'P(etrus) A(baelardus)'—he explains that, because Christ is the Wisdom, *sophia*, of God, the word 'philosopher' fits Christians especially, because they are lovers of Christ, just as it fits the ancient philosophers, whose way of life and teaching accords with that of Christians, and who openly taught the doctrine of the Trinity.[27] The other theme shows Abelard in similar fashion bringing together reasoning and Christian doctrine, but in a much more carefully reasoned manner. He begins (I.2) the *Theologia Summi Boni* by declaring that, for God to be

<hr/>

[23] *TSB* I.43; *TChr* I.106; *TSch* I.166; cf. chapter 6.

[24] *TChr* I.54; *TSch* I.94.

[25] *TSB* I.30 refers merely to 'the reason of philosophy itself' leading them to the understanding (a Trinitarian one) of the one God.

[26] *TChr* I.54; *TSch* I.94. Valente (2011, 40–41) presents just this strand of Abelard's thinking.

[27] Peter Abelard 1984, see esp. 887. Cf. *TChr* II.43.

Father, Son and Holy Spirit, is 'as if we were to say that the divine substance is powerful, wise and benevolent (*benigna*)'. He then goes on (I.3) to argue that 'the whole perfection of the good consists in these three—power, wisdom and benevolence'. On its own, each of them is of little worth, but 'that in which these three come together, so that it can fulfil what it wishes, and, because benevolent, wishes well, nor steps over the measure of reason because it is wise—that is indeed is clearly good and perfect in all things'. It seems, then, that someone has only to think about what is involved in God's being entirely good to arrive at the fact that he is powerful, wise and benevolent, and by doing so, this person will have grasped the Trinity. Abelard repeats these claims in the *Theologia Christiana*, and says substantially the same in the *Theologia Scholarium*, although with a little more reserve about the equivalence between the two formulations.[28] In all three versions, he includes a paragraph in which he says that, since for God to be Father, Son and Holy Spirit is for him to be powerful, wise and benevolent, and no one of any intelligence—neither Jew nor Gentile—doubts this, 'it seems that this faith is lacking to no one'.[29] Abelard accepts this conclusion, and in the *Theologia Christiana* and the *Theologia Scholarium* he adds a paragraph explaining that, because of this concurrence, it should be easy to persuade those outside the faith, since they hold the same as Christians, although they use different words to express their belief. On this view, then, it should be no surprise at all that the ancient philosophers believed in the Trinity, since it is obvious to anyone who thinks about God at all.

What is the relationship between the first idea—that 'the very reason of philosophy' led the Philosophers to the Trinity—and the second one, according to which they knew about the Trinity through a revelation they had earned? Since Abelard expresses the two views together (in the same sentence, indeed), it seems that he must have believed they could be reconciled. One way, suggested by Jean Jolivet, is to equate the so-called revelation made to the philosophers with the gift of reason.[30] But how would that be a revelation, and, in particular, how could it be a revelation given specially to the philosophers on account of their ascetic lives? Perhaps—although it is certainly not worked out very clearly—Abelard had it in mind that all people at all times, by just a little thought, can come to the idea of God as a trinity of power, wisdom and benevolence and, in this sense, the philosophers and others are led to this truth by 'the very reason of philosophy'. In addition, as his exegesis of the Platonic texts on the World Soul shows, Abelard believed that some of the philosophers at

[28] *TChr* I.4–5; *TSch* I.30–33.
[29] *TSB* III.100; *TChr* IV.159; *TSch* II.183.
[30] Jolivet 1980, 108.

least had a much fuller knowledge of Trinitarian relations; this, he might have thought, they owed to the special revelation they had earned.

Knowing about the Trinity at all means knowing about the Son, as a divine Person—what Abelard calls his 'divinity'; but it need not include knowledge of his Incarnation. The passage in all three versions of the *Theologia* which says that everyone of any intelligence, whether Jew or Gentile, knows that God is a trinity of power, wisdom and benevolence continues by saying that 'they have perceived by reason what pertains to divinity (*ad diuinitatem*), because reason teaches these things about God naturally to everyone. For which reason, when (as quoted above) Augustine presented the views of the Platonists, he stated only that he had found in them what pertains to the divinity of the Word of God and nothing about the mystery of the Incarnation'.[31] For Abelard, as will become clear, knowledge of the Incarnation is of supreme importance for salvation. The comment just quoted does not rule out the possibility that ancient philosophers and others had knowledge of the Incarnation. Rather, it says that the Incarnation is not something which people of all times could have known about simply through using their reason. Although many of the pagan testimonies to the Trinity which Abelard presents contain no indication that the second Person would become a man, the Sibyl's utterances are explicitly recognized as prophesying the Incarnation and the Passion.[32] The existence of this prophecy is used by Abelard as a reason for saying that it cannot be shown that the ancient philosophers did *not* know about the coming of Christ. The fact that they do not talk of it openly in the writings may have been a deliberate choice, like that of the translators of the Septuagint, 'who, rendering the Law for non-Jews, kept silent about almost all the hidden things of the faith'.[33] In the *Theologia Christiana* (II.16), Abelard even suggests that Plato, read allegorically, can be taken to have written about the Crucifixion, when he talks in the *Timaeus* about making the earth by forming two lengths into the cross shape of the Greek letter chi and then bending them to form a globe. He drops this idea from the *Theologia Scholarium*, however, and, even in the *Theologia Christiana*, Abelard is very clear that knowledge of the Incarnation was exceptional among the philosophers. He begins his defence of them (II.15) declaring boldly that 'all the philosophers were Gentiles perhaps by nation, but not by faith', but with regard to their belief in the Incarnation he confines himself to showing that there is no reason to rule out the possibility in some cases. 'And who could assert that the faith in the Incarnation was revealed to none of them?', he

---

[31] *TSB* III.100; *TChr* IV.159; *TSch* II.183.
[32] *TSB* I.60; *TChr* I.26; *TSch* I.189.
[33] *TChr* II.15; *TSch* I.110.

asks, mentioning the Sibyl and explaining why they might have known about it but kept silent. Later in the same book (II.44), he says that the teaching of the Gospel fitted the philosophers' own thinking very closely, and 'it was perhaps not in disharmony in anything, except perhaps those things which pertain to the mysteries of the Incarnation, sacraments and Resurrection'.

ABELARD'S PHILOSOPHER: MORAL KNOWLEDGE WITHOUT REVELATION

Knowledge of Christ's Incarnation and Passion is central to Abelard's thinking about salvation. But before looking at that part of his think-ing, and his closely related consideration of virtue, there is another figure who needs to be examined: the Philosopher of the *Collationes*. He has not been discussed yet, because Abelard says almost nothing about his God. Even the basic knowledge of the Trinity as power, wisdom and be-nevolence is not explicitly attributed to him, though, from what Abelard says elsewhere, he can hardly have lacked it. Rather, Abelard concentrates on—not his moral behaviour, nor the possibility of his salvation—but the level and nature of his moral knowledge.

The Philosopher is one of four characters. In the first part, he is in dialogue with a Jew; in the second with a Christian. All three are figures in a dream, and the fourth, the dreamer himself, Abelard, has a walk-on role as the judge (who never delivers his judgement). Each of the par-ticipants has what might be called an 'autobiographical' identity, an ac-count of his background that can be established from what he says, and a 'theoretical' identity, the perspective from which he develops his posi-tion. The autobiographical identity of the Christian is bland: he is simply any highly educated Christian theologian; his theoretical identity is also straightforward: his perspective is like Abelard's own. Through a vivid account of his way of life and its hardships, the Jew is given a sharply focused autobiographical identity as a member of a Jewish community in Christian Europe. The Jew's theoretical identity, however, has nothing to do with the realities of Jewish living, worship or thought in the twelfth century. For a medieval Christian, even a rare one, like Abelard, able to portray their difficult existence as if from the inside, contemporary Jews were people who refused to recognize that Christ was their promised Messiah and clung, wrongly, to the Old Law, when it had been replaced by the New Law. Had Abelard written a dialogue between the Jew and the Christian, he could hardly have avoided these themes, which were at the centre of a large literature of Jewish-Christian dispute. Instead, it is the Philosopher who debates with the Jew who, he argues, gains nothing by following the Old Law rather than Natural Law, discovered by reason

alone. The discussion thus becomes one about whether the Old Law can
be justified for the Jews in its own terms, disregarding the fact that it has
now been replaced by the New Law. As a theoretical figure, then, the Jew
belongs to the period before Christianity, although he is given an attitude
to argument and a general view about the importance of intention in
morality close to Abelard's own.[34] The Philosopher is split in a similar
way. Autobiographically, Abelard connects him with the Islamic world,
and it is possible that he may have heard that in Islam there were, or
had been, thinkers who carried on the tradition of ancient, reason-based
philosophy (a gross simplification, but with some basis in reality).[35] Theo-
retically, however, the Philosopher belongs to the ancient world, like the
philosophers Abelard writes about in his *Theologia*.

Unlike most of them, however, he is not a Platonist.[36] The main reason
is probably that Abelard wants to use the imaginative space allowed by
the dream vision to conduct a thought experiment in how someone who
relied only on reason would think—a thought experiment that departs
from real history since, in Abelard's view, there was Christian revelation
even in the ancient pagan world and it was the Platonists, especially, who
took advantage of it. Moreover, by turning to two other schools of ancient philosophy, Abelard is able to respond to Augustine's position on
the question debated in this second book: granted that, absolutely speaking, God is the Highest Good, what is the Highest Good for humans?

The two ancient schools to which Abelard's Philosopher is made to
belong are an unexpected combination. The Philosopher is at once a Stoic
and an Epicurean.[37] He is given two positions which mark him out as a
Stoic. He holds that the wise do not feel pity, and that all virtuous people
are equally virtuous.[38] This second view is developed by using Cicero's
work, the *Paradoxes of the Stoics*, and is then subjected to a fierce attack
by the Christian, who succeeds in making the Philosopher abandon it.[39]
But the Philosopher also shows himself to be a follower of Epicurus. Epicurus tended to be reviled, both by members of other ancient schools of
philosophy and by Christian thinkers, for making pleasure the Highest
Good, though a few writers, such as Seneca, recognized that he meant

[34] See discussion in Peter Abelard 2001, xlvi–l and von Moos 2005.
[35] See Jolivet 1963 (connections with Islam), but cf. Peter Abelard 2001, l–liv.
[36] Diogenes and those who figure only in anecdotes, without having any doctrines attributed to them are an obvious exception; another exception is Seneca (*TSch* I.198), who
is included because of his supposed epistolary exchange with St Paul. There is also the Stoic
who figures in Aulus Gellius's anecdote about the philosopher in a sea storm (see below),
but his identity as a Stoic is lost in Abelard's reference.
[37] See Marenbon 2012a, 13–16.
[38] *Collationes* secs. 128 and 98–99, respectively.
[39] *Collationes* secs. 100–106.

tranquillity, not carnal delight. Abelard is the first of an important minority groupy of medieval authors who take a positive view of Epicurus.[40] Referring to Seneca, the Philosopher explains that Epicurus understood pleasure, not 'as the unworthy, shameful delights of bodily enticements, but a certain inner tranquillity of the soul'. He then declares that pleasure, understood in this sense, and virtue are *both* the Highest Good for humans—not because they are different parts of it, but because 'having a tranquil soul' and 'excelling in the virtues' are different words for the same thing (secs. 81–82). It is not, however, explained how this can be so, and it is in fact by placing more emphasis sometimes on virtue, sometimes on tranquillity that the two men continue to agree as their argument moves forward.

Since the Philosopher accepts the immortality of the soul, the Christian (secs. 83–84) argues, in the spirit of Augustine, that he should agree that there is greater happiness in Heaven, where there is no pain or suffering, and so it will be there that the Highest Good—'that by which, when someone attains it, he or she is happy'[41]—is to be found. The Philosopher does not immediately agree because, although he also retains the idea of the Highest Good as tranquillity, he insists that it is also virtue: only by becoming better can a person be more happy. In the end, however, the Christian persuades him that the life of Heaven must be the Highest Good, because sinning there is impossible, and non-moral evils, such as death, sickness and want, are absent. The Philosopher does not, however, believe that, by accepting this position, he is moving to a specifically Christian understanding. When the Christian argues (sec. 90), again repeating a point made by Augustine, that the pagan philosophers said that virtues should be pursued for their own sakes, whereas for Christians they are followed out of hope for something better, the Philosopher replies that pursuing virtue for its own sake means without consideration of earthly comforts and pleasures, but it does not rule out reward for merits. He then goes on (sec. 92) to suggest that by 'pleasure' Epicurus meant the same as what Christ did by 'the Kingdom of Heaven'. He can therefore claim that the Christian's reasoning has merely helped him to understand Epicurus (whose denial of immortality Abelard either does not know, or has chosen to hide) better. But he has clearly, though without explicit acknowledgement, regrouped the Stoic and Epicurean elements in his understanding of the Highest Good, so that the virtues become ways to gain, as a reward, perfect tranquillity.

[40] See Marenbon 2012a, 11, 14–15 and, for the most complete and balanced survey of medieval Epicureanism, Robert 2013.

[41] *Collationes* sec. 80, taken verbatim from Augustine, *CG* VIII.3 (see above, p. 36).

There are more twists and turns in the argument—partly, it seems, a contrivance to allow the Philosopher to put forward the Stoic theory of the equality of the virtuous, and the Christian to show why it is wrong—but the interlocutors seem (sec. 109) to have come to agreement: the Highest Good is the 'quietness of life in heaven' and the virtues are 'sufficient for happiness' in the sense that they are the *paths* to gain this quietness. But, after the Philosopher has been allowed to set out the nature of the individual virtues and their subdivisions, the Christian produces an argument against this position and against the corresponding one about the Greatest Evil for humans, which it identifies as punishment in the afterlife (secs. 147–49). The Christian points out that the guilt for which someone deserves punishment is something worse in him than the punishment itself, and so it, not the punishment is the Greatest Evil: rather, it is the hatred for God, with which those being punished burn. In the same way, the Highest Good for humans is not the life of Heaven but the love for God which the blessed feel there. This final position, apparently accepted by the Philosopher, harmonizes Augustine's views and the Philosopher's, and indeed it harmonizes the Stoic and Epicurean elements within his opinion better than he himself had done.

Augustine had insisted that the value of the virtues is in the struggle with vice which is never absent from earthly life: they lead to, but do not constitute, the Highest Good, salvation, which brings the true happiness found only in Heaven. There is a gulf between identifying the Highest Good for humans in terms of qualities like the virtues, which it seems to be good that people should have, but not obviously good for the people who have them, and in terms such as 'quietness', 'peace' or 'salvation', which denote obvious benefits for those who enjoy them. The Stoic view maintains that this gulf is apparent, because we are really most benefited simply by being virtuous, but this is denounced by Augustine as a sort of moral fanaticism. He and the Epicureans (even unadulterated Epicurus, to say nothing of the Philosopher's version of him) side together in proposing that people are right to set up what obviously benefits them as the Highest Good. But through the idea of love, which does not feature in ancient pagan ethics in this way, though it certainly does in Augustine, Abelard recognizes and yet overcomes the gulf. Love for God is both something virtue-like, which it is good for people to have—indeed, for both Augustine and Abelard it is the foundation of virtue (see below)—and yet it is also an obvious benefit, a more vivid and dynamic way of picturing the quiet of Heaven.

Through this sequence of argument, Abelard implies a second-order point about pagan moral knowledge. Augustine had argued that the main pagan schools were in intellectual error about the Highest Good for humans. By including the Epicureans, but adapting them, Abelard is able to show that their underlying position can be brought close to the Christian one. But the Philosopher's exegesis of his tradition's view is developed only through the Christian's questioning, and the final position, which harmonizes all the various elements, is the Christian's own. Not only this strand in the discussion, but the whole of the second dialogue of the *Collationes* suggests that the Philosopher, relying on natural reason, is on the path to the truth, but only the Christian—the rationalizing, Abelardian Christian—fully reaches it.

TRUE PAGAN VIRTUES

Abelard does not have to consider whether the Philosopher of *Collationes* is virtuous in practice, nor whether this figment of his imagination will be saved. But these questions loom large in his portrayal of the real philosophers of antiquity in *Theologia Christiana* II and elsewhere.

Abelard clearly sets out to portray the ancient philosophers as, for the most part, not merely virtuous, but virtuous in an extreme, exemplary fashion. The larger part of *Theologia Christiana* II is a commented dossier of quotations, texts and stories, designed to show that the ancient philosophers (and some other Greeks and Romans, but they are very much an afterthought) lived so virtuously as to put Christians to shame by comparison (II.43–115). This discussion is organized loosely around the three of the four cardinal virtues—justice, courage and temperance. (Abelard thought that the fourth, prudence, is a precondition for virtue rather than a virtue itself.) Abelard observes (II.27) that the Church Fathers took over the definitions of justice, courage and the other virtues from the philosophers. In showing how the philosophers' lives exemplified these virtues, Abelard concentrates in each case on an extreme form of the virtue. Rather than simply their courage, he concentrates on the magnanimity of the philosophers. He praises their justice as shown by the cities which, as he believes, they ruled. But the comparison is not with an ordinary civic community, but a monastery. And the monastic theme is continued by treating temperance in terms of its extreme manifestations— abstinence (giving up comforts and possessions) and sexual continence. In each case, Abelard wants to show that the ancient philosophers outdid the Christians of his own time, even the monks.

Abelard's main sources are the two pagan Platonic texts that had been known since the ninth century (the *Timaeus*, Macrobius on the *Dream of Scipio*), Valerius Maximus's collection of anecdotes from Roman legend and history, and especially Jerome's *Against Jovinianus* and some of his letters and Augustine's *City of God*. He handles them with great ingenuity and freedom. The *Timaeus* is mined for the information it contains about another work of Plato's, *The Republic*, which is summarized at its beginning, because it is supposed to have been the dialogue which took place the previous day. Abelard, who takes Plato's ideal scheme as if it were a description of real cities that ancient philosophers had established and ruled, is particularly impressed by the requirement that all goods be in common. In this way the city, he says (II.45), became a brotherhood and both prefigured the life of the first Christian apostles, and set an example for the monks of his own day.[42] Jerome wrote *Against Jovinianus* to attack a Christian who, among other heresies, denied the value of sexual continence and virginity, and of abstinence in food. One way Jerome attacks him is by showing that these ideals were pursued by pagans as well as Christians. He illustrates his point with *exempla* of ancient philosophers, such as the story of Diogenes who throws away a cup, his sole possession, once he finds out that he can drink using his hands, or of Crates, who throws his gold into the sea. For Abelard, Jerome's treatise was, therefore, an excellent source for his account of the virtues of pagan philosophers. He quotes Jerome's words and he borrows his stories, adding to them from Valerius Maximus and providing the first medieval example of a type of writing which would become popular: accounts of the ancient philosophers and their lives, sometimes consisting mainly of such anecdotes.[43]

The *City of God* seems to be a strange source to use in a eulogy of the ancient philosophers, since it is above all a critique of the civilization to which they belonged. To some extent Abelard may just be following the common medieval tendency to take passages from Augustine out of context to back up a whole variety of views. The praise of Socrates and the Platonic philosophers he quotes is genuine, but just one aspect of the complex position taken in the *City of God*. At other times, the partial nature of the quotation is more blatant. Where Augustine cites Aulus Gellius's story and discussion about the passions in order to correct the Stoic view presented, Abelard simply cites the Stoic view, as part of his praise of the pagan philosopher's courage.[44] Immediately afterwards, Abelard tells the story from *Against Jovinianus* of Diogenes, who cut his own throat rather than continue suffering from a fever.[45] But he then asks whether this is real or merely apparent courage. Suicide, he suggests (II.79), can

[42]Abelard quotes Acts iv, 32. He says (150:644; cf. 150:636) that those who now follow this way of life are the monks. See Marenbon 2007c.

[43]See below, chapter 6.

[44]*TChr* II.76, citing (with abbreviations), Augustine, *De civitate Dei* IX.4. For a detailed discussion of the *exemplum*, see Casagrande 2006, though she does not mention Abelard's use of it.

[45]*TChr* II.77; *Contra Jovinianum* II.14; *PL* 23, 305C–306B.

be condoned only if, as in the case of Samson, it is a divine command. He quotes from the *City of God* where Augustine writes against suicide, and puts Cato's and Lucretia's killing themselves down to pride. But (II.86) he ends by saying that, though suicide is to be condemned, Diogenes and other suicides can nevertheless be used as examples of 'contempt for this life and desire for eternal life', as if he refuses to take Augustine's point that these suicides were not just wrong, but also done for the wrong reasons. A little later on (II.107), when he is specifically praising conjugal chastity, Abelard returns to Lucretia, quoting a brief account of her story from Valerius Maximus, prefaced by the remark that 'she stands out as an example—she on whom almost all the Romans, poets as well as historians, have tried to bestow just praises for her love of chastity'. Here Augustine's quite other view seems implicitly to be rejected. These cases might suggest that Abelard sees the whole of this book as an anti–*City of God*, in which Roman and Greek civilization becomes part of sacred history. But his relation to Augustine turns out to be even more complex, as becomes clear once the question is posed of how Abelard's presentation of the virtuous lives of the pagan philosophers is compatible with his theological obligations and commitments.

Abelard accepted unquestioningly the truth of the Bible, and so he had to take account of the famous passage in Romans, where Paul says that, having come to know God through visible things, the philosophers became vain, turned to idolatry and moral degradation.[46] His usual strategy (one example of it has already been mentioned) is to say that Paul's words apply just to 'some' or 'a few' of the philosophers and to point out that Solomon, who was venerated as a biblical patriarch, had fallen in the same way.[47] Much more difficult to tackle was a problem raised by Abelard's theory of salvation. William of Champeaux—Abelard's teacher and then one of his great enemies—had considered that it was enough for people before Christian times to believe in God as the repayer of good and evil. Abelard did not accept this view, nor did he follow some of the theologians of his own generation, who thought that it was enough for those living under natural law to have a faith in Christ 'shrouded in mystery', which did not include knowledge of the Incarnation.[48] Rather, he insists on explicit knowledge of the Incarnation for all who are saved,

---

[46] See above, p. 20.

[47] *TChr* II.15 'some' (*nonulli*); *TSch* I.110 'a few' (*paucis potius quam multis imputandum uidetur*)—he had said a few paragraphs before that Paul blames 'many' (*plurimi*) of them for becoming corrupt. The comparison with Solomon is introduced at *TSB* I.33; *TChr* I.59, II.15; *TSch* I.104.

[48] See above pp. 65–66 (William of Champeaux) and below pp. 168–69 (theologians of Abelard's generation).

at any time. He blames a contemporary who held that 'many were saved before the Incarnation of God and redeemed by his Passion, who never believed in either his Incarnation or his Passion' for departing from the faith of the Church.[49] Moreover, in all three versions of the *Theologia* he states very clearly that it is certain that 'the whole sum of human salvation consists in the mystery of the Incarnation and the other things [the Trinity] are believed in vain without it'.[50]

This may seem just to be a problem about salvation, but it also presents a central difficulty for Abelard's theory of the virtues. Abelard holds, in common with Christian doctrine, that those who have charity are saved.[51] He also apparently holds that no one is virtuous without charity—indeed, in the proper sense of the word, virtue either is charity, or derives from charity.[52] But if everyone with charity is saved, and no one can be saved without explicit knowledge of Christ, then no one can have charity, and hence no one can be virtuous, without explicit knowledge of Christ. Yet Abelard makes it clear that most of the philosophers lacked such knowledge. It is this point which rules out an otherwise plausible reading of Abelard's position given by István Bejczy. According to Bejczy, Abelard's philosophers are Christians in all but name, and so, in presenting them as morally outstanding, Abelard is saying nothing about natural virtue: 'Abelard did not extend the virtues beyond the realm of faith and grace; he rather extended faith, grace and the virtues beyond the world of the chosen people'.[53] But, if virtue were, as Bejczy contends, confined to the realm of faith and grace, then according to Abelard most of the philosophers, because of their ignorance of the Incarnation, would be excluded from it. And to argue that Abelard meant to limit the virtuous philosophers just to those, apparently few, who knew about the Incarnation would not only go against the obvious sense of his writing. It is also directly contradicted by a passage in the *Theologia Christiana*, where Abelard suggests that, because of the excellence of their lives and worship of the one God, the philosophers may have had revealed to them what is necessary for salvation—that is to say, the Incarnation.[54] From this it is clear that Abelard thought that ancient philosophers who did not (yet) know of the Incarnation lived excellent lives, which were worthy of reward from God.[55]

[49] *TChr* IV.78.
[50] *TSB* III.100, *TChr* IV.159; *TSch* II.183. This passage comes at the end of the passage quoted above, p. 79.
[51] See *Collationes* sec. 105, where the Christian says that no one with charity is damned.
[52] *Sententie* sec. 251.
[53] Bejczy 2005, 139.
[54] *TChr* II.115. This passage is discussed in more detail below.
[55] For a fuller discussion of these points, see Marenbon 2011a.

In face of this textual evidence, the only reasonable conclusion is that Abelard did not achieve consistency between his clear recognition, on the one hand, of the virtues of the ancient philosophers and the fact that many of them did not know of the Incarnation, and, on the other, his view, following Augustine, which makes charity the basis of the virtues. Or, rather, he develops a shadow-theory—implied by what he says, but never acknowledged—according to which there are two sorts of virtue. There is virtue proper, virtue with charity, available only to those who are fully Christian (and so know of the Incarnation). But there is also what might be called 'true pagan virtue', the virtue demonstrated by the ancient philosophers who did not know of the Incarnation: not only do its divisions correspond exactly to those of virtue proper, so that the Christians were able to take them over without change, but also it is considered meritorious by God—meritorious enough both to deserve a revelation of the Trinity and to give a hope, at least, that some of those who are virtuous in this way will be given the revelation of the Incarnation they need in order to be saved. Abelard's implied true pagan virtues compare revealingly with Augustine's false pagan virtues. Both thinkers consider that the divisions of pagan virtue provide the model for those of Christian virtue, though Abelard alone brings out the point explicitly. Augustinian false virtues differ structurally from true virtues because they are pursued for their own sake, not for the sake of God. By contrast, Abelard believes that the pagan philosophers' valuing virtues for their own sake can be interpreted as loving them for the sake of God. Commenting on the line from Horace he has used to characterize their moral attitude, 'The good hate to sin because of their love of virtue', he writes,

> If it seems to contribute less to merit for salvation that it says 'because of their love for virtue' and not 'because of their love for God'—as if we could have virtue or any good work which was not according to and for the sake of God himself—it is easy to find this too among the philosophers, who set up the Highest Good, that is, God, both as the principal—that is the origin and efficient cause—and as the end—that is the final cause—of all things, so that all things, which derive from his gift, might come into being from his good love.[56]

And, most important of all, while for Augustine, however good they might appear, pagan virtues are false and certainly useless for salvation, Abelard believes—as the passage just quoted, among others, makes clear—that

[56] *TChr* II.28; cf. the way in the *Collationes* (sec. 91) the Philosopher does not accept the Christian's characterization of philosophical view as being that virtues are to be valued only for the sake (see above, p. 83). Bejczy (2003, 4n14), failing to notice that the Philosopher corrects the Christian's view, uses this passage (sec. 90) to suggest that Abelard thought that the pagan view of virtues was inadequate.

true pagan virtues do earn merit. No one can be saved just by them, but they can make people worthy to receive the knowledge of the Incarnation which will make them properly virtuous and open the possibility of salvation for them.

THE SALVATION OF PAGANS

Abelard's position on the salvation of pagans before the time of Christ will have already become apparent. As explained, his contemporaries, basing themselves on Patristic thought and with the patriarchs of the early books of Genesis and Job in mind, had elaborated a theory of how, before baptism, there were sacraments through which people could purge Original Sin and follow a path to salvation. For the Jews, the sacrament was circumcision of men, and it was not a universal obligation, but imposed only on Abraham's progeny. For those living under not the Old Law but natural law, prayers and sacrifices could play the same role. Abelard took up this idea, but unlike his contemporaries applied it to the ancient Greeks and Romans, especially their philosophers.[57] When, in the *Theologia Christiana*, he makes his provocative statement that the philosophers were Gentiles 'by nation, not by faith', Abelard immediately compares them to Job and his friends (II.15), and he quickly goes on (II.17), with another comparison to Job, to explain that they cannot be criticized for not taking up the 'sacraments which existed before the coming of the Saviour'—meaning circumcision and the other ritual precepts of the Old Law, because unlike the Gospel, the Old Law was not universal but intended only for the Jews. Very many of the philosophers were also thought by Abelard to have believed in God and the Trinity, but knowing the Trinity does not amount to knowing about the Incarnation, explicit knowledge of which was necessary for salvation. Abelard suggests two ways in which the philosophers might be saved, even given this requirement. First, *some* of the philosophers, at least, may well have known about the Incarnation during the course of their lives, because it had been prophesied. As he puts it in a passage already mentioned from the *Theologia Scholarium* (I.110), 'if someone should object that they cannot be saved without faith in the one to come (Christ), how can it be proved that they did not believe in him?'— and he goes on to mention the Sibylline prophecy. Second, Abelard suggests that, as a result of their good lives, philosophers might have been granted a special revelation. The passage (in the *Theologia Christiana*) where he advances this idea most explicitly has already been mentioned.

---

[57] See above for the one exception (probably Ralph of Laon).

Abelard has been talking about people who lived after the coming of Christ, and he continues,

> Now, if these people, after the announcement of the Gospel, and without faith in Jesus Christ or the grace of baptism, obtained such things from God for the merits they had performed before in their lives, what compels us to doubt that the philosophers from before the coming of Christ, who were so outstanding in both their faith and their life, gained indulgence, or that their life and worship of the one God . . . did not acquire for them gifts from God both in this life and the future one and that God showed them the things necessary for salvation?[58]

What about the pagans who lived after Christ? The two examples Abelard had been discussing immediately before the passage just quoted were both Roman emperors: Valentinian and Trajan. Valentinian was a Christian catechumen, who had formed the intention to be baptized but died before the ceremony could take place. These are rather special circumstances, and even the usually severe Augustine would probably have supported Jerome's view. But Abelard uses the story to make the point that he received pardon and salvation because of 'the good works he had performed before in his life'.

He also talks in the same way about Trajan. Abelard's source was not the earliest life of Gregory the Great, but a hagiography written a century and a half later, by the cultivated Roman Deacon, John (Hymnodites).[59] One important difference between their approaches is the context: for Abelard but not for John, the story of Gregory praying for Trajan, after hearing of his doing justice for the widow, is an example of how good works performed in their lives can profit even people who died without the faith or the grace of the sacraments. Abelard differs too over the theology of salvation. John had been struck by the apparent theological ineptitude of the anonymous author's account, which was his source here. 'But whilst no Roman doubts any of the miracles told above', he wrote, 'what is read among the Saxons—that Trajan's soul was freed from the torments of Hell by [Gregory's] prayers, seems to be dubious especially because such a learned man would never presume to pray for a pagan: in the fourth of his *Dialogues* he himself teaches that, for the very same

---

[58] *TChr* II.115. Earlier in the same book (II.19), Abelard uses exactly the same turn of phrase ('We seem therefore not to be compelled by any reason to doubt the salvation of such gentiles who, before the coming of the Redeemer, taught by no written law, "by nature", as St Paul says, "do those things that are of the law; these are a law to themselves, who shew the work of the law written in their hearts, their conscience bearing witness to them"'); it is reasonable to think that he has in mind principally the same mode of salvation.

[59] On the earliest *Life*, see above. John's *Life* is dated to 873–76 (cf. Limone 1978, 44 and references there) and edited in Gregory the Great 1849 (*PL* 75), 59–242.

reason as the saints will not pray, at the Last Judgements for the sinners damned to the eternal fire, so now holy men should not pray for those who die as impious infidels'.[60] But John finds a way out of these difficulties, which plays down the extent of the miracle. The Whitby life does not say that Gregory prayed, but merely that he wept, he explains. Moreover, it does not say that Trajan's soul was 'freed from Hell and placed in Paradise—which seems entirely incredible' because of the requirement for baptism, 'but it is said that his soul was only freed from the tortures of Hell'. Just as the same fire of Hell burns one sinner more than another, so John thinks that, by God's mercy, a soul could be in Hell but not feel its tortures.[61] Abelard repeats John's central idea, but alters its implications through his phrasing. According to John, it is credible that Trajan should have stayed in Hell, but had his pain relieved, whereas Abelard states that his 'soul was plucked out of the places of punishment, although—as we read [in John's account]—*we are not therefore compelled to believe* that he entered into the Kingdom of Heaven, lest perhaps we go against the words of Truth, by which it is said: "Unless a man be born again of water and the Holy Ghost, he cannot enter into the kingdom of God"'. Since the story of Valentinian and Jerome gives grounds for thinking that this verse of Scripture need not be interpreted literally, Abelard seems to suggest a strong possibility that Trajan *was* in fact saved.[62]

In the *Problemata Heloissae*—a set of replies to theological questions sent by Heloise probably near the end of his career—Abelard writes,

> It accords with piety and reason that whoever, recognizing by natural law God as the creator and rewarder of all, adhere to him with such zeal that they strive in no way to offend him through consent, which is the proper name for sin: such people, we judge, should by no means be damned; and what is necessary for them also to learn in order to be saved will be revealed to them by God before the end of their lives, either through inspiration, or through someone sent by whom instruction may be given about these things, as we read was done in the case of Cornelius about faith in Christ and receiving baptism.[63]

This remark—the earliest clear pronouncement of the idea of special inspiration which would be of immense importance in discussions of pagan salvation in the following centuries—seems to apply to people at any

---

[60] Gregory the Great 1849, 105C.

[61] The possibility of the alleviation of suffering in Hell had Augustine's backing and was held by many theologians until about 1200: see Augustine, *Enchiridion*, chaps. 110 and 112; and cf. Landgraf 1952–56, IV.2, 255–95.

[62] Whatley (1984b, 51–52) gives a well-nuanced account of Abelard's position and emphasizes how Abelard turns the focus from Gregory to Trajan himself.

[63] *PL* 178, 696A.

time, before or after the coming the Christ, and the mention of Cornelius suggests that it is particularly relevant to those living after him.

In *Scito teipsum* (or the *Ethics*), probably written just a little after the *Problemata*, Abelard mentions the case of Cornelius again, in the context of those who cannot be blamed for their lack of belief in Christ, because they have had no chance to hear about him. Although, says Abelard, Cornelius already 'recognized and loved God by natural law, and from this he deserved to have his prayer heard and for his charity to be acceptable to God', yet had he died before his faith in Christ 'we would not at all dare to promise him life, however good his works seemed to be, nor would we number him among the faithful, but rather among those without faith, however keenly he had worked for salvation'.[64] There is nothing here which contradicts what Abelard says in the passage just quoted, since it is merely a counterfactual possibility that Cornelius was not taught about Christ, and the principle suggested by the *Problemata* is that, given his good life, he would be taught about Christ. Abelard is simply insisting that this explicit teaching did have to take place in order for him to be saved. But he does, by what he goes on to say, suggest a qualification to his position. He looks at the case of the towns of Tyre and Sidon, where Christ chose not to preach, though he knew that they would have been receptive to his words. People in those towns who might have been saved will have been damned as unbelievers, but it is unclear to us why Christ should have left them to remain in their blindness. Abelard believes very firmly that, as he says in the *Problemata*, a sin takes place if and only if someone consents to an action he or she knows to be against divine command and thereby shows contempt for God. He acknowledges that the unbelief of people such as the citizens of Tyre and Sidon, which arises from non-culpable ignorance, cannot be considered sin in this proper sense, although perhaps, since it leads to their damnation, it must be described as a sin, but one without fault (*culpa*). Abelard's position seems to be, then, that in principle a pagan, after the coming of Christ, who lives excellently by natural law and who is non-culpably ignorant of Christ, will have revealed what is needed for salvation, but that this is not a rule which binds God.

His insistence on explicit knowledge of the Incarnation as a precondition for salvation means, then, that Abelard makes little distinction between the salvation of pagans before and after the coming of Christ. Although for those living in Christian times he also needs to explain how they can be saved without baptism, he has good patristic backing for the position that faith in Christ and charity are enough, if there is no opportunity for physical baptism. In order to explain how these pagans come

---

[64] *Scito teipsum* 64:20–23.

to know about the Incarnation, he resorts to what seems to be the *deus ex machina* of a heavenly guided messenger or 'internal inspiration'. This artifice, however, fits within a highly rationalized theology. Abelard insisted on explicit knowledge of the Incarnation for salvation not just because he thought it the orthodox view, but also because it was required by his understanding of how Christ's Crucifixion redeems humanity. Although his whole explanation is broader and more complex, an important aspect of it is the great love for God instilled in us once we know that Christ suffered on the cross and gave up his soul to redeem humankind, which enables us in our turn to love God more fully.[65] But this inspiration to love God will apply only to those who know explicitly that God became incarnate and, indeed, that he was put to death. It makes perfectly good sense to imagine a pagan as filled with love for God, but having this love raised to the even higher level needed for salvation by knowing about Christ's life. Moreover, the heavenly messenger or inspiration comes as a direct result of a person's following natural law and avoiding sin— even if, as the passage from *Scito teipsum* shows, Abelard held back, but with apparent reluctance, from insisting that sufficiently good conduct would always lead to such enlightenment. In this way, Abelard succeeds in making pagan goodness continuous with Christian goodness: a virtuous pagan, though fit to be held up as an example to most Christians in many ways, is not yet a good Christian who will be among the saved, but, through the pagan virtues, he is well on the way to becoming one.

[65] Cf. *Comm.Rom.* 118:256–62; *Sententie* sec. 174.

CHAPTER 6

John of Salisbury and the Encyclopaedic Tradition

ABELARD WAS NOT THE ONLY TWELFTH-CENTURY THINKER FOR WHOM the Problem of Paganism was central. But the contemporaries who might have been expected to share this concern—the thinkers usually associated with Platonism and the School of Chartres—turn out to have had little interest in it.[1] William of Conches (d. after 1155), the outstanding commentator of the period on texts from the Platonic tradition, was criticized at the time for sharing one of the doctrines which Abelard used to vindicate the importance for Christians of the ancient philosophers: the view that the persons of the Trinity can be adequately understood as power, wisdom and benignity (or, for William, will).[2] But the passage which earned him this criticism is a brief episode in a short section at the beginning of the *Philosophy of the World* on those things 'which exist but are not seen'. William's predominant concern (occupying more than 90 per cent of this treatise, and most of his other work) is with 'what exist and are seen': the physical world. When he revised the work into a treatise he called the *Dragmaticon,* he formally retracted his identification of persons of the Trinity with attributes, except for the scripturally attested description of the Son as Wisdom.[3] The same pattern can be seen in the area where recent scholars have especially linked Abelard and William: the identification of Plato's World Soul with the Holy Spirit.[4]

---

[1] For general discussion of twelfth-century Platonism (and its relationship to the school at Chartres and the rather murkier notion of the 'School of Chartres'), see Marenbon 2000b, 2000c and 2012e, 412–14.

[2] On William, see Obrist and Caiazzo 2011. For the criticism, see William of St Thierry 2007. Appropriating the terms 'power', 'wisdom' and 'benignity' to the persons of the Trinity was common in the twelfth century, often under the influence of the impeccably orthodox Hugh of St Victor (Poirel 2002, 283–420). Abelard's position was heterodox, because it presented these terms as adequate and primary characterizations of the Trinity, and at the beginning of his *Philosophia mundi* (I.2.8; William of Conches 1980, 20; quoted at William of St Thierry 2007, 61:20–21, 62:24–27) William of Conches presents this view in a stark form.

[3] 1.3.2; William of Conches 1997, 12:14–15.

[4] See Dronke 1974, 55–62; Marenbon 2004a, 35–38. There is an extended discussion of the possible relations between Abelard and William of Conches, which reaches different conclusions from those here, in Stover 2011, 187–94.

One of the most extended discussions in each version of the *Theologia*, when Abelard is presenting Old Testament and pagan philosophical testimonies to the Trinity, is dedicated to showing that when Plato talked of the World Soul, he was referring to the Holy Spirit. Already in the *Theologia Summi Boni*, it occupies about a quarter of book 1, and Abelard extends it in the two later versions.[5] Abelard also returns to the subject later on in each version, arguing that, despite Macrobius's wording, he and the other Platonists recognized that the World Soul, by which was meant the Holy Spirit, was not created.[6] Obviously, Abelard attached great importance to this identification, and continued to do so up to his last writing on the subject. It was required by an important element in his view of pagan wisdom: the claim that the Platonists had an understanding of all three persons of the Trinity, not just—as many patristic and early medieval writers held—the Father and the Son. William of Conches, too, considered the identification of the World Soul and the Holy Spirit, but his attitude to the idea could hardly have been more different. In the earliest of his commentaries, on Boethius's *Consolation*, he suggests, though without insisting, that the World Soul mentioned by Plato, which is the 'natural power' (*naturalis vigor*) by which living things have their life functions, 'is, as it seems to me, the Holy Spirit . . . which is well called natural power, because all thinks are born and flourish by divine love'.[7] In the commentary on Macrobius, William distances himself a little from the identification: 'according to some', he writes, the World Soul is the Holy Spirit.[8] In his next work, the *Philosophy of the World*, William repeats that the identification with the Holy Spirit is made by some, and he distinguishes this view from the one (held by 'others') with which he had initially combined it, that the World Soul is 'the natural power within things'.[9] And after that, glossing the *Timaeus*, William adds an extra note of reserve: 'Some say that this spirit is the Holy Spirit, which we neither deny nor affirm'.[10] In the *Dragmaticon*, written as much as two decades later, the World Soul is not even mentioned.[11]

William, then, is favourable to the syncretistic outlook implied by identifying the World Soul and the Holy Spirit, but it is not a view which

[5] *TSB* I.36–56; *TChr* I.68–116; *TSch* I.123–79 (about one-third of the book in these last two cases).
[6] *TSB* III.94–99; *TChr* IV.140–51; *TSch* II.169–80.
[7] William of Conches 1999, 168:522–170:531.
[8] See Marenbon 2004a, 37 and 44n71 for more material on the parallels and divergences between William and Abelard here. Jeauneau gives some quotations in his note on the text from the *Timaeus* commentary: see below.
[9] I.4.13; William of Conches 1980, 22–23.
[10] LXXI; William of Conches 2006, 124:13–14.
[11] Southern 2001, 74–77 gives a full survey of the different attitudes taken to the identification of the World Soul and the Holy Spirit in William's works and some related ones.

matters much to him, and he is prepared to draw back from and then drop it—as he can easily do, because it is not an essential part of a wider view about pagan wisdom, as it is for Abelard. There is another striking difference between the two thinkers' approach to this topic. Abelard emphasizes that the identification of the World Soul with the Holy Spirit is a matter of interpreting an *involucrum* (or, as he occasionally calls it, *integumentum*, a roughly synonymous word)[12]—an extended metaphor, and he discusses at length the reasons why philosophers veil their meaning in this way.[13] The metaphorical character of the interpretation is something, then, that Abelard wants to emphasize (and he almost never uses the terms *involucrum* or *integumentum* elsewhere). It can even be said that he never really *identifies* the World Soul with the Holy Spirit, but rather makes the claim that the ancient philosophers having understood the nature of the Holy Spirit as part of a triune God used the expression 'World Soul' to talk about it in a veiled way, deliberately concealing their knowledge.[14] By contrast, explaining ancient texts by unravelling their metaphors (*integumenta*) is one of William's favourite procedures, and the whole discussion in the *Timaeus* of the World Soul is presented by him as an *integumentum*.[15] But nowhere does William suggest that the World Soul is an *integumentum* for the Holy Spirit. For him, either the World Soul is literally the Holy Spirit, or—as he finally seems to decide—it is not to be identified with the Holy Spirit at all.

William does not in general see *integumenta* as ways in which specifically Christian truths are covertly presented in writings by pagan philosophers. Rather, they are instances where myth (the stories of Hercules or Orpheus and Eurydice) or figurative language (as in the case of the World Soul) is used to veil scientific ideas or moralizing thoughts, which reflect the ambiance of Christian ethics but only occasionally explicitly biblical doctrine. The strategy of discovering *integumenta* is a way of continuing the dominant approach to Platonic texts in the preceding centuries, making them comfortable within a Christian world, neutralizing ideas inconsistent with the faith, but only rarely actually Christianizing.

Altogether, then, William was a user of ancient philosophical texts, as well as some more recent Arabic scientific writings, inclined to think that Plato and his followers were rarely at variance with Christian truth, but without a wider view of pagan wisdom and virtue. The same is more

---

[12] Both words mean, literally, a covering; for their synonymy as terms for an extended metaphor, see Jeauneau 1957, 130, and on the history of the terms (especially *involucrum*), see Dronke 1974, 56n2.

[13] *TSB* I.30–44; *TChr* I.98–107; *TSch* I.158–67.

[14] This view is argued in Gregory 1955, 136–37.

[15] LXXIV; William of Conches 2006, 130:15 and see the exposition in the pages following.

obviously true of another celebrated twelfth-century Platonist, Thierry of Chartres. The commentaries which relay his teaching of Boethius's *Theological treatises* indicate him as a thinker who looked back admiringly to the ancient philosophers—the Platonists especially, but also Hermes Trismegistus. He is generally willing to accept their wisdom, but does not commit himself to any definite position about their relation to Christianity.[16] In his treatise *On the Work of the Six Days*, he does, however, in passing assert that what Plato called 'the World Soul' is what Christians call 'the Holy Spirit'; though, in a work mainly concerned to provide physical explanations of the creation story, he does not develop its implications.[17]

In his most widely read work, the *Cosmographia*, which he dedicated to Thierry of Chartres, a third well-known twelfth-century Platonist, Bernardus Silvestris, shows—more firmly, though implicitly—the same attitude: there are few or no incompatibilities between the wisdom of the Platonists and the doctrine of the faith, so that Christians can unproblematically make use of ancient pagan philosophy.[18] Where William of Conches used the mythic, integumental character of the Platonic texts to find scientific meaning in them and neutralize any unacceptable ideas, Bernardus is himself a myth-maker. He tells of the creation of the universe and man, in terms heavily influenced by the *Timaeus* and Calcidius's commentary, though not entirely borrowed from them. The actors in this cosmic prosimetrum either personify central ideas in Plato's dialogue, such as Intellect (*Nous*) and formless matter (*Silva*—the drama's quickly reformed villain), or—as with celestial existence (*Urania*) and earthly existence (*Physis*)—are used by Bernardus to develop his story. They all belong to a non-Christian, vaguely Platonic world, and the work begins with an account, close to the *Timaeus*, of how formless matter is given form and beautified. This opening does not, however, commit Bernardus to teaching that the universe is eternal and uncreated, and that the role of the divine is merely to give it form, since nothing is said to rule out an initial act of creation by God, as Christian teaching requires. Later, when Bernard is telling of the future events and characters prefigured in the stars, he mixes allusions to the classical world, its rulers, poets and thinkers, with a reference to the virgin birth of Christ, 'the true Godhead'.[19] In the second part of the prosimetrum, Urania and Natura, seeking divine

[16]These commentaries are printed in Thierry of Chartres 1971, but they should not be considered, as by their editor and most scholars, to be works written by Thierry himself: see Marenbon 2012e, 416.

[17]Sec. 27; Thierry of Chartres 1971, 566:44, 567:52.

[18]There is no fully critical edition of the *Cosmographia*, but Peter Dronke gives a reliable and carefully presented text—Bernardus Silvestris 1978.

[19]III, lines 53–54; Bernardus Silvestris 1978, 105.

consent for their plan to make the first human, enter a realm of 'pure and unsullied light', where they pray to a threefold God.[20] Since Bernardus's philosophical creation story is clearly a myth, there is no danger of its seeming heretically to rival or contradict the faith, and these occasional allusions to Christ and the Trinity make the Christian reader comfortable, even in surroundings which might otherwise seem pagan.

By contrast, in his poem, *The Astrologer* (*Mathematicus*)—not so widely read in the Middle Ages as the *Cosmographia*, but still quite popular[21]—Bernardus thinks himself into a pagan world. The story, taken, much extended and adapted, from an ancient declamation, is that of a couple in ancient Rome whose long awaited son, they learn from an astrologer, will grow up to be outstanding in looks, intelligence and virtue and become ruler of the city, but will kill his father. The father orders that the baby be killed at birth, but the mother secretly saves the child, whom she calls Patricida. He grows up to be the paragon described by the astrologer, saves Rome from the Carthaginian enemy and becomes its ruler. Reunited with his parents, and learning the astrologer's prediction, Patricida resolves to commit suicide, since it is the one way he can escape his fate and save the purity of his character. Interpreting this somewhat bizarre tale is not straightforward.[22] Nothing, however, could be clearer than Bernardus's insistence on the pagan setting, with its gods or, from time to time, God, referred to in terms that could have come from an ancient philosopher. Patricida, like a good Platonist, looks forward to the return of his soul to the stars; there is not even a hint of the Christian view that suicide is a sin, or that this pagan is any less than entirely virtuous.[23] In this work, though, the Problem of Paganism is considered merely by implication.

JOHN OF SALISBURY

One contemporary reader certainly aware of Bernard's deliberate decision, as narrator of *The Astrologer*, to take a classical, pagan view was John of Salisbury. In his *Policraticus*, he quotes a couplet said by the

[20] V.1–4; Bernardus Silvestris 1978, 127–28.
[21] There are about fifty surviving manuscripts of the *Cosmographia*, nearly twenty of the *Mathematicus*.
[22] See the differing readings offered in Dronke 1974, 126–39 and Godman 1990. The work is edited with English translation in Bernardus Silvestris 1996.
[23] Is Bernardus deliberately portraying the pagans as fatalists, unaware that God's power can overrule that of the stars? See the interesting discussion in Dronke 1974, 139–43, but note (cf. Burnett 1977) that the material from what is supposedly a work called the *Experimentarius* which he connects with Bernardus may well not be linked with him at all.

narrator in *The Astrologer*, 'Blind fate overturns the ridiculous works of men; our world is jest and sport for the gods', attributing it to 'a certain excellent writer of our own time' who, however, 'is using the words of pagans'.[24] It is not surprising that John should be sensitive to the approach Bernardus takes since, in all likelihood, he himself also followed it in one episode, though in a less open, more complicated way.[25] But for him, as for Abelard, who was briefly his teacher, the Problem of Paganism is a constant concern, which is addressed explicitly. Unlike Abelard, however, John does not make his own views on it immediately obvious. This reticence has misled many historians.[26] John's devotion to the Latin classics, manifested in an impressive breadth of reading and citation, and a polished, allusive style, is undoubted. But this long-time student, then courtier, who ended his life as a bishop, is considered to have combined love for antiquity with his religion in the more or less untroubled way that is labelled 'Christian humanism'.[27] His two works especially concerned with antiquity are both heterogeneous discussions. The earlier of them (c. 1155), the *Indicator of the Doctrines of the Philosophers* (*Entheticus de dogmate philosophorum*), is a didactic poem mainly about the shortcomings of contemporary education, courtly life and its vanity, the value of philosophy and the various ancient philosophers and their schools. The same subjects, along with political theory, loom large in his vast, rambling and yet beautifully written prose treatise, the *Policraticus* (c. 1159). On the surface, both works offer two lines of thought about pagan philosophy and its value, which fit with the comfortable picture of a Christian humanist, who offers even less for the subject of this book than William of Conches and Thierry and Chartres.

The first line of approach is put very clearly in the *Indicator*. Philosophy is valuable, John says, but only when it is based on grace, which the pagans lacked: without it, the reason and genius of speech is sterile, born rotten and degenerating further; cleansed by grace, nature is able to bring forth noble work from the bosom of genius.[28] Grace sharpens reason, and 'philosophy transcends the world, when it is certain that faith is at

[24] *Policraticus* III.8; John of Salisbury 1909, I, 194:21–25; cf. Godman 1990, 598–99.
[25] See below, pp. 104–5.
[26] Two scholars who, however, have delved appreciatively into John's subtle way of thinking are Peter von Moos (especially von Moos 1988b) and Christophe Grellard, whose new book (Grellard 2013) makes the case for seeing John as a serious and consistent sceptical thinker.
[27] See Liebeschütz 1950 and many of the essays in Wilks 1984, which also give a good idea of the range of John's classical reading, the sophistication of which is even more evident in von Moos 1988b. For a critique of the idea of John as a Christian humanist, see Marenbon 2012a, 21–22.
[28] *Entheticus* lines 223–24, 237–38; John of Salisbury 1987, I, 121.

the beginning of it'.[29] The long account which John goes on to give of the different schools of ancient philosophy and of individual thinkers, such as Socrates, Aristotle, Plato, Cicero and Seneca, can, on this reading be seen as framed by these comments and his concluding remark, describing them all as pagans (*gentiles*) whom error has driven astray: 'All reason', he continues, 'fails without faith; only those who worship Christ are wise'.[30] John makes some similar remarks in the *Policraticus*,[31] and he often refers there to the passage from Romans, where Paul accuses the pagan philosophers of having found God through his creation but turned their backs on him: whereas Abelard tried to explain away this condemnation, John appears to accept that the philosophers made themselves 'inexcusable'.[32] In his presentation of Plato's philosophy, he takes account of how much the Platonists have in common with the Christians, only to turn it against them by saying, echoing the Pauline condemnation, that therefore 'they are entirely inexcusable for turning the truth of God to a lie'.[33] It seems then, from this approach, that pagan philosophers are merely sources for thinking which, in the right Christian hands, can lead to wisdom.

The other line of approach, developed in the *Policraticus*, is linked to his preference among the ancient schools of philosophy not, as might be expected, for the Platonists or the Aristotelians, but rather for the Academic sceptics. Right at the start of the work, he declares that he does 'not blush to declare' himself an Academic, following 'their footsteps in those things which can be doubted by a wise man'.[34] He justifies this preference by inventing a prehistory of pagan philosophy, which fills in, and somewhat alters, the details behind Paul's condemnatory remarks in Romans (alluded to again here). The philosophers made wonderful discoveries about nature and its causes, from which we still benefit, John explains, and even in some way contemplated the Creator. In their self-confidence, relying on free will, they 'declared war on the grace of God'. They are compared to the builders of the tower of Babel. Just as God punished them by disunifying human language, so for the philosophers as a result of their pride the 'unity of the unchangeable and unfailing truth' was obscured for them, and consequently they split into a variety of sects, such as the Stoics and Epicureans. Under these circumstances of enforced ignorance, John argues, it is right to prefer the Academics who,

---

[29] *Entheticus* lines 309–10; John of Salisbury 1987, I, 125.

[30] *Entheticus* lines 1269–71; John of Salisbury 1987, I, 187.

[31] See, e.g., *Policraticus* VII.13; John of Salisbury 1909, II, 145:15–20.

[32] See, e.g., *Policraticus* III.3, III.9, VII.5; John of Salisbury 1909, I, 174:8–22; 196:22–27; II, 110:22–25.

[33] *Policraticus* VII.5; John of Salisbury 1909, II, 110:9–10.

[34] *Policraticus* Prol.; John of Salisbury 1909, I, 17:7–9.

rather than recklessly accepting uncertainties as true, show appropriate epistemological modesty and subject everything to doubt.[35]

Both of these approaches are undoubtedly taken by John, yet there are aspects of his attitude to pagan philosophy which run beyond, or even contrary to them, and where John turns out to be closer to his one-time teacher, Abelard, than anyone else of his time writing about antiquity. John's theological justification for scepticism, based on the fall through pride of the ancient philosophers, ends by blurring the very distinction between erring pagans and enlightened Christians which gives rise to it. For John insists that the epistemological modesty of Academic scepticism remains as necessary in his own Christian times as it did in the period of pre-Christian ignorance. He is careful to rule out the position of the extreme sceptic, who doubts everything and so cannot even claim to know that he does not know, and to leave room for faith, which—though not bringing knowledge—can bring certainty.[36] But he ends up by giving a long list of the sort of subjects in which he, in his own Christian present, prefers to follow the Academics and remain in doubt: they include most of the grand themes of philosophy and theology—providence, the nature of the soul, chance and free will, time, place and matter, universals, virtues, angels and the divine attributes.[37]

Moreover, as an alternative to his hostile, theological, Pauline account of the origin of the different ancient philosophical schools, John also provides a Boethian account. He compares the way in which the different sects flowed from 'the words of Plato and Socrates' to the way in which, according to the *Consolation of Philosophy*, all people seek the same goal of happiness, but by different paths.[38] Then, taking Boethius's idea literally rather than using at as a metaphor, John adds that, though we seek happiness, the way to gain it is through virtue, and virtue is what philosophy teaches, and without philosophy 'anyone on the path aiming at happiness is like a blind person who, presumptuously aiming to reach the heights, falls on the slippery ground'.[39] Where, in the other account,

[35] *Policraticus* VII.1; John of Salisbury 1909, II, 93–95. This line of thought has been discerned and explained in Grellard 2007, 24–25; Grellard 2008, 43–45 (with the relevant text translated in an appendix); 2013, 40–42.

[36] *Policraticus* VII.2; John of Salisbury 1909, II, 96:1–11.

[37] *Policraticus* VII.2; John of Salisbury 1909, II, 98:20–99:11.

[38] *Policraticus* VII.8; John of Salisbury 1909, II, 118:4–9; cf. Boethius, *Consolation* III.2. Grellard (2008, 45) points to this passage in order to justify the idea that Socrates—and Socrates alone—is thought by John to be 'a pre-lapsarian' philosopher, who preceded the Babel-like division of the sects. But John is clearly talking about both Socrates and Plato, and he is presenting the history of ancient philosophy in a way that cannot be reconciled with the account given in VII.1.

[39] *Policraticus* VII.8; John of Salisbury 1909, II, 119:7–9.

philosophizing leads to pride, here it is seen as pride to go without philosophy. That John has ancient, pagan philosophy in mind (principally, or at least as well as philosophy practised in his own, Christian times) is made clear when he adds that, though at least some of the ancient philosophers believed in the immortality of the soul, they had received no doctrine about the life to come, and so they set up virtue as the Highest Good, something he presents, not in Augustinian fashion as a mistake, but as an approximation to the truth: clearly nothing is better than virtue, he says, save for the enjoyment of the Highest Good. John even sees the different proximate goals of the various schools (contempt of life for the Stoics, enquiry into the truth for the Peripatetics, pleasure for the Epicureans) as so many paths by which they each tried to gain virtue.[40] Both here in the *Policraticus* and in the *Indicator*, John's discussion of each of the schools contains a mixture of praise and criticism which fits better with his Boethian account of their origins than with the Pauline one.[41] For example, in the *Indicator*, what seems as though it will be a description of how Aristotle was overcome by vainglory ('Aristotle conquers other people, but vainglory conquers him') unexpectedly turns into an account of how he struggles against this vice, over which philosophy is finally victorious.[42] And, although John seems to accept the popular view of Epicureans as indulgers in sensual pleasure, frequently using the term to describe the worldly courtiers whose way of life he is attacking, he shares with Abelard a respect for Epicurus himself as a man and as a philosopher. He recounts Seneca's praise of Epicurus's simple and austere life, distinguishing it sharply from that of his swine-like followers.[43] In the *Indicator*, he accepts as good teaching Epicurus's view that all is subordinate to pleasure, so long as the pleasure (*voluptas*) is pure—the true tranquillity reached after toil by a soul intent on pious ends. This view of Epicureanism recalls that of the Philosopher in Abelard's *Collationes*, who equates Epicurean tranquillity with the Christians' Kingdom of Heaven.[44] John does add, however, that this rest can be gained only through grace, and he goes on to attack a drunken, gluttonous version of Epicurus, who advocates materialism, the power of chance and the mortality of the soul.[45]

John may well have been following Abelard in his treatment of Epicureanism. In his handling of Trajan and his legend, he goes beyond him.

[40] *Policraticus* VII.8; John of Salisbury 1909, II, 121:26–122:11.
[41] See Marenbon 2012a, 18–21.
[42] *Entheticus* lines 873–76; John of Salisbury 1987, I, 163.
[43] *Policraticus* VIII.8, 11; John of Salisbury 1909, II, 275:30–276:18; 294:4–14.
[44] See chapter 5.
[45] *Entheticus* lines 527–82; John of Salisbury 1987, I, 141–43.

Since Trajan lived in Christian times but had remained a pagan, Abelard is unwilling, despite his virtues, openly to claim that Pope Gregory's intervention led to his release from Hell: he repeats John the Deacon's theologically-sanitized version of the story, though implying the possibility that Trajan was saved.[46] The *Policraticus*, however, does not mention John the Deacon's comments, but talks of Trajan as having been set free from the punishments of Hell because of his outstanding merits.[47] It would be possible to read this description as implying no more than John the Deacon allowed: that Trajan remained in Hell, but without being punished. Perhaps indeed this possibility is being deliberately left open, but no reader would be likely to observe it, and a normal reader would conclude that Trajan's soul went to Heaven.

Trajan is more for John than just a figure in an exemplum: he is also the ruler to whom, supposedly, the philosopher Plutarch sent his *Institutio*—the *Institutio Traiani* from which John claims that he has cited, or more often summarized, the core of his political doctrine. If this text ever existed, it was certainly not written by Plutarch or sent to Trajan. But there is very good reason to think that it is a fiction, and that John has put himself into the mental world of a pagan writer, not to tell, like Bernardus Silvestris, a story about destiny and overcoming it, but so as to present his political ideals for Christian rulers.[48] And 'Plutarch's' paganism is something John will not let his readers forget, reminding them, for instance, that when he speaks of priests being charged with the ceremonies for the worship of God, Plutarch says 'gods' and then saying that he will omit Plutarch's discussions about the worship of idols.[49] A little further on, John roundly criticizes Plutarch for his discussion of the pagan Gods, which 'is unworthy of a philosopher', and speculates that perhaps he was merely pretending to share the beliefs of his audience.[50] To the naïve reader, such comments will be seen as markers intended to distance a pagan source. To the knowing reader, who sees the game which John is playing, the effect may be, rather, to expose how easily good teaching can take a pagan, or a Christian, dress. John undercuts the clear distinctions which would have ordered and bounded his field of vision, had he been a straightforward Christian

[46] See chapter 5.

[47] *Policraticus* V.8; John of Salisbury 1909, I, 317:1–318:10; at the end of the passage Trajan is said simply to have been 'set free' (*liberatus*). On this passage in general, see Whatley 1984b, 32–26, though Whatley does not bring out that, contrary to John the Deacon's account, the implication here is that Trajan's soul is saved.

[48] The view, held by most experts on John of Salisbury today, that the *Institutio Traiani* is a literary fiction, is very well put in von Moos 1988b, n. 462, and pp. 464–65 n. 922, and in more detail in von Moos 1988a; for a contrary view, see Kerner 1988.

[49] *Policraticus* V.2; John of Salisbury 1909, I, 282:15–16, 283:27–284:3.

[50] *Policraticus* V.4; John of Salisbury 1909, I, 294:14–24.

humanist. Timidly and indirectly, he asserts an even bolder view of the unity of knowledge, pre-Christian and Christian, than Abelard had done.

THE ENCYCLOPAEDIC TRADITION

John of Salisbury's role in addressing the Problem of Paganism is not limited to his own, partly concealed but audacious way of approaching it. His *Policraticus* is at the beginning of an important side-stream in the medieval treatment of ancient philosophers: the encyclopaedic accounts of the lives and sayings of the philosophers. Behind John of Salisbury, it is probably right to see his teacher, Peter Abelard, who had brought together in the *Theologia Christiana* flattering stories about the ancient philosophers to back up his account of their virtues. There is a striking correspondence between the *exempla* of philosophers in the *Theologia Christiana* and those rehearsed in the *Policraticus*.[51] Whereas the *Theologia Christiana* itself was hardly known, the *Policraticus* was quite widely read in the Middle Ages, and its accounts of philosophers were also influential indirectly, through the *Chronicle* of Helinand of Froidmont, which was the source for this material in Vincent of Beauvais's very popular *Mirror of History*, part of his vast encyclopaedia, *The Great Mirror*, compiled in the mid-thirteenth century.[52] The aim of the *Mirror of History* is to provide an account of outstanding events and people, from all the ancient sources, biblical and pagan, in chronological order. Philosophers (and also poets) are no less important for Vincent than kings or military leaders, and so the whole account of antiquity is scattered with chapters on the pagan philosophers, from Pythagoras to Seneca. The underlying source for his account of ancient philosophy is Augustine's *City of God*, but the exemplary stories, repeated from John of Salisbury (usually through the intermediary of Helinand) add an important, eulogistic strand. Vincent aims, on the basis of his wide reading, to collect as much information as he can find about the lives and doctrines of each thinker, adding for the most famous a list of sayings and a florilegium from their works.[53] He is willing, on occasion, to take a critical view of

[51] See Marenbon 2006, 133 (Appendix 2).

[52] On Vincent, see Lusignan and Paulmier-Foucart 1997, Paulmier-Foucart 2004 and Paulmier-Foucart et al. 1990; and for full bibliographic information, the Vincent of Beauvais web page at http://www.vincentiusbelvacensis.eu. *Speculum historiale* exists in five versions, the earliest written in 1244, the latest, after 1254; Vincent of Beauvais 1624 gives the latest version; cf. Voorbij 1991, 344–46. On Vincent's aims, see Smits 1986.

[53] Piaia 1983, 50 describes the work as a sort of medieval Ueberweg; on 54–60 he gives a valuable list of the philosophers treated in the *Speculum historiale* and the sources used. On the range and limits of his knowledge of Aristotle, see Hamesse 1990.

the pagan philosophers: he infers, for instance, from a passage in Orosius that Socrates, 'misled by his daemon' took the poison before his executioner gave it to him 'either from love of popular glory or from fear of greater punishment'.[54] But the general effect of Vincent's search for comprehensiveness is to transform the underlying source, the account of ancient philosophy in the *City of God*, into a generally flattering picture (even Epicurus is presented in a benign light, although the account does end with a mention of where he erred).[55] Moreover, Vincent's decision to present a single chronology, merging biblical and pagan sources, undoes without polemic Augustine's theology of history and makes the philosophers part of a unified picture of pre-Christian times.

The most remarkable of the medieval accounts of ancient philosophy is, however, by a Franciscan, John of Wales, writing a little after Vincent's time. In his *Breviloquium* ('Short Account of the Virtues of the Ancient Rulers and Philosophers'; 1260–70) he uses the exempla of these pagans to illustrate the cardinal virtues, and the *Compendiloquium* ('Compendious Account of the Lives of the Illustrious Philosophers'; after 1272) is a work entirely about the lives, manners, virtues and sayings of the ancient philosophers, including even a chapter on philosophers' clothing (pt. 2, chap. 3) and a whole section (pt. 5) on the perfections of philosophers in, for instance, hating vices, taming the passions and mortifying the flesh.[56]

John's aim in presenting all this material was partly to provide *exempla* for those preaching sermons, but he also envisaged readers who would study his *Compendiloquium* as a whole. These readers were university *philosophers*, that is to say the students and Masters of Arts who devoted themselves to an Aristotelian curriculum. In writing the *Compendiloquium*, John looked back to the tradition of Franciscan hagiography, but he transformed it, dropping many of the specifically Franciscan virtues, so as 'to put forward to the philosophers a moral project based on their own heritage'.[57] It would be tempting to see this work, far more than any of the previous encyclopaedic accounts, as harking back to Abelard's golden world of ancient philosophy, which his contemporaries are invited to emulate. But Abelard believed that the ancient philosophers really were virtuous and that many of them were saved, whereas

[54] *Speculum historiale* III.66; Vincent of Beauvais 1624, 107.

[55] *Speculum historiale* IV.39–41; Vincent of Beauvais 1624, 127–28.

[56] See Swanson 1989, 13–14 for dates. I discuss John of Wales in Marenbon 2012a, 23–25. The texts are in John of Wales 1511: *Breviloquium de virtutibus antiquorum*, ff. 200–217; *Compendiloquium*, ff. 140–94.

[57] Ricklin 2006b, 221. See the whole article for Ricklin's convincing account of the relationship between the *Compendiloquium* and Franciscan hagiography and its intended audience. On the Arts Masters and philosophy in the 1260s and 1270s, see chapter 8.

John explains the value of these *exempla* at the beginning of the *Brevilo-quium of the Virtues of the Ancients* by saying that 'if those ancients, who were neither illuminated by faith nor ordered by charity nor confirmed by hope were so virtuous in their deeds—and this was out of desire for glory or worldly benefit or uprightness of life, how many things should be done by the faithful, who are enriched with the virtues of grace; and how many things should they scorn for eternal happiness?'[58] By directing attention here to pagan desire for glory and worldly benefit, John seems to subscribing to Augustine's view that their virtues were not genuine, because they were misdirected—an impression strengthened by the fact that he then quotes a passage from the *City of God* (V. 20) saying that it is no better to be virtuous for the sake of human glory than for the sake of pleasure. John begins another work of his, also called *Breviloquium*—but *of the Wisdom of the Saints*—by saying that the saints are the true philosophers, illuminated by true wisdom, and (echoing Romans i, 21) he calls the Gentile philosophers fools who lacked knowledge of God, although they thought themselves wise.[59]

Although the *Compendiloquium* enjoyed a modest popularity, the text to which later medieval readers turned out of preference for information about the ancient philosophers was *On the Lives and Manners of the Philosophers*, written in the early fourteenth century and misattributed to the distinguished logician and philosopher Walter Burley.[60] Here, for the first time in the Middle Ages, the famous ancient philosophical dox-ography, the *Lives of the Philosophers* by Diogenes Laertius, is used as a source. For the most part, however, the pseudo-Burley writes in the tra-dition of Vincent of Beauvais and the *Compendiloquium*, which is used extensively.[61] But the author has abandoned John of Wales's moralizing programme and, although he gives the sayings of some philosophers, he places less emphasis than Vincent of Beauvais on giving an account of their doctrines, and there are no florilegia.[62] The attitude towards the ancient philosophers is generally approving, to some extent because of material taken from the earlier tradition. The author even suggests at one point that Aristotle, who was 'eager to inquire into the writings of

[58] *Breviloquium de virtutibus antiquorum*, f. 216v.

[59] Swanson (*John of Wales*, 194–95) considers that John wrote about the virtues of the saints only from a feeling of duty and perhaps even as a result of external pressure. She does not take into account the Augustinian colouring that John admits elsewhere, despite his interest in gathering classical exempla.

[60] On date and authorship, see Grignaschi 1990.

[61] See Piaia 1983, 118–19; Ricklin 2005.

[62] Ricklin (2006b, 221–22) draws the contrast with John of Wales and compares the number of surviving MSS of the *Compendium*—27—with the 272 MSS catalogued of the *De vita et moribus philosophorum*.

all wise people' and who says in the *Secret of Secrets* that 'God revealed the hidden things of his wisdom to his holy prophets', perhaps knew of some of 'our books'.[63] None the less, the imaginative evocation of a golden world of ancient philosophy, passionately set forth by Abelard and echoed to some extent by John of Salisbury, Vincent of Beauvais and John of Wales, is here replaced by a list, rich in anecdote but lifeless.

[63] *Liber de vita et moribus philosophorum* 53; Walter Burley 1886, 244. On the pseudo-Aristotelian *Secreta secretorum*, see chapter 9. Even in this pseudonymous work, the exact sentiment which pseudo-Walter cites cannot be found: see the editor's note (a) on 244–45.

CHAPTER 7

Arabi, Mongolia and Beyond: Contemporary Pagans in the Thirteenth and Fourteenth Centuries

NOT ALL THE PAGANS MEDIEVAL PEOPLE READ OR HEARD ABOUT WERE those long-dead, from Greece and Rome, or the Old Testament. Brief accounts of paganism in Eastern and Northern Europe had circulated from the eleventh century.[1] In the mid-thirteenth century, when the Mongols had conquered a vast empire, stretching from China to the edges of Europe, two Franciscan travellers, John of Piano Carpini and William of Rubruk, were received by the Great Khan and wrote about the life and traditions of a pagan society at first hand.[2] Medieval readers also knew a mass of partly fantastical material, much of it inherited from antiquity, about the remote lands of Asia and their pagan inhabitants. In the mid-fourteenth century, an anonymous writer wove this material together with the reports of genuine travellers into *The Book of John Mandeville*, a medieval best seller which takes a surprisingly deep and original look at the Problem of Paganism. But this chapter begins by looking at *Willehalm*, a Middle High German poem written c. 1210–20 by Wolfram von Eschenbach.[3]

---

[1] See above, pp. 68–72.

[2] Another important account of the East, including China, is the *Description of the World* (*Le divisament dou monde* or *Il milione*), written by the merchant Marco Polo and the romance writer Rustichello in the last years of the thirteenth century. It contains many descriptions of pagan ceremonies, but lacks the strong interest in the religious beliefs of the pagans found in the Franciscans' accounts.

[3] References to *Willehalm* are by the number of the thirty-line section, and the line within it, with the book number given as a roman numeral: e.g., 'IV.193, 6–11' indicates lines 6 to 11 of section 196 in book 4. The text used is Wolfram von Eschenbach 1991 (with parallel modern German translation; there is a good English translation: Wolfram von Eschenbach 1984).

ISLAM AS PAGANISM: WOLFRAM VON ESCHENBACH'S *WILLEHALM*

Willehalm, however, seems as though it has no place in the present book. Its tragic central character, Giburc, is daughter of the 'Amirat'—that is to say, Emir, the grand Islamic ruler Terramer, and was married to King Tiburc, until she eloped from the city of Arabi with the Christian captive Willehalm, was baptized and married him. It is a story then, apparently, about Christians and their nearest non-Christian neighbours: Muslims not pagans. Yet, on scrutiny, its subject—and that of the whole *chanson de geste* tradition from which it stems—is rather the relation between Christians and pagans, where paganism is conceived so broadly that it covers every sort of non-Christian except for the Jews. The well-educated distinguished Muslims from the pagans, ancient or contemporary, but popular opinion held otherwise. There was not, however, a sharp break between the learned and the popular views, but rather a continuum, stretching from the detailed theological discussions of a Peter the Venerable to the tradition of French epic poetry inaugurated by the *Chanson de Roland* (written down in the late eleventh century), celebrating Christian encounters with an enemy who, though historically Muslim, is depicted as consisting of idolaters, worshipping a counter-Trinity of Mahumet, Tervagan and Apollin.[4] A few of the poems occasionally give the enemy some more specifically Muslim characteristics, but the tendency is to merge all non-Christians, not just linguistically, by using the terms 'pagan' and 'Saracen' indifferently, but also geographically. In poems like the *Chanson de Roland* itself and *Aliscans*, the source for *Willehalm*, where lists of enemy leaders are given, many come not from the lands of Islam, but from pagan areas in Eastern Europe or Asia.[5] In *Willehalm* itself, some of the pagans come from as far away as India and China, whilst the one who is singled out as especially virtuous is king of Scandinavia.[6]

---

[4]Norman Daniel (1993, Appendix A; 1984) makes a very sharp division between the version of Islam presented in the *chanson de gestes* (which he regards as pure invention, intended for entertainment) and learned accounts. Tolan (2002, 105–34) shows the links between that version and Crusading ideology, and Akbari (2009, 200–203) stresses the relations between learned and popular accounts of Islam. On the names of the gods, see Daniel 1984, 142–45.

[5]The *Chanson de Roland* names rulers from what were at the time pagan lands in Eastern Europe (see lines 3221, 3226). *Aliscans* (Boutet 1996, 308–445), the immediate source for *Willehalm* (see below), has leaders of the pagans from India (lines 30–31) and Slav ones (line 1697, cf. line 850); cf. also Daniel 1984, 66–67, 263.

[6]See *Willehalm* I.41.15–16 (India); I.26.25 ('Seres'). For Matribleiz, king of Scandinavia, see below. The use of contemporary country names such as 'India' and 'China' needs, however, to be qualified. 'India' was generally taken to cover the whole of the East, and although 'Seres' refers to the Chinese in classical and medieval sources, there was throughout the Middle Ages some vagueness about the location of the *serica regio*, and it was often thought

The *chanson de geste* tradition can be used, therefore, as evidence of medieval ideas about pagans. But, in general, its productions offer almost nothing for the discussion of the Problem of Paganism. On the one side, the poets simply dismiss the pagans' religion as wrong: *paien unt tort e chrestiens unt dreit* ('pagans are wrong, Christians are right'), as Roland's emblematic statement puts it;[7] on the other side, the life and habits of the Saracen soldiers are depicted as indistinguishable from those of the Christians, and the best of them have every sort of martial virtue.[8] *Willehalm* is a different case. Wolfram borrows his plot and its wider setting from the *chanson de geste* tradition, and he shares with it a delight in scenes of battle and heroism. The plot itself, taken from *Aliscans*, is simple. A vast pagan army has come to Orange, to defeat Willehalm and punish Giburc. The Christians are heavily defeated, with many casualties. William goes to Laon, with difficulty persuades his brother-in-law, King Louis the Pious, at Laon, to raise an army, with which he returns and wins a decisive victory. But Wolfram's consciousness of the human and intellectual difficulties raised by this story is of a different order from that of the writers of *Aliscans* and the other *chansons de geste*.

Although much of the poem describes military heroism, Wolfram makes the central character a woman, Giburc, who blames herself for being the cause of such bloodshed and whose kin die on both sides of the fighting. Her position as a Christian convert gives her an interest in theology rare in martial poetry, and her pagan background and family an unusual boldness in the positions she takes. While Willehalm is at Laon and she is holding Orange, besieged by the enemy, she talks to Terramer, her father, who wants her to renounce Christianity. She replies with a sermon on the Fall and Redemption. She tells her father that, at his age, he should know about this, and she mentions as prophets the Sibyl and Plato.[9] Wolfram is drawing here on the tradition, seen so clearly in Abelard, which makes Plato and the Sibyls pagan prophets of the Christian truth. He makes Giburc cite them, in particular, so as to suggest that Christianity is the destination for the enlightened pagan tradition: she is asking her father to accept, not something new and strange, but what was already part of his, and her own, culture. Later in the poem, Giburc speaks to the Christian soldiers, who are about to fight the pagan armies led by her father. She urges the Christians to recognize the pagans as God's creations and, if they defeat them, not to kill them—a view echoed by the narrator

---

to be a different place from 'Cathay', the name used by, for instance, Marco Polo for China. It was not until Matteo Ricci, in the late sixteenth century, that the identity of the two was established: see Mungello 1985, 50.

[7] *Chanson de Roland*, l.1015.

[8] See Daniel 1984, 23–93; Raucheisen 1997, 75–82.

[9] *Willehalm* V, 218.10–14.

himself later in the poem: 'to slay them like cattle is a great sin; it is God's handiwork'.[10] She goes on to argue—against the general assumption in the poem that the Christians' enemies are destined one and all for Hell—that the unbaptized are not inevitably damned. She cites as examples Enoch and Elijah who, as one of her previous comments recalled, are said by the Bible to have been assumed into Heaven and so *cannot* be among the damned.[11] They were Old Testament Jews, but in addition she names genuine pagans—Noah, a patriarch from before the time of Abraham, the three Magi and Job.[12] She also alludes—as many theologians do, when discussing natural law, the Old Law and the New Law—to the Jewish equivalent of baptism, circumcision.[13] And, by putting forward the idea that, because the babies in the wombs of Christian mothers are unbaptized, they are pagan, she seems deliberately to be blurring in her comments, as she does in her person, the distinction between Christian and pagan. Without stating anything definitely, the implication of her speech overall is to question, the necessity—even in her own, Christian times—of baptism for salvation.[14]

Willehalm also presents pagan virtue in a way that goes beyond the usual acknowledgement in the *chansons de geste* that among the enemy there are high-born, strong and courageous fighters. After his victory, Willehalm singles out one of his captives, King Matribleiz of Scandinavia, praising his virtues in extravagant terms, endorsed by the narrator, and trusting his word. Matribleiz is not merely courageous, but loyal, constant and generous.[15] There is also the perplexing story of Rennewart. The son of Terramer (and so Giburc's sister), Rennewart was abducted as a child by merchants and ends up employed in Louis the Pious's kitchens. Wolfram complicates his position through an alteration he makes to his source. In *Aliscans*, Louis refuses Rennewart baptism; in *Willehalm*, Louis offers baptism to Rennewart insistently (and the implication is that, were he to accept it, his social status would be greatly improved),

[10] *Willehalm* IX, 450:17–19, taking up what Giburc had said at VI, 306.28.
[11] *Willehalm* VI, 307:1, cf. V, 218.18.
[12] *Willehalm* VI, 307:3–14.
[13] *Willehalm* VI, 307:23–24.
[14] The final five lines of this part of the speech (*Willehalm* VI, 307:26–30) have occasioned great dispute among interpreters (see McFarland 2002 for an account of the discussion, and his own theory), because it is not clear whether or not Giburc is talking about God as the Father and reinforcing the point she has just made about not all pagans being damned. Von Moos (2013a, 9n24) 'hesitates' to include this speech in his discussion of the salvation of heathens, because—he implies—Giburc wants the enemy, if defeated, to be spared so as to be converted. None the less, for the reasons stated here, through Giburc's words Wolfram does indeed also seem to be raising doubts about whether only those in the Church will be saved.
[15] *Willehalm* IX, 462.1–9; cf. 461.9–13—the narrator's praise.

but Rennewart refuses it, because 'it does not suit him'.[16] Rennewart becomes Willehalm's greatest support in battle and, despite the burlesque elements in his character—his violent temper, superhuman strength and the ungainly club which is his preferred weapon—he, though wilfully a pagan, is the poem's male hero almost as much as Willehalm. His religious views are somewhat uncertain. When he first speaks to Willehalm, he declares that he has turned from Mahmet, because of that god's failure to help him in his distress and has turned to Christ.[17] Later, however, when he is talking to his sister, and she asks what God she might have but 'the one who has born of a virgin', he replies that 'he knows three gods, Tervagant, Mahumet and Apolle and he willingly follows their commandments'.[18] Yet the dramatic situation here is very complex. Rennewart knows that Giburc is his sister (and hints so to her), but she does not recognize her brother. Rennewart may be professing this pagan belief, which he no longer holds, as a sort of test, and also, perhaps, because he feels she has too easily renounced her heritage. Wolfram's portrayal of Rennewart does not support any position as such about paganism, but has an extraordinary power to raise questions about it, even anticipating some of the problems raised by the pagans of America and China centuries later. Even if, as most specialists hold, *Willehalm* is unfinished, and by the end of the poem, as in *Aliscans*, Rennewart would have been baptized, the treatment of his baptism earlier on remains no less disturbing and provocative.[19]

REAL MONGOLIA

Under Chinggis (i.e., 'Genghis') Khan (d. 1227), the Mongols built themselves a vast empire in Asia. Between 1235 and 1242, Mongol forces led by Chinggis's grandson Batu devastated large areas of Russia, Poland and

---

[16] *Willehalm* IV, 193.16–22; cf. IV, 191.2–6 on Louis's unsuccessful attempts to persuade Rennewart to be baptized. Compare *Aliscans* 3271–73. The difference from *Aliscans* is noted by Lofmark 1972, 133–34.

[17] *Willehalm* IV, 193.6–11.

[18] *Willehalm* VI. 291.21–24.

[19] Lofmark (1972, 210–43) gives a thorough account of the reasons why *Willehalm* is unfinished (but compare the balanced discussion in Wolfram von Eschenbach 1984, 268–73). Yet, if the ending comes where it does in most of the manuscripts, it is supremely well placed, emphasizing the story's tragic shape and—since the last scene concerns the preservation and return of the dead pagan kings' bodies—the rare openness to the Problem of Paganism. It does indeed seem anachronistic for a medieval poem to end in this abrupt fashion, with the loose ends (including Rennewart's whereabouts) untied, but perhaps our view of what might or might not be medieval is too narrow. The ending of Bernardus Silvestris's *Mathematicus* provides an interesting comparison.

Hungary. Christians in Western Europe feared that they too would soon be invaded. The pope, Innocent IV, decided to send two ambassadors, by different routes, to make contact with the Khan and deliver papal letters to him. One of them, John of Piano Carpini, a sixty-year-old Franciscan who had been one Francis of Assisi's original followers, wrote an account of what he found, the *History of the Mongols*, which provides a remarkably detailed, systematic and dispassionate description of a pagan society and its religious practices.[20]

John's approach is especially remarkable, because the picture of the Mongols given in nearly all the various accounts of their devastations in the 1230s is of a semi- or subhuman race, unlimited in cruelty and violence. 'The men are inhuman and bestial, and rather to be called monsters than human beings, thirsting for blood and drinking it, tearing to pieces and devouring the flesh of dogs and of humans', runs one of the many reports Matthew Paris collected in his *Chronicle*, and the tone of the others is similar.[21] It is not merely that they are characterized by particular vices ('they are greedy, full of rage, deceitful and pitiless more than all others'), but they are entirely without law ('their law is to be lawless').[22] Moreover, they are without anything recognizable as a religion. 'They are pagans, who have no knowledge of God, but neither do they worship idols, but live like beasts'.[23] 'They fear nothing, they neither believe in nor adore anything except their king, whom they call the King of kings and the Lord of lords', writes Alberich of Trois-Fontaines in his chronicle for 1239; Matthew Paris report that 'they call the leaders of their tribes gods'.[24] John's *Historia* is not a traveller's narrative—an account of the course of his journey and his reception is postponed until the final chapter—but a report. Much of it is about the matters which

[20] Cf. Hyde's judgement in his valuable discussion (Hyde 1991, 171–83, at 181) that John 'raised Western ethnography . . . to a level hardly surpassed until the present century'. The *Historia mongolorum* is best edited in John of Piano Carpini 1989; an earlier edition is in Wyngaert 1929; English translation in Dawson 1955, 3–72; useful commentary in John of Piano Carpini 1930 (and German translation) and John of Piano Carpini 1965 (and French translation).

[21] Matthew Paris 1872–83, IV, 76; see Bezzola 1974, 65 for further citations from Matthew. For a full account of the early reactions, see Bezzola 1974, 36–109 and Klopprogge 1993, 19–186.

[22] Matthew Paris 1872–83 IV, 275, 272 (and cf. 109); these comments are from a letter by Ivo of Narbonne, on whom see Bezzola 1974, 82–86.

[23] From the report of Richard, a Dominican from Hungary, ed. in Dörrie 1956, 151–61, at 157 (sec. 4.4). See also Simon of Saint-Quentin 1965, 34–35 (section XXX.74) for another account in this vein, although (see below, p. 119) it is based on first-hand knowledge.

[24] For Alberich, see Bezzola 1974, 61n230; Matthew Paris 1872–83, IV, 275 (Ivo of Narbonne).

would especially concern the pope in planning his political engagement with the Mongols: their administrative and political organization, their armies and techniques of conquest. But he begins with a description of their country, their clothes, dwellings and kinship structures, before going to a chapter specifically devoted to their worship of God and religious rites, and a following one on their morals and customs. 'Kinship structures' seems anachronistic—as if this thirteenth-century Franciscan were analysing what he saw like an ethnographer. But this is exactly what he does, explaining the number of wives each man can have, and who is allowed to marry whom—it is forbidden only to marry one's own daughter, mother or full sister, but not, after the father's death, a sister who had a different mother. And he goes on to explain how the women are bought as wives, and how it is difficult for them to remarry.[25]

John starts off his account of their worship in a way which surprises, given the precise, factual observations he has previously been making: 'They believe in one God, whom they believe to be the maker of all things visible and invisible, and they believe that he is the giver both of good things in this world and of punishments'.[26] For a moment, John looks at the Mongols' beliefs through the verbal framework of the Nicene Creed, and decides that they believe what, as followers of natural law, they should do—although he is probably accurate to say that in some sense they believe in one deity.[27] But then he immediately adds, 'They do not however worship him through prayers, praises or any sort of rite'. He proceeds to give a clear, detailed and dispassionate account of their ritual practices, which involve idols. He describes the different sorts of idols in detail, how they are made and for what they are used. For example, he explains that a particularly honoured sort of idol is made of silk cloth and that, when one has been made, a sheep is killed, its flesh eaten and its bones burned; these sort of idols are made when a boy is sick and are put on his bed.[28] He discusses how they offer food and drink to the idols, and also to the sun, moon, fire and water. He is also an acute observer of their various prohibitions ('customs handed down, which they say are sins'), such as touching fire with a knife, because 'they believe that in this way the head of the fire will be cut off', or touching the threshold of a leader's dwelling or spitting out food—both of them

---

[25] *Historia* 2.3. References to the *Historia* are to the chapters and sections, which are followed in John of Piano Carpini 1989 (as well as the older edition of the text, in Wyngaert 1929).

[26] *Historia* 3.2.

[27] See William of Rubruk 1990, 22; cf. also below, p. 118, on William of Rubruk and Buddhist monotheism.

[28] *Historia* 3.3.

capital offences.[29] He notes that 'they know nothing of eternal life and perpetual damnation'—that is to say, of the Christian understanding of the world to come, since he adds immediately that they believe that 'they will live in another world after death, increase their flocks, eat, drink and do the other things which are done in this world by living people'.[30] John also describes their rites of purification by fire,[31] and he goes into great detail about their burial customs.[32]

Immediately after his account of their ritual prohibitions, John makes the point that, while such actions are counted as sins, 'to kill people, invade the land of others, take the things of others in whatever unjust way, fornicate, do injury to others and to act against God's prohibitions and commandments is no sin among them'.[33] This seems, at first, to be an uncharacteristic intrusion of his own judgement, as a Christian, into his usually descriptive and explanatory account. But perhaps it should be seen, rather, as expressing a certain relativism: an acknowledgement that the Mongols' ways of evaluating behaviour do not at all correspond to Christian concepts. This relativism is limited, however, to describing their own evaluative scheme. When John comes to give his own evaluation of their behaviour, he does not hesitate to use the values he and his readers share to give what turns out to be a very balanced account, divided between their good ways and their bad ways. He notes their obedience, the lack of arguments or quarrels, absence of theft, good humour in enduring hardships, absence of envy and community-mindedness; the chastity and modesty of the women; and the fact that, even when the Mongols are inebriated, they do not become abusive or violent.[34] Only then does John go on to describe their bad practices. They despise all other races, are easily angered, and they are deceitful (he is here talking about their behaviour to foreigners, since he has made it clear that among themselves they are honest and honourable). They become drunk, throw up and then go on drinking; they are greedy and avaricious; they 'count for nothing killing other men', and, John concludes, 'it would take too long to put all their evils down in writing'.[35] John is certainly not trying to give a picture of virtuous pagans, but manages to be aware both that they have a quite different system of values from his own, and yet that there are a number

---

[29] *Historia* 3.7.
[30] *Historia* 3.9; compare Peter of Dusburg's account of the beliefs of the pagan Lithuanians, above, chapter 4.
[31] *Historia* 3.10, 15.
[32] *Historia* 3.12–13.
[33] *Historia* 3.8.
[34] *Historia* 4.2–3.
[35] *Historia* 4.4–6.

of his own moral categories by which they can in some way be assessed. And on this assessment they do not turn out be wholly evil, nor wholly good. On one occasion, he suggests that the Mongols are deceived by devils, when they engage in divination.[36] But his general picture is far from that of a people diabolically possessed.

Another exceptional discussion of the Mongols and their beliefs comes from William of Rubruk, who visited the courts of various Mongol leaders in the 1250s. Like John, William was a Franciscan but, unlike him, he was not a papal emissary. Although he was acting in a covert, semi-official capacity for King Louis IX of France, to whom he addressed his account, he presented himself, and in the main considered himself, as a straightforward missionary, aiming to convert unbelievers to Christianity. And his *Journey* (*Itinerarium*) is not, like John's text, a report, but rather a travel story, and one which, despite the merely workmanlike Latin, is of a very high literary order.[37] Where John's skill is to make himself invisible as an individual and simply to recount and analyse what he observes, William understands that a travel narrative needs a central character, and his own personality, as he artfully portrays it, beautifully fills the role. William is the determined, principled but ever resourceful, adventurer, long-sufferingly enduring hunger and cold in a way which, in his presentation, seem to have more to do with masculine bravado than Franciscan asceticism. William's eye for ethnographic detail is as sharp as John's, but he does not draw together and order this material in the same analytical way. Rather, the observations escape in the course of his story and add to its drama. So, for example, William mentions the threshold taboo, and then, before he and his companion, Bartholomew, enter Mangu (Möngke) Khan's tent, he says that they are explicitly told about it. But the hapless Bartholomew stumbles on the threshold and is led away to Bulgay, the court official who judges those who are condemned to death. William, unaware of what has happened, thinks Bartholomew has been taken to be given lighter, more comfortable clothing. Only later does he learn what has happened and thinks up a convenient half-truth—'They had no interpreter with them, so how could they know?'—which saves his companion from the executioner.[38]

At times, William will pause for a while to describe an aspect of Mongol religious practice, and he is the first European observer to describe a

---

[36] *Historia* 3.10.

[37] References are to the chapters and sections of the edition in Wyngaert 1929, 147–332. There is an excellent translation, with introduction and commentary, which follows these chapter and section divisions: William of Rubruk 1990.

[38] See *Itinerarium* 15.6, 29.28–29, 29.36–37.

Buddhist temple.[39] Usually, though, in line with his missionary aims and the centring of the narrative around him and his actions, he is less concerned to describe the Mongols' beliefs than to explain how he engaged them and others in argument about God. The most ambitious of these occasions was a dispute in the presence of Mangu Khan between Christians (himself and the Nestorians), Muslims and Buddhists. At his insistence, the discussion is about God. William proclaims that there is one God, and the Buddhists—on his account—reply that there are many; they believe, as they will go on to explain, in a supreme God, but many inferior ones. William, so he reports, easily manages to defeat their position by introducing the concept of omnipotence: when they deny that any of their gods is all powerful, he can then retort that there is none of their gods who can help them in every danger. When the Muslims are invited to speak, William tells us that they refused, saying that they acknowledged the truth of the Christian law and they constantly prayed to die a Christian death.[40] This claim is hard to believe. But at least the Christians and Muslims would have had enough in common in their conception of religion to be able to dispute about God. So far as the Buddhists are concerned (and the same probably goes for the Khan and the other Mongol onlookers), their views of religion and, especially, of God are so different, that to present the difference as about whether there is one God or many, as William insists, misses the point (as, most probably, does William's view that there is a special group of Buddhists who, influenced by their 'frequent disputations' with Christians and Muslims, hold that there is one God).[41] William himself seems aware of the problem, in a world-weary manner: 'They all heard and no one said anything in contradiction [to the account of Christian beliefs which the Nestorians went on to give], and yet no one said: "I believe. I want to become a Christian". Then the Nestorians and the Muslims sang loudly, the Buddhist priests were silent, and afterwards they all drank a lot'.[42] Neither William of Rubruk's vivid story of travel and adventure, nor John of Piano Carpini's scientific ethnography won a wide medieval readership. Few people, apart from Roger Bacon, seem to have known William's work.[43] John's *Historia* was, however, used as a source in Vincent of Beauvais's extremely popular *Speculum Historiale*, along with the account of the embassy by Simon of Saint-Quentin of

---

[39] For example, there is a detailed description of their rituals before drinking 2.8 (more detailed than in John's account: cf. *Historia* 3.3); of divination 29.27; of the *divini* (shamans) 35; for the Buddhist temple, see 24.5–25.6.

[40] *Itinerarium* 33.13–21.

[41] *Itinerarium* 26.1; 33.22.

[42] *Itinerarium* 33.22–23. On this debate, see Southern 1962, 47–52 and Tardieu 2010, secs. 10–15.

[43] Cf. below, pp. 129–30.

the embassy of Ascelin, the other Franciscan sent by Innocent IV.[44] But the account of Mongolian paganism becomes much less interesting and less dispassionate. Perhaps for political reasons, Vincent makes selective omissions, leaving out the idea that the Mongols recognized one supreme God, and stressing their animism and superstitious practices. The Mongols end up seeming hardly human, and Vincent's readers could scarcely discern John's extraordinary effort to describe, even if he could not understand, an approach to the sacred totally different from that of his own culture.[45]

In the decades after William, the Franciscans expanded their missionary work in the East, and John of Montecorvino (1247–1328) set up a Franciscan mission in China. In the period between 1318 and 1331, his confrere, Odoric of Pordenone, made a long journey to India, South East Asia and China. The *Account* which he wrote of it was far more popular than the works of John of Piano Carpini or William of Rubruk, perhaps just because Odoric was more credulous than they were. Although he claims to be giving a truthful account of what he saw himself or heard 'from trustworthy sources', he allows elements from traditional accounts of the monstrous races of the East (such as the dog-headed men, well known since Pliny)[46] to slip into or colour his account, and is quick to accept stories of cannibalism and human sacrifice. Yet a good deal of the material does apparently come from his own observation, even if he distorts or misunderstands what he has seen, and as a missionary he has a special interest in pagan religious practices. Although, unlike John and William, he is quick to add reproving comments, he also records some apt replies made by pagans to his criticisms. He describes, for example, a conversation with Buddhist monks about reincarnation; when he objects that the cattle in front of him are beasts and cannot be the souls of 'noble men', the monk explains how the souls of noble people enter animals such as cows, whereas those of rustics go into vile animals.[47] When Odoric describes how, on the Island of Dondin, people kill and eat their closest relations when they are sick and it is prognosticated that they will not recover, the story may seem like a fantasy; but he goes on to recount his reproach to the islanders—'Even dogs and wolves

[44] Simon of Saint-Quentin's narrative of this, far less resourceful ambassador's trip, survives only from the extracts in the *Speculum historiale*. It has been extracted from there and edited in Simon of Saint-Quentin 1965.

[45] See C. Kappler, 'L'image des Mongols dans le "Speculum historiale" de Vincent de Beauvais' in Paulmier-Foucart et al. 1990, 219–40.

[46] On Pliny and the monstrous races of which he tells, see Chibnall 1975.

[47] References are to the chapter numbers of the Latin text (in Yule 1913) and those of Jean le Long's French translation, which was used in the *Book* by 'John Mandeville': Latin 33; French 23.

do not eat their own kind'—and then their very apposite reply, that they eat them rather than letting the worms do so, which would cause their souls pain.[48]

Sir John Mandeville

The most far-fetched, yet also the most reflective discussion of pagans in the East is a work which, although called the *Book* (or more commonly, and less correctly, the *Travels*) *of Sir John Mandeville*, may or may not have been written by someone really of that name. Whichever is the case, the 'Sir John' of the *Book* is a fiction, in the sense that he did not really make the lengthy journey, a medieval world tour, from England to the Earthly Paradise (and back), which he describes. The *Book* is written, not from experience, but from other books. It is a collage made up from different sources, with two in particular accounting for the bulk of the text: the account written in 1336 by William of Boldensele, a Dominican, of 'certain regions beyond the Mediterranean' for the Holy Land, and, for the remoter parts of the fictional journey, Odoric of Pordenone's *Account*. Despite this unpromising mode of composition, not only was Mandeville's *Book* one of the most widely read of all medieval vernacular texts—in different versions of the original French, and in translations into Latin, English and many other languages—it is also, in many ways, intellectually the most original. The descriptions are taken from others, but the ideas they are used to put forward are the author's own. Borrowed material is given a new meaning by the ways in which it is ordered and juxtaposed; and the author also practises 'overwriting', where in copying from a source he makes a series of small verbal changes which adapt or alter the sense of the original.[49]

Although the writer frequently claims (falsely) to have witnessed all he reports, the *Book* is not written for the most part as a travel narrative, but rather as a guidebook—indeed, sometimes alternative routes will be sketched out—and as a geography.[50] Another of the author's aims is to use the description of distant parts and the experiences and conversations Sir John has there to criticize religious practices and social arrangements in his own Europe; as most obviously in the speech he puts into the sultan's mouth about the failure of Christian priests to behave in a Christian way.[51] But another of his purposes is to talk about

[48] Latin 26; French 20.
[49] 'Overwriting' is a term taken from Higgins 1997.
[50] See Deluz 1988.
[51] *Book* 15; John Mandeville 2000, 278–80. References to the *Book* cite the chapter, and then the page numbers of Deluz's critical edition of the Insular Version of the French. There

religious diversity, and what apparently different religions have in common. This interest stretches beyond his well-informed and sympathetic account of Islam to paganism. Pagan forms of worship are discussed especially in two places. First, there is a series of chapters, in the section based on Odoric, which tell of various different peoples and their beliefs.[52] Although he inserts extra material, especially some about the Plinian monstrous races, for the most part the author follows the French version of Odoric quite closely, and yet through small changes he gives a completely different impression. Odoric presents an account of cruel, revolting pagan practices, which he deplores, although he will occasionally put down an explanation for them he has been told. The *Book* suggests, rather, that there are often parallels with Christian practices, and frequently good sense behind what the pagans do, however horrifying or disgusting.

In one land, for example, Odoric tells how they 'worship a cow as god' and goes on to describe how the priests wash in its urine. The *Book* retains this picturesque detail, but it explains that 'in this country the people worship a cow because of its simplicity and gentleness and because of its usefulness, and they say that it is the holiest animal on earth'.[53] Further on, Odoric gives an outraged description of the fanatical devotion shown in the Kingdom of Mobar to an idol: some worshippers throw themselves under the cart on which it is wheeled 'and so wickedly lose their lives, their souls and their bodies', whilst others have themselves cut up and thrown at the idol, and then their bodies are cremated and they are considered to be holy.[54] In the *Book*, the idol worshippers throw themselves under the idol cart in just the same way, but the authorial comment is quite different: 'They do all this for love of their god, with great devotion, and they think that the more pain and tribulation they suffer for love of this idol, the closer they will be to God and the more joy they will have in the world to come'. And, just to reinforce the point, the author goes on: 'In brief, they do such

---

is an excellent translation (with supplementary material): John Mandeville 2011. The various different versions of the *Book* often differ significantly, in a way that shows different reactions to the material by various translators and redactors. These variations have led Higgins to speak of the *Book* as a 'multi-text', and he studies these variations sensitively in Higgins 1997 (cf. also Tzanaki 2003). The story of the transmission of the *Book* is not studied here (but see below, note 76). It should also be noted that there is debate over whether the Insular Version or the Continental Version of the text is the author's original, but the differences are not very important for the matters discussed here.

[52] Chaps. 18–22, based on Odoric 9, 11–20 of the French, which will be cited here, because it was the text usually used by the author. There is a fine account of the *Book*'s strategies, as well as the way they are adapted in different versions of it, in Higgins 1997, 143–55.

[53] *Account* 16; Jean le Long 2010, 22:28–37; *Book* 18; John Mandeville 2000, 321.

[54] *Account* 12; Jean le Long 2010, 26:62–27:89.

penance and make their bodies suffer such pain for love of their idols that hardly any Christian would dare to do a tenth part of it for love of his Christ'.[55] Even the worst behaviour is presented in the most favourable way. The inhabitants of Lamory, for example, are cannibals. Odoric says that 'they are very evil and very cruel. They eat human flesh', and he goes on to explain how they buy children from merchants and kill them to eat. In the *Book*, after a generally favourable account of the people, the author adds simply, 'But they have one bad custom—they like to eat human flesh more than any other sort of meat'.[56] On the people, mentioned in the discussion of Odoric above, who kill their closest relations when they are sick and are said to be going to die, the *Book* adds the idea that 'when the flesh is too lean, the friends of the dead person say that they have done great wrong to have let him suffer so much pain for no reason. And when they find the flesh fat, they say that they have done well to send him to Paradise quickly and they have not let him suffer too much pain'.[57] Cannibalism is thus turned into high-minded euthanasia. The reply these people made to Odoric's reproaches—about saving the souls from the pain of being eaten by worms—is not needed here and is re-used to better effect earlier in the text as an explanation for why bodies are cremated, rather than buried.[58] Especially telling is the way the author adapts the account of the dog-headed people. Odoric, in Jean le Long's translation, pictures a primitive, savage, idolatrous race: naked, 'all black', very cruel in battle—they eat prisoners who cannot pay a ransom—and worshipping a cow.[59] In the *Book*, the 'Canophelez' still go naked and eat their prisoners of war, but they are no longer described as black or cruel, and a comment about the lack of crime in this country, missing in the French, is taken from the Latin, with the added remark that 'this king is very upright according to his law'.[60] There is an equivalent shift of emphasis in how their religion is presented. The phrase 'they worship a cow for their God', copied from Odoric, takes on a different meaning when it is preceded by the words 'They are a rational people of good understanding'. Odoric had reported that their king has a pearl necklace, like our amber prayer beads, and every day he makes three hundred prayers 'to his gods'. In the *Book* not only does the king pray 'devoutly' to his god (singular), but the prayer-bead comparison

[55] *Book* 19; John Mandeville 2000, 328.
[56] *Account* 13; Jean le Long 2010, 28:19–23; *Book* 20; John Mandeville 2000, 332.
[57] *Book* 22; John Mandeville 2000, 357.
[58] *Book* 18; John Mandeville 2000, 322.
[59] *Account* 18; Jean le Long 2010, 33.
[60] *Book* 21; John Mandeville 2000, 350–52.

is developed, so that he counts the beads 'in the way that we say *Our Father* or *Hail Mary*'.[61]

Although the author of the *Book* has often been held up as a liar, because he never visited the countries he claims to have seen, he seems to have held strictly to a certain conception of scientific honesty. He treats what Odoric and others relay as his empirical evidence, the (supposedly) factual content of which he is not at liberty to alter, even when it sits awkwardly with his general outlook. His main interpretative tool is not, as for modern ethnologists (or one of their predecessors in spirit, like John of Piano Carpini), analysis, but rather imaginative retouching and addition of details. Through this method he is certainly able to offer a sympathetic look at the immense diversity of customs and beliefs, especially religious, and perhaps, incidentally, he is making a plea for tolerance, but more than anything the author succeeds in bringing out the deep unity in religious experience between Christians and almost every variety of pagan.[62] Such thinking does not, however, lead to a naturalistic view of religion, Christianity included, as a mere human practice. Indeed, although he shapes his descriptions suggestively, he refrains at this point from any explicit theological comment. It is only near to the end of the book when, in his second main discussion of pagan religion, he describes the Brahmans, that he proposes a definite doctrinal position.

By Mandeville's time, there was already a long history of treating the Brahmans (*bragmanni*), or as they were also called, the *gymnosophistae*, as virtuous pagans. At the origin of these accounts was a real encounter between Alexander the Great and some ascetic Indian philosophers in the Punjab.[63] Augustine and Jerome mention them, acknowledging their asceticism, though making it clear that they could not be saved without Christ.[64] In the Middle Ages, the Brahmans' asceticism could be read

---

[61] *Book* 21; John Mandeville 2000, 351; cf. Higgins 1997, 146–47, who also notes the 'almost Christian fashion' in which the king's devotion is portrayed.

[62] Greenblatt, who (1991, 26–51) gives an interesting reading of the *Book*, rightly (45–46) cautions that the engagement with these distant and in some cases imaginary peoples is too distant to be called tolerance. He invokes, rather, Hans Blumenberg's idea of 'theoretical curiosity'. But when he goes on to follow Blumenberg in describing such curiosity as 'heterodox', because it presents a narrative which does not 'secure the rock-like centrality of the Christian order', he is oversimplifying, as some of the other chapters in this book will show. In any case, the *Book* does, in its own way, assert the centrality of this Christian order.

[63] On the background to the Brahman material and its relationship to both Indian and Greek thought, see Stoneman 1994, 1995 and 2008, 91–95 (modifying to some extent his earlier conclusions).

[64] Jerome, *Commentary on Ezechiel*, IV (to Ezechiel, xiii, 17ff.); Augustine, *CG* XV.20.

about both in the many versions of the Alexander romance,[65] and in an exchange of Latin letters supposedly between their king, Dindimus, and Alexander.[66] Alcuin knew these letters,[67] whilst Abelard, though suspicious about their authenticity, used them as the basis for praising the life of the Brahmans as 'unequalled by that of other people, however religious, in innocence and abstinence'. From a passage in the *Letters*, he claims that they had knowledge of the Trinity and so can be put beside Nebuchadnezzar, David and Solomon as ancient witnesses to the doctrine.[68] The Brahmans reappear fleetingly a little later, when Abelard is discussing the unknowability of God, and remembering how, in the *Letters*, Dindimus attacks religious ceremonies, he refers to their way of sacrifice as 'prayers and tears'.[69] The Abelardian view reappears in James of Vitry's book on the East and, from there, in Thomas of Cantimpré's *On the Nature of Things* (1228–44), where the Brahmans are said to lead lives of marvellous innocence and to have written of the Son of God before the Incarnation.[70] Albert the Great (c. 1250), in similar vein, refers to their doing without external goods and calls them 'the greatest philosophers'.[71]

The *Book* tells, not of Brahmans or Gymnosophists, but of two islands, Bragmey and Gynosophe, following the French prose romance of Alexander, its main source, along with the *Letters* as reproduced in Vincent of Beauvais's *Speculum historiale*.[72] The author deliberately selects his material so as to present the (indistinguishable) peoples of both islands as ideal types of good pagans.[73] All the elements of primitivism in the traditional account of them—nakedness, no agriculture, commerce or cities—are omitted, as is the exaggerated asceticism which Alexander attacks in the *Letters*; there is retained just the idea that 'they lead a better life than any monk or friar and fast everyday' and that 'they have no care for earthly things'. The law-abidingness of Bragmey, 'the land of Faith', is

[65] Ross 1988 provides a guide to the complex tradition; detail is added in Cary 1956. An overview of the whole tradition is provided in Stoneman 2008, 199–216.

[66] See Ross 1988, 31–32; Cary 1956, 13–14. One version of the text is edited in Julius Valerius 1888, 169–89, and there is a translation in Stoneman 1994, 57–66. The letters balance Dindimus's own presentation of his people's way of life with Alexander's criticisms of it.

[67] See above, p. 63.

[68] Abelard, *Theologia Christiana* I.131–33 (taken over in the *Theologia Scholarium* I.195–97). Abelard refers explicitly to Jerome's *Contra Jovinianum*.

[69] *Theologia Christiana* III.45. See also Cary 1956, 93; Hahn 1978, 221–22.

[70] *De natura rerum* 3.4; Thomas of Cantimpré 1973, 98. See Pfister 1941, 75–77 (pages according to reprint); Hahn 1978, 229.

[71] *Super Ethica* X.16.1; Albert the Great 1987, 771.

[72] 4.66–71; Vincent of Beauvais 1624, 135–37.

[73] *Book* 32; John Mandeville 2000, 456–59.

emphasized, as is the goodness of the inhabitants. They do not have perfect law (that is, the revealed New Law), but through following natural law they avoid all the seven deadly sins and follow the Ten Commandments. At the end of the account, the author adds the idea—introduced originally by Abelard, who had inferred it from certain turns of phrase in the *Letters*—that 'in these Isles they prophesied the Incarnation of our Lord Jesus Christ, how he would be born of a virgin, three thousand years before Our Lord was born of the Virgin Mary. And they believe in the Incarnation perfectly, but they do not know the way in which he suffered and died for us'.[74] Before adding this information, the author has come out with his own, doctrinal assertion:

> Although this people does not have the articles of faith which we have, none the less for their good natural faith and their good intention I believe that it is certain that God loves them and that God looks on their service favourably, as he did for Job, who was a pagan, and none the less he accepted him as his loyal servant. Therefore, however many different laws there may be throughout the world, I believe that God loves all those who love and serve him virtuously and loyally, and who scorn the vain glory of this world, just as these people do, and Job also did.[75]

The author goes on to give a string of scriptural authorities which are said to justify this generous view of God's attitude to pagans.[76]

In one way, there is nothing surprising about the idea that the inhabitants of the two islands are accepted by God as his servants and so may well be among the saved. The author has described their behaviour and beliefs in a way that fits exactly one of the main models for the salvation of pagans: they follow natural law and they have implicit faith—they do not know the full details of Christ's life and Crucifixion, but they have a minimum (indeed somewhat more than the minimum requisite) knowledge of the coming of a Redeemer.[77] But there is a big difference from Job, to whom they are compared. These people are living now, in Sir John Mandeville's own time, more than a thousand years after Christ. Accepted Christian teaching distinguished sharply between the time before the Incarnation, when implicit faith was sufficient, and the period afterwards, when an explicit knowledge of Christ's redeeming work, and

---

[74] *Book* 32; John Mandeville 2000, 461.

[75] *Book* 32; John Mandeville 2000, 459–60.

[76] Higgins 1997, 234–38 examines the reception of this portrait of good pagans by the various redactors and translators of the *Book*. Some, including the Latin translation, make changes which indicate clearly very different views about pagan goodness, but the others do retain the emphasis the author gave to his account.

[77] See above, p. 66, and for a fuller discussion, chapter 8.

the intent, at least, to receive baptism, was needed. The author has, therefore, made yet another of his adaptations, turning a perfectly orthodox
line of doctrinal thought into a theological innovation.

He returns to the same theme a few pages later, at the very end of the
Book, declaring that among all the peoples 'of diverse laws and beliefs'
which he has described, there is 'none, because they have reason and
understanding, which does not have some of the articles of our faith and
some of the good points of our belief, and who do not believe in God who
made the world'.[78] He goes on to explain that they do not know how to
speak of the Son or the Holy Spirit, but they do know how to speak of
the Bible, especially the Old Testament—presumably meaning that their
ideas coincide with the ones expressed there. He explains, as he had done
earlier, that their idolatry does not in fact involve worshipping physical
objects,[79] but continues by drawing a sharp contrast between Christian
and pagan images, and by suggesting, in line with widely held Christian
views from Augustine onwards about idolatry, that when they hear idols
speaking to them they may be hearing the voices of devils. The author is
not, however, retrenching from his position in the chapter on Bragmey
and Gynosophe. These final comments apply to all pagans, not just to exceptionally good ones. For the mass of pagan peoples—many of whom,
clearly, fall far short of being excellent followers of natural law—he
wants to make clear that the unity in diversity of religious feeling must be
understood in terms of more or less inchoate understanding of the true
God: they grasp his existence and understand some of his laws. Only for
the exceptionally virtuous pagans will he give the reassurance that God
loves them and regards them as his servants.

[78] *Book* 34; John Mandeville 2000, 477.
[79] See Higgins 1997, 226–27 for an analysis of this discussion.

CHAPTER 8

Aristotelian Wisdom: Unity, Rejection or Relativism

IN THE THIRTEENTH CENTURY AN INSTITUTIONAL DEVELOPMENT TOOK place which wrote the Problem of Paganism into the very structure of higher education by making one of the constituent faculties of the universities an institution dedicated to knowledge not gained through revelation, especially as set out by one great pre-Christian author, Aristotle. When the loosely organized schools of Paris became a university, around 1200—and at much the same time the University of Oxford took shape— the rather loose and uncertain arrangements found in the early medieval schools were replaced by a highly organized system of faculties. The Arts Faculty, devoted to secular learning, was where all students had to begin, usually when they were about fifteen, and where most finished even before they had completed the seven-year course, after which they would be required, as part of their degree, to spend two years as Arts Masters.[1] Only then could a student begin a course in one of the 'higher' faculties: law, medicine and theology. This institutional rigidification of a pattern of study already loosely established might not, on its own, have had much effect on approaches to knowledge. But the first fifty years of the Paris and Oxford universities also coincided with the rapid assimilation of Aristotle's non-logical writings. Many of them were at first prohibited from being taught in the Paris Arts Faculty, but by the middle of the thirteenth century, the Arts Faculties in both Paris and Oxford based their teaching almost entirely round Aristotle's works of logic, natural science, psychology, metaphysics and ethics.[2] Although it was possible, as the sequence

---

[1] There was an exception to this rule, but it is less important than it may first seem. Members of the mendicant orders (such as Dominicans and Franciscans) did not study in the Arts Faculties, but they followed a similar course, in their own houses of study, which were often in university towns. For an introduction, with bibliography, to the rise of the universities and the position within them of the mendicant orders, see chaps. 4 (Marrone) and 5 (Luscombe) in Pasnau 2010, I, and Friedman 2012, 196–201.

[2] See Friedman 2012, 194–98 with up-to-date bibliography.

of a student's career indicated, to see the arts simply as a propaedeutic to studying sacred doctrine, the curriculum based around the near complete Aristotelian corpus was in no ordinary sense a preparatory training for something else. On the contrary, the various texts (sometimes supplemented by pseudepigrapha, such as the *Book of Causes*)[3] seemed to offer an impressively comprehensive system of knowledge, complete with a theoretical account (in the *Posterior Analytics*) of the systematization. Without its having been planned that way, universities each had among their faculties one dedicated, and officially restricted to, pagan knowledge: what could be learned without the help of Christianity, as exemplified pre-eminently in the writings of an Athenian from the fourth century BC.

The search for knowledge within such a faculty could only ever achieve a qualified autonomy, given the presumptions shared by everyone, including the Arts Masters themselves, about the pre-eminence of the faith. But even a qualified autonomy for such pagan knowledge raised serious problems, and there were some Paris Arts Masters, especially among those who chose to teach in the faculty for far longer than the statutory two years, who were very eager to advocate it. But before looking at the central discussion among these Arts Masters and the theologians, who supported, differed from or opposed them to different degrees, it is worth pausing to consider two university figures who, though detached from this debate, gave especial prominence to thinking about paganism: Roger Bacon and Albert the Great.

ROGER BACON AND ALBERT THE GREAT

Bacon's long life—he was born sometime between 1210 and 1220 and died in 1292 or shortly afterwards—spans the period covered in most of this chapter.[4] In his early years, Bacon was much involved in the leading current of the intellectual life of his times, studying Aristotle at Oxford (where there were no prohibitions as in Paris) in the 1230s and teaching as an Arts Master in Paris in the following decade. But for ten years from the late 1240s, he devoted himself to private study—for which he had private means—especially in languages (learning some Greek, dabbling in Hebrew and Arabic), and developing strong interests in what he called *scientia experimentalis*, something nearer to astrology, alchemy and magic than to experimental science in the modern sense. Bacon then

[3] A text based on Proclus, but often attributed to Aristotle.
[4] An up-to-date survey of Bacon's life and a careful study of the aims of his work, with a stress on their missionary nature, is given by Power 2013.

decided to become a Franciscan. Although he seems to have been in both Oxford and Paris, he had never studied in the Theology Faculty, and so he could not, like the secular master Alexander of Hales, who became a Franciscan, teach there. Rather, his major text, finished in 1267, the *Greater Work (Opus Maius)*—along with its two accompanying shorter pieces (*Opus minus, Opus tertium*)—was written by special request for the pope, Clement IV, whom Bacon had come to know before his elevation. In a way that has little to do with the subtle questions of doctrine which fascinated and divided professional theologians, and little connection with the Parisian controversies explored below, Bacon set out a scheme of knowledge including mathematics, optics, *scientia experimentalis* and what he called 'moral philosophy', designed especially to provide a way of converting all peoples to Christianity.[5]

Bacon's missionary aims made the Problem of Paganism not just a historical question, but a matter of immediate, contemporary concern to him. As the rest of this chapter will show, the university Arts and Theology Masters had almost no interest in the contacts with contemporary pagans of the sort discussed in the last chapter. Their pagans were Greeks and Romans—and usually Greek or Roman philosophers. By contrast, although Bacon did develop distinctive views about the ancient pagan philosophical tradition, the various different peoples inhabiting the world and their beliefs interested him deeply, and he was one of the few readers of the *Journey* to the Mongols by William of Rubruk, whom he met, and he had also read Carpini's *History*.[6] Using these sources and his general wide reading, in the *Moral philosophy* which formed the final part of his *Greater Work*, Bacon drew up a systematic account of the different types of religion (or 'sects', as he called them) which, he believed, included all those which existed or could exist.[7] As well as Christians, Jews and Muslims ('Saracens'), Bacon identifies three other groups: Tartars, Pagans and Idolaters. He classifies them according to their knowledge of God (God is naturally known to everyone, he believes, but some sects know him less well than others),[8] their manner of worship and their views about the afterlife. He places the 'Pagans' (or 'pure pagans'), such as the Lithuanians,

[5]Bacon did, however, take a definite view about the influence of Averroes, whom he considered wrong in many respects and placed well below Avicenna: see Hackett 2005, and see below for the controversy in general.

[6]On the meeting, see Power 2013, 62 (with further references) and, for references to the *Journey* (Bacon calls it *On the Manners of the Tartars [De moribus Tartarorum]*) *Moralis philosophia* IV, d. 1, 1.6; IV, d. 1, 3.5–6; IV, d. 2, 5.4–10; Roger Bacon 1953, 190:8; 194:11–20; 213–14; and for reference to John of Carpini, *Moralis philosophia* IV, d. 1, 1.7; Roger Bacon 1953, 190:13–15.

[7]Or, strictly, up until the coming of the sect of Antichrist: IV, d. 1, 1.4; Roger Bacon 1953, 189:20–21. The classification follows: IV, d. 1, 1.5–2.6; Roger Bacon 1953, 189:22–193:6.

[8]IV, d. 2, 1.14; Roger Bacon 1953, 198:24–199:4.

lowest: they have no priests and make whatever they care to choose their God, worshipping what they wish and sacrificing as they like. He adds that they take natural things, such as the sun, moon, animals, groves or water and worship them from love, and what is frightening from fear.[9] These pagans, he says (in line with the reports on, for instance, the Lithuanians), believe that they will continue in the afterlife to enjoy the pleasures and riches of their earthly life, which is why at their death they burn their possessions, friends and families along with their own bodies. The Idolaters have places of worship, ceremonies and sacrifices, and believe in many gods, none of them omnipotent. They too hope to enjoy the goods of this world in a future life, although their priests remain chaste and abstinent. The Tartars worship one omnipotent God, but they also venerate fire and the threshold of their dwellings; and Roger recounts, from Rubruk and Carpini, the rites of purification by fire and the death sentence imposed on those who tread on a threshold. Bacon also believes that the characters of nations and hence the nature of their belief in God and religious practices are determined astrologically, although 'the rational soul may not be compelled to anything'.[10] Bacon seems to have been fascinated by the material he collected about the different sorts of pagans and at one moment, drawing the parallel between the Mongols' threshold taboo and the very same taboo recounted in the Old Testament about the priests of the Philistine God Dagon, he is unselfconsciously engaging in comparative ethnography.[11] None the less, he is always careful to direct his discussion towards his practical, missionary end. By starting from their present beliefs, Bacon believes that Christian missionaries can persuade the unbelievers—Jews, Muslims and the various sorts of pagans— that they are rationally obliged to accept a set of philosophical views about God and salvation which accord with Christian doctrine, and also that revelation is necessary and has been made to one sect, and finally that this sect is Christianity.

It is this idea of a common *philosophical* basis, rationally convincing to all sects and to which revelation can be added, which lies behind Bacon's thinking on the wisdom of ancient pagans. Anyone who has read about Ficino and other thinkers of his time will know about *prisca theologia* or the Ancient Theology, the idea that certain figures who lived long before the Greek philosophers, such as Zoroaster, Orpheus and Hermes Trismegistus had access to revealed truths by contact with the Old Testament tradition. Bacon is a less direct precursor of this tradition, already foreshadowed by Abelard, than he may at first seem. His account of the

[9] IV, d. 1, 3.9; Roger Bacon 1953, 195:6–10.
[10] IV, d. 1, 3; Roger Bacon 1953, 193:7–195:10; cf. Power 2013, 227–32.
[11] IV, d. 2, 5.6; Roger Bacon 1953, 213:17–20; cf. 1 Samuel v, 5.

history of philosophy begins in remotest antiquity and discusses Hermes Trismegistus and Zoroaster, and he uses, as Ficino would do, Josephus's *History of the Jews*, as well as Augustine.[12] But, as the context suggests, Bacon is not setting up an Ancient Theology but rather what might be called an Ancient *Philosophy*. The point to be established by the chapter in his *Greater Work* where these discussions occur is that the 'fullness of philosophy' was given to the same people as those to whom God gave the law: that is to say, the Jews and their Old Testament predecessors. In his *Compendium of Theology* Bacon is even clearer. First, he says, God gave 'the truth of philosophy' (which has been explicitly distinguished from 'divine wisdom') to some patriarchs, prophets and other just men among the Hebrews, 'after whom there followed the men who were called 'philosophers', especially the Greeks, who received the principles of the sciences and arts from the Hebrews'.[13] The idea behind the Ancient Theology would be that ancient peoples other than the Jews had access to revelation, though through the Old Testament tradition, and so parts of Greek philosophy conform to revealed truth because it was shaped by it. By contrast, Bacon wishes rather to insist that Old Testament figures such as Noah, his son Ham, Abraham, Joseph and Moses were skilled philosophers and that, due to them, there had been, as he quotes Averroes as saying, 'a complete philosophy' in times before Aristotle.[14] Aristotle himself was left trying to complete philosophy again, catching up on a tradition of philosophizing from Old Testament times which was the basis of Greek philosophy, but had been only partially transmitted. This Ancient Philosophy extends to many aspects of Christian doctrine, such as the Trinity, the Incarnation and the immortality of the soul—as Bacon shows from a variety of sources, including the Hermetic writings, Pliny, Apuleius, Aristotle, Arabic writers such as Abu Mashar and Avicenna (who are taken to be part of the tradition) and one very surprising 'pagan' source, the philosopher Ethicus, 'in his book of divine, human and natural things, which he wrote in the Hebrew, Greek and Latin language, because of the magnitude of its secrets': that is, the *Cosmographia*

---

[12] *Opus Maius* II.9–13; Roger Bacon 1900, 53–67. Note that references are to the revised edition of parts I–III, which Bridges published in 1900 as volume 3 of his edition, and not to his earlier edition in volume 1.

[13] 2.13; Roger Bacon 1988, 44:20–24. At the beginning of the previous section, Bacon says that most people have always erred in both *philosophia* and *sapientia divina*. Then he explains how they have erred in *sapientia divina* and, in the passage here, he comes on to discuss, by contrast, the errors of the majority in philosophy (44:18—*Similter possumus videre in philosophia*). The *Compendium*, according to the author himself (2.14; cf. 4.86; Roger Bacon 1988, 46:16, cf. 86:31), dates from 1292, quite possibly the year of his death, but it is based, though not slavishly, on material in the *Greater Work* from twenty-five years earlier; cf. Roger Bacon 1988, 8–9.

[14] *Opus Maius* II.9; Roger Bacon 1900, 54–55.

of Aethicus Ister.[15] There is an element of revelation in this knowledge—Bacon refers, for instance, to the Sibylline prophecies and remarks that 'if such weak little women spoke in this way, it is far more to be believed that the wisest philosophers tasted these truths'[16]—but even it is also derived from reason.

Bacon emphasizes philosophy in his account of ancient pagan wisdom, because of the role it can play in his own day in persuading the unbelievers to become Christians. Since philosophical thinking, as carried forward by the Greeks and now transmitted to his own times, began along with the Old Testament roots of the Christian tradition, it shares much common ground with Christian thinking. Christians should use this philosophy, but add to it their knowledge of revelation to complete and surpass what antiquity has handed to them. In doing this, they do not, however, move out of philosophy into theology. They remain philosophers, because they put forward only what is common to Christians and the unbelievers (even if their grasp of it comes from revelation), and which it can be shown that those learned in the philosophy of the unbelievers cannot deny.[17] As Bacon says explicitly, 'the person who completes philosophy through these truths should not on that account be called a theologian, nor should he transcend the bounds of philosophy, because he can safely treat those things which are common to philosophy and theology, and those which are accepted in common by the faithful and the unbelievers'.[18] And it is precisely this set of truths, 'common to philosophy and theology, to the faithful and unbelievers, given by God himself and revealed to the philosophers so that the human race would be prepared for the special divine truths' which Bacon wishes his philosopher-missionaries to use in converting the world.[19] So far as Bacon's theoretical stance, shaped by these practical aims, is concerned, he is at the furthest extreme from making a contrast or separation between pagan philosophy and Christian thought. Pagan philosophy has its origins in the Old Testament tradition and Christian philosophers who develop it are merely taking back what is their own, but they are able, whilst remaining philosophers, to develop it further. They should do so, he insists, not just because of their aims as philosophers, but 'on account of their Christian conscience, which asks them to bring all truth back to divine truth, so as to make it subject to it and serve it'. Outside the

---

[15] *Moralis philosophia* I.2–8; Roger Bacon 1953, 9–35. See I.2.8 (Roger Bacon 1953, 12:12–14) for the description of Ethicus, on whom cf. above, chapter 4.

[16] *Opus Maius* II.17; Roger Bacon 1900, 74.

[17] *Opus Maius* II.19; Roger Bacon 1900, 77.

[18] *Opus Maius* II.19; Roger Bacon 1900, 78.

[19] *Moralis philosophiae* IV, d. 2, 1.5; Roger Bacon 1953, 196:21–25.

context of its relationship to Christian truth and, ultimately, divine truth, pagan philosophy ('the philosophy of the unbelievers') is without value and entirely harmful.[20]

Like Bacon, Albert the Great enjoyed a long life—he was born c. 1200 and died in 1280—which spanned the dramatic developments in philosophy during the thirteenth century. He was also, in a certain way, an outsider: after studying and teaching theology at Paris at much the same time (1242–48) as Bacon was teaching the Arts there—Albert returned to Cologne. He spent the rest of his life away from Paris, teaching and writing prolifically, and he seems to have been somewhat detached from the Parisian Arts Masters and the theologians there in the 1260s and 1270s.[21] And, Aquinas apart, Albert's main followers would form a distinctively German school of philosophy. But, although not involved in them, Albert was arguably one of the most important factors in these very conflicts, because of the enormous influence his method had not on his pupil, Thomas Aquinas, who took a different approach, but on the Arts Masters. Albert was the great advocate of distinguishing between the spheres of natural reasoning, based on pagan authors and Arabic ones writing in the pagan, philosophical tradition and theology. His most famous dictum to this effect ('When I am discussing natural things, God's miracles are nothing to me')—adapted from, of all people, Bernard of Clairvaux—would be repeated by Arts Masters such as Siger of Brabant and John of Jandun.[22] Albert used this phrase to answer the hypothetical objection that God might choose at some moment to end the process of generation and corruption which, on an Aristotelian view, is eternal. Albert does not reject this possibility, but asserts that, when he is discussing nature, it is of no concern to him. Similar statements abound in his work: for him, the job of someone investigating the natural world is to investigate what can take place according to natural causes; the task of someone expounding Aristotle's ethics, similarly, is not to explore questions such as what happens to souls after death, a subject about which philosophers do not have sufficient knowledge.[23]

Albert had a voracious interest in natural knowledge. Along with Bacon, he was one of the pioneers of the newly available Aristotelian

[20] *Opus Maius* II.19; Roger Bacon 1900, 79.

[21] On these conflicts, see below. Albert has been thought to have written a work (*De unitate intellectus*) directed against the use made of Averroes by some of the Arts Masters, but Alain de Libera (1994, 13–21; 2003, 78–82) has shown that the work was written before this period of conflict and subsequently adjusted, superficially, in the light of it.

[22] See de Libera 2003, 75nn115–19. The phrase is found in Albert's *De generatione et corruptione* I.1.22.

[23] See de Libera 2003, 75–78, 265–66.

works in natural sciences and metaphysics, and he wrote a long series of paraphrase commentaries to them. And, from the information he found in Averroes's commentaries and other Arabic writings he knew in translation, he believed that he had a wide knowledge of the various ancient schools. But, unlike the Arts Masters who would adopt his approach of separating investigation into nature from revelation, Albert was himself a theologian, and he fitted his attitude towards philosophy into a wider framework. On the one hand, he considered that, just as each discipline in philosophy should be structured as an Aristotelian science, so theology too has its own scientific structure, in which revealed truths, rather than self-evident ones, provide the foundation. This view underwrote his separation of spheres: theology is no less a rational, argumentative pursuit than philosophy, but it has a completely different starting point. On the other hand, for Albert theology carried out according to the usual university practice of commenting on the *Sentences* of Peter the Lombard was just one half of the subject. The other half consisted of a theology based on pseudo-Dionysius, which aimed at a contemplation of God even in this life, in preparation for the vision of him in Heaven. What is more, Albert thought that, just as the theologian's work, based on revelation, has this mystical side which led to contact with God, so too philosophers, through their speculations, without revelation, can also come to a contemplation of God. In his commentary on Aristotle's *Ethics*, he explains the differences between the two types of contemplation:

> Theological contemplation is the same as philosophical contemplation in one way, and different from it in another. . . . For they are the same in that in theological contemplation too there is the inspection of some spiritual things without the obstruction of the passions from the subject, and without the obstruction of doubt from faith, which is ordered so as to find its peace in God, the highest happiness. But it differs with regard to disposition, end and object. It differs with regard to disposition because theological contemplation contemplates through a light infused by God, but the philosopher contemplates through an acquired disposition of wisdom. It differs with respect to end, because theological contemplation places the final end in the contemplation of God in heaven, but the philosopher places it in the vision by which God is seen in some way in the course of earthly life. It differs in object also . . . because the philosopher contemplates God as a conclusion to a demonstration, but the theologian contemplates him as existing above reason and intellect. And for this reason there is a different way of contemplating, because the philosopher has the certainty of a demonstration, on which he relies, but the theologian

relies on the first truth on account of itself and not on account of reason, although he has reason, and so the theologian wonders, but not the philosopher.[24]

Since, when Albert talks of the philosopher's contemplation, he has in mind what was possible for pagan thinkers, such as Aristotle himself, he is giving pagan wisdom an enormous scope. It can reach even to God himself, he insists, although he carefully refrains from saying anything here about the fate of the philosophers' souls in the next life.[25]

Behind Albert's idea of contemplating God there lie two main traditions. The first, as the source of the passage just quoted might suggest, is Aristotle's *Ethics*. In book 10 of the *Nicomachean Ethics*, when he comes to consider the happiest life for human beings, Aristotle insists that, since happiness consists in activity according to virtue, the happiest life will be activity in accord with the virtue of the highest part of human beings, their intellect, and that this activity is found to the highest degree in theoretical contemplation, when we think scientifically about unchanging things.[26] Whilst readers today tend to feel uncomfortable at the way Aristotle devalues the life of practical moral virtue, to which he devotes the previous books of the *Ethics*, in favour of the ivory-tower existence of a research professor, this vision of the happiest life chimed with many medieval readers. So, for example, the Byzantine commentator Eustratius (d. 1120), whose commentary on books 1 and 6 was widely read in Latin translation, sees the *Ethics* as teaching that we should be led by reason to moderate our passions, and that the person who strives for perfection should utterly mortify the passions, so that 'reason alone should operate in him, unhindered in any way by irrationality, and by this the person's soul, through the continuous and uninterrupted operation of reason, will become intellect and be made intellectual in form, that is an intellect by participation, and then also Godlike in form as it is united with God, according to the one thing within it which the great Dionysius called the flower of the intellect'.[27] Eudemus himself tended to Christianize the *Ethics*, but it was open to Albert and others, who held a clear boundary between philosophy and revelation, to retain this contemplation-centred approach whilst repaganizing Aristotle's text.

The other strand is related, although more distantly, to another of Aristotle's works, *On the Soul*. For ancient and medieval philosophers, a soul

[24]X, lectio 16.(6); Albert the Great 1987, 774–75.

[25]For Albert's views about the salvation of pagan philosophers, see below, chapter 9, note 71.

[26]*Nicomachean Ethics* 10, 1177a. On Albert's commentary on the *Nicomachean Ethics* as a turning point in his thought, see Sturlese 1993, 332–42.

[27]Prologue to bk. 1; Mercken 1973, 6:42–47.

is simply a life principle, that on account of which a thing has its life activities. Every living thing, therefore, has a soul: a plant's soul explains its capacity to grow and reproduce, a non-human animal's soul also explains its capacity for sense perception (including memory and manipulation of sense images), and the human soul also explains the human capacity for rational or intellectual thought, about universals, as when we grasp the truth that man is a rational animal. Aristotle distinguishes between the potential (or 'possible') intellect and the active intellect which, he says, produces all things and is distinct, unaffected and unmixed.[28] While commentators until Averroes seem to have accepted that the possible intellect is each human's capacity to engage in intellectual thought, they disagreed from the start about the active intellect. Was it a capacity of individual humans, or was there just one active intellect? The Arabic Aristotelian tradition, starting with al-Fârâbî in the tenth century, was strongly influenced by the later Platonists' theories of emanation and, tracing a series of Intelligences emanating ultimately from the One and each responsible for the movement of a celestial sphere, they identified the active intellect (or as they usually called it, the Agent Intellect) with the last of these Intelligences, which is responsible, not for a sphere, but for the sublunar realm, that is to say, the earth and its inhabitants. The Agent Intellect is a storehouse of universal forms—the sum of all worthwhile knowledge (since knowledge of particulars was thought unimportant), derived ultimately from the source of all being. Although, there is an important role for bottom-up investigation, starting with sense impressions, sorting and abstracting from them, intellectual knowledge itself can come only top-down from the Agent Intellect, with which the individual human's potential intellect conjoins itself. The philosopher's final aim—the highest human happiness as set out in the *Nicomachean Ethics*—is to assimilate his intellect so far as possible to the Agent Intellect. Albert adopted this way of thinking within his writings on natural philosophy. Nowhere is this more evident than in his *On the Intellect and the Intelligible*, where he describes the stages of perfecting the human intellect. Through study, a person reaches the state of having an 'acquired intellect' (*intellectus adeptus*), when all the intelligibles which it is in potentiality to understand are actually understood by it; and only at this stage, Albert believes, does a person really know himself.[29] Beyond this stage, there is the 'assimilative intellect' (*intellectus assimilitivus*) 'in which a person in so far as it is possible and right rises in proportion to the divine intellect, which is the light and cause of all things'.[30]

[28] Aristotle *On the Soul* III.5 (430a10–17).
[29] *De intellectu et intelligibili* II.8; Albert the Great 1890–99, IX, 515.
[30] *De intellectu et intelligibili* II.9; Albert the Great 1890–99, IX, 516; cf. de Libera 2005, 300–311.

Although, then, Albert distinguishes sharply between the spheres of natural science and revelation, he allows a genuine knowledge of God, and even a close, quasi-mystical closeness and assimilation to him, to philosophers working outside revelation.

THREE APPROACHES TO PAGAN KNOWLEDGE

Among the mainstream of university thinkers, there were three main approaches to the problem of pagan knowledge, one of which owed much to Albert, but was quite different from his. They could choose the path of unity, maintaining that, although Aristotle had been ignorant of Christian mysteries such as the Incarnation and the Trinity, understood properly he is almost entirely correct in everything he proposes, and so Arts Masters are right to follow him, and theologians to use him without reserve, although adding their knowledge of revealed truths to their picture of the world. This path was championed above all by Thomas Aquinas. The opposite approach, followed by many other thirteenth- and fourteenth-century theologians, was the path of selective rejection. There was no question of rejecting the whole Aristotle: even those keenest on pointing to his weaknesses remained imbued with his language, his method and many of his assumptions. But certain individual doctrines and even important principles or whole areas of his thought could be recognized as wrong. Third, there was a limited relativism, which allowed scholars to explore Aristotle in his own terms and, as his expositors, assert his conclusions, whilst also accepting the truth of Christian doctrine where it is contradicted by them. Pagan wisdom is granted a certain space, not as a historical fact, but a living reality. It is this approach which looks back to Albert the Great, but its main exponents were Arts Masters.

UNITY OR SELECTIVE REJECTION: AQUINAS AND THE THEOLOGIANS

The outstanding advocate for the path of unity was Aquinas. Aquinas sets out a theoretical basis for his position most clearly in his commentary on Boethius's *On the Trinity* (c. 1259). He says that 'although the natural light of the human mind is insufficient to make manifest those things which are made manifest by faith, it is however impossible that the things which are divinely handed down to us by faith should be contrary to those which are within us by nature. For it would be necessary that one or the other be false, and since both are for us from God, God would be responsible for making us believe something false—which is impossible'.[31] He then draws the conclusion that if any position in a philosophical text is contrary to the faith, it is 'not philosophy, but rather the abuse of philosophy from the failure of reason'. Just as there are doctrines of the faith which cannot be proved demonstratively, so these sorts of philosophical errors sometimes cannot be demonstratively shown to be false, but it can be shown 'that they are not necessary'—that is to say, that they cannot be demonstrated to be true.

Aquinas, then, recognizes a two-sided compatibility between Christian doctrine and philosophical reasoning. Reason cannot show that those revealed truths (such the Incarnation or, for Aquinas, the Trinity) it cannot discover are *false*; whilst nothing reason demonstrates to be *true* can contradict Christian teaching. His most personal exposition of the whole of theology, the *Summa contra Gentiles* (1259–65), bears out this position. The first three books are dedicated to talking about God, creation and providence in ways which do not require knowledge available only from revelation, which forms the basis for his discussions in the fourth book. It used to be thought that Aquinas adopted this organization because the work, as suggested by its title '*Textbook against the Pagans*', was designed for use by missionaries preaching to non-Christians, a hypothesis that now seems unlikely.[32] Rather, Aquinas is expressing the confidence, central to his work, that without revelation reason, rightly used, will show the falsity of heretical doctrines and arrive at many of the truths of Christian theology, which, on the basis of revelation, it can extend harmoniously.

The selective rejectionists did not, in fact, dispute this compatibility, but they differed from Aquinas over how they related reason to philosophy. When Aquinas thinks about reason and its capacities, he turns immediately to 'the philosophers' whose teaching 'is founded on the light of natural reason'. The philosophers he has in mind are the ancient pagan philosophers, above all Aristotle, who used their reasons without the benefit of revelation. He does, indeed, accept that their reasoning might go astray—in which case revealed doctrine will correct it—but his assumption is that ancient philosophy developed and reached a near perfect form in Aristotle, who almost always uses his reason well and reaches correct conclusions. By contrast, the selective rejectionists, more or less fully and explicitly, held that, in order to function properly, reason needed to be *based on* faith. John Pecham, talking about the creation of the world in time, puts the position very clearly and firmly: 'The creation of the world

[31] *Super De Trinitate*, pars 1, q. 2, a. 3, co.

[32] See the balanced summary in Torrell 1993, 153–56. The work's title—which would in any case be very strange were it intended for missionaries to the Muslims (since there was little of a missionary movement to the genuine *gentiles*, that is to say, pagans)—is very unlikely to be Aquinas's: see Gauthier 1993, 110–12.

in time can, it seems, be investigated by reason, although it is an article of faith. Nor is there any prejudice to faith in doing so, since it is not because of reason that assent is given to faith, but rather by the merit of faith that we come to its understanding. Therefore those who have spoken about the creation without faith have all erred: either they have said less than they ought, not attributing it to God, or more than they ought, attributing it to something other than God'.[33] The attitude of the selective rejectionists—that acceptance of Christianity by faith is a prerequisite to proper rational understanding—has its roots in Augustine. It was formulated by Anselm in his formula of faith seeking understanding (*fides quaerens intellectum*) and is a theme in many thirteenth-century accounts of knowledge. Where Aquinas envisages the pagan philosophers as having been on a quest for truth parallel to that of Christians like himself, though one which left important truths undiscovered and might need occasional correction in the light of faith, for Pecham and the majority of thirteenth-century theologians, only the Christians were on the path to the truth; the pagan philosophers, though of course not wrong in everything, had been bound to misuse their reason.

Aquinas demonstrated his respect for Aristotle both by devoting himself, not as a beginner but in his later years, to a precise, sentence-by-sentence exposition of his major texts, and by various Aristotelian positions he followed (for example, on the soul and body—see below; on the will and intellect) where most of his contemporaries and successors chose to be less faithful. The quotation from Pecham which so vividly illustrates the view opposed to Aquinas's comes from a discussion about the eternity of the world. This is the topic which most clearly shows in practice how Aquinas's path of unity differed from the selective rejectionism practised by most of his colleagues in the Faculty of Theology—and it does so precisely because it was one of the very few topics where even Aquinas could not simply accept the Aristotelian view. Aristotle's world (that is to say, his whole universe of the celestial spheres with, at their centre, the earth) is an eternal one, and in the *Physics* (VIII.1) he argues explicitly that there cannot be a first motion, and (VIII.8) that the celestial spheres are in eternal, continuous circular motion.[34] Christians (and Muslims and Jews), however, believe that the world is not eternal, but has a beginning. They do not mean by this that it began at a certain point within time: as the Lateran Council of 1215 put it, God created spiritual and bodily creatures from nothing 'from the beginning of time' (*ab initio*

---

[33] John Pecham, 'Utrum mundus potuit ab eterno creari' (c. 1270), responsio, ed. in Dales and Argerami 1991, 81.

[34] See also *On the Heavens* I.10–11.

temporis).[35] Time begins only with the world. It might seem, then, that there is no real difference from Aristotle, since Christians accept that the world is eternal in the sense that there is no moment of time at which the world does not exist. Although such reasoning was indeed used by some theologians to dissolve the problem, it fails to do so, as became evident when Aristotle was better known.[36] There is a real incompatibility, which Aquinas and his contemporaries had to face, between the Christian view and Aristotle's position, since Aristotle holds not just that the world has no beginning within time, but that it has no beginning whatsoever: before every change, there was another change, and so on, without end.

From his earliest discussion of the problem, in his commentary on the *Sentences* (1253–56; II, d. 1, q. 1, a. 5) to his last in the little treatise devoted to it (*On the Eternity of the World*, 1271), Aquinas maintains that reason can show neither that the world has a beginning nor that it lacks one. That the world is not eternal is a revealed truth, just like God's triunity, which Christians should accept on faith. When he talks of what can be shown by reason, Aquinas has in mind Aristotelian demonstration, where a conclusion is reached by logical reasoning from self-evident premises. A piece of reasoning which falls short of demonstration can always be 'solved'—that is to say, shown not to be a valid demonstration. By the time Aquinas was writing, a number of arguments were circulating both for the eternity of the world and against it (these included some sophisticated pieces of reasoning, going back to John Philoponus [d. 570s], which turn Aristotle against himself by claiming that various paradoxes of the infinite result if the world is supposed to be eternal world).[37] In his three set-piece discussions of the problem, in his *Sentences* and the two *Summa*s, Aquinas therefore chooses to present arguments both for and against the world's eternity, and solutions to both the arguments for *and those against it*.[38] Although the arguments against it lead he believes, to a true conclusion, they are not demonstrative, and so, like the ones against it, they can be 'solved'. For most of his career, Aquinas held in addition that Aristotle himself also believed that there were no demonstrative ar-

[35] *Denzinger* 1976, no. 800 (428). Aquinas is particularly clear on this point: cf. *Summa Theologiae* I, q. 46, a. 3, ad1 and his commentary on *Physics* VIII, lectio 2, n. 20.

[36] Dales 1990 traces this way of dissolving the problem back to William of Conches (29–30), who is dealing with Plato's *Timaeus* and Boethius's *Consolation* rather than Aristotelian texts, and it is taken up by Philip the Chancellor (58, 63–64), Alexander of Hales (68–70) and Roger Bacon (191).

[37] The main sources were the Latin translations of al-Ghazâlî's *Intentions of the Philosophers* (in fact, al-Ghazâlî himself strongly rejected the eternity of the world, but this text is a near translation of a short encyclopaedia in Persian by Avicenna, designed to present the philosophers' opinions) and Maimonides's *Guide of the Perplexed*.

[38] Commentary on *Sentences* II, d. II, q. 1. a. 5; *Summa contra Gentiles* II, 32–38; *Summa Theologiae* I, q. 46, a. 1 and 2.

guments to show the eternity of the world. Looking back to Maimonides (an important influence on his treatments, especially the earlier ones, of this question), he pointed to a passage in the *Topics* (I.11; 104b15–16) where Aristotle gives the eternity of the world as a problem so vast that 'we have no argument'. He explained that the arguments Aristotle gives in *Physics* VIII for the eternity of the world are all ad hominem, directed against pre-Socratics such as Anaxagoras and Empedocles, and following their assumption that the cause of the world is like any other particular cause, which causes through changing; they are not intended to be demonstrations.[39] When, in his last decade, he came to write his close commentary on the *Physics* (1268–69), he realized that Aristotle did in fact believe that he had demonstrated the eternity of the world and even uses it, as a proven truth, in demonstrating the existence of God.[40] But, in his last word on the subject, the brief *On the Eternity of the World*, Aquinas concentrates on showing that, although the world had a beginning, it is possible that God could have created it without one.

By contrast, the selective rejectionists make the question of the world's eternity an opportunity to show the pagan philosophers' inadequacy. Grosseteste uses all the sources at his disposal, both Latin and Greek, to show that Aristotle did not, as some were arguing, recognize a beginning for the world. He and the other ancient philosophers failed to do so, continues Grosseteste, because their mental gaze had not been purged of its love of worldly things and so could not grasp the idea of eternity as unextended. Not, therefore, being able to understand that God's eternity is something of a different kind altogether from temporality, they concluded that the world's duration must be coextensive with it.[41] In the 1260s, the Franciscan William of Baglione has no hesitation in asserting the soundness of the very Philoponian arguments that the world has a beginning, which Aquinas had from the beginning refused to accept as demonstrations.[42]

These arguments had already been used by various theologians, notably Bonaventure in his *Sentences* commentary.[43] Bonaventure may seem, however, to be closer to Aquinas. He says that, whilst to argue that the world was created ex nihilo but eternally would be so irrational that he cannot believe 'any philosopher, however small his understanding, would have posited it', to argue that the world is eternal, presupposing that matter is eternal, is rational. But, in the previous article, Bonaventure has presented creation ex nihilo as a truth not reached by any of the philosophers, even—though he is tentative about this claim—by Aristotle,

[39] See especially *De potentia* (written 1265–66) q. 3, a. 17, cor.
[40] Commentary on *Physics* VIII, lectio 2, n. 16.
[41] *Hexaëmeron* VIII.4–5; Robert Grosseteste 1982, 60–61.
[42] See the *Questions* edited in Brady 1972.
[43] Book II, d. 1, pt. 1, art. 1, q. 1.

but rather one which is declared by Scripture. So does he not, just like Aquinas, hold that belief that the world has a beginning rests on faith, not demonstrative reason?[44] But Bonaventure does not present creation ex nihilo as a truth that is in principle knowable only through revelation, but rather one which none of the pagan philosophers in fact managed to reach, where—as he puts it—'their skill failed'; he even says explicitly here that this Scriptural revelation is supported by reason. He therefore seems to take the Philoponian arguments as demonstrative and, by sharp contrast with Aquinas, to see the question as one where the pagan philosophers draw the wrong conclusion, because of the deficiencies, not of reason itself, but of *their* power of reason.

In any case, Bonaventure's criticisms of the pagan philosophers soon became much more strident. In his *Collationes* on the Ten Commandments (1267), he sees the philosophers' 'wicked daring' as a type of idolatry, which leads them to assert the eternity of the world and deny the immortality of the soul.[45]

LIMITED RELATIVISM

Although the most sophisticated defence of limited relativism was made in connection with the eternity of the world (see below), the disputed doctrine with which the position became especially linked for medieval readers—and from which many of its exponents would be named—concerns the soul. As interpreted by the ancient commentators and most of the Arabic tradition, Aristotle considered that each human has a potential (or 'possible') intellect. But a different interpretation had been proposed by Averroes (d. 1198), who was, along with Avicenna, the best known Arabic philosopher in the Latin world, where he was often referred to simply as 'the Commentator', because translations of his commentaries were indispensable instruments for understanding Aristotle's texts. Throughout his career, and over the course of three commentaries, Averroes grappled with the often elusive text of *On the Soul*: in his Long commentary, the only one translated into Latin, he put forward his most radical reading. Not only did he hold, like his Arabic predecessors, that there is only one Agent Intellect, but he also insisted that the potential intellect, too, is one for all humans—that is to say that individual humans do not each have their own intellects. The individual human soul, like that of other animals, is responsible for growth, movement and sensation, including the refining and ordering of mental images, but not for

[44]As Michon 2004, 51–54 argues.
[45]II.25; Bonaventure 1882–1902, V,514.

grasping and reasoning with universals. Reasoning is carried out by the single active-and-potential intellect, but individual humans are attached to the process, because (in line with Aristotle's insistence that all intellectual thinking requires imaginary forms) the one intellect uses the imaginary forms which they have prepared in their sensible souls.[46]

This view of Averroes, according to which there is only one potential intellect, was not discussed by the Arts Masters of the earlier thirteenth century. It first appears around 1250, mentioned in writings by Bonaventure and Aquinas.[47] These theologians present the position only to dismiss it, not only as contrary to Christian faith—as it clearly is, since it denies individual immortality and so reward and punishment after death—but as contrary to reason. But, sometime between 1265 and 1270, Siger of Brabant, an Arts Master, put forward, as his reading of *On the Soul*, Averroes's position. Whilst other Arts Masters may also have held these views at the time, a good case has been made for seeing Aquinas's *On the Unity of the Intellect, against the Averroists*, written in 1270, as directed very precisely against Siger.[48] It is not surprising that Siger's views should have produced so powerful a response from Aquinas in particular, since they presented an obvious challenge to the way of unity: on a central philosophical question, where Aquinas considered that Aristotle, the best of the philosophers, and Christian doctrine had reached similar conclusions, Siger insisted that there was a contradiction. *On the Unity* tries to show both that Averroes's teaching is philosophically unacceptable, since it entails that no individual human thinks, and even more emphatically that it is a misinterpretation of Aristotle, contradicted point for point by the text, and at odds with the whole interpretative tradition. (There is a telling contrast with Bonaventure's remarks on the subject in 1273, in his *Collations on the Hexaemeron*, where he blurs the distinction between Aristotle's views and Averroes's reading of them.)[49]

That Averroes's view goes against Christian teaching is beyond any doubt, but it is worth pointing out why, despite its apparent bizarreness,

[46] Averroes's *Long Commentary* on *On the Soul* survives only in its Latin translation by Michael Scotus (Averroes 1953; see chap. 5 for the theory of the one intellect; cf. Averroes 2011). Davidson 1992 provides a learned and thorough guide to the whole area.

[47] See Bonaventure, Commentary on *Sentences* (1250) II, d. 18, a. 2, q. 1; Bonaventure 1882–1902, II, 444–48; Aquinas, Commentary on *Sentences* (1252–56) II, d. 17, q. 2, a. 1. Aquinas returns to the subject in, among other works, the *Summa contra gentiles* II, 73, 75; *Summa Theologiae* I, q. 76, a. 2. Albert discusses it in his *De unitate intellectus* (1263, but based on work done in the previous decade).

[48] Thomas Aquinas 1997, 51–58 (Alain de Libera).

[49] In the *Sentences* commentary (II, d. 18, a. 2, q. 1 cor), the unity of the intellect is described as a position Averroes imposed on Aristotle; in the *Collations on the Hexaemeron* (VI.4), he simply remarks without comment that this error is attributed to Aristotle by Averroes.

144 • CHAPTER 8

and the common-sense force of Aquinas's main objection, it had such attraction, in the thirteenth century and later, for dedicated Aristotelians. As Siger observes at the beginning of his argument that there is one intellect for all humans, 'no immaterial form, which is one in species, is numerically multiplied. But the intellect *is* an immaterial form, which is one in species'.[50] For Aristotle, numerical individuation is due to matter, but the intellect, everybody agreed, is immaterial, and so, as Siger goes on to say, 'it is not in the nature of the intellect to be numerically multiplied'.[51] Bonaventure and Aquinas do indeed each have ways to overcome this difficulty, but they are not without cost and problems. With the help of Averroes, Siger has identified a real weakness in the standard medieval adaptations of Aristotle's psychology. As for the charge that the position goes against the everyday belief that each human being thinks, Averroes has not ignored something so obvious: in his account individual humans are involved in each act of thinking, and it is then a point for argument as to whether the involvement is adequate to account for the everyday belief, or whether, indeed, given that thinking is not any sort of cogitation but just reasoning about universals, the everyday belief is not true without qualification.

Siger's limited relativism is the direct result of his decision that Aristotle had taught that there is only one possible intellect, and his underlying assumption that Aristotle's views are those at which reason arrives. In his earliest commentary on *On the Soul*, he simply proposes Averroes's interpretation as the correct one, without further qualifications. He does not make clear what is his attitude, as a Christian, to the truth of what, as an Arts Master, he is expounding. But, in the teaching (very probably his) attacked by Aquinas in *On the Unity*, after asserting that God *cannot* make there be many intellects, because that would imply a contradiction, he added, 'By reason I conclude of necessity that the intellect is one in number, but by faith I firmly hold the opposite'.[52] As Aquinas immediately goes on to point out, from these statements it follows that the faith holds what is not merely false, but impossible because even God cannot make it so. Whatever Siger's own words may have been, this cannot be what he wanted to say. The way he frames the discussion of the unity or multiplicity of the potential intellect in his questions *On the Intellective Soul*, written a few years later (1273–74), may give a better idea of his meaning, except that by then Étienne Tempier, the Bishop of Paris, had condemned, on pain of excommunication, the view 'that the intellect for all humans is one and the same in number', and so not surprisingly his

---

[50] *In Tertium de anima*, q. 9 (Siger of Brabant 1972, 25:7–26:9).
[51] *In Tertium de anima*, q. 9 (Siger of Brabant 1972, 26:23–24).
[52] Chap. 5.

attitude is submissive, in a way it was unlikely to have been earlier.[53] Siger begins by saying that he will be considering the problem 'in so far as it pertains to the philosopher and as it can be understood by human reason and experience, seeking in this the opinion of the philosophers rather than the truth, since we are proceeding in a philosophical way'. He then says that 'according to the truth, which cannot lie' there are as many intellective souls as human bodies, 'but some philosophers think the contrary, and through the path of philosophy the contrary seems to be the case'.[54] Siger wants to insist that, as an Arts Master, he can investigate a question such as this 'in a philosophical way' even if his investigation ends in a conclusion which contradicts Christian doctrine, which he accepts as true. The justification he gives, that he is not seeking the truth, but just trying to set out the philosophers' opinions, without—as he puts it at the beginning—'asserting anything for myself', probably concedes more than Siger would have done before the condemnation. He seems to be trying to set out a position which would allow him and his fellow Arts Masters to be consistent Aristotelians, without either uttering heresies or entirely disowning their own pronouncements. Sometime in the 1270s his colleague in the Arts Faculty, Boethius of Dacia, succeeded far better in describing and vindicating exactly the limited relativism which Siger had sought to formulate.

Boethius's subject, as already mentioned, is the eternity of the world. Much of Boethius's treatise follows Aquinas's line. It cannot be *demonstrated* either that the world is eternal or that it is not eternal; but Christians should accept from faith that it has a beginning and so is not eternal. Boethius accordingly gives the various arguments to show that the world is eternal and replies to each, showing that it is not conclusive; and he gives the common arguments supposed to demonstrate that the world has a beginning, and, although he concedes them, because their conclusion is correct, he adds that 'they can be solved, since they are sophistical';[55] and he also gives a set of arguments—most of them close to Aquinas's *On the Eternity of the World*—to show that the world could have been eternal. He leaves these arguments unanswered and presumably considers them sound. But, in the body of the question, Boethius focuses not

---

[53] Denifle and Châtelain 1889, I, 487 (no. 432).

[54] *De anima intellectiva* 7 (Siger of Brabant 1972, 101:5–12). After the discussion, he declares himself uncertain what position should be held on the matter 'by the way of reason' and what Aristotle thought it should be: 'in such doubt', he concludes (108:86–87), 'we should adhere to the faith, which surpasses all reason'. Siger seems, by this stage, to have been on his way to adopting a less problematic interpretation. It remains controversial whether this intellectual journey ended, as many scholars have thought, with his acceptance of views near to Aquinas's.

[55] Boethius of Dacia 1976, 364:803–4.

on the problem itself, but on the position and the role of philosophers, by whom he means, not the thinkers of antiquity but the Arts Masters like himself, teaching the Aristotelian curriculum. He distinguishes three sorts—the natural scientist (*physicus*), the mathematician (whose subject embraces astronomy) and the metaphysician. He shows easily that none of them can demonstrate, starting from the principles of their subject, that the world is not eternal. In the case of the natural scientist, however, he goes further—and it is this step which makes his treatise into a vindication of limited relativism. The other two sorts of philosopher can, as philosophers, say that 'The world is eternal' is a statement which they will neither affirm nor deny, since neither its truth nor its falsity can be demonstrated; they are not, therefore, placed in a position of conflict with their belief, as Christians, that the world has a beginning. By contrast, Boethius insists that the natural scientist must *deny* that the world has a beginning, because the position that the world has a beginning contradicts the principles on which natural science is based and so destroys it.[56]

This view faces an immediate difficulty. Since Boethius admits that it is not just the truth of the Christian faith, but the truth *without qualification* that the world has a beginning, then how can natural science, which is based on principles contradicted by this truth, and so false, provide knowledge? Boethius answers that natural scientists are talking about the operations of natural causes and that what they say is true so far as these are concerned. The natural scientist is not denying that things are possible by supernatural causes which are impossible by natural ones.[57] Boethius's justification of the value of natural science is, then, not unlike that which might be made for Newtonian physics as against Relativity: Relativity provides a correct account of things, but within its more limited sphere, Newtonian physics gives true results.[58] But what about the truth-value of the natural scientist's statements, in particular those where he denies a revealed truth of Christianity? If the natural scientist insists, as he must, that it is false that a human is resurrected from the dead, is he not thereby saying something which is false and contradicting an article of the faith? No, says Boethius, because whatever the natural scientist denies or concedes, he does according to natural principles, and there is no contradiction between asserting a proposition, and denying the same proposition 'according to something'.[59] One way of construing this posi-

[56] Boethius of Dacia 1976, 351:438–352:1. See above for the Aristotelian idea of sciences built on fundamental principles.
[57] Cf. Boethius of Dacia 1976, 352:475–353:480.
[58] See Pinborg 1974, 175–81. There have been many interpretative studies of Boethius's treatise, but this and the introduction by Luca Bianchi to Boethius of Dacia 2003 are the most valuable.
[59] Boethius of Dacia 1976, 352:457–75.

tion is to say that, for Boethius, every utterance made by someone working in science S carries with it the automatic rider: 'according to the principles of S'. On this reading, however, scientists never succeed in talking directly about the world, since every proposition they express ends up, because of the rider, being about their science.[60] A better way, then, is to take Boethius as laying down the rules, not for what propositions scientists express, but for how their utterances are to be interpreted when they are considered outside the sphere of their science. When a natural scientist says 'The world is eternal', his words express the proposition that the world is eternal, which is what he means to convey. If we consider his statement outside the context of his science—suppose, for instance, we ask ourselves how a Christian can say such a thing—we should interpret it charitably as applying only to natural causes and so not at variance with Christian faith. Natural scientists engaged in their work are a little like actors in a play. When the hero says 'It is snowing', we do not rebuke him for lying, although outside it is a fine dry night; we know that he is speaking according to how things are in the play, but we do not add on to everything he utters the qualification 'according to how things are in the play', as if it were part of the meaning of his sentences.

The importance of Boethius's position for the Problem of Paganism rests on the fact that the philosophers he is discussing are, as mentioned, not ancient pagans, such as Aristotle, but contemporary Christian followers of Aristotle. Most scholars of the time accepted that Aristotle reasoned correctly so far as natural causes are concerned. It is a sentiment which many of the selective rejectionists, Bonaventure included, expressed, and it underlines the importance of the first, qualifying word in their descriptive label.[61] Boethius, by contrast—perhaps inspired to some extent by Albert the Great, but working from a very different perspective, since unlike Albert he was himself an arts master—provided a very moderate-seeming justification for a far more disturbing position. Even where it contradicts the faith, the wisdom of pagan philosophers should be followed and cultivated by those Christians of Boethius's time who are by profession philosophers.

Boethius did not merely justify the methods of the Arts Faculty philosophers. He wrote a short treatise *On the Highest Good*, in praise of the life of the philosopher, strongly influenced by the ideal of the contemplative life put forward by Aristotle at the end of the *Nicomachean Ethics*. The philosopher's consideration of nature leads him step by step to

[60] This is the interpretation which I (Marenbon 1990, 268) and others (Putallaz and Imbach 1997, 89–90) have proposed. It is pertinently criticized by Bianchi in his introduction to Boethius of Dacia 2003, 50–55.

[61] Dales (1984) draws attention to this current of thought, but does not see that Boethius's position is different.

knowledge of the first cause. Since 'there is delight in speculation, and the more delight, the more noble are the intelligible things', the philosopher therefore lives an 'extremely pleasurable life'.[62] Moreover, the philosopher who is engaged in contemplation will also be good morally, because he will be living an austere life in which he scorns the pleasures of the senses.[63] The philosopher's, Boethius contends, is the life that humans were born to live, and 'whoever does not have it, does not have the right life'.[64] Other Arts Masters wrote similar works. For example, near the beginning of his *Philosophia* (c. 1265), Aubry of Rheims writes, referring to Averroes, that 'the being of humans in its ultimate perfection and completeness is being perfect through the speculative sciences' and adds that the word 'man' is equivocal between a man so perfected and others, just as it is between a real man and a painted man.[65] It was almost certainly not just Aristotle's *Ethics*, but Albert the Great's reading of them which led the Arts Masters to this way of thinking, but there are important differences. The only one of these texts in which Albert's idea of assimilation to and union with God appears is the supposed work by Siger of Brabant, *On Happiness*, reconstructed from what might be citations from it in the sixteenth-century writer Agostino Nifo's *De intellectu*. But it is doubtful whether Siger ever wrote such a work.[66] Moreover, in *On the Highest Good*, Boethius seems—very possibly deliberately—to mark a difference with Albert. Albert distinguishes the theologian's contemplation from the philosopher's by saying that the philosopher's is without wonder. By contrast, Boethius—though dispensing with the apparatus of assimilation—stresses that the philosopher's speculation does involve wonder at, and love for, God: 'Considering all these things, the philosopher is led into wonder (*admiratio*) at this first principle and into love for it, because we love that from which goods come to us, and we love most that from which the greatest goods come to us'.[67]

Siger of Brabant gives some details about this philosophical life in one of his *Moral Questions*. Asked whether the virginal or the married state best suits a philosopher, he replies that 'the philosopher has as a final goal the cognition of the truth, and that state which hinders less the

---

[62] Boethius of Dacia 1976, 375:184–376:185.

[63] Boethius of Dacia 1976, 374:149–375:164.

[64] Boethius of Dacia 1976, 377:239–40.

[65] Aubry's treatise is edited in Gauthier 1984, 29–48. For this passage, see 29:12–17, and for other similar works from the time, see Gauthier 1984, 6.

[66] The attribution was first made in Nardi 1945. On the reasons for doubt about Siger's authorship, see Agostino Nifo 2011, 18–24. On the absence of assimilation and conjunction in Boethius's *On the Good* and other Arts Masters' texts, see Fioravanti 2005, 10–12 and Bianchi 2005.

[67] Boethius of Dacia 1976, 377:226–29.

cognition of the truth suits most and is appropriate for philosophers', and this, he goes on to argue, is the state of virginity, because 'the married state carries many worldly cares, about one's wife and children'.[68] Siger's answer shows both how, in line with his functions as an Arts Master, he defends virginity without any appeal to its virtuousness within the Christian framework, and how the ideal of *Nicomachean Ethics* X can start to be expanded into a whole way of life. This is indeed one of the texts on which Luca Bianchi drew when he put forward the idea that intellectual happiness—the state which Arts Master philosophers alone could reach—became a sort of 'profession' and way of life in the Paris University of the 1260s and 1270s.[69] Did the Paris Arts Masters of the 1260s and 1270s, as Bianchi, Alain de Libera and others have argued, defend not just the practice of reasoning like pagan philosophers, but a broader ethical conception of a philosophical life, aiming at goals set by reason and not the Christian faith? Some of the best, though most debated, evidence for answering this question is found in the very document which was intended to put an end to the movement led by Siger and Boethius.

THE 1277 PROHIBITIONS

On 7 March 1277, Stephen Tempier, Bishop of Paris, published a document, hastily drawn up by a commission of theologians, listing 219 propositions which he forbade, on pain of excommunication, from being held or defended.[70] Among them are over forty, which are clearly (though not always accurately) based on the teaching of Siger of Brabant and Boethius of Dacia.[71] Overall, the prohibited propositions fall into four groups: (1) Aristotelian positions (such as the eternity of the world, God

---

[68] *Quaestiones morales* q. 4; Siger of Brabant 1974, 102–3.

[69] See Bianchi 1987. An important influence on Bianchi was the work of Maria Corti—especially Corti 1982—and behind his ideas, and the further developments of them made by Alain de Libera (see below) were two very influential French thinkers: Pierre Hadot and his idea of philosophy as a way of life in antiquity, and Jacques Le Goff and his book (Le Goff 1957) on medieval 'intellectuals'; cf. Fioravanti 2005, 2–6.

[70] Piché 1999 provides a critical edition of the text, numbered according to the original order in the decree. As well as giving these numbers, I give (in square brackets, preceded by 'H') the numbers assigned in Hissette 1977, who usefully classifies the propositions by subject and comments on each. See Bianchi 1998, 93–96 on how Tempier himself probably intended to prohibit the discussion of certain theses, rather than to condemn them.

[71] Hissette 1977, 314 lists thirty articles which relate directly (and another fourteen possibly) to Siger, and thirteen (and another three possibly) to Boethius. There is often a close textual correspondence with Boethius's *On the Eternity of the World*: see 17 [H215], 18 [H216], 90 [H191], 145 [H6], 154 [H2] (cf. Hissette 1977, 308, 309, 285, 24–25, 19, respectively).

acting of necessity, God's not knowing singulars, the determination in humans of the will by the intellect) judged incompatible with Christianity; (2) characteristic teachings of Arabic Aristotelians (especially the system of emanated cosmic intelligences and Averroes's theory that there is only one potential intellect) judged incompatible with Christianity; (3) a few more theological doctrines (on God's knowability and angels, for instance); and (4) views about morality and religion which are obviously unacceptable—indeed, often shocking—to Christians. These include the denial of central Christian dogmas, such as the Trinity and creation ex nihilo (and the assertion that there are fables in Christianity as in other religious laws), and also the repudiation of Christian morality and practices, including the sinfulness of sexual activity and the need for prayer, confession and humility, and the view that happiness is in this life and there is nothing to fear after death.[72] This fourth group presents special problems (see below). The articles in the other three groups betray the mentality of the selective rejectionists, trying to draw attention to the aspects of ancient Arabic teachings which clash with Christian teaching, as well as to views developed by Christians, theologians especially, which they judge to have been too greatly influenced by them. It is as if Bonaventure's most hostile pronouncements on non-Christian learning have been given legal force. The Arts Masters such as Siger and Boethius are not named, but they are clearly under attack. Moreover, in his preface to the Condemnations, Tempier echoes the charge which Aquinas had made against (the also unnamed) Siger: 'For they say these things are true according to philosophy, but not according to the catholic faith, as if there were two contrary truths, and as if, against the truth of sacred scripture there were the truth in the sayings of pagans who are damned'.[73] Yet,

---

[72] Some of the most important articles in this group are (the content of each is summarised, not translated verbatim): (On Christian doctrine) Denial of Trinity 1 [H185]; it does not matter if one says heresies 16 [H201]; denial of Resurrection 17 [H215]; no torture of separated soul by fire 19 [H219]; there can be no accident without a subject 139 [H198], and 141 [H197]—an attack on the doctrine of transubstantiation; (On Christian morality) humility not a virtue 171 [H211]; we have happiness in this life, not in another 176 [H172]; the only virtues are acquired or innate 177 [H200]—this rules out the infused, theological virtues; death is the end of terrible things 178 [H213]; (General attacks on theology and reliability of Christian doctrine) a naturalistic explanation of visions 33 [H177]; theological utterances are based on fables 152 [H183]; people learn nothing more by learning theology 153 [H 182]; there are fables in the Christian law, as in others 174 (181); the Christian law obstructs people from learning 175 [H180]; (Attacks on Christian practice) confess only for the sake of appearances 179 [H203]; don't pray 180 [H202]; (Sexual morality) continence not essentially a virtue 168 [H208]; completely abstaining from sex corrupts virtue and the species 169 [H210]; the pleasure of sexual acts does not impair acts of the intellect 172 [H207]; fornication between two unmarried people is not a sin 183 [H205].

[73] *Prologue letter* 5; Piché 1999, 74.

despite borrowing his strategy against Siger, most historians now agree that Tempier also had Aquinas himself in his sights.[74]

About the meaning and importance of these prohibitions there is more controversy than consensus among specialists; the 219 articles give an intellectual form to deep political differences no less today than in the thirteenth century.[75] For their bearing on the Problem of Paganism, there are two main questions about the prohibitions which need to be answered. First—to take up the question raised at the end of the last section—what do they tell about the thinking, especially the ethical views, of the Arts Masters they are attacking? Second, what was their effect on the three ways of treating pagan philosophy—unity, selective rejection, limited relativism—in the following decades and century?

The answer to the first question depends on the extent to which it is supposed that the propositions condemned by Tempier, especially those in fourth category above, reflect positions or ideas really held by some Arts Masters. No one would suppose that they actually and explicitly held them, but they could be a caricatured version of views towards which they were tending. Did Tempier and his commission capture something important about the intellectual life of the Arts Faculty in the very act of trying to destroy it? Historians used to be dismissive of the commission's work, representing it as an attempt to ban all sorts of positions which were not in danger of being held by anyone. The Condemnations are not therefore, they believed, a guide of any sort to what has happening.[76] Recently, some scholars have found the 219 articles far more informative. According to Alain de Libera, Tempier is 'the inventor of the thirteenth-century philosophical project' in the sense that he saw clearly the vision of philosophy and its place which remained inchoate for its advocates:[77] 'The censor can speak of the future, speak of a way which no one would

[74] A set of theses advanced by Giles of Rome (in many respects a follower of Aquinas) was condemned later in March 1277, and it seems that Tempier had been preparing a (posthumous) condemnation of some of Aquinas's views, but was stopped. The exact interpretation of the evidence is much debated: see Bianchi 1999, 210–12; 2003, 210n13. On 18 March 1277, at Oxford, the Archbishop of Canterbury, Robert Kilwardby, condemned thirty propositions which included three definitely linked to Aquinas's view that humans have only one substantial form.

[75] In addition to the works by Hissette and de Libera cited in the following notes, and the studies with which Piché accompanies his edition of the Condemnations (Piché 1999), Luca Bianchi has studied every aspect of the events of 1277 in depth (Bianchi 1987, 1998, 1999, 2003, 2009). Aertsen and Speer 1998, 71–121, 371–434 contains detailed discussions of the Condemnations, and Aertsen, Emery and Speer 2001 is a very large collection of papers entirely devoted to the Condemnations, their context and their effects. Important new light is thrown on the purpose of the condemnations and how they were compiled in Calma 2011.

[76] See, for example, Hissette 1990, as well as his edition of the articles (Hissette 1977).

[77] De Libera developed this interpretation of the 1277 condemnations in de Libera 1991, esp. 143–245 and he has extended and refined it in de Libera 2003, 174–230.

dare to name, nor perhaps even to conceive'.[78] That is not to say that the articles as they stand spell out this project straightforwardly. They need interpretation. For example, although at first sight the condemned positions about sexual morality seem to advocate permissiveness by contrast with Christian renunciation, according to de Libera the underlying pattern of thought, confirmed by the Arts Masters' own pronouncements (such as that by Siger discussed above), is almost the opposite: they take over from Christian teaching an idea of asceticism, but it is asceticism in the service of philosophy, of the path to intellectual happiness, accepted voluntarily, because sexual love is not a sin 'but a possible way of life that the philosopher goes beyond by living according to the intellect'.[79]

Altogether, de Libera sees the Condemnations as providing proof that the Arts Masters' never more than inchoate project aspired to a philosophical way of life, strongly influenced by Albert the Great (and behind him the Arabic Aristotelian tradition) and his ideas of conjunction with the Agent Intellect and assimilation with God. Whilst there are doubts about whether some of these more idiosyncratic features of Albert's thinking were widely shared, there is good evidence that what de Libera now prefers to call 'intellectualist aristocratism'—the view that philosophers could reach a true human happiness unattained by other people—was the fashion among the avant-garde of Arts Masters in the 1260s and 1270s; and it makes good sense to see the Condemnations as confirming this judgement, rather than dismissing them as being aimed at straw men.[80] From the perspective offered by the Problem of Paganism, however, it might seem that the idea of a philosophical *way of life* needs some qualification. The Aristotelian programme of the Arts Faculty could not but be an intrusion of pagan philosophizing into the Christian world. Moderate Arts Masters sought to make it an untroublesome and useful intrusion, whereas men like Siger and Boethius seem to have delighted in the friction it generated. But did even they think of their roles as philosophers fully and seriously as a way of life, in the manner that an ancient Greek or Roman might have adopted Epicureanism or Stoicism as his guide to living? It is hard to think so, because Christianity gives a way of life, in this sense, to those who follow it, and there is no reason to think that Siger, Boethius and their colleagues were not all believing and observant, if not perhaps very pious, Christians. Christianity can allow almost any degree of enthusiasm for philosophy as practised and handed on by

[78] De Libera 1991, 236.

[79] De Libera 1991, 243.

[80] On reasons to be sceptical, though, about the influence of ideas about conjunction, see the works cited in note 66 above and de Libera 2003, 321–28 (his own self-criticism). For a general critique of de Libera's and Bianchi's approach, see the editors' preface to Aertsen, Emery and Speer 2001, 9–10.

pagans, but it cannot, it would seem, accommodate philosophy as a complete way of life. It may be better to think along the lines which Boethius of Dacia's own analysis of the relation between philosophy and the faith suggest. The Arts Masters did not want to make philosophy their whole way of life, but they wanted to mark out a space, that of their profession as interpreters of the Aristotelian curriculum, within which they could pursue purely philosophical aims and the happiness which, they claimed, philosophers alone could reach.

What was the effect of the Condemnations on the three main ways of treating pagan philosophy outlined in this chapter? Although officially limited to Paris and directed at Arts Masters, the 219 articles certainly had a long-lasting effect, throughout Europe, on theologians probably more than Arts Masters, by proscribing certain positions which might otherwise have been held.[81] Yet, in one very important way, the Condemnations seem to have failed completely in their prime objective. Bishop Tempier specifically targeted the approach described here as 'limited relativism' by echoing Aquinas in condemning those who hold some things 'to be true according to philosophy, but not according to the catholic faith' as well as in many of the particular doctrines condemned.[82] Yet, although the Condemnation put an end to the work of Siger's and Boethius's generation of radical Arts Masters, limited relativism survived, and indeed flourished, as a method of approach for Arts Masters. One version of it leant heavily on Averroes, as the best expositor of Aristotle and adopted, as the best rational explanation, his characteristic theory of the unity of the possible intellect—and its exponents are often called (even at the time, especially by their opponents, 'Averroists').[83] One of the most famous and influential of these limited relativists was John of Jandun (1285/9–1328), who was teaching in the Paris Arts Faculty from 1310 to 1326 and wrote a widely read series of commentaries on Aristotle. John is described as an 'Averroist' even by those who think that

[81] See Bianchi 1999, 203–30.

[82] In some cases, the condemned articles were statements of the form 'P is true, but not-P should be held by faith', or implied this sort of thinking: e.g., That creation is not possible, although the contrary should be held by faith 184 [H189]; Resurrection should not be conceded by philosopher, because impossible for reason 18 [H216].

[83] 'Averroism' is a controversial term in the historiography of medieval philosophy. Few specialists now accept the older idea that Latin Averroism can be traced back all the way to Siger of Brabant and Boethius of Dacia, but most will use the label for writers like of John of Jandun and some of the Arts Masters in Italy and elsewhere from the fourteenth century onwards, although they stress that these writers often changed Averroes's views: cf. Imbach 1991. I have myself defended the traditional label of 'Averroist', even as applied to Siger and Boethius (Marenbon 2007a). For the purposes of understanding the Problem of Paganism, however, it is clearer to think about the general category of limited relativists, to which Averroists and other others who were not Averroists belong.

label inappropriate for earlier Arts Masters such as Siger and Boethius. In fact, although Averroes was an important authority for him, as interpreter of Aristotle, John frequently departed from his views to answer the questions which had been raised about them by, especially, Aquinas.[84] All the same, he follows the limited relativism of Siger and Boethius and puts forward, as the best interpretation of Aristotle and the best rational answer to various questions at issue, positions which are incompatible with Christianity. Rhetorically, however—and probably no more than that—his relativism is more limited, in that he explicitly states that, because of God's power, of which natural reasoning cannot take account, his philosophical conclusions are false, and Christian doctrine true: 'I assert that this conclusion [that of Christian teaching] is true without qualification and I hold it without any doubt by faith alone. And I would like to reply to the arguments against this opinion briefly, stating that all those things which these arguments show are impossible are possible for God'.[85] John of Jandun's close associate, Marsilius of Padua, follows a similar line in his *Defender of the Peace* (1324). He sets out a scheme of political society, in which priests and religion serve a purely social function, but he recognizes that there is, for Christians, the promise of heavenly happiness, which it is beyond his competence, working within an Aristotelian framework, to treat. John of Jandun and Marsilius were both Paris Arts Masters, who cut short their careers by fleeing to join the opponent of the pope, Emperor Ludwig of Bavaria, when they were condemned, not because of their Averroism, but on account of the political views expressed in the *Defender*. But the Averroist version of limited relativism flourished in many universities, especially Italian ones, in the later Middle Ages.[86]

The survival of limited relativism becomes even clearer from looking at an arts master who was not in any sense an Averroist (he rejected, for instance, Averroes's views on the intellect as a mistaken interpretation of Aristotle), John Buridan. Buridan taught in the Paris Arts Faculty for no fewer than forty years, from 1320 onwards, and his influence on his own and the next century was vast. He was happy, it seems, to accept the prohibition, as laid down in the 1272 statutes, of Arts Masters from disputing on theological topics, and even, sometimes, to take the further step of finding arguments to refute philosophical teachings which went against the faith.[87] In general, however, Buridan developed his teaching in strictly Aristotelian terms, whilst freely admitting, wherever there were

[84] See Brenet 2003.
[85] Commentary on *De anima* III, q. 5. John often explains himself in similar vein.
[86] See Kuksiewicz 1965 and Niewöhner and Sturlese 1994.
[87] See Sylla 2001.

contradictions, the truth of Christian doctrine and the insufficiency of philosophy to reach it. So, for instance, he argued that the most plausible and rationally convincing interpretation of Aristotle's views on the soul was that of Alexander of Aphrodisias, according to whom the human soul is a generable and corruptible material form, like that of other animals, which does not survive after death.[88] On creation ex nihilo, he makes it clear that it can be accepted only on biblical authority. And, like the Arts Masters of the 1260s and 1270s, he believes that the greatest human happiness—apart from beatitude in Heaven, which it is outside his sphere to consider—comes from the perfection of intellectual contemplation, available to philosophers alone, and he sees this contemplation less as a mystical joining with God than as the simple practice of philosophical speculation itself.[89]

THEOLOGIANS AND PAGAN PHILOSOPHY AFTER 1277

Whereas limited relativism survived, and indeed flourished after the late thirteenth century, Aquinas's way of unity did not, until its gradual revival in the fifteenth and sixteenth centuries. From Henry of Ghent in the 1280s onwards, the university theologians became generally far more pessimistic than Aquinas had been about the powers of unaided human reason, as exemplified by pagan philosophers and supremely by Aristotle, to reach a true, though admittedly incomplete, conception of God. The Condemnations are both evidence that this change had already begun by the 1270s, and one of the causes for its continuation. As theologians became more deeply acquainted with Aristotle and the implication of his positions, many began to think that his conception of God—and, it seemed, any reached purely by natural reason—was not merely incomplete, as Aquinas thought, but wrong in a number of important respects. In particular, Aristotle's God was seen to operate as a natural, necessary cause, as the source of unchanging physical laws, whereas the Christian God is a contingent cause, who makes the universe as it is according to his will, which might have been otherwise. This emphasis on God's contingent causality, and its denial by Aristotle, links one major theme in the Condemnations with a position emphasized throughout his work by the greatest and most influential of all the post-1277 theologians, Duns Scotus (d. 1308).

Scotus begins his commentary on the *Sentences* with a long discussion of the need for revelation, which he presents in terms of a conflict

---

[88] *Quaestiones de anima* III, qq. 3–6.
[89] See Biard 2001.

between the philosophers (he means Aristotle and his followers) 'who hold the perfection of nature and deny supernatural perfection' and the theologians 'who know the deficiency of nature, the need for grace and supernatural perfection'.[90] The philosophers, according to Scotus, maintain that no revelation is necessary, since in the soul there are naturally the passive intellect, which is able to receive any intelligible, and the active intellect, which can act with regard to any intelligible. So long as they are not impeded, therefore, there is nothing which together they cannot understand. Moreover, since we are naturally able to grasp the first principles of the sciences, there is nothing to stop us reaching all the conclusions contained in those principles (and so having perfect scientific knowledge).[91] Scotus is not making the philosophers claim that we do in fact understand all things, but that, through a process of enquiry and reasoning, we might in theory do so. The philosophers are, however, wrong, he believes. We can, indeed, intellectually grasp every concept, but there are many propositions which we need to know which, without supernatural revelation, are either unknown or remain dubious to us.[92] So far from 'vilifying' human nature by holding that it needs supernatural aid, Scotus believes that he gives it more dignity by claiming that the intellect's passive power is even greater than its active power, so that as well as what it has naturally, it can naturally (but through supernatural agency) receive something superior.[93] The reason why we can be sure that this supernaturally given knowledge is necessary is provided by what the philosophers themselves say. Consider what is most important to humans: knowledge of their end and how to reach it. We gain happiness, Scotus explains, as a reward from God, given contingently, and not by natural necessity following our actions. But the philosophers deny this, claiming that everything which comes directly from God comes of necessity. Moreover, the philosophers, reasoning without revelation, *cannot* know the truth in this matter.[94] Scotus does not criticize their reasoning. Working from the effects back to the cause, it is most reasonable to conclude that the first immaterial cause in not threefold, and that it causes naturally, not contingently; and to conclude about the world that it is eternal and comes about by necessity.[95] But these conclusions are wrong—as Scotus knows—*because of his faith*. What argument, then, can he give to

---

[90] *Ordinatio* I Prol. 1, q. unic. n. 5; John Duns Scotus 1950–, I, 4:15–17.
[91] *Ordinatio* I Prol. 1, q. unic. nn. 6, 9–10; John Duns Scotus 1950–, I, 5:7–15, 7:1–12.
[92] *Ordinatio* I Prol. 1, q. unic. n. 62; John Duns Scotus 1950–, I, 38:3–15.
[93] *Ordinatio* I Prol. 1, q. unic. n. 75; John Duns Scotus 1950–, I, 45:20–46:10.
[94] *Ordinatio* I Prol. 1, q. unic. nn. 17–18; John Duns Scotus 1950–, I, 11:18–13:7.
[95] *Ordinatio* I Prol. 1, q. unic. n. 41; John Duns Scotus 1950–, I, 24:2–25:2.

convince the philosophers that they are wrong? Scotus's reply is simple: none. As he puts it,

> It cannot be shown by natural reason that there is anything supernatural within people in this life, nor that it is necessarily required for their perfection. . . . Therefore it is impossible to use natural reason here against Aristotle. If the argument is based on what is believed, it is not a reasoning against the philosopher, because he does not accept the premise which is held through belief. And so the reasonings that are made here against him have as one of their premises either something believed or shown through something believed. They are therefore merely theological persuasions, from beliefs to a belief.[96]

Scotus, then, is as eager to separate the spheres of philosophical and theological enquiry as the boldest Arts Master, though he, as a theologian, has little interest in the philosophical sphere in itself, much as he will use Aristotle (and his own, perhaps equally fine philosophical brain) in pursuit of revealed truth within theology.

Scotus's wish to differentiate philosophy and theology was shared by many theologians in the following decades of the fourteenth century, and in the next century it would be the formative principle of the *via moderna*.[97] In the 1320s, William of Ockham would propose an even lower estimate of the power of natural reason to grasp God: for, whereas Scotus developed one of the most elaborate proofs of the existence of an infinite God, Ockham argued that the existence of such a deity could not be demonstrated.[98] At least two distinguished thinkers, however, took a rather different approach to pagan knowledge, attributing a high level of knowledge about God to the ancient philosophers, but explaining it by their contact with the revelation to the patriarchs of Genesis and the Old Testament prophets. They were thus exponents of an idea already proposed by Abelard, adapted by Roger Bacon and which, as the 'Ancient Theology' would be an important theme in sixteenth- and seventeenth-century thought.[99] Both were members of a circle, gathered around the wealthy bibliophile, Richard de Bury, which cultivated an interest in antiquity and its literature unusual among scholastic theologians.[100] One of them was Robert Holcot, an English Dominican who

[96] *Ordinatio* I Prol. 1, q. unic. n. 12; John Duns Scotus 1950–, I, 9:3–10.

[97] See chapter 12.

[98] Scotus develops his proof in book I, d. 2, q. 1 of his *Ordinatio* and elsewhere: see Cross 1999, 160–61n3 for further references and bibliography. For Ockham's views, see, e.g., his *Quodlibet* 1, q. 1.

[99] See chapter 5 and chapter 12.

[100] See Smalley 1960.

taught in Oxford and Cambridge in the 1330s and 1340s. Holcot wrote not only a commentary on the *Sentences*, quodlibetal disputations and other treatises, but also a widely read commentary on the biblical book of Wisdom, directed to a wider audience, yet maintaining his characteristic concerns and positions. Following Ockham, Holcot holds that neither the existence of God, nor indeed that of anything incorporeal, can be demonstrated by natural reason.[101] Yet he does not conclude that the philosophers and others who lived under natural law were for that reason ignorant about God or denied his existence.

> They accepted the faith, because of the fact that from the beginning of the world some people worshipped God—Adam and some of his children, for example, and Noah and his children after the flood. Also, there were without break prophets who taught divine worship, and their fame reached to the Egyptian, Arabic (!), Greek and Chaldaean philosophers. And so God's prophets preceded all human and earthly wisdom, as Augustine declares in the *City of God* XVIII, 47. . . . And so it is sufficiently established that knowledge of the worship of God had come through the patriarchs and prophets (and knowledge of their lives and observances) to the cognizance of the philosophers who lived many thousand years after them.[102]

It is by reference to this knowledge acquired from tradition, rather than the use of natural reason, that Holcot explains Paul's insistence on the ability of the ancient philosophers to know God from his creation. 'As a result of the ancient revelation', says Holcot, 'it has been diffused to all peoples living under a law that God exists', and 'what is known to all seems to be known by nature'.[103]

The other holder of a similar position was Thomas Bradwardine, who finished his great treatise *The Case for God against the Pelagians* (*De causa Dei contra Pelagianos*) in the mid-1340s. Like Holcot, Bradwardine stresses the extent of prophecy before the coming of Christ (though he also sees reason as a powerful tool, able to grasp the existence and main attributes of God).[104] He illustrates his views about prophecy by pointing to various figures other than Jews about whom there is evidence, biblical or other, that they must have received divine revelation: they include Job,

---

[101]The sentence immediately preceding the passage just quoted reads, 'it has not been demonstrated by any reasoning up until now that God exists or is creator of the world'; for other instances where Holcot denies that even the existence of God can be proved, see Marenbon 2005, 62n15.

[102]Commentary on *Sentences* III, q. 1 tertium dictum; SS); Robert Holcot 1518 (unnumbered folios). See also the passage from Lectio 157 in Smalley 1960, 328.

[103]Commentary on Wisdom, Lectio 157; Robert Holcot 1489 (these folios unnumbered).

[104]See pp. 185–86 below.

Nebuchadnezzar (after he had been humiliated and repented), Cornelius the Centurion (before his baptism) and, less expectedly, Alexander the Great.[105] This coupling of Holcot and Bradwardine will turn out to be both a surprising and a revealing one, when their views about pagan virtue and salvation—the subject of the next chapter—are considered.

[105] *De causa Dei*, chap. 1—corollarium, 32; Thomas Bradwardine 1618, 59–60, 62E.

CHAPTER 9

University Theologians on Pagan Virtue and Salvation

PAGAN KNOWLEDGE, IT IS CLEAR FROM THE LAST CHAPTER, BECAME A contested notion in the late thirteenth- and fourteenth-century universities, and the optimistic attempts of thinkers such as Roger Bacon, Albert the Great and Thomas Aquinas, in their different ways, to combine a very high estimate of pagan wisdom with their doctrinal aims as theologians were generally abandoned, although Arts Masters were left surprisingly free to develop thinking on the basis of natural reason, so long as they accepted its falsehood where it went against the teaching of the faith. The present chapter explores the different trajectories taken by discussions among (mainly) university theologians of pagan virtue in the first section, and salvation in the three sections following: the second section is on the theories devised in the period up to Ockham in the early fourteenth century, the third section on discussions about the salvation of particular pagans (such as Aristotle himself) and the final section about the theoretical developments which took place in the mid- and later fourteenth century and set the stage for the debates which would go on to 1700 and even later.

Pagan Virtues from Peter the Lombard to Ockham

Abelard implied, but did not explicitly put forward a notion of real pagan virtues.[1] He accepted, following Augustine, that properly speaking virtues are founded on charity and so no one can be virtuous in the proper sense without Christian faith, which is a prerequisite for charity. But he was also highly impressed by the accounts of the excellent and austere lives of the ancient philosophers, and he could not accept Augustine's view that their virtues, and those of other outstanding men and women of antiquity, were false. No theologian in the following two centuries admired antiquity so fervently as Abelard. None the less, in the decades after his

---

[1] See above, chapter 5.

death a theory came to be evolved, and then very widely held, which stated explicitly what he had apparently not dared to propose openly: that there are genuine pagan virtues. One difference between this theory and Abelard's is that its exponents always insist that these pagan virtues do not bring merit—that is to say, they do not contribute to a person's salvation. By contrast, Abelard had suggested that pagan virtues might lead to salvation, indirectly, by gaining those who cultivate them a special divine revelation of the articles of faith. Even this contrast though, it will turn out, may not be absolute.[2]

The basis for this post-Abelardian theory was the Roman Neoplatonist Macrobius's discussion, in his Commentary on the *Dream of Scipio*, of the 'political virtues'. Macrobius had made, following Plotinus, a division of levels of virtues. The lowest are political virtues: they enable humans to be political and social animals, as Aristotle had characterized them, and Macrobius goes on to describe them as the virtues by which the good of towns and commonwealths is preserved, and family and neighbourly relationships are sustained. They include all the four cardinal virtues: prudence, temperance, courage and justice: 'by these virtues', he says, 'a good man is made into the ruler, first of himself and then of the commonwealth, governing justly and with foresight, and not leaving human things'.[3] This distinction was taken up by later twelfth-century theologians, especially those influenced by Gilbert of Poitiers, such as Simon of Tournai (c. 1130–1201) and Alan of Lille (d. c. 1203). They distinguish between political virtues, the firm habit of mind to carry out duties for the commonwealth, and catholic virtues, the firm habit of mind to perform the duties set down by the Catholic religion, for the sake of God and in order finally to enjoy him. Simon, rather more than Alan, is willing to regard the political virtues as genuine virtues, although insufficient for salvation.[4] Unbelievers (Jews and pagans) can have political, but not catholic virtues.[5] The twelfth-century theologians usually thought that, in the case of a Christian, the political virtues could develop into catholic virtues. By the early thirteenth century, however, most theologians

[2]The fundamental studies for doctrines of the virtues in the twelfth and thirteenth centuries remain the chapters in Lottin 1949, 1954 and 1961. They are now complemented by Bejczy's fine, wider-ranging study (2011). I fully agree with Bejczy's view that Lottin at times exaggerates the difference in this area between Aquinas and other theologians of his time.

[3]Commentary on the *Dream of Scipio* 1.8.5–8; Macrobius 1970, 37:25–38:18.

[4]See Lottin 1961, 77. (The chapter to which this and subsequent references to this book are made appeared originally as Lottin 1953.)

[5]This summary is based on a passage from Simon of Tournai, quoted in Lottin 1949, 107:26–39, but the doctrine is in most important respects the same in texts Lottin discusses by Alan of Lille, and is taken up by other theologians in the early thirteenth century: see Lottin 1949, 105–15.

believed that the catholic virtues are given to infants when they are baptized, even though they are not yet able to practise them.[6]

Parallel with the distinction between political and catholic virtues was a distinction between those which were acquired and those which were infused. The ancient tradition considered virtues, such as the four which came to be described as 'cardinal' (prudence, justice, courage and temperance) to be acquired by people through their behaviour and efforts. By contrast, Christian theologians held that the three 'theological' virtues, necessary for salvation, faith, hope and charity, are infused by God. Given that all the theologians, even Abelard, the great champion of ancient philosophy, accepted that the cardinal virtues in the highest sense, which confer merit to Christians, depend on the infused virtue of charity, the idea of acquired virtues presents them with a problem. Abelard, admittedly, defines virtue (he is thinking of the cardinal virtues) as 'a mental disposition (*habitus mentis*), that is a good quality of the mind which has become a disposition through application of the mind and can hardly or never be separated from it'.[7] But he has only a few lines before declared, following Augustine, that 'every virtue is charity or from charity'.[8] This second view is more consistent with the definition of virtue that would be put forward by Peter the Lombard and was widely adopted: '. . . a good quality of the mind, by which one lives well and which no one can use badly, which God alone works in a human being'.[9] Peter the Lombard's definition leaves no room at all for acquired virtues. The distinction between political and Catholic virtues enabled thinkers to retain acquired virtues—the political ones—while allowing that the Catholic cardinal virtues which confer merit are infused, just like the theological virtues, or at least dependent on the infused theological virtues. This terminology was not, however, always followed. For example, William of Auxerre distinguishes between 'habitual (*consuetudinales*) political virtues', which are those that Aristotle talks of and can be possessed by people in mortal sin, and political virtues in the sense of the cardinal virtues which depend on faith, hope and charity and are discussed in the Bible, in the book of Wisdom.[10]

In Aquinas, most of his contemporaries and most of the later Dominican school, the result of this way of thinking is a very complicated system of virtues, since the acquired cardinal virtues of prudence, justice, courage and temperance are doubled by a set of infused cardinal virtues,

---

[6] See Lottin 1949, 116–42. According to Bejczy (2011, 192–96) this view did not exclude the idea that acquired, political virtues could also be elevated by grace to Catholic ones.

[7] *Sententie* sec. 252; Peter Abelard 2006, 133:2996–98.

[8] *Sententie* sec. 251; Peter Abelard 2006, 132:2985–86.

[9] *Sentences* II, d. 27, 1.1; Peter the Lombard 1971–81, I, 480.

[10] *Summa Aurea* III, tr. 40.2; William of Auxerre 1980–87, III, 770:40–54.

which bear the same names, but in which infused prudence plays the role played by acquired prudence in the acquired virtues.[11] In some cases, at least, the behaviour characteristic of the acquired virtue is different from, and incompatible with, that attached to the infused virtue of the same name: following acquired temperance, we eat moderately and healthily, whereas by infused temperance we chastise the body by fasting.[12] The exact relationship intended by Aquinas between acquired and infused virtues in a Christian is, then, a difficult problem, and one that exercised his commentators.[13] Not surprisingly, some theologians began to question whether it was necessary to posit separate infused virtues, as opposed to seeing the acquired virtues working under the aegis of the infused theological virtues. At the end of the thirteenth century, both Henry of Ghent and Duns Scotus argued against maintaining a real distinction between acquired and infused virtues, and they were followed by most theologians outside the Dominican tradition.[14] But these complications concern the moral lives of Christians; with regard to pagans, the majority of the later thirteenth- and early fourteenth-century theologians accepted that they could be virtuous by acquired, political virtues, which are genuine though not perfect virtues, and which do not lead to salvation. The four greatest theologians of the time, Aquinas, Henry of Ghent, Duns Scotus and William of Ockham, illustrate this common view.[15]

When Aquinas poses himself the question whether there can be true virtue without charity, he answers it in the negative: that is to say, only the infused virtues can be true.[16] Similarly, he says that, although there are acquired virtues without charity (possessed by many pagans), virtues 'fit the definition of virtue perfectly and truly' only if they bring about good which is ordered to the ultimate supernatural end of humans,

[11] See Aquinas, *De virtutibus* q. 1, a. 10; Commentary on *Sentences* III, d. 33, q. 1, a. 2, qc. 3; *Summa Theologiae* IaIIe, q. 65, a. 2. For the infused virtues in Aquinas and their background, see Lottin 1949, 459–535.

[12] Aquinas, *Summa Theologiae* IaIIe, q. 63, a. 4; and cf. Commentary on *Sentences* III, d. 33, q. 1, a. 2, qc 4, ad 2.

[13] The most thorough study is Bullet 1958. The tendency of many philosophical studies on Aquinas's ethics is to concentrate on what he says about acquired virtues and treat his comments on infused virtues as a side-line. But he clearly thinks of the infused virtues as central to a Christian moral life, which is the focus of his interest: for a philosophical discussion which does justice to Aquinas's views on both types of virtues, see Kent 2002.

[14] See Lottin 1954, 739–807.

[15] See also Bejczy 2011, 194–95. There also developed a tradition, outside the mainstream of university theology, in which an ethics based on natural virtues is developed especially for the laity. It goes back at least to Martin of Braga in the late sixth century (see above, p. 61); a striking later example of it is the *Speculum virtutum* of Engelbert of Admont (1308–13): cf. von Moos 2012, esp. 126. I am grateful to Peter von Moos for drawing this theme and the references to my attention.

[16] *Summa Theologiae* IaIIe, q. 23, a. 7.

and such virtues 'cannot be acquired by human acts but are infused by God'.[17] But Aquinas steps back from calling all acquired virtues false, although he certainly considers them imperfect. Just as perfect virtue is directed to what is without qualification the highest good, so a virtue which is directed to some particular, genuine good, such as the preservation of the city, can be called true, if imperfect, by contrast with, for instance, the courage or temperance a miser shows in keeping his wealth, since here the end is not a less than final good, but an illusory good, and so the virtue is false.[18] The example, as Aquinas notes, is Augustine's, from his *Against Julianus*.[19] But where Augustine is trying to efface any distinction between such obviously false virtues and any virtue without charity, Aquinas is drawing one. Aquinas refers to *Against Julianus* again in the same article, citing Augustine's view that the act of an unbeliever (*infidelis*)[20] in so far as it is that of an unbeliever, is a sin, even if the act is clothing the naked or feeding the hungry. Aquinas does not disagree with Augustine directly, but he makes a distinction. The non-Christian lacks charity, but his acts might either be directed towards that through which he lacks charity—his not being a Christian, in which case they are always evil, whatever they are; or, alternatively, directed to another good, which might be a good of nature, since this good has not been entirely removed by Original Sin. Such an act can be good 'of its kind' (*ex suo genere*), although not perfectly good. As he explains in a different question, denying that every act someone outside the faith performs is a sin, 'it is clear that unbelievers cannot perform the good works which come from grace, that is to say, meritorious works, but they are able to in some way to perform the good works for which the good of nature suffices'.[21]

Henry of Ghent considers the same passage in Augustine's *Against Julianus* even more carefully than Aquinas. He explains how 'the philosophers and rulers of the commonwealth among the unbelievers' can have political virtues: their moral actions were elicited from their free will by a good intention, which was 'to live in the exercise of the moral virtues according to the rule of prudence *and so for the sake of God*'. Henry then explains this final phrase as meaning: 'in reaching God through a certain likeness of him, in which they placed the end of man and the political happiness of man, but not from the intention of directing them to God as

[17] *Summa Theologiae* IaIIe, q. 65, a. 2.
[18] *Summa Theologiae* IIaIIe, q. 23, a. 7.
[19] *Against Julianus* IV.3; see above, p. 37.
[20] *Infidelis* is a word which includes heretics, as well as non-Christians, and Aquinas does indeed mention as the goods less than charity for which an *infidelis* might act 'other gifts of God, such as faith and hope'.
[21] *Summa Theologiae* IIaIIe, q. 10, a. 4.

saviour and rewarder in the happiness of eternal life'.[22] Henry recognizes
that, for Augustine, the fact that they did not direct themselves to God in
this way means that the pagans lacked true moral virtues, and he quotes
from *Against Julianus*, where Augustine insists that virtues which do not
contribute to true beatitude are not true virtues, and that even the best
pagans are merely less bad than the worst. Henry answers by making the
same sort of distinction as Aquinas had done, but adding an extra element. One can perform an act of the right sort but not for the right end
in two ways: by performing it for an end contrary to the right end, or by
performing it for the right end, but envisaging that end under the wrong
description.[23] An example of the first way is someone who comes to the
help of an innocent person in danger out of vainglory. An example of the
second way is someone who comes to the help of an innocent person in
danger 'for the sake of God, in the way by which philosophers and the
rulers of states (*politiae*) did such deeds, from natural uprightness (*pietas*)
and the judgement of right reason regulated by natural law, so that they
conformed themselves in this with God and reached him in so far as it
was possible'.[24] Henry has to accept that according to Augustine even
those following the second way sin, but it is a sin of omission, and so
he can say that they do *not* sin and are *not* evil in their actions, but only
their omissions: in what they do, they are good as political agents, but,
because they are outside the faith, not good without qualification. Henry
gives a more satisfactory response than Aquinas had done, since his virtuous pagans do not, like Aquinas's, aim at a different end from the right
one, which is also good, but at the right end, envisaged in a different way.

Henry recognizes that Augustine would have been unlikely to accept
his conclusions, since Augustine's insistence that there can be no good
fruit from a bad tree implies that the actions of a non-Christian are in
no way good. But he sticks to his own position: '*I* say that he does good
things and does them well in so far as they are directed towards the
good end, and to this extent the tree is good and it produces good fruits'.
Henry feels able to sustain this position against Augustine by making a
distinction absent from *Against Julianus*. Augustine anticipates, and rejects, the retort that a person can be considered a good tree, not in that
he is a non-Christian, but in that he is a human being. By this qualification, he points out, every human would be a good tree, since everyone is
good as a human being, since humans are the work of God. Henry's good
pagan, however, is not good in that he is a human being but in that he is

---

[22] *Quodlibet* 13, q. 10; Henry of Ghent 1985, 73:32–74:38.

[23] 75:71–72: '. . . because he does for the sake of that [that for which it ought to be done]
not according to the description (*ratio*) according to which it should be done for the sake
of that . . .'

[24] 75:72–76.

a human being 'who acts according to right natural reason to a good end, although not as he should, for the reason stated' (because he is not aiming at God *qua* giver of happiness in eternity).[25] Henry ends his discussion by saying that, whilst in the context of attacking Julianus's extreme view that the pagans have true and perfect virtues, Augustine's unqualified assertions are 'well and truly said', they stand in need of being expounded and nuanced in the way he has just shown—a comment that may not be entirely straight-faced, coming as it does after this masterpiece of deconstructive interpretation, which draws from an author the opposite of what he wished to say.[26]

Where Aquinas and, even more, Henry are obviously keen to insist on the genuine virtue, albeit less than perfect, of pagans, Scotus accepts that there can be true virtues without charity more for reasons of definition. According to him, a virtue is a 'disposition with regard to choice according to right reason' (*habitus electivus secundum rectam rationem*), and on such a definition charity is not required in order for something to be a virtue.[27] The onus is therefore for the Augustinian to explain why charity should be required by virtues. Scotus ventures such an explanation. In so far as virtues are the instruments for perfecting a human being, they should order him to his final end. They can do this only by means of the virtue the nature of which is to regard the final end—and that is charity. This consideration, Scotus agrees, means that virtues are imperfect without charity, but it does not prevent each individual virtue from being perfect in its species without charity, since none of the other virtues is of a sort which, by its nature, orders those who have it to the final end.[28] By this characteristically abstract formulation, Scotus means that someone who has, for instance, courage without charity—a pagan, for instance—can in principle have perfect courage, since as a virtue courage is simply the disposition to courageous acts (not a disposition which, in itself, is concerned with a human's supernatural end). But even if such a person had perfect courage, perfect temperance, perfect justice and perfect prudence, he or she could not be perfectly virtuous as a whole without charity.

Writing a couple of decades after Scotus, William of Ockham distinguishes a grade of virtue which, alone, is 'perfect and true moral virtue about which the holy writers (*sancti*) speak'. Such a grade (grade 4) is

---

[25] *Quodlibet* 13, q. 10; Henry of Ghent 1985, 76:4–6.

[26] *Quodlibet* 13, q. 10; Henry of Ghent 1985, 77:38–78:43. Lottin 1961, 100–101 misreads Henry's discussion as simply accepting Augustine's position.

[27] *Ordinatio* III, d. 36, q. unica, nn. 80, 104; John Duns Scotus 1950–, X, 254:551–52, 262:709–10.

[28] *Ordinatio* III, d. 36, q. unica, n. 105; John Duns Scotus 1950–, X, 262:711–263:721.

reached when a person does not merely (grade 1) perform the just deeds which right reason says are to be done under the circumstances, because of the worthiness of these deeds, or for the sake of peace or suchlike, nor (grade 2) with, added, the intention not to desist from the deeds even at the cost of death, if that is what right reason dictates, nor (grade 3) with it added that he wills the deeds just because they are required by right reason. In order to have grade 4 virtue, the agent must in addition be acting just out of the love of God.[29] From these distinctions, Ockham would seem, through the differentiation he makes between grades 3 and 4, to have a view about pagan virtue close to that found in Aquinas, Henry of Ghent and Scotus: it is genuine virtue, but distinct from perfect Christian virtue because not directed towards God. Ockham emphasizes, however, that when a pagan philosopher engages in abstinence, because of its intrinsic worth or for the 'conservation of nature', he thereby makes the act good from its circumstances though he does not make it good from a 'principle worthy of merit', as a Christian does when he is continent not just because of right reason but also to the honour of God.[30] And Ockham does not stop at the fourth grade virtue, but includes another, fifth grade, and his treatment of it suggests that he goes even further than his predecessors in accepting pagan virtues as genuine and, indeed, admirable. Grade 5 virtue is, as Ockham himself calls it, 'heroic virtue', in which someone exceeds the common condition of humans, doing or suffering something beyond human nature. In defining it, Ockham is careful to make clear that pagans as well as Christians can be heroically virtuous: the end for which deeds of such virtue are done might be God or might be ('I say this with regard to the intention of a philosopher') for worthiness or peace, and Ockham gives, alongside the example of a martyr who is willing to bear death for the sake of the faith, someone who is willing to be burned or incarcerated rather than do injustice, stating that such a person, exactly as the one (the Christian) in the first case, is 'perfectly heroic'.[31]

---

[29] *De connexione virtutum*. q. 7, a. 2, distinctio 3; William of Ockham 1984, 335:115–336:142.

[30] *De connexione virtutum*. q. 7, a. 2, distinctio 6; William of Ockham 1984, 339:221–24.

[31] *De connexione virtutum*. q. 7, a. 2, distinctio 3; William of Ockham 1984, 336:152–337:180. Ockham does add later (*De connexione virtutum*. q. 7, a. 2, conclusio 7; William of Ockham 1984, 355:326–29) that, whereas the Christian's heroic virtue is incompatible with any vice or culpable defect from the same reason, the heroic virtue of a philosopher is compatible with vice. Bejczy 2011, 195–96 wrongly thinks that the fifth grade of virtue is only for Christians. King 1999, 233–35, to whom he refers, presents Ockham's views correctly and explains why, in spite of the value given to pagan virtues, he believes that Christian belief can add to the moral value of people's acts.

THE SALVATION OF PAGANS: THREE THEORIES

Almost all medieval university theologians believed that they needed to give an explanation of how pagans—people living under natural law, without the benefit of the Old or the New Testament—could be saved. Usually, they were thinking about biblical people, living before the time of the Old Law, and some non-Jews, such as Job, who lived during that period. A few theologians (most important, Thomas Aquinas) also, though fleetingly, considered how these ideas about salvation might apply to figures from classical antiquity.The most used theory was one about implicit faith. In the early twelfth century, as has been explained, there was a straightforward opposition between William of Champeaux, Anselm of Laon and their followers on the one hand, and Abelard on the other.[32] William and the others believed that, although a few people had an explicit belief in how God would redeem mankind, for those living under natural law the Pauline minimum—belief in God as the repayer of good and evil—was all that was required for salvation. By contrast, Abelard insisted that no one could be saved without explicit knowledge of the Incarnation. A serious problem for William's view is that Augustine very clearly insisted that no one can be saved except by faith in Christ. In the 1130s or 1140s, some of the followers of Anselm and William raised the problem directly, citing Augustine, and repeating William's idea that, for most people under natural law, the Pauline minimum was enough for salvation, but with the additional idea that, none the less, 'all the good people did have faith with regard to Christ, although for some it was closed in mystery'.[33] This addition is important because it means that the author accepts that faith in Christ is necessary, but contends that someone who will be saved can have, so far as explicit faith is concerned, merely the Pauline minimum, and yet also the necessary faith in Christ but 'clothed in mystery'.[34]

At much the same time, Hugh of St Victor was developing William of Champeaux's ideas in a similar direction, but with greater sophistication and cogency.[35] Hugh insists that the faith by which people are saved must be the same faith in all periods. But he does not at all agree with those, such as Abelard (not mentioned by name), who require that everyone

---

[32] See chapter 4 and chapter 5.

[33] *Sententie Anselmi* (probably from Paris in the decade after 1135; see Flint 1976); Bliemetzrieder 1919, 80.

[34] The *Sententiae Atrebatenses*, probably from the same period (Section 8; Lottin 1959, 417:36), put forward the same idea, although without talking of mystery. According to this author, to believe in the Pauline minimum was indeed to have 'the faith of Christ, that is of the Redemptor'.

[35] *On the Sacraments* 2.6–7; *PL* 176, 335A–41A.

who was saved, even in the earliest times, had explicit faith in the Incarnation. According to this approach, Hugh argues, either very few people would be saved before Christian times—something he thinks unworthy of God—or else a large number of people must be assumed to have benefited from special divine inspiration. If the latter were true, then people in this early period would have been better provided with the faith than those of later times, who have to rely on oral testimony, and so 'the coming of Christ not only brought no illumination to the faithful, but took away from them a more certain and better knowledge'.[36] Hugh proposes instead that, whilst the faith remains the same at all times, knowledge of it increases. In consequence, many could be saved under natural law and the Old Law without knowing about the Incarnation, although it was included in the faith by which they were saved. But how can people have faith in what is unknown to them? Hugh explains that some people (though, he insists, not many) in every period *did* have full knowledge of the faith. The majority of simple people at the time of natural law believed no more than the Pauline minimum, the existence of God as a redeemer, and yet they could also be said to have faith in the birth, passion, resurrection and ascension of Christ 'because they adhered to those who believed and knew these things, with faith and devotion, in hope and expectation of this same redemption, although they did not know in the same way the manner of this same redemption'.[37] According to Hugh, then, people can be said to have faith in what is affirmed by a proposition *p*, without holding or even contemplating *p*, if they accept a general proposition, of which *p* is an instantiation, and they also place their trust in other people who actually believe that *p*.

In his *Sentences*, Peter the Lombard follows Hugh closely. He brings out clearly that the Pauline minimum is not enough and was *never* enough for salvation, giving a string of citations from Augustine and Gregory the Great which demand faith *in Christ* for salvation.[38] What, then, he asks himself about the simple people before Christian times (the context makes it clear he is thinking just of the Jews) 'to whom the mystery of the Incarnation was not revealed, who piously believed what was handed down to them?'[39] Peter answers by saying that to all of those who were saved a revelation had been made, but 'Abraham, Moses and other of the 'greater ones' (*maiores*) benefited from a distinct revelation, whereas for the simple people or 'minor ones' (*minores*) the revelation was 'veiled': 'to them it was revealed that those things should be believed which the

---

[36] *On the Sacraments* 2.6; PL 176, 339A.
[37] *On the Sacraments* 2.7; PL 176, 340A.
[38] *Sentences* 3, d. 25, chap. 2, 2–3; Peter the Lombard 1971–81, 153:4–154:22.
[39] *Sentences* 3, d. 25, chap. 2; Peter the Lombard 1971–81, 154:24–26.

greater ones believed and taught, but they do not grasp them distinctly'.[40] The two elements of Hugh's theory—that the lesser ones have an indistinct grasp of the redemption and that they place their trust in those greater ones who know distinctly how it will take place—are both there.

Peter the Lombard's *Sentences* became the textbook for the theology faculties in the medieval universities. On most subjects, it provided basic doctrines which were then subject to enormous refinement and which excited debate and the development of rival theories. On this question of faith before the New Law, however, Peter the Lombard's view—reinforced and extended by direct reference to Hugh's *On the Sacraments*—became a standard theory, accepted by almost every important thirteenth- and earlier fourteenth-century theologian. In the *Summa fratris Alexandri*, put together by the disciples of Alexander of Hales between 1236 and 1245, the one development is to use the terms which from then on become standard, 'implicit' to describe the indistinct faith of the lesser ones, and 'explicit' to describe the distinct faith of the few greater ones.[41] Bonaventure, for example, follows Hugh and the Lombard closely. Before the coming of Christ, there were only a few to whom the details of his life were revealed, and it was sufficient for others to believe implicitly, which was 'to await the future redeemer, but to believe how and in what way it should be according to that which those believed to whom it had been revealed by the Lord'.[42] Albert the Great is unusual, because although he makes a distinction between implicit and explicit belief, he rather blurs it, by saying that the *minores* are not required to believe even implicitly anything but what they are taught by the *maiores*, to whom it has been revealed, and which falls within their powers of understanding.[43]

Aquinas follows the standard theory. Faith in the Incarnation and Passion of Christ is necessary for salvation, but before the time of Christ, only some people needed to have it explicitly, others could be saved by implicit faith.[44] His account of what is meant by 'implicit' may give the impression of being rather different from the usual one, but it turns out not to be. In his *On Truth*, he explains that when many things are contained virtually in something, then they are said to be in it 'implicitly'. He gives as an example the way in which, when we know universal principles, we have 'implicit cognition' (*cognitio implicita*) of all the

[40] *Sentences* 3, d. 25, chap. 2; Peter the Lombard 1971–81, 155:3–5.

[41] *Summa Fratris Alexandri* 3, inq. 2, tr. 2, q. 1, chap. 4, art. 1; (Alexander of Hales) 1924–48, IV, 1120.

[42] Commentary on *Sentences* III, d. 25, a. 1, q. 2; Bonaventure 1882–1902, III, 540.

[43] Commentary on *Sentences* III, d. 25, a. 4; Albert the Great 1890–99, XXVIII, 480.

[44] Commentary on *Sentences* III, d. 25, q. 2, a. 2, qc. 2; *On Truth* q. 14, a. 11; *Summa Theologiae* IIaIIe, q. 2, a. 7.

particular conclusions. When we actually consider these conclusions, we have explicit cognition of them. Similarly, he goes on, 'we are said to believe things explicitly when we actually adhere to them in cogitation, but implicitly when we adhere to certain things, in which they [the things believed implicitly] are contained as in universal principles'. This sounds as if Aquinas is not thinking of implicitness in the usual terms of relying on someone else's beliefs. But he immediately adds, giving an example, 'as when someone believes that the faith of the Church is true, in this he or she as if implicitly believes the individual things which are contained in the faith of the Church'.[45] Implicit faith is, then, for Aquinas as for other theologians, a matter of taking something on trust, and in his commentary on the *Sentences*, he had explained why. There he puts to himself the objection that the faith of someone else is not a proper object for implicit faith, since faith should follow the model of knowledge (*scientia*). When we speak of the implicit knowledge someone has, we do not mean knowledge implicit in someone else, but in the universal of the knowable thing. (When—to give an example, unlike Aquinas here—we know that game fowl is healthy, our knowledge that pheasant is healthy is implicit in the universal Game Fowl, not in a nutritionist.) Aquinas answers by saying that, in the case of scientific knowledge we can draw the conclusions from the principles without being taught, and so we can be said to have implicit knowledge of the conclusions in the principles; yet even here we also have implicit knowledge in someone else who knows, in so far as we do in fact need the help of a teacher. But 'it is not the same with regard to knowledge (*scientia*) as to faith, because there are no principles naturally within us from which the articles of faith derive. Rather, faith in us is determined entirely by teaching, and so we must have implicit faith in the cognition of ‹some other› human being'.[46]

Few other theologians go into so much detail as Aquinas, but the standard theory of implicit faith he proposes continues to be widely followed. It is put forward, for example, by Richard of Middleton in the next generation, and Duns Scotus and Durandus of St Pourçain at the turn of the fourteenth century.[47] But there are some changes: although Durandus's solution follows Aquinas's quite closely, and he does clearly think of implicit faith as a matter of the *minores* taking on trust what the *maiores* believe, his explanation of what is meant by 'implicit' is given in terms of the particular being implicit in the universal, without any reference to the

[45] *On Truth* q. 14, a. 11.
[46] Commentary on *Sentences* III, d. 25, q. 2, a. 1, qc. 4, arg 1 and ad 1.
[47] Richard of Middleton, Commentary on *Sentences* III, d. 25, a. 3, q. 1–2; Richard of Middleton 1591, 277–79. For Scotus, see his *Lectura* on the *Sentences* III, d. 25; John Duns Scotus 1950–, XXI, 159:77–80; 167:238–45.

faith of others.[48] This slide in meaning is even more apparent in the way the very widely-read biblical commentator, Nicholas of Lyra (d. 1349) puts a view which, otherwise, is like Aquinas's. Those who believe in God as a rewarder must in consequence, he argues, believe in divine providence, and the way in which in fact God provided for the providence of humans was the Incarnation.[49]

Implicit faith provides the main medieval theory for how, in principle, good pagans can be saved, but it was not the only theory. There was an alternative approach, based on the idea of special inspiration and first put forward by Abelard, to how pagans both before *and after* Christ could be saved. Unlike most of the other theologians of his own time and later, Abelard rejected altogether salvation by any other than explicit faith. But other theologians would adopt the Abelardian solution mainly, it seems, to explain—as the theory of implicit faith could not—how salvation might be possible for pagans after the coming of Christ. In the *Problemata Heloissae*, Abelard explains that those who recognize by natural law God as creator and rewarder of all (the Pauline minimum) and strive to sin in no way will have revealed to them explicitly what they need to know in order to be saved.[50] This is the only text of Abelard's which contains this idea, but in a commentary on the Pauline Epistles written by a follower, exactly the same view is presented,[51] whilst in a mid-twelfth-century question-and-answer commentary on them, Abelard is cited as saying, about the ancient philosophers, that 'they were worthy of being saved, that is that there should be given to them that from which they might be saved; because, if they did as much as they could (*si fecissent quantum possent*) God would never permit them to depart ‹this life› without faith'.[52] This approach implies that non-Christians are able to act in a way which is not just morally good, but also brings God, as a matter of 'piety and reason', to provide—through a teacher or special inspiration— what they need in order to be saved. Although Abelard deliberately holds back from saying that God is bound by it, the theory is bolder than the one based on implicit faith. Not only can it apply to all non-Christians at any time (so long as their lack of faith is purely negative: they do not know about Christ and could not have found out about him by diligent

[48] Commentary on *Sentences* III, d. 25, q. 1, n. 8–9 (for Aquinas's theory); n. 5 for definition of implicit faith; Durandus of St Pourçain 1571, f. 258v.

[49] Gloss to Hebrews xi, 6; *Bibliorum sacrorum* 1603, col. 922; cf. gloss to Acts x, 35; *Bibliorum sacrorum* 1603, col. 1105.

[50] The text is quoted above, chapter 5, p. 92.

[51] *Commentarius Cantabrigiensis* to Romans 10; Landgraf 1937, 144, cited by Landgraf 1952–56, I.2, 38n29b.

[52] *Quaestiones in epistolas Pauli* no. 39, *PL* 175, 440CD; this passage is noted both by Capéran (1934, 77) and Landgraf (1952–56, I.1, 251).

enquiry); it also makes a link between their good deeds and their salvation. The link is indirect, since they do not earn salvation, but rather the
knowledge they need in order to be saved. Yet it is hardly compatible with
an Augustinian insistence on the complete gratuity of grace.

Abelard's approach did not die with him. It remained an element in
thirteenth-century discussions of salvation, though at their edges. In the
Summa Fratris Alexandrii, from the mid-thirteenth century, there is no
mention of it in the detailed treatment of faith and salvation, but in the
discussion earlier of culpable and non-culpable ignorance, the question is
raised about someone who is locked up from early childhood in 'a Saracen prison': is he culpably ignorant 'of the things which are of the faith'?
The writers answer on lines quite similar to Abelard's:

> Such a person, when he comes to adulthood, does not entirely lack
> the power to believe, because, if he does what is in him, God will illu-
> minate him, either through hidden inspiration or through an angel or
> through a human. . . . To do what is in him is to use reason, through
> which he can understand that God exists and he can call on God's
> help. . . . If he uses his intellect in so far as it is in him, he will be told
> about the Incarnation and the Redemption by an interior voice, even
> if not an external one.[53]

Writing at much the same time, in his *On Laws*, William of Auvergne
argues that those who are ignorant of God's laws are always culpably
so, because they could find them if they tried. He has in mind the basic
knowledge about the Christian God needed for salvation. He considers
that, by using our mental talents, we are all in a position to know that
our creator is God and he should be honoured and worshipped; and, if
we do well with what we can find, God will add the other requisite beliefs, through inspiration, teaching or preaching.[54] Albert the Great introduces the theme into his main discussion of faith in his Commentary on
the *Sentences*. He poses the question about someone before the coming
of Christ who follows the dictates of natural law and has heard nothing about a mediator. It is impossible, he answers, 'that there should be
someone who did what was in himself sufficiently to prepare himself,
and who did not receive a revelation from God, or a teaching from men
who had been inspired, or a sign of the mediator'.[55] Although Albert's
answer is definite, his main way of explaining salvation before the time
of Christ is in terms of implicit faith. The case is put forward here in a

---

[53] IIaIIe, inq. 3, tr. 2, sec. 1, q. 2, tit. 1, cap. 8 (n. 325); (Alexander of Hales) 1924–48,
III, 331.

[54] *De legibus*, chap. 21; William of Auvergne 1674, 58.

[55] Commentary on *Sentences* III, d. 25, a. 2, 6 and ad 6.

very hypothetical way, and the answer is not presented as if it provided a common route to Heaven.

Albert's pupil, Aquinas, follows him in introducing this discussion into his main treatment of faith in his own earliest major work, the commentary on the *Sentences* (1253–56). He does not limit himself to the period before Christ—indeed, he seems to be talking about a person who might be living in his own times who 'is born in the forest or among non-Christians (*infideles*)'. He states firmly that 'God never is or was lacking to a person who seeks him in what are necessary for salvation, except in so far is the person is to blame' and so to such a person he will provide the necessary knowledge either 'divinely' (by special inspiration) or through a preacher.[56] The same question is posed, and a similar answer given in the slightly later *Questions on Truth* (1256–59). But there is a small, though perhaps significant change. In his earlier work, by saying that the person in question might be anyone who grows up among non-Christians (and does not know about Christianity), Aquinas suggests that he is dealing with possibly a large class of people, but this phrase does not recur in the later work, which instead talks of someone 'brought up in the forest or *even among wolves*'—emphasizing that the circumstances are exceptional.[57] The discussion is absent from the *Summa Theologiae*, but it recurs in his commentary on the Pauline Epistles from the same period in the years just before his death in 1274. Here too it is just someone growing up 'in the forest' who is envisaged because, as he explains here, Aquinas believes that the Gospel has been preached to all peoples, though not to every individual member of them. The answer is the same as before except that an important qualification is added: 'But, however, the fact that some people do what is in them, that is to say, they turn themselves to God, comes from God who moves their hearts to the good'.[58] This qualification—about what, in any case, is presented as a very exceptional sort of case—removes much of the boldness from the special inspiration theory.[59]

As some of the quotations in the paragraphs above will have indicated, a phrase that often occurs in discussions of this theory of salvation is 'doing what is in oneself' (*faciens quod in se est*): those who 'do what is in them' will be given the means for salvation. The idea came to be summed up in the neat tag: *facientibus quod in se est, deus non denegat gratiam*

---

[56] Commentary on *Sentences* III, d. 25, q. 2, a. 1, qc. 1, arg 2 and ad 2. Durandus of St Pourçain (III, d. 25, q. 1, n.9; 1571, f. 258vb) writes in similar vein.

[57] *De veritate* q. 14, a. 11, arg 1 and ad 1. See Torrell 2006, 20–21 for a presentation of why Aquinas thought that, by his day, it was hard to find anyone who had not heard the Gospel.

[58] *On Romans* 10, lectio 3. See Capéran 1934, 196–97 for a discussion of Aquinas's position about the dissemination of the Gospel as indicated by this passage.

[59] See also Capéran 1934, 198–99 (who plays down the importance of Aquinas's qualification of his position) and McGrath 2005, 111–12 (who emphasizes the change).

('God does not deny grace to those who do what is in them'), which would have a long history in medieval theology.[60] It would be wrong, however, to gather that the special inspiration theory of salvation was, therefore, widespread, since usually the idea that God rewards those who 'do what is in them' is used in the context of those who are already Christians, in an attempt to make some link between desert and receiving grace which does not bind God or imply that grace can be earned. A reason for believing that, in the thirteenth and fourteenth centuries, little emphasis was placed on the special inspiration theory is provided by the treatment of a biblical episode which could be used to exemplify it—the story of Cornelius. Cornelius was a Roman centurion who, though apparently pagan, is described in Acts (chap. 10) as God-fearing, making many charitable gifts and always praying to God. Shortly after Christ's life, and when his followers are still all Jews, Cornelius is visited by an angel who tells him that his prayers and acts of charity 'are ascended for a memorial in the sight of God'. Peter is then sent to teach him about the faith and baptize him. As already mentioned, Abelard used the story precisely to illustrate the process by which a pagan, because of his moral goodness, could have Christianity revealed to him by a special, divinely directed minister: 'he had beforehand through natural law known and loved God, from which he merited to have his prayer heard and for his charity to be acceptable to God'.[61] Peter the Lombard, however, following Gregory the Great and Augustine, was anxious to avoid any suggestion that Cornelius had been rewarded for his goodness by faith since, as the celebrated verse from Hebrews insists (xi, 6) 'Without faith it is impossible to please God': faith cannot therefore be a reward for goodness, since it is required before God gives any reward. Peter the Lombard therefore goes further than his sources to suggest that Cornelius already knew 'by revelation from God' about the Incarnation, though not whether it had already taken place.[62] This interpretation of the Cornelius story, which removes the notion (central to Abelard's idea of special inspiration) that natural goodness can earn revelation, was widely accepted. But both Albert the Great and Thomas Aquinas say that, although in fact Cornelius already had explicit faith, it would have been sufficient for him to have implicit faith.[63] This is a strange comment, however, since implicit faith in the Incarnation is normally in itself sufficient for salvation, but only before the Gospel was preached. In general, it seems that Albert and Aquinas, but

[60]Landgraf 1952–56, I.1, 249–64 studies the early origins of the motto; see also Oberman 1963, 132–34.
[61]*Scito teipsum*; Peter Abelard 1971, 64.
[62]*Sentences* III, d. 25, chap. 4; Peter the Lombard 1971–81, II, 156–58.
[63]Albert, Commentary on *Sentences* III, d. 25, a. 8; Albert the Great 1890–99, XXVIII, 486; Aquinas, Commentary on *Sentences* III, d. 25, q. 2, a. 2, qc. 4, expos.

few other theologians, were sympathetic to the special inspiration theory, but unsure about it and not willing to place much weight on it.

There is also a third approach to be found in Aquinas specifically to the question about the salvation of a non-Christian *after* the Incarnation. Any Christian child coming to the age of reason would have been baptized and so would, at that stage, be free from Original Sin. Aquinas considers a non-Christian child, reaching this age, and asks whether he or she could ever be in the position of having only Original Sin (because this has not been removed by baptism) and venial, but not mortal sin. He says that

> before a person comes to the years of discretion, his lack of years, which prohibits the use of reason, excuses him from . . . sin. Now, when he begins to have the use of reason, he is not entirely excused from venial and mortal sin. But the first thing which it occurs to such a person to think about then, is to deliberate about himself. And if, indeed, he orders himself to the due end, the remission of Original Sin through grace will follow. If, however, he does not order himself to the due end, since at that age he is capable of discretion, he will sin mortally, not doing what is in him.[64]

In answering one of the arguments, Aquinas goes on to make clear what is involved in this 'ordering himself to the due end'. A person reaching the age of reason will be guilty of a mortal sin of omission, from which he will not be freed 'unless, as quickly as possible, he turns himself to God. For the first thing that happens to a person when he has discretion is that he thinks about himself, and he orders other things to himself as the end'.[65]

This can hardly be called a theory of Aquinas's about the salvation of pagans. It is an incidental idea, which Aquinas had already mentioned early in his career, but treated even more incidentally then, giving it in a three-line answer to an objection. But in later centuries it would become an important *Thomistic* contribution to the discussion of pagan salvation.[66]

The Salvation of Pagans in Practice: The Philosophers, Aristotle and Trajan

The theories about the salvation of pagans leave it very unclear who might in fact have been saved: the patriarchs of Genesis certainly, but

---

[64] *Summa Theologiae* IaIIe q. 89, a. 6; cf. Commentary on *Sentences* II, d. 42, q. 1, a. 5 ad7).

[65] *Summa Theologiae* IaIIe, q. 89, a. 6, ad 3.

[66] See below, chapter 14.

what about the Greek and Roman philosophers? And what, in practice rather than principle, about pagans living in Christian times? There are a few discussions of the salvation of the ancient philosophers, and of the famous case of Trajan, a pagan who lived after Christ, which throw light on thirteenth- and fourteenth-century views.

The theory of implicit faith, as developed by Hugh of St Victor, was ill-suited to apply to pagans outside the biblical framework, since it envisages a class of 'greater ones' with prophetic, explicit knowledge of Christ. Even for a pagan such as Job there would be the same difficulty. The *Summa Fratris Alexandri* turns, rather, to the special inspiration theory (with scripture as one of its possible vehicles) in order to save some of the ancient philosophers. Answering the question of whether these philosophers would all be damned, because the Incarnation was not revealed to them, the authors explain that the philosophers divide into the bad ones, who were inflated with pride, as Paul says in Romans, and who are damned, and the good ones, about whom they suggest that that 'a revelation was made to them, either through Scripture, which the Jews had, or through prophecy or through internal inspiration, as was the case for Job and his friends'.[67]

By contrast, Bonaventure is happy to conclude from the fact that none of the philosophers had even implicit faith in the mediator, but rather 'held on to their merits and virtues', that they were accordingly 'separated from the members and merits of Christ, as proud people, and excluded from the joys of paradise'.[68] Bonaventure's insistence on the damnation of the philosophers is firm: in his late *Collationes* on the *Hexaemeron*, where he makes a distinction between philosophers who taught misleading doctrine (such as Aristotle) and the ones who were illuminated, he maintains that even these ones went to Hell.[69] Bonaventure's stern views commanded support among other Franciscans in the late thirteenth century. For example, in his *Questions on Faith*, Matthew of Aquasparta responds unhesitatingly to the argument that the philosophers reached what was needed for salvation, because they had perfect knowledge, and so would have acted with perfect virtue: the philosophers had merely worldly wisdom and, although he accepts (with almost everyone of his time) that they had 'political virtues', he explains that these were not true virtues; salvation is beyond the limits of human nature and so, without the guidance of divine illumination, the philosophers could not direct themselves to it or act in a way which would lead to it.[70]

[67] *Summa Fratris Alexandri* III, inq. 3, q. 2, tit. 3, pars 2 (n. 707); (Alexander of Hales) 1924–48, IV, 1141.

[68] Commentary on *Sentences* III, d. 25, a. 1, q. 2; Bonaventure 1882–1902, III, 541.

[69] See chapter 8.

[70] *Quaestiones disputatae* 3, 14 and ad 14; Matthew of Aquasparta 1903, 104–5.

With one exception, the most generous of the thirteenth-century theologians towards the ancient philosophers was Aquinas.[71] He sets his views out in greatest detail in his *Sentences* commentary, and repeats the main lines of them in the rather later *Questions on Truth*.[72] Like Abelard before him and Robert Holcot and Thomas Bradwardine in the following century, he believes that prophetic knowledge of Christ was to some extent available to non-Jews, as the example of the Sibyls show (and he also cites a Roman miracle in which Christ's coming is prophesied). But he accepts that there were some to whom no special revelation was made, and he puts forward a way in which they were able to be saved by implicit faith. On the one hand, they did not sin by failing to follow the Old Law, which, unlike the New Law, applied only to the Jews. On the other hand, as he puts it in the *Questions on Truth*, the philosophers should not, despite their worldly wisdom, be thought of as instructors in the divine faith, and so they can be considered among the lesser ones, for whom implicit faith is enough. But in whom was their faith implicit? He answers in the *Sentences* commentary that it was implicit 'in the cognition of God' (in *Questions on Truth* 'divine providence') or 'of those who were taught by God—whoever they might be, indeterminately (just as the greater ones among the Jews so far as those things which had not yet been revealed to them were concerned), so long as they did not pertinaciously hold themselves against the preaching of the faith'.[73] It was enough, then, for pagan philosophers who believed in God, as they did, to accept as their own belief whatever God himself knew about the truth, or it was sufficient for them to say that they accepted as their own the belief of whoever it might be who knew more of God's ways than they did.

Occasionally, a thinker would not confine himself, as Aquinas does, to considering the general possibility of the salvation of ancient philosophers, but would hazard an opinion about one in particular. The figure who held particular fascination was Aristotle, because of the dominant position of his writings in the universities. To us today Aristotle seems to have been very far in his views from Christianity—much further in many

[71] The exception is his teacher, Albert the Great. It is argued very plausibly (Anzulewicz 2012, 78–83) that Albert thought that the souls of those philosophers who had achieved union with the agent intellect could enjoy happiness after their bodily death, although he distinguished this state from the salvation to be gained by Christians.

[72] Commentary on *Sentences* III, d. 25, q. 2, a. 2, qc. 2, 3 and ad 3; *De veritate* q. 14, a. 11, 5 and ad 5.

[73] In the *Questions on Truth* he merely says 'in the faith of the Law and the prophets'. This formulation sounds fantastical at first sight—it is as if Aquinas believed that Plato or Aristotle said, 'I put my faith in the Jewish prophets or the Jewish law'. But the Commentary on the *Sentences* explains what is behind this idea. The people in whom the philosophers put their faith are, in fact, the Jewish prophets, but the philosophers do not know this—they simply put their faith in whoever knows the ways of God better than they do.

ways than Plato—and so an unlikely candidate to pick out especially for salvation. But, as the last chapter showed, Aristotle's views were thought, especially in the first two-thirds of the thirteenth century, to accord with Christianity on the immortality of the soul and to a considerable extent on the nature of God; even the eternity of the universe was usually thought to be a view Aristotle did not definitively hold.[74] Aristotle's suitability as a candidate for salvation was raised further by two rather strange works associated with him. The *Secret of Secrets* is a Mirror-for-Princes-cum-astrological-treatise, translated from the Arabic, which was attributed to Aristotle and was immensely popular inside and beyond the universities from the thirteenth century, when it was first completely translated into Latin.[75] Its preface is full of the most extravagant praise of Aristotle, such as that God called him an angel rather than a human, and that he ascended into Heaven in a column of fire. The other text is *The Book of the Apple*, written originally in Arabic, and then translated into Hebrew and thence into Latin in about 1255.[76] Also widely read, it presents Aristotle in a death-bed dialogue, modelled on Plato's *Phaedo*, in which the philosopher upholds the immortality of the soul, denies the eternity of the world, and which ends with the comment from those assembled: 'May he who gathers the souls of philosophers gather your soul and place it in his treasury, as is worthy for the soul of an upright and perfect man, as you are'.[77]

Roger Bacon was so impressed by the *Secret of Secrets* that he prepared his own edition of it, with glosses; it dates from about 1275, though Bacon was by then elderly and his thinking is closer to that of the 1250s. He reacts to the idea that Aristotle ascended to Heaven by explaining that 'this is the view of the pagan philosophers, but it is not permitted to us Christians to think or affirm this, because he could not have been saved unless he had the faith of Christ revealed or was instructed by the prophets'. He goes on to say that 'we do not know what God did to him and other worthy prophets and philosophers to whom he gave mighty works of wisdom'. The gloss then makes the case that knowledge of the Trinity was widespread among the philosophers, and

[74]The relation between the question of Aristotle's salvation and the views he was supposed to have held is discussed in detail in von Moos 2013a, in connection with Lambertus de Monte (on whom see below, chapter 14), and in the essays in Bianchi 2011 (the editor's introduction provides a useful survey of recent scholarship).
[75]See Schmitt and Knox 1985, 54–75 and Williams 2003.
[76]Edited in Plezia 1960; Schmitt and Knox 1985, 51–52. It is translated in Rousseau 1968, and there is a German translation, along with the Latin text, introduction and additional material in Acampora-Michel 2001. The Hebrew and then Latin texts abridge and alter the original, which is more faithfully represented by a Persian translation, an English version of which is reproduced in Rousseau 1968, 60–76.
[77]Plezia 1960, 64.

that Aristotle had an even better grasp of this mystery than Plato; and some of the philosophers also knew about Christ. Still, he concludes that they merely had 'some preludes of faith, but that we ought not to claim that they had sufficient faith, nor however should we affirm the damnation of a number of very worthy men, because we do not know what God has done with them, even though, just like the blessed Job, they were not under the Old Law'.[78]

Early in the fourteenth century, an anonymous writer, probably a Franciscan, wrote a *quaestio* on 'Whether Aristotle is saved'.[79] The single argument for the positive answer is provided by the *Book of the Apple*: according to it, Aristotle preached the truth, and so it can be argued that he will be saved. The author answers it by rejecting the authenticity of that work—and he also rejects the comments in the preface to the *Secret of Secrets* which have Aristotle taken to Heaven or compared to an angel: that book too is not authentic and no trust should be placed in it.[80] Most of the *quaestio* is concerned, following the lead of Duns Scotus, and the more general movement of thinking after the time of Aquinas and Albert, with the limitations of natural knowledge in general, and in particular of Aristotle's grasp of the truth—he is said, for example, to have been uncertain about whether there is an afterlife.[81] So far from Aristotle's having come near to grasping Christian truths, this theologian collects comments from Augustine to suggest that he was an idolater and so clearly condemned to Hell.

The case of Trajan differed sharply from Aristotle's, not just because he lived in Christian times, but more importantly because his post-mortem destiny was supposedly known, from the story of Pope Gregory's intervention.[82] In the form in which the legend was found in Latin Europe up to the mid-twelfth century, going back to the Whitby *Life*, there was room to argue, as John the Deacon had done, that he had not actually been saved. By contrast, most, though not all, discussions of Trajan from after 1200 assume that he has been saved—the result perhaps of a newly available Greek sermon, misattributed to John of Damascus, which indicates his salvation rather less equivocally.[83] When, as they usually do,

---

[78] Roger Bacon 1920, 36–37.

[79] The text is edited, with an introduction and commentary, in Imbach 1994. See also Chroust 1945.

[80] *Utrum Aristotiles*, 0.2; III.2, 4; Imbach 1994, 304, 309–10.

[81] *Utrum Aristotiles*, II.5; Imbach 1994, 308.

[82] Gordon Whatley (1984b, 36–40) provides a very thorough and finely analysed account of how the story of Trajan was used in his period, but I am wary of his distinction between a 'hagiographical' and a 'humanist' side to the legend.

[83] For the sermon, see *PG* 95, 247–78 at 262D–63A. God's voice says that he 'grants pardon' to Trajan. This version was already known by Hugh Etherianus in about 1170 (*Liber de anima corpore exuta*, *PL* 202, 200); it is cited explicitly on this subject (as the work of

these theologians and other writers hold that Trajan was saved, most explain that he was first recalled to life and then was able to be saved. Whilst Philip the Chancellor, writing in 1225–28, does not say anything to indicate such a revivification, and the *Summa Fratris Alexandri* seems to rule out in principle anything but a suspension of punishment for such souls, William of Auxerre, writing at much the same time in his *Summa Aurea* (1215–29) talks of Trajan as someone who was 'neither absolutely and irrevocably saved or damned' but was 'revived and called back to the state of the present life by the prayers of the blessed Gregory'.[84] The resuscitation version of the story became that most commonly followed by theologians, including William of Auvergne (c. 1240), Aquinas, Albert the Great and, in the early fourteenth century, Durandus of St Pourçain. Other versions of the story were also considered. On one of the two occasions when he raises it in his *Sentences* commentary, Aquinas mentions the possibility that Trajan's soul was not absolved from guilt and so from eternal punishment, but merely that his punishment was suspended (an idea John the Deacon had suggested), and only until the Day of Judgement.[85] The very widely read *Golden Legend*, by Jacob of Voragine (before 1267), gives the resuscitation story, as the view of some, but also three other views about what happened, all them involving the remission of his punishment: according to the first, punishment was suspended until the Day of Judgement (apparently following Aquinas); according to the second, attributed to John the Deacon, who is cited explicitly, he remains in Hell but does not feel its tortures; according to the third, 'eternal punishment consists in two things, the punishment of the senses and the punishment of loss, which is being without the vision of God': Trajan was spared the first, but remained subject to the second.[86]

Despite this variety, there is in fact a large measure of agreement among thirteenth-century authors over the Trajan story. Almost all consider that Trajan's soul was not simply transferred from Hell to Heaven (as John of Salisbury had probably held).[87] This attitude is not surprising

---

the Damascene, by Aquinas [Commentary on *Sentences* IV, d. 45, q. 2, a. 2, qc. 1, ad 5; *De veritate* q. 6, a. 6, ad 4]).

[84] Philip the Chancellor, *Summa de bono* III, q. XVI; Philip the Chancellor 1985, I, 150–51; *Summa Fratris Alexandri* I, 1, tr. 4, q. 2 membrum 2, cap. 2; (Alexander of Hales) 1924–48, I, 221, talking in general of those 'freed from Hell through the prayers of the saints'; *Summa Aurea* I, tr. 11, cap. 5; William of Auxerre 1980–87, 211–13; see also IV, chap. 4, q. 1, a. 1; William of Auxerre 1980–87, 527–39.

[85] Commentary on *Sentences* IV, d. 45, q. 2, a. 2, ad 5 (Aquinas refers to the resuscitation version of the story at Commentary on *Sentences* I, d. 43, q. 2, a. 2, qc. 1, ad 5 and briefly, without making it clear which version, at *De veritate*, q. 6, a. 6, 4 and ad 4.)

[86] *Legenda aurea* 46; Jacob of Voragine 1890, 196–97.

[87] Durandus of St Pourçain, probably writing early in the next century, gives the resuscitation story, but also mentions that his pardon might be considered 'a singular privilege

in view of another common feature of these accounts. Trajan is not regarded, as he clearly was by Abelard and John of Salisbury, as a virtuous
pagan, but as a wicked one. The change may well be due to the pseudo-
Damascenian text, which talks of Trajan being redeemed despite his having been responsible for putting to death many Christian martyrs (Aquinas and Jacob of Voragine both mention this point). Moreover, the story
of Trajan and the widow, which illustrates his justice, is not mentioned
in the theological discussions, although perhaps it was known. It makes
sense, then, that William of Auvergne should envisage the resuscitation as
the beginning of an extended second life, lasting 'many years', in which
'doing penitence for his vices and for the sins of idolatry in which he
had lived, he became a Christian and placated his creator with regard
to himself and, finally, brought his life to the best close'—that is to say,
he died in a state of grace.[88] Indeed, the theologians do not bring up the
story of Trajan in connection with the post-mortem fate of pagans. The
context is sometimes that of the efficacy of prayer and its limits, and more
often that of divine justice in relation to divine power, encapsulated in the
question of whether God could damn Peter (the worthiest of the disciples,
who is Heaven) and save Judas (Christ's betrayer, who is in Hell). Trajan
appears as an example of someone who goes from Hell to Heaven, but
the resuscitation story shows why this is not contrary to divine justice,
since he gains salvation only when he dies a second time in a state worthy of it.

After Ockham: Holcot and the Augustinian Revival

It has been argued that Ockham and the next generation of English theologians, in particular Robert Holcot, put forward a more optimistic view
about the salvation of virtuous pagans than their predecessors, basing
themselves on the idea that God does not deny grace to those who do
what is in them.[89] But Holcot's positions on pagan virtues and salvation seem, in fact, to have been little different from those held by many
thirteenth-century writers, except perhaps for being less clear. He accepts

of divine grace from which no consequences can be drawn' (Commentary—third redac-
tion—on the *Sentences* IV, d. 45, q. 2; Durandus of St Pourçain 1571, 405v–6v). Even if
this second suggestion would involve Trajan's going straight from Hell to Heaven, it is not
at all because of his own virtues—Durandus mentions that he put many martyrs painfully
to death.

[88]William of Auvergne 1674, II (supplementum) 190a; cf. Whatley 1984b, 39.

[89]This view has been especially popular among specialists in Middle English literature,
giving the background to the work of Chaucer and Langland: to name just two of the most
widely-learned, see Coleman 1981a, esp. 117–26; 1981b, 249–51; Minnis 1982.

the anti-Augustinian view held by most since the time of Aquinas, that pagans can be genuinely good when they perform acts such as feeding the hungry and clothing the naked. He even says that they are 'meritorious', but he immediately adds that what is merited is 'not eternal life but a lessening of eternal punishment or good in this life'—something even Augustine would have accepted.[90] In his commentary on the *Sentences*, he distinguishes between some philosophers 'who practised the worship of God according to various rites and declarations and were saved' and others who, as described by Paul in Romans, despite their knowledge of God indulged in wicked behaviour and turned to idolatry.[91] Holcot goes so far as to name some individual philosophers and groups: Socrates, Plato, Aristotle and many of the Stoics (and he also mentions Job), but he does not say exactly *how* they were saved.

Does he, then, like the authors of the *Summa Fratris Alexandri* a century earlier, believe that the philosophers were saved by some sort of special inspiration? A passage from the Commentary on Wisdom may seem to indicate so:

> God will communicate a sufficient knowledge of himself, enough for them to be saved, to those who behave innocently towards God and strive to use their natural reason, and do not offer an obstacle to divine grace. There are examples of this—the example of Cornelius, to whom Peter was sent, and Paul, to whom Ananias was sent, who so disposed themselves that they merited having a revelation or an inspiration of the one God. And so it should be said that it will never happen that a man who has the use of reason will, without fault, lack knowledge of God, at least as much as is necessary for salvation.[92]

In context, however, this passage must refer just to some exceptional cases. As already indicated, Holcot had a different way of explaining how the ancient philosophers could have had the knowledge they needed in order to be saved: through their acquaintance with the revealed teaching given to the patriarchs of Genesis and the Old Testament Jews.[93] His references to special inspiration seem, then, to be designed to take care of special cases where, for some reason, a person was not taught externally about God. And, just because special inspiration fills in any possible gap

---

[90] *De imputabilitate peccati*, answer to tenth principal point; Robert Holcot 1518 (unnumbered folios).

[91] Commentary on *Sentences* III, q. 1 (quartum dictum; TT); Robert Holcot 1518 (unnumbered folios).

[92] Commentary on Wisdom, lectio 155; Robert Holcot 1489, Liii ra (for this passage, there is a better text, which I have used, from Oxford, Balliol College 27 in Smalley 1960, 327).

[93] See above, chapter 8.

in the knowledge available before the coming of Christ, Holcot can also use the principle that God does not deny grace to those who do what is in them negatively. The fact that some people did not know what is necessary for salvation is evidence of their moral fault—not doing what is in them—because otherwise God *would have* ensured they did not lack this knowledge.[94]

A far more generous attitude to the salvation of pagans is found in the work of a contemporary of Holcot's, who shared and took further the idea of a tradition of revealed knowledge. Bradwardine is usually contrasted with Holcot, since he was one of the fiercest representatives of an Augustinian reaction to the teaching about natural virtue and grace held by many in the early fourteenth century, including Holcot. A central theme in this reaction was the rejection of any attempt to lessen the gratuity of grace and suggest that, in a certain way (*de congruo*), those out of a state of grace could earn merit.[95] Although Bradwardine's main concern here was with Christians, it also led him back to Augustine's own black-and-white division between true Christian and false pagan virtue. 'No philosophical or moral virtue is true virtue, right without qualification, without being perfected by charity and grace. . . . No deed by anyone which does not have the true virtue of charity and grace, is without qualification virtuous, right or just; on the contrary, any such deed is in some way a sin'.[96] Bradwardine may be a little more qualified than Augustine himself, but he goes on to accept literally the very passages from *Against Julianus* that Aquinas and Henry of Ghent had interpreted away. And, where Ockham made a place for a pagan heroic virtue, Bradwardine considers that Aristotle must have had true Christian virtue in mind when he mentioned it.[97]

Yet, despite this Augustinian assessment of pagan virtues as false, Bradwardine turns out to have an extremely generous view about the salvation of pagans, based on his idea of their access to ancient revelation. It is, indeed, an Augustinian theme that some people, at all times and in all races, are among the elect, but Bradwardine is unlike Augustine in that he apparently considers such salvation widespread. Moreover, he differs from almost every other medieval writer by not simply condemning those

[94] For further discussion of Holcot's views about pagans, see Marenbon 2005. Such negative, hypothetical uses of the principle became common in the sixteenth century: see below, chapter 14.

[95] *De causa Dei*, chap. 39; Thomas Bradwardine 1618, 325–64. On merit *de congruo*, see above, introduction, note 11.

[96] *De causa Dei*, chap. 39; Thomas Bradwardine 1618, 327CD.

[97] *De causa Dei*, chap. 39; Thomas Bradwardine 1618, 327D. For the approving citation of *Against Julianus*, see 327E—328.

pagans who were idolaters, but finding a way to explain their idolatry as a sort of true worship. He explains that, in the same way as 'we Christians adore images' of Christ, God and the saints, so they may have been worshipping idols not for themselves, but for God: some of the idolaters, he conjectures, may have known God but worshipped 'the highest God under the name and through the idol of Jupiter'.[98] Even though, Bradwardine continues, their way of worship was defective, this was a result of ignorance, not malice, and so it is reasonable to think that God accepted their 'sincere love, holy intention, and benevolent wish'. These considerations lead Bradwardine to state that 'I believe firmly that God, who is pious and just, reveals at some time to a person who loves him before all other things and who efficaciously wishes to venerate him through worship and through what is due, and who perseveres in offering the diligence which is due, the religion which is due and necessary for salvation, that is, the Christian religion, implicitly or expressly'.[99] Given Bradwardine's very clearly and frequently expressed condemnation of any idea that grace could be earned, or that humans could, through their natural abilities, love God beyond all things, this statement should not be taken to mean that pagans, acting well according from their unaided natural powers, were rewarded by God with the revelation by which they could be saved, but rather that God graced many apparent pagans. His comment also differs from the usual special inspiration theory by allowing that the faith inspired might be merely implicit (and, presumably, that even so it would be sufficient for salvation). This concession made it much easier to hold, as Bradwardine did, that such special inspiration was widespread, in spite of the lack of evidence for explicit faith (and even in spite of the evidence for idolatry, given Bradwardine's indulgent views about it). Bradwardine's position shows that there was no necessary link between being 'anti-Pelagian' (as he described it) and holding that many ancient pagans were saved.

In the period after Bradwardine, the two opposing tendencies in his thought about pagans were championed (though without obviously direct connection with him) by two different thinkers. Uthred of Boldon (d. 1396) a Benedictine monk, took to an extreme his view that many pagans are among the saved. But, whereas Bradwardine had used and extended a traditional Augustinian explanation and seems to have been thinking

---

[98] *De causa Dei*, chap. 1—corollarium, 32; Thomas Bradwardine 1618, 61B. The Mandeville author, writing a decade or so later than Bradwardine, would offer a charitable, but less boldly excusing, view of idolatry. It is not until Las Casas, in the sixteenth century, that a similar attempt to see idolatry as a way of worshipping God is made, and even then it is carefully qualified: see chapter 12.

[99] *De causa Dei*, chap. 1—corollarium, 32; Thomas Bradwardine 1618, 62D.

just of antiquity, Uthred brings salvation into the reach of contemporary pagans (and Jews and Muslims), through an innovative but theologically problematic idea. At the moment of death, every soul—including those of newborn and unborn babies—is given a clear vision of God: all who accept God at this point are saved, whatever their previous faith; those who reject God are damned. Few details of the theory survive. It does avoid the unfairness of people being condemned to Hell for no reason other than where or when they were born, and this consideration may well have motivated Uthred's line of thought. But theologically it wreaks havoc on the doctrine of baptism (as Uthred admits), and philosophically it leaves unexplained how and why someone would ever reject God in a clear vision, and how this choice is linked to his or her previous life. Uthred's views were duly condemned by the Archbishop of Canterbury; they had only limited publicity and were quickly forgotten.[100]

By contrast, Gregory of Rimini (c. 1300–1358) would be read until the sixteenth century—the Augustinian against whom Thomists pitched their very different views about salvation. Like Bradwardine, he condemned as Pelagians those recent thinkers who in any way compromised the gratuity of grace.[101] Again, like Bradwardine, he accepted Augustine's position in *Against Julianus* and others of his late works that non-Christians can do nothing genuinely good, and consequently their virtues are not true virtues. Although he constantly uses Augustine as an authority to back up this position, Gregory reaches it through reasoning, supported by Aristotle and other philosophers, from what he takes to be self-evident premises.[102] To be morally good, an act must be in accord with right reason. An act is not, however, in accord with right reason if it is failing in any of its due circumstances, and the most important of these is its intention. An act's intention is the will for its end, and the end—so Gregory contends all those discussing the problem accept—is the final end 'for which something is willed and which itself is willed only for its own sake'. This final end is love of God for his own sake. From this reasoning, Gregory contends, it follows that 'no act of those who are without qualification non-Christians . . . is morally good. This is clear, because no act ‹by such people› is done from love of God or finally for the sake of God, because they do not know that he is to be loved for himself and all other things for him'.[103] Gregory goes on to emphasize the position that pagan virtues are not true virtues in the most uncompromising way,

[100] See Knowles 1951.

[101] *Lectura* on *Sentences* II, d. 26–28; Gregory of Rimini 1980, 17–114.

[102] *Lectura* on *Sentences* II, d. 38–41, q. 1; Gregory of Rimini 1980, 281–315.

[103] *Lectura* on *Sentences* II, d. 38–41, q. 1; Gregory of Rimini 1980, 311:29–34; cf. 310:23–313:4.

emphasizing Augustine's points where so many thirteenth-century theologians had tried to soften them. They do not even, he contends, have true political virtues, because their dispositions with regard to political life are imperfect in their kind.[104] Although his doctrinal framework is similar to Bradwardine's, for him neither is God's grace much at work in the ancient world, nor revelation there widespread.[105]

---

[104] *Lectura* on *Sentences* II, d. 38–41, q. 1; Gregory of Rimini 1980, 314:21–33.
[105] See, for example, *Lectura* on *Sentences* II, d. 26–28, q. 1; Gregory of Rimini 1980, 74:12–75:30, 80:8–81:8.

CHAPTER 10

Dante and Boccaccio

DANTE'S VIRGIL INTRODUCED THIS WHOLE STUDY, BECAUSE HE EPITO-
mizes the Problem of Paganism. In his great poem, the *Divine Comedy*,
begun near the beginning of the fourteenth century and finished near to
the time of his death in 1321, Dante describes his journey through the
three realms of the world to come, Hell, Purgatory and Heaven, where
souls (those of ancients, figures from history and his contemporaries) are
punished or rewarded according to the way they lived their lives on earth.
Virgil is his guide for more than half of this journey, and Dante's reverence for him could not be greater. Yet, as soon as he is introduced, Virgil
is made to explain that he will lead Dante through Hell and Purgatory,
but then his place will be taken by a worthier guide because

> . . . quello imperador che là sù regna,
>   perch'i' fu' ribellante a la sua legge,
> non vuol che 'n sua città per me si vegna.

> *The emperor who reigns up there because I was a rebel to his law*
> *does not want his city to be entered by me.*[1]

The indication here that Virgil is a rebel to God's law and so among the
damned is confirmed in the next canto, when he places himself among
those who are *sospesi*—suspended in the Limbo of Hell.[2] It quickly

---

[1] *Inferno* I, 124–26. It would be a pity to substitute even the best English translation for
the eloquent precision of Dante's verse. The *Commedia* is therefore quoted in the original
(the text is Petrocchi's, in Dante 1966–67, as reprinted in Dante 1991–94, the best of the
commented versions available), followed by my own literal English translation. Both the
Convivio and the *Monarchia* are cited according to standard book, chapter and section
numbers. There are new critical texts of each, published by the Società Dantesca Italiana:
Dante Alighieri 1995, ed. Franca Ageno (*Convivio*); Dante Alighieri 2009, ed. Prue Shaw
(*Monarchia*). For the *Convivio*, the commentaries by Cesare Vasoli (in Dante Alighieri
1988) and by Francis Cheneval, Thomas Ricklin and Ruedi Imbach (in Dante Alighieri
1996–2004) are particularly valuable, and for the *Monarchia* that by Ruedi Imbach and
Christoph Flüeller in Dante Alighieri 1989. English translations of all these works are available (including ones freely downloadable from the web).
[2] *Inferno* II, 52.

becomes clear that Virgil is not an unlucky exception. Hardly any pagans from Graeco-Roman antiquity are in Heaven, or in Purgatory (and so on their way to Heaven). Many readers of Dante, and even Dante scholars, unfamiliar with discussions of the Problem of Paganism in other texts, assume that Dante is simply putting forward what they regard as the standard medieval Christian view: that pagans, even those who lived before Christ, are damned. For anyone who has read this book up to here, however, it will be clear that this was by no means a standard position, and that it was usually avoided by those who, like Dante, knew and admired classical antiquity. Augustine was an exception to this rule, but he condemned the ancient pagans to Hell because he believed that even the best of them had only apparent virtues, not real ones. By contrast, for Dante, it will become clear, Virgil and many other ancient pagans were genuinely and outstandingly virtuous—and yet they are in Hell.

So far from presenting a standard view, Dante's position is then unusual and, at first sight, highly paradoxical: it is discussed in detail in the two sections which follow. The chapter will then go on to explain why he adopted it, by looking at Dante's attitude to pagan wisdom and its relation to Christianity, especially his adoption, but transformation, of the position of limited relativism which strictly separates the spheres of philosophical enquiry and Christian doctrine. The damnation of virtuous pagans turns out to be the price required by this approach, which remains deliberately paradoxical, despite Dante's innovation of placing them in a special part of Hell, where there are no physical torments.[3] The final section of the chapter looks at another aspect of Dante's discussion of paganism, his treatment of Epicurus and his followers, and links it to a comparison with his great admirer and commentator, Boccaccio.

Virtuous Pagans in Hell

Wicked pagans, of course, as well as many Christians are placed by Dante into one or another of the circles of Hell where sins of a particular sort are punished: Alexander and Dionysius of Syracuse, for instance, among the tyrants, Brutus and Cassius, with the betrayers, Diomedes and, less

---

[3] The fate of Virgil and other virtuous pagans in the prose works and the *Commedia* has been much discussed by Dante scholars. Some of the most important detailed work is found in the commentaries mentioned in note 1 above: in addition Padoan 1977; Foster 1977, 156–253; and Carron 2010, 884–901. A particularly detailed and careful treatment is given in Corbett 2013, 122–73. Like me, he sees a close connection between the position of the virtuous pagans and what he calls Dante's 'dualism'—his sharp distinction between the ends of earthly and heavenly happiness.

obviously perhaps, Ulysses with the fraudsters.[4] Virgil and those like him
are in a different position. They are in Hell: in a specially privileged part
of it, the 'Limbo', that is to say the margin, but it is Hell, none the less.
The figures named as being there along with Virgil fall into three groups:
four other great poets of antiquity (Homer, Horace, Ovid and Lucan);[5]
heroes and heroines from Roman history, and its Trojan prehistory (with
the one exceptional addition of the chivalrous crusading Sultan of Egypt,
Saladin);[6] and the ancient philosophers—at their head, and named merely
as 'the Master of those who know', Aristotle, close by him Socrates, Plato
and a group of pre-Socratic philosophers Dante would have known
through doxographies, Cicero, Seneca, Euclid, Ptolemy, Hippocrates,
Galen and two recent Islamic Aristotelian philosophers, Avicenna and
Averroes.[7]

Although the life stories of some of the Roman characters, such as
Lucretia (whose suicide Augustine had condemned) and Julius Caesar,
might suggest otherwise, Dante presents all the inhabitants of Limbo as
virtuous pagans in a very strong sense—as exemplified by their spokes-
man, Virgil. For, as he explains, they are not guilty of any of the sins
for which other souls are being punished: their only sin is not to have
had faith.

Dante makes this point most clearly in a passage from *Purgatorio*,
when Virgil explains to the poet Sordello,

> Io son Virgilio; e per null' altro rio
>   lo ciel perdei che per non aver fé.
>
> . . .
>
> Non per far, ma per non fare ho perduto
>   a veder l'alto Sol che tu disiri
>   e che fu tardi per me conosciuto.

> *I am Virgil, and I have lost heaven for no other fault than through
> not having faith. . . . Not for doing, but for not doing I have lost the
> chance to see the high Sun, which you desire and which was known
> by me too late.*

[4] *Inferno* XII, 107–8; XXXIV, 64–67; XXVI.
[5] *Inferno* IV, 88–90. To this group Dante and most of his contemporaries would add
another, Statius, to whom Dante gives a special, happier fate: see below, pp. 194–95. In his
conversation with Statius (*Purgatorio* XXII, 97–114), Virgil names some further ancient
poets, heroes and heroines who are in Limbo.
[6] *Inferno* IV, 121–29.
[7] *Inferno* IV, 130–44.

And he goes on to say that he is in Limbo along with

> . . . quei che le tre sante
> virtù non si vestiro, e sanza vizio
> conobber l'altre e seguir tutte quante.

> . . . *who were not clothed with the three sacred virtues, and without
> vice knew the others and followed them all.*[8]

It seems most unlikely that Dante has put misleading information into
Virgil's mouth, and so these comments show that, in his view, the virtuous pagans were indeed virtuous—as he says, they lacked the theological
virtues of faith, hope and charity, but followed the cardinal virtues without vice. They are damned, not for anything they did, but for something
they failed to do—to have Christian faith; but this omission is not itself
to be considered a sin, since we are told clearly that 'they did not sin'.
This point should be stressed, because most theologians who hand over
the virtuous pagans to damnation make it clear that they were not really
virtuous.[9]

The genuine virtuousness Dante attributes to these pagans is closely
linked to his central political idea. The Roman Empire, Dante believed,
was the ideal political society, and his aspiration was for universal rule to
be restored under a new Roman emperor. The Empire had been founded
on right and through divine providence, as the birth of Christ (and
Mary's participation in the census) in the reign of Augustus, Rome's apo-
gee, indicates. This theme is important in the *Divine Comedy*, and was
already announced in the earlier *Convivio* and developed most explicitly
in the *Monarchia*.[10] Although the *City of God* is one of his main sources
for Roman history, Dante reconstructs—with the help of late ancient and
medieval intermediaries—the heroic story which Augustine had taken
apart and exposed as deceitful.[11] Not surprisingly, the Romans who carried out these rightful and divinely sanctioned conquests are portrayed
by Dante as showing outstanding virtue and, just as in Abelard, any

---

[8] *Purgatorio* VII, 7–8, 25–27, 34–36.

[9] See Corbett 2013, 124–25 for a well-drawn contrast between Aquinas's position, according to which no adult, without grace, can be without sin except for original sin, and
cf. chapter 8.

[10] *Convivio* IV.5; *Monarchia* II. On the endorsement of the rightfulness of the Roman
Empire by Christ's time of birth and Mary's participation in the census (which Dante conjectures may have been divinely inspired through Caesar), see *Monarchia* II.10.

[11] For the use of Augustine and the intermediaries, who include Augustine's contemporary, Orosius, and Dante's (probable) master, the Dominican Remigio de' Girolami, see
Davis 1957, 40–86.

suggestion that they acted through vainglory is removed.[12] It is no accident, then, that the virtuous pagans Dante singles out for mention, except for the great poets and philosophers, are from the extended Roman history presented in the *Aeneid*, nor that their special representative is its author, Virgil.

An earlier passage, where Virgil is addressing Dante when they arrive at Limbo, as well as confirming these pagans' lack of moral fault, attempts to give a theological account of why they are, none the less, denied salvation:

> Or vo' che sappi, innanzi che più andi,
>
> ch'ei non peccaro; e s'elli hanno mercedi,
>   non basta, perché non ebber battesmo,
>   ch'è porta de la fede che tu credi;
>
> e s'e' furon dinanzi al cristianesmo,
>   non adorar debitamente a Dio:
>   e di questi cotai son io medesmo.
>
> Per tai difetti, non per altro rio,
>   semo perduti, e sol di tanto offesi
>   che sanza speme vivemo in disio.

> *Now I want you to know, before you go further, that they did not sin, and though they have merit, it is not sufficient, because they did not have baptism, which is the door of the faith which you believe; and if they were before Christianity, they did not worship God duly. And I myself am one of these. For such defects and through no other fault, we are lost and afflicted only in this, that we live in desire without hope.*[13]

This passage explains that, if the pagans lived after the coming of Christ, then they lacked baptism; if they came before, then they did not worship God duly (*debitamente*). After Christianity was preached, baptism was considered to be a requirement for salvation—though medieval theologians accepted that someone who desired baptism, but was prevented from undergoing the physical ceremony, could be considered to be baptized. Before the preaching of Christianity, the people of the early chapters of Genesis, and then the Jews, were generally considered to have had ceremonies—sacrifices and then circumcision for males and the rites of

---

[12] *Convivio* IV.5.10–20; *Monarchia* II.5.8–17.
[13] *Inferno* IV, 33–42.

the Jewish Law, which had the function which baptism would hold of reconciling humans with God and making their salvation possible (although they could not actually go to Heaven until, at his Resurrection, Christ released them from Hell).[14] When Dante says that they did not worship God duly, he seems to be pointing out that the virtuous pagans did not follow these rites.

Looking at Dante's Limbo against the background of the theology of his time, there is an obvious omission. During the thirteenth century, as explained above, a doctrine of implicit faith had been developed, which would have provided a simple way of saving the virtuous pagans who came before Christ, such as Plato, Aristotle and Virgil himself. Although the doctrine was developed to explain how the Old Testament Jews, and not just their prophets and leaders, were saved, it could be extended, as Aquinas showed, to cover people, such as the philosophers, from the Graeco-Roman world. Dante obviously rejected the idea of extending implicit faith in this way, since he says nothing about it and pointedly does not use it to save these illustrious figures of antiquity.[15] For (what was considered to be the exceptional case of) pagans living in Christian times, who did not have the chance to hear anything of the Gospel, there was a different way of allowing the possibility of salvation—the special inspiration theory, which can be traced back to Abelard and was taken up by Aquinas.[16] This line of thinking was certainly alive in the Italy of Dante's day. Giorgio Padoan cites (without noting its dependence on Aquinas) a very similar passage from a sermon given in Florence on 26 December 1303, by Giordano da Pisa.[17] But Dante does not simply omit this idea: he explicitly rejects it. In the *Paradiso*, Dante puts into his own mouth a question about someone—he thinks of an Indian, perhaps because of the traditional idea that the Brahmans there (*bragmanni*) led excellent lives according to natural law:[18]

> . . . Un uom nasce a la riva
>   de l'Indo, e quivi non è chi ragioni
>   di Cristo né chi legga né chi scriva;

[14]This seems rather clearly to be Dante's meaning here, and it is how, for example, Chiavacci Leonardi (Dante Alighieri 1991–94, I, 111) explains it. Those excluded because of lack of baptism would, then, be just the pagans listed, such as Averroes, who came after Christ (cf., e.g., Foster 1977, 209; Carron 2010, 890n550). Other commentators have, however, given different and less convincing explanations.

[15]Foster 1977, 181–89 explains very clearly the absence of a notion of implicit faith in Dante's discussion.

[16]See above, chapter 8.

[17]Padoan 1977, 109–10.

[18]See chapter 7.

e tutti suoi voleri e atti buoni
  sono, quanto ragione umana vede,
  sanza peccato in vita o sermoni.

Muore non battezzato e sanza fede:
  ov'è questa giustizia che'l condanna?
  ov'è la colpa sua, se ei non crede?'

[Dante asks:] A man is born on the banks of the Indus, and there is nobody there who speaks or teaches or writes about Christ; and all his volitions and acts are good, so far as human reason sees—he is without sin in his life or speech. He dies unbaptized and without faith: where is this justice that condemns him? Where is his guilt if he does not believe?[19]

To this question, the expected answer according to the special inspiration theory is that God would find a way to save him. Instead, the Eagle, made up of beatified souls, gives the authoritative reply:

'Or tu chi se', che vuo' sedere a scranna,
  per giudicar di lungi mille miglia
  con la veduta corta d'una spanna?'

Now you—who are you to place yourself on the seat of judgment to judge what is happening a thousand miles away when your sight is the shortness of a span?[20]

Although this reply does not rule out the possibility that the anonymous Indian will be saved, the rhetorical force of the answer and its continuation suggests that there is no reason to assume that he will, and it makes clear that it is not, as the character Dante had asserted, a matter of justice that the Indian should not be condemned.

Pagans in Paradise? Exceptions That Prove the Rule

Dante names just four apparent pagans among the saved, in Purgatory or Heaven. One of them is Statius, who is in Purgatory. But Statius, although known only as the pagan poet of the *Thebaid*, is in Dante's invented afterworld, as he explains, someone who was baptized—led to his faith by Virgil's prophetic words in his fourth eclogue—but hid his

---

[19] *Paradiso* XIX, 70–78.
[20] *Paradiso* XIX, 79–81.

Christianity from fear of persecution.[21] It was thus only apparently that he was a pagan when he was saved. The same is true, though less straightforwardly, for two of the others, Trajan and Ripheus.

By putting Trajan in Heaven, Dante is simply following the theological tradition from the time of William of Auxerre onwards, which, unlike some of the earlier accounts, accepted the story told by Gregory's earliest hagiographer that Trajan's soul had been saved and found an acceptable theological explanation for it.[22] But, in the way he tells the story of his salvation, he underlines that it provides no basis for the salvation of just pagans. He explains that Trajan

> . . . de lo 'nferno, u' non si riede
> già mai a buon voler, tornò a l'ossa;
> e ciò di viva spene fu mercede:
>
> di viva spene, che mise la possa
> ne' prieghi fatti a Dio per suscitarla,
> sì che potesse sua voglia esser mossa.
>
> L'anima glorïosa onde si parla,
> tornata ne la carne, in che fu poco,
> credette in lui che potëa aiutarla;
>
> e credendo s'accese in tanto foco
> di vero amor, ch'a la morte seconda
> fu degna di venire a questo gioco.

> *returned to his bones from Hell, from where no one ever returns to be able to will well, and that was the reward of living hope, which gave the power to the prayers offered to God to raise it, so that Trajan's will could be moved. When the glorious soul of which we are speaking had returned to the flesh, in which it spent a short time, it believed in him that he could help it, and, believing, became enflamed in such a fire of true love that, at its second death, it was worthy to come to this joy.*[23]

This is the 'Resurrection' version of the story, used by a number of thirteenth-century theologians, which turns the *exemplum* from being about the reward for virtue into one about God's ability, miraculously, to

---

[21] *Purgatorio* XXII, 89–91; cf. lines 63ff. for the story of his conversion.

[22] See above, chapter 9.

[23] *Paradiso* XX, 106–17.

act beyond the ordinary order of nature:[24] it is no special tribute to Trajan and his virtue that, granted the exceptional privilege of returning to life, he should have hoped, believed and been enflamed with charity. He goes to Heaven, as Dante emphasizes, not at all as a virtuous pagan, but as a Christian. Dante's source seems to have been Jacob of Voragine's *Golden Legend*, and so he choose this version in deliberate preference to the earlier form of the story, found there too, which lacks the resurrection and emphasizes Trajan's virtue. Indeed, Dante goes even further to remove any credit from Trajan for his own salvation. Before telling Trajan's story, he explains,

> *Regnum celorum* vïolenza pate
>   da caldo amore e da viva speranza,
>   che vince la divina volontate:
>
> non a guisa che l'omo a l'om sobranza,
>   ma vince lei perché vuole esser vinta,
>   e, vinta, vince con sua beninanza.

> *The Kingdom of Heaven suffers violence from hot love and living hope which defeat the divine will, not in the way that one human overcomes another, but they defeat it because it wishes to be defeated, and defeated, it is victorious with its benevolence.*[25]

While this comment does bring human, as well as divine, agency into Trajan's salvation, the actor is not Trajan. It is Pope Gregory whose love and hope 'defeats' God's will, as the telling of the story makes clear. Nor is there any reference here to the story of Trajan and the widow—the instance of virtuousness which, in the legend, moved Gregory to pray for Trajan. The story is, in fact, told much earlier in the *Commedia*, in *Purgatorio*, but even here the phrasing is telling, since Dante writes of a sculpture which tells (X, 74–75) the story of 'the high glory of the Roman ruler, whose worth moved Gregory *a la sua gran vittoria*'. Trajan's virtue is here acknowledged, but the 'great victory' is not Trajan's, but Gregory's.

There is another unexpected soul presented to Dante alongside Trajan's in Paradise. It is that of Ripheus, a figure who was known only from two and a half lines of Virgil's *Aeneid*, where he, 'the justest among the Trojans and he most kept fairness', is described among those who are

---

[24] See chapter 9.
[25] *Paradiso* XX, 94–99.

killed.[26] Dante's choice of this figure is entirely his own, but the manner in which he describes his salvation is based on a long tradition:

> L'altra, per grazia che da sì profonda
>   fontana stilla, che mai creatura
>   non pinse l'occhio infino a la prima onda,
>
> tutto suo amor là giù pose a drittura:
>   per che, di grazia in grazia, Dio li aperse
>   l'occhio a la nostra redenzion futura;
>
> ond'ei credette in quella, e non sofferse
>   da indi il puzzo più del paganesmo;
>   e riprendiene le genti perverse.
>
> Quelle tre donne li fur per battesmo
>   che tu vedesti da la destra rota,
>   dinanzi al battezzar più d'un millesmo.

> *The other, through grace which wells from a fountain so deep that no creature ever penetrated with his eyes to the first wave, placed all his love on rightness, through which, from grace to grace, God opened his eyes to our future redemption, and so he believed in it, and no longer put up with the mire of paganism and reproached the wicked people for it. These three ladies [i.e., Faith, Hope and Charity] whom you saw on the right wheel counted as baptism for him more than a thousand years before there was baptizing.[27]*

And so Ripheus, just like Trajan, is merely a seeming just pagan, since he too, thanks to a less theatrical miracle, died as a Christian:

> D'i corpi suoi non uscir, come credi,
>   Gentili, ma Cristiani, in ferma fede
>   quel d'i passuri e quel d'i passi piedi.

> *They did not, as you believe, leave their bodies as Gentiles, but as Christians, in firm faith, this one in the feet that would suffer and that in the feet that had suffered.[28]*

[26] *Aeneid* II, 426–28; he has also been mentioned at line 339 of the same book.
[27] *Paradiso* XX, 118–29.
[28] *Paradiso* XX, 103–5.

The internal inspiration that leads Ripheus to Christian belief and baptism of the spirit is exactly what Aquinas and Albert were talking about
when they described the case of the virtuous pagan invincibly ignorant
of revelation and saved according to the special inspiration theory. They
would not disagree with Dante that such a movement to God needs to be
initiated by grace, but they do not altogether share Dante's emphasis on
the pure gratuity and utterly exceptional character of this sort of salvation, which he brings out in how he concludes the episode:

> O predestinazion, quanto remota
> è la radice tua da quelli aspetti
> che la prima cagion non veggion *tota*!
>
> E voi, mortali, tenetevi stretti
> a giudicar . . .
>
> *O predestination, how far is your root from the vision of those who*
> *do not see the first cause entire! And you, mortals, hold back from*
> *judging* . . .[29]

The last remark clearly refers back to the reproach addressed to the character Dante when he asked about the virtuous Indian. The implication cannot
be that the Indian, like Ripheus, will be saved, because he is just, but rather
that it is beyond us, who do not know God, the first cause, in his fullness,
to judge these matters. Some virtuous pagans may be saved, but we must
not think that their deserts in themselves provide a reason why they should
not be damned. Indeed, Ripheus and the explanation of his salvation put in
dramatic form an idea from Augustine's *City of God*, that some members
of every people at every time have been among the elect and inwardly inspired by God so that they became Christians in all but externals.[30]

The fourth pagan among the saved is Cato, guardian of the shores
of Mount Purgatory.[31] Whereas Trajan, Ripheus and even Statius are
introduced mainly so as to explain why and how they are saved, Cato's
salvation, in so far as it is not already implied by his office in Purgatory,
is indicated in passing—Virgil talks about the glory of his body on the
Day of Judgement.[32] This absence of explanation creates a problem,

---

[29] *Paradiso* XX, 130–33.

[30] See chapter 2.

[31] A very full study of Dante's presentation of Cato is given in Carron 2010, 709–922;
see also Corbett 2013, 129–33.

[32] *Purgatorio* I, 75: 'la vesta ch'al gran dì sarà sì chiara'. A remark by Cato himself a little
further on (line 90) shows that he went, along with Adam and other Old Testament figures,
into Limbo until the Harrowing of Hell, when he was released.

because there is nothing explicit to show that Cato was anything but a pagan when he died—and a pagan who killed himself. More than any other ancient figure, perhaps, Cato enjoyed the reputation of moral perfection; it was queried by some of the Fathers, but usually upheld by medieval writers, and Dante himself had praised him in the most hyperbolic way in the *Convivio*—'what earthly man is worthier to signify God than Cato', he asks rhetorically?[33] In the *Purgatorio*, Cato's face is bathed in the light of the four stars, which represent the cardinal virtues.[34] While his suicide was condemned by Augustine, for Dante it seems to have been a reason for his salvation, rather than an impediment to it. In the *Monarchia*, he calls it 'an indescribable sacrifice', which Cato, 'the strictest upholder of true liberty' made in order to set alight love of liberty in the world, by preferring death to life without liberty.[35] And here, in the *Purgatorio*, Virgil's address to Cato has the same theme: Dante, he tells him, is seeking liberty 'ch'è sì cara,/come sa chi per lei vita rifiuta' ('which is so dear,/as he knows who gives up life for it') and then he talks of Cato's own suicide.[36] There remains, none the less, the problem of how, given Dante's theology, Cato could avoid, at best, the fate of Virgil. The two recent scholars who have thought most carefully about the problem suggest that he, like Ripheus, could have been secretly inspired and so, despite appearances, he too died a Christian.[37] At the least, Dante's way of thinking (and even Augustine's harsh views) left room for such a possibility, if the question were pressed—but Dante is clearly not pressing it, and he is certainly not arguing, as a general principle, against the evidence provided by Virgil and his companions in Limbo, that outstanding merits without belief will be rewarded by Heaven.

[33] *Convivio* IV.28.15. Earlier in the book (IV.5.16), Dante talks of 'the most sacred breast' of Cato.

[34] *Purgatorio* I, 22–27, 37–39. The stars have not been seen 'since the first people (*la prima gente*)', which most modern commentators take to be Adam and Eve before the Fall, though some of the medieval commentators took the description more widely, to embrace a Golden Age at the beginning of the world, or even ancient (pagan) times, when the cardinal virtues were especially cultivated (the anonymous Lombard commentary of c. 1325 first identifies the *prima gente* with those in the Old Testament, but then adds, 'for those wise men, as were Aristotle and Cato and many others, flourished more in these four virtues than people now. But after the coming of Christ, faith hope and charity flourished, which were unknown earlier to the first peoples').

[35] *Monarchia* II.5.15.

[36] *Purgatorio* I, 71–72, cf. 73–75. See Scott 1996, 69–74; Imbach in Dante Alighieri 1996–2004, IV, liv–lxiv; and Carron 2010, 770–805, 853–66.

[37] Carron 2010, 878–901; Corbett 2013, 132 (Corbett points out [n. 37] that one of the earliest commentators, Pietro Alighieri, suggests this solution). Scott (1996, 76–78) argues that Cato is saved by implicit faith. But, if Dante had allowed for implicit faith, then it is completely puzzling that many more pagans (such as Virgil) were not saved by it.

Dante and Pagan Wisdom

To understand why Dante took such an attitude to pagan salvation, his views on pagan wisdom need to be examined. They are developed especially in two of his prose works, the Italian *Convivio*, written in 1304–8, just before he started the *Divine Comedy*, and the Latin *Monarchia*, which dates from 1314, the time he was writing the *Paradiso*, if not later.[38]

The *Convivio* has an unusual form: after an introductory book, explaining and justifying his rationale, Dante comments on three of his own *canzoni*. He tells (in what need not be taken as literal autobiography) how, after the death of his beloved Beatrice, nothing comforted him until he happened to read Boethius's *Consolation* and Cicero's *On Friendship*.[39] These two works—both based on philosophical reasoning, not religious doctrine, although Boethius was a Christian—so inspired Dante with enthusiasm for philosophy that he compares himself to someone who, searching for silver, finds gold. The lady to whom his *canzoni* are addressed is Philosophy, and the commentary on the poems is an introduction to philosophy and its benefits. The main exponents of philosophy are seen as the leaders of the ancient schools. Like John of Salisbury, Dante has praise for each of them; unlike him, he does not at the same time point out deficiencies in each of their doctrines. On most things they are presented as concurring in truth. But for Dante—as he would confirm by his depiction and placing of him in the *Inferno*—there is one supreme philosopher, Aristotle.[40]

Through its rootedness in the Aristotelian tradition, and its aim of introducing and commending philosophy, the *Convivio* can be compared to the works by Arts Masters, such as Boethius of Dacia and Aubrey of Rheims, on the Highest Good and how philosophers can reach it. But there is an important difference: it is not the work of a professional university master exalting his discipline, but the story of a brilliant layman's own intellectual discoveries, deliberately written in the vernacular to

---

[38] At *Monarchia* I.12.6, Dante makes an explicit reference to his *Paradiso* (Canto 5, lines 19–24). Only if it is regarded as an interpolation can the *Monarchia* be dated—as many earlier scholars wished—to before c. 1314. The phrase is indeed absent from the *editio princeps*, but this edition presents the work as being not by Dante the poet, but by a different Dante, who was a contemporary of Poliziano (1454–94); it is hardly surprising that such a reference is omitted from it, and exhaustive study of the MSS tradition shows that there is no sign at all that the reference to the *Paradiso* was interpolated: see Dante Alighieri 2009, 355 and cf. Prue Shaw's introduction.

[39] *Convivio* II.12.1–3.

[40] See *Convivio* III.14.15 (also discussed below); IV.6.8–16, where the supremacy of Aristotle is emphasized; IV.22.15. At IV.22.4, Dante decides to leave behind the opinions of Epicurus and Zeno on the good for humans and go straight to the true, Aristotelian account. On Dante and Epicurus, see below.

reach an audience outside the universities.[41] And, in line with this difference of origin, there turns out to be a profound difference in the way the shared goal of following and commending philosophy is conceived.

The Arts Masters approach their task in a spirit of exclusivism and triumphalism. Although in no way repudiating Christianity, they put it aside for the moment, whilst they manifest an unlimited confidence in the powers of philosophy to bring them to true wisdom and happiness. By contrast, so far from avoiding specifically Christian language in the *Convivio*, Dante seems to delight in melding biblical allusions with discussion of the philosophers, even to the extent of comparing three of the ancient philosophical schools to the three Marys who went to Christ's tomb.[42] In his treatment of the number of angels, Dante combines a wish for syncretism with a willingness to abandon the ancient philosophers' teachings when, he feels he can show, they conflict with his better reasoning, and with Scripture. He equates the angels with the intelligences of Arabic Aristotelianism (and explains how the non-philosophers in the ancient pagan world worshipped them as gods); emphasizing the harmony of different beliefs, he declares that no one—'no philosopher, pagan (*gentile*), Jew, Christian or any sect'—doubts that these intelligences enjoy perfect happiness. But he has a rational argument to show that there are more angels/intelligences than indicated by the movements of the heavens, and he then goes on to back up this view from the Bible; as he says, the ancients went wrong though lack of both reason and teaching (*ammaestramento*).[43]

Dante is willing to welcome Christian truth, in harmony, addition or correction to philosophical teaching, which he believes has very strict limitations. We can, indeed, gain the 'perfection of reason' for the sake of which all other human activities, such as growth and sensing, take place; and 'when this is perfect, so are they, so that a human being, in so far as he is a human being, sees every desire fulfilled and so is happy'. Yet we still do not know God, eternity or prime matter: we know that they exist, but not what they are; at best we see them 'as if in a dream'.[44] How seriously he takes this position can be seen from the answer he gives to a problem it raises. How can a wisdom which leaves some things unknown make people happy, since they will still desire naturally to know what

---

[41] Cf. Imbach 1996, 135; on these works in praise of philosophy, see chapter 8.

[42] *Convivio* IV.22.14–15.

[43] *Convivio* II.4–5; for the sources, see Ricklin's commentary in Dante Alighieri 1991–94, II. Dante is closer to Aquinas than to other writers, but the central argument to show that there are more Intelligences/Angels than is evident from the heavenly motions is his own.

[44] See especially *Convivio* III.15.4–6 and Cheneval's commentary in Dante Alighieri 1996–2004, III. The reference to dreaming depends on an emendation.

is beyond their knowledge and so be unsatisfied? Dante might have followed the solutions given either by Aquinas or by the Arts Masters, who shared the view that humans have a natural desire for knowledge which includes grasping what God is; and that, since nature does nothing in vain, there must be a way for this desire to be fulfilled. Aquinas believed that this sought-for knowledge will never be reached in this life. Humans must wait for the beatific vision in Heaven for the fulfilment of their desire.[45] The Arts Masters thought that, in some sense at least, humans in this life could, through philosophy, fulfil their desire to grasp the highest good.[46] By contrast, Dante resolved the problem by rejecting the shared premise: according to him, 'the desire which is naturally in each thing is measured according to the possibility of the thing desiring'—it is in this way that nature avoids vainly producing an unfulfillable longing. We therefore do *not* (as humans in this life) desire to know God and other things which are impossible for our nature.[47]

It fits this earthbound, human-centred view of philosophy that, contrary to the usual Aristotelian understanding, which places metaphysics at the head of philosophy, Dante makes ethics (which includes politics) the branch without which all the others would be useless and there would be no happiness.[48] Similarly, he describes the three main sects of ancient philosophy—the Epicureans, Stoics, Peripatetics—as sects of 'the *active* life'. Philosophical reasoning can, however, indicate analogically that there is a higher realm of understanding. From the fact that it can demonstrate to us many things which, in its absence, would seem to us miraculous, we are led by it to believe that for every miracle—even those which philosophy cannot explain—there is a reason in God's mind. And this thought is the root of the faith, hope and charity which will lead us to Heaven, where there is no discord between schools of philosophy.[49]

[45] See *Summa Theologiae* I–II, q. 3, a. 8. Nardi 1960, 66–75 brings out very clearly Dante's differences from Aquinas here.

[46] Cheneval assembles texts from Boethius of Dacia, Siger of Brabant and John of Jandun to illustrate this point in his introduction in Dante Alighieri 1996–2004, I, lxxv–lxxvi.

[47] *Convivio* III.15.8–10. Following and going beyond Nardi, Dante's originality here is noted by Imbach (1996, 148) and discussed at length by Cheneval in his notes and his general introduction (in Dante Alighieri 1996–2004, I).

[48] *Convivio* II.14.14–18. Cf. Imbach 1996, 137–38, Cheneval in Dante Alighieri 1996–2004, I, lviii–lix.

[49] *Convivio* III.14.14–15. The text in the archetype is obviously corrupt at this point, and there is some disagreement about how to emend it, but the account I have given fits a conservative reconstruction. In his commentary (Dante Alighieri 1996–2004, III) Cheneval insists that Dante is talking not about the Christian theological virtues, but a different triad of faith, hope and charity, which is infused directly into the philosophers. The most natural way to read the passage is, however, to see it as showing how Dante's Christian readers can be inspired by philosophy not just to the fulfilment of their limited, natural desires, but in a parallel movement towards charity. The section ends by saying that 'through these three

In the *Monarchia*, Dante brings out even more clearly the idea that philosophy is a discipline operating within its own sphere—a limited relativism, then, in the manner of some Arts Masters; but he further emphasizes—quite contrary to their view—its practical, political and communal nature. He could not be more explicit about the division of responsibilities:

> Indescribable providence has therefore set before us two goals to aim at: the happiness of this life, which consists in the activity of our own powers and is represented figuratively by the earthly paradise; and happiness of eternal life, which consists in the enjoyment of the vision of God (to which our own powers cannot ascend unless they are aided by God's light) and which is signified by the heavenly paradise. We must reach these two kinds of happiness, which are like different conclusions, through different middle terms. For we come to the first through the teachings of philosophy, when we follow them by acting in accord with the moral and intellectual virtues; whereas we attain the second through spiritual teachings which transcend human reason, when we follow them by acting in accord with the theological virtues (faith, hope and charity). These conclusions and middle terms have been shown to us on the one hand by human reason, which has been entirely made known to us by the philosophers, and on the other hand by the Holy Spirit, who through the prophets and sacred writers, through Jesus Christ the son of God, coeternal with him, and through his disciples, has revealed to us the supernatural truth which is necessary for us.[50]

Dante goes on to explain that, because of greed, humans need 'twofold guidance' to overcome their irrational natures and pursue their two goals: 'the supreme Pontiff, to lead mankind to eternal life according to revealed truth, and the Emperor, to guide mankind to temporal happiness according to the teachings of philosophy'.[51] In itself, the idea of a twofold end is something which Aquinas, for example, accepted. But Dante insists

---

virtues we rise so as to philosophize in that celestial Athens, where the Stoics and Peripatetics and Epicureans, through the light of eternal truth, come together harmoniously in one will'. If this is taken to mean that ancient Stoics, Peripatetics and Epicureans are all in Heaven, then it certainly represents a completely different view about pagan salvation from the one Dante would put in the *Commedia*, and Cheneval is probably right to reject this reading. But Dante need not be taken as saying that these ancient philosophers are literally in Heaven, but merely that, in the fullness of God's truth, the differences between their philosophies disappear.

[50] *Monarchia* III.15.7–9. In Aristotelian logic, syllogistic arguments are constructed by finding premises with a common 'middle term' (e.g., 'man' in 'Every man is mortal', 'Every philosopher is a man'). What the conclusion is depends on the middle term.

[51] *Monarchia* III.15.9–10.

on a disciplinary separation in a manner quite contrary to Aquinas's path of unity, and he claims that reason, which leads to earthly happiness, is made known to us *entirely* (*tota*) by the philosophers, whose teaching the temporal ruler, the Emperor, must follow.

The treatise begins with a demonstration, based purely on supposedly self-evident premises and rational argument, to show that the end for which humanity exists will be frustrated unless the whole world is ruled by a single monarch who, as book 2 will show, must be the Roman emperor. In order to make this argument, Dante poses a question which is similar in form to a basic Aristotelian one, but significantly different in content. Aristotelian ethics is based on establishing what is the end or goal of human life—that is to say, for each individual human. Aristotelian politics considers the goals of groups of humans—households, villages, cities. But for his purpose Dante needs to do something unprecedented within this tradition (though anticipated in ways by Stoic cosmopolitanism): he needs to ask what the aim is of humankind taken as a whole, of the entire species. He believes that, since nature does nothing in vain, he can find something's aim by considering its 'proper' activity, that is to say, the activity of which just that item, and no other, is capable. In the case of humankind this activity is apprehension through the possible intellect: other animals do not engage in intellectual activity, whilst the other intellectual creatures, the angels, engage in perpetual intellection and so there is nothing 'possible', that is to say potential, in their activity. But no individual or grouping of individuals less than the whole of humanity is enough to put into act the whole potency of the possible intellect. So Dante can confidently conclude that 'the proper work of humankind taken as a whole is to actuate always the whole power of the possible intellect'.[52] He then goes on to argue that, for humankind to do this work, peace is necessary, and peace requires a universal ruler; but the step which really makes his advocacy for universal rule plausible is the initial one, setting up a goal for humanity *as a whole*.

The goal is, of course, just one of the two which Dante carefully distinguishes: the goal of earthly happiness under the Emperor's philosophically instructed rule. This limitation may help to explain one of the most puzzling features of this argument. In order to identify the goal for humanity as a whole, Dante speaks of 'the possible intellect' as a single entity. The view that there is just one possible intellect for all humans is the characteristic Averroist doctrine which a succession of Arts Masters, from Siger of Brabant, advanced as the correct interpretation of Aristotle, and the best rational theory, though, as they all added, it is to be

---

[52] *Monarchia* I.3.6–1.4.1.

rejected because it clashes with Christian doctrine by denying individual immortality. When a Dominican, Guido Vernani, wrote an attack on the *Monarchia* in 1329, he accused Dante of holding Averroes's doctrine of the one potential intellect (and pointed out that he refers explicitly to Averroes's long commentary on *On the Soul*), but this judgement is generally regarded as a wild misrepresentation, and interpreters of the *Monarchia*, whatever their other differences, agree that this cannot have been the position its author intended.[53] But, if not, it is hard to know what Dante is supposed to be saying. Dante's whole position makes no sense unless the possible intellect is one for all people: its activation as a whole is the collective task of humanity. Perhaps the phrase could be taken as what philosophical jargon terms a *façon de parler*—a way of putting things, which should not be presumed to carry its apparent ontological weight. It would fit better, though, with the methods of the time to suppose that Dante is here deliberately writing as a philosopher, who accepts—though purely for the purpose of philosophical discussion—the Averroistic position. He can use it here, because he is putting forward this argument wholly within the sphere of philosophy. Of course, he accepts it as the unqualified truth that possible intellects are individualized and individuals are immortal—a belief expressed by almost every line of the *Commedia*, and he even explicitly corrects Averroes's error in *Purgatorio*, though with an acknowledgement of his wisdom and without offering any counterargument.[54]

If this way of understanding his method here is correct, this passage can be added to various other indications that Dante did not simply go through a phase when he followed some of the doctrines and methods of

[53] In Marenbon 2001a, I give details of the ways in which different Dante scholars have rejected the idea that he is talking about a unitary possible intellect, in the manner of Averroes, and I give a step-by-step analysis of Dante's argument, which shows that it does assume such a single possible intellect. Brenet (2006, 467–68) refers to my article and says (468–69) that his identification of the particular passage of Averroes in question—see below—'implicitly challenges the idea that he is referring in general to the thesis of the unity of the intellect'. Brenet is quite probably right that it is not a general reference; but the particular view to which Dante refers *presupposes* the unity of the possible intellect, as does the transformation of this view by Dante, so acutely described by Brenet himself. Zyg Baranski, in a valuable and wide-ranging article (Baranski 2013), also rejects my reading on (I believe insufficient) general grounds that Dante is unsympathetic to 'those contemporary philosophers who wished to insulate their thinking and conclusions from the higher insights provided by revelation'.

[54] At *Purgatorio* XXV, 63–65, Statius refers to the error of disjoining the possible intellect from the individual soul. He does not name Averroes, but calls him 'one wiser than' his interlocutor, Dante himself. He gives Averroes's reason for taking his view that 'there is no bodily organ taken up (*assunto*) by the intellect', which is indeed a central argument for his position; and he offers no counterargument.

Siger of Brabant and Albert the Great.[55] Rather, at the end of his career, even more definitely than at the time of the *Convivio*, Dante took up the limited relativism of the Arts Masters (labelled 'Averroists' by their adversaries) and where appropriate adopted, without the Christian corrections and additions of the *Convivio*, the perspective of natural reasoning.[56] But it was an influence Dante adapted to his own terms. In the passage of the commentary on *On the Soul* to which Dante probably intended his explicit reference to point, Averroes is saying that the possible intellect is always thinking, because although any individual human is thinking only at some times, there is always, at every time, some member of the human species engaged in thought.[57] Within this framework, Averroes thought of striving to actualize the possible intellect in terms of an individual's conjunction with it, and Averroes also suggested that there will always, at any time, be at least one perfect philosopher, whose conjunction with the possible intellect explains its being in act.[58] By contrast, Dante has in mind a communal cognitive goal, achievable only in conditions of peace, which alone the rule of a single Emperor can bring. Moreover, he is not envisaging all humans rapt in intellectual speculation. The activation of the potential intellect involves the 'extension' of the speculative intellect to the practical one.[59] True to the view of the *Convivio* which gives moral philosophy pride of place, Dante thinks of people accomplishing humanity's

[55] Bruno Nardi (1930, 241–305; 1960, 37–150) and, later, Maria Corti (1982, 77–101) argued that Dante stopped following these ideas by the time he was writing the *Commedia*. But not only are they found in the *Commedia* itself; the *Monarchia*, which Nardi especially used as evidence for Dante's thought in its 'Averroist' phase, has now clearly been shown to be a late work (see note 38 above).

[56] The most important of the other indications are (1) that he places Siger of Brabant along with Aquinas and Albert the Great in Paradise (*Paradiso* X, 133–38)—see Dronke 1986, 96–102 (a very fine discussion, which successfully challenges attempts to deny that Dante was in some sense endorsing Siger's radical position); Marenbon 2001a, 367–69 (with discussion of the scholarly controversy); Baranski 2013 (expresses doubts about the reading proposed by Dronke and accepted by me); (2) passages in the *Monarchia* and the *Paradiso* where he follows views on angels proposed by Boethius of Dacia and Siger of Brabant, which had been condemned in 1277: see Imbach 1996, 145–47. (In Baranski 2013 it is argued that Dante is not saying anything out of the ordinary in these passages, but Imbach's points are not tackled.)

[57] The passage, identified by Brenet 2006, 472, is from Commentary 20 (Averroes 1953, 448:136–44). Nardi (Dante Alighieri 1996, 300–303) and Imbach and Flüeler (Dante Alighieri 1989, 268) cite a different passage, from Commentary 5 (Averroes 1953, 407:605–408:623), but its subject matter is similar. It is not absolutely certain that Dante has either of these passages, or any specific passage, in mind: see Marenbon 2001a, 364–65.

[58] See Brenet 2006, 477–81. Dante's idea of the noble man which he developed in *Convivio* IV is probably related to this theme, but it lacks any echo in the *Monarchia*.

[59] *Monarchia* I.3.9, I.4.1. The idea of this extension, based on a misreading of Aristotle's text, was widely used (see Minio-Paluello 1955, sec. 1), but Dante's way of using it is special to him.

intellectual aim through how they act and what they make, as well as by theoretical speculation. And, given his view of the limitations of humans' capacity, and their desire, for knowledge, Dante perhaps conceived the earthly happiness brought by a universal Emperor ruling according to philosophical teachings not so much as contemplative beatitude but a well-ordered society of virtuous people satisfied in their grasp of the limited knowledge for which they strive. For they would also be seeking, not socially or politically, but ecclesiastically, a different, unbounded heavenly beatitude, under the guidance of Scripture and the pope.[60]

DANTE'S LIMBO AND THE PUNISHMENT OF VIRTUOUS PAGANS

To this rigid distinction between the teachings of philosophy and those of scripture, the purviews of the Emperor and the pope, Dante sacrificed in his vision of the hereafter the pagans he admired so much, even while he emphasized their virtue. They represent the earthly virtue and happiness political society can achieve, and for the return of which under a restored Empire Dante aspires. But, as Dante's separation of the spheres of philosophy and faith requires, this path to earthly happiness does not, however well it is followed, lead at all to heavenly happiness. He can allow for a few miraculous instances of salvation, celebrated as in the case of Trajan, or unknown like that of Ripheus, but there is no normal way in which pagans, before or after Christ, can be saved. In particular, the most obvious way of allowing at least pre-Christian virtuous pagans to be saved, through implicit faith, becomes hard to use. Aquinas's most considered explanation of implicit faith sees it related to the same faith made explicit as if they were the two ends of the same argument: it is like the principle compared to its conclusions.[61] But, according to Dante's statement at the end of the *Monarchia*, 'We must reach these two kinds of happiness, which are like different conclusions, through different middle terms': to follow the end set by philosophy is like making a different argument, with a different middle term and conclusion, from that made by following Christian doctrine.

Dante's attitude to pagan wisdom—his idiosyncratic version of limited relativism—explains why his position with regard to pagan salvation is paradoxical, since he fully accepts the virtuousness of pagans whom he consigns to Hell. But it does not show how Dante resolves the paradox,

[60]That Dante transforms the ideas of Averroes and the Latin Arts Masters influenced by him in his own, special political direction has been recognized since the time of Gilson and Nardi (cf. Marenbon 2001a, 365–66); especially valuable recent discussions are Imbach 1992; Imbach 1996, 173–89; Brenet 2006.

[61]See above, pp. 170–71.

for the good reason that Dante leaves the paradox unresolved—not by oversight or incapacity, but deliberately. It is an aspect of the division Dante wishes to make between the sphere of reasoning and that of faith that certain aspects of God's ordering of the world are simply incomprehensible to reason, unless it is aided by faith in what is said in Scripture. When, in the *Monarchia*, he wishes to give an example, he immediately chooses this very point: 'no one, however perfect in moral and intellectual virtues, both as dispositions and in practice, can be saved without faith, ‹even› when he has heard nothing about Christ'—this, says Dante, 'human reason through itself cannot see as just, though it can when aided by faith'.[62]

Dante, however, does not, as the discussion so far might have suggested, put the virtuous pagans in Hell proper. They are placed in Limbo, where they suffer no physical tortures but merely the punishment of 'desire without hope'.[63] In the theology of Dante's time, Limbo was well established as the place where the souls of the patriarchs, prophets and good people of the Old Testament went until Christ released them, when he descended to Hell after his Crucifixion; and also as the place for the souls of unbaptized babies, who died before they could sin. Dante's Limbo has both these traditional functions, but the extra role it is given, as home for the virtuous pagans, is his innovation.[64] Dante's early readers were acutely aware of the idea's novelty, to the extent that most of the early commentators of the *Commedia* explained that this description is not supposed to be taken literally, as an account of what happens in the hereafter, but allegorically as a way of recognizing the everlasting fame of these pagan heroes, rulers, poets and philosophers.[65] Given that the constraints, not of Christian doctrine in his time but of his own approach to the distinction between philosophy and faith, required him to damn Virgil, Aristotle and so many other pagans he admired, Dante, it might seem, has attempted to make their damnation as comfortable as possible. Here there is no weeping, only sighs; grief, but no physical punishment.[66] Although the noble castle, surrounded by a beautiful

[62] *Monarchia* II.7.4–5.
[63] *Inferno* IV, 41–42.
[64] Virgil describes the moment, not long after his own coming to Limbo, when Christ releases these souls (*Inferno* IV, 52–63). In *Purgatorio* VII, 31–33, when he is describing Limbo to Sordello, Dante says that he is there 'with the innocent babies devoured by the teeth of death before they had human sin [i.e., original sin] removed from them [by baptism]'. On the innovative character of Dante's Limbo, see Padoan 1977, 103–24. Corbett (2013, 124) points out that Augustine (*Contra Iulianum* 4.3.26) brings up the idea of the heroes of ancient Rome being sent to a place intermediate between Heaven and Hell, but rejects it as a shameless suggestion.
[65] See Ricklin 2011, 282–83.
[66] *Inferno* IV, 26–28.

river, and the enamel-green of the meadow (borrowed from the Elysian Fields of *Aeneid* VI) may have allegorical significance, they also lend beauty and dignity to the place where the heroes and philosophers, slow and grave of eye, authoritative in countenance, speak sparingly in their sweet voices.[67]

Are these virtuous pagans not being allowed to enjoy an eternity which, although not filled with joy, is free of pain, marred only by a disappointment like that which someone in this life would experience if he knew that he would always be denied the vision of God in Heaven? In fact, Dante intends something far less bearable—and some early commentators do indeed stress the severity of these pagans' suffering, most strikingly Boccaccio, who thought it so severe that, if the spirits were mortal, they would kill themselves rather than endure such despair.[68] The punishment is especially cruel because, unlike Aquinas, and unlike many of the Arts Masters, Dante did not believe on earth we naturally desire to know what God is—the beatific vision—in such a way that our desire is frustrated by lacking this knowledge. As the *Convivio* explains, our desire is proportioned to our capacities.[69] But God has given the virtuous pagans in Limbo a desire *disproportionate* to their capacities, a desire which could only be fulfilled by seeing God. Virgil makes this clear in *Purgatorio*. He begins by emphasizing the limitations of human intellect in this life: humans who are not content to know just that God exists, but want to grasp by reason the nature of the Trinity are, he says, 'mad'. He continues,

> . . . ché, se potuto aveste veder tutto,
> mestier non era parturir Maria;
>
> e disïar vedeste sanza frutto
>   tai che sarebbe lor disio quetato,
>   ch'etternalmente è dato lor per lutto:
>
> io dico d'Aristotile e di Platone
>   di molt' altri . . .
>
> . . . *because, could you have seen everything, there would have been no reason for Mary to give birth, and you see those desiring fruitlessly, with a desire which is given to them eternally for their grief,*

---

[67] *Inferno* IV, 112–14.
[68] See *Espozioni* (*Inferno* IV) II.13–14; Boccaccio 1965, 266–67.
[69] See above, p. 202.

*who [were humans able to see everything] would have their desire
fulfilled—I mean Aristotle and Plato and many others . . .*[70]

Aristotle, Plato and 'many others' (including Virgil himself) have been
given, to their grief, a desire which they would only be able to fulfil in the
counterfactual world where humans were created all-knowing. Dante's
God is an artist of the *contrapasso*, of the punishment which, not just
in its degree of severity, but its character, fits the crime, and nowhere is
the suffering more carefully adjusted to its victims than here. The virtuous pagans he mentions have intellectual capacities greater than all other
humans, and it is these very capacities which become the instruments for
inflicting pain on them, since, however much and however well they use
their powers, these souls will never succeed in fulfilling the desire they
have been given for something beyond their reach. But for what are they
being punished? Virgil is not saying here (and Dante the author nowhere
suggests) that the ancient thinkers overreached themselves and they (as
opposed to some foolish people now) wanted to know more than humans can do. His point is very different, as the lines on the Incarnation
indicate. Adam was not created with perfect knowledge and so he could,
and did, make the wrong choice and bring sin into the world. God's plan
of redemption took shape in history, with Mary's giving birth to Christ as
its central, dividing moment. The sole crime of Aristotle, Plato and Virgil
himself is to have lived on the wrong side of this division.[71] No wonder
that Dante thought that the damnation of just pagans is something which
human reason by itself *cannot* understand.

Epicurus, Dante and Boccaccio

One eminent ancient philosopher is not in Dante's Limbo, but suffering
even worse punishment in Hell, where he is confined to an open tomb,
which will be closed on the Day of Judgement—a fitting punishment for
holding that the soul dies along with the body. He is Epicurus, and it is
Dante's innovation to make Epicureanism consist simply in this denial
of human immortality.[72] In this Canto (*Inferno* 10), Dante meets Epicu-

[70] *Purgatorio* III, 38–43.

[71] For the post-Christian souls in Limbo, such as Averroes, their crime is to have lived
on the wrong side of the division geographically, just like the good pagan on the banks of
the Indus.

[72] See Marenbon 2012a, 30–37. It was, indeed, a common charge against Epicurus that
he denied life after death, but this was just one of many aspects of a philosophy which some
regarded as a creed for sensual indulgence, but other medieval writers treated in a more nuanced and accurate way. On medieval Epicureanism, see Pagnoni 1974; Marenbon 2012a,
9, 13–15, 28; Corbett 2013, 9–18; and Robert 2013.

rus's followers of his own day, who are presented as dignified and high-minded, but tragically misguided: unambiguously infernal counterparts to the virtuous pagans of Canto 4.[73] They include Farinata and the older Cavalcanti, father of Dante's friend, the famous poet Guido Cavalcanti. Guido was known as a philosopher, especially interested in natural science, and he was thought to deny the immortality of the soul. Although Guido was still alive at the supposed time of Dante's vision, the text suggests that he will be joining his father and the other Epicureans in Hell.

Giovanni Boccaccio was not only one of the other great Italian writers of the *trecento*, but Dante's admirer, biographer, editor and commentator. Yet in his *Decameron*, he makes what most recent critics have seen as a riposte to this Canto. In day 6, story 9, a party of young Florentines are angry that the intellectually exclusive Guido Cavalcanti prefers to spend his time alone, studying and thinking, rather than joining them in their merriments. Moreover, says the narrator, 'because he held something of the opinions of the Epicureans, it was said among the common people that the sole point of all these speculations of his was to find a way of showing that God does not exist'. The party surprises Guido deep in thought among the tombs of a cemetery. 'You are at home here', Guido says, and, vaulting over a sepulchre, he makes his escape. Most of the party are puzzled by his comment, but one of them explains that compared to the learned like him, ignorant people of our sort are no better than corpses.[74]

Boccaccio clearly has *Inferno* X in mind, but is he in fact questioning Dante's judgement on Cavalcanti? The idea that he is fits with a view developed by some recent writers of Boccaccio as an Averroist, who sides with Cavalcanti whilst the supposedly more orthodox Dante condemns him.[75] But the contrast is misleading. Dante himself, though certainly not an Averroist, was arguably an idiosyncratic follower of the limited relativism associated with Averroism. Once he is seen not just to condemn but also, though in a strictly relative sense, to admire the Epicureans of *Inferno* X, the story in the *Decameron* emerges as, not a criticism of Dante but a rephrasing of his very point—in a lighter tone, but not without a sardonic edge. Cavalcanti may have the last laugh at the expense of

[73] Corbett 2013 develops an impressive interpretation along the lines crudely sketched here.

[74] On this story, see especially Baranski 2006 and 2008.

[75] On Boccaccio the Averroist, see Gagliardi 1999. There are, in fact, good reasons for associating Boccaccio, not with the Averroist separation of philosophy and theology, but rather with the early humanist attempt to discover, like some twelfth-century authors, hidden ideas in pagan texts which are either Christian or at least acceptable to Christians: see Papio 2012.

the young Florentines, but if he is destined for an entombed existence in eternity, his laughter is hollow, to say the least.

At the end of his life, Boccaccio began a long commentary on the *Divine Comedy*. His treatment of the virtuous pagans shows him as a loyal follower of its author, willing to defend the theological innovation of their presence in Limbo rather than, like most commentators, explaining it away as mere allegory, but unable to accept the shocking inexplicability of their fate which results from Dante's stark separation between the realms of philosophy and revealed religion. Rather, he devises an ingenious and legalistic theory, which emphasizes strongly the traditional distinction, elided by Dante, between pagans before and after Christ. Moreover, where good pagans, such as Virgil, were wholly virtuous for Dante, Boccaccio depicts them in the more usual language of the political virtues: they live morally, hating dishonesty, violence, lust and treachery and strive to excel in knowledge, soldiery, doing well for the commonwealth and 'in becoming glorious among humans' (there is an un-Dantesque touch of Augustinian sarcasm here).[76] In keeping with this view, Boccaccio does not find it necessary to explain why the good classical poets, heroes and philosophers are not simply saved (for example, by implicit faith, as in Aquinas), but rather why, although damned, they suffer only the same punishment as unbaptized infants. The reason they are damned is for an omission: they lacked faith. But are they not guilty for this omission, and so worse than infants who are personally guiltless? Boccaccio answers by citing a legal distinction between 'ignorance of the law'—when a law has been properly promulgated and someone remains ignorant of it—and 'ignorance of the fact'—when a law has been decided on but not made public (suppose, he suggests, that the pope and the College of Cardinals have made a ruling, but have not announced it).[77] Boccaccio then looks at the three periods of sacred history in the light of this distinction. Before God chose and gave a law to the Jews, there was only the natural law, which was known to all nations. The Old Law, Boccaccio says, was given to the Jews and not promulgated publicly to all nations, and so other peoples, such as the Greeks and Romans, who did not follow it, were non-culpably ignorant of a fact. By contrast, when Christ came the New Law was publicized everywhere, and so those who ignorant of it are culpably ignorant of the law. The Greeks and Romans from before Christian times are, therefore, no more guilty than unbaptized

[76] *Esposizioni* (*Inferno* IV) II.41; Boccaccio 1965, 273. The *Esposizioni* were written in 1373–74.

[77] *Esposizioni* II.19–21; Boccaccio 1965, 268. The distinction is rather different from the theologians' common one between culpable and non-culpable infidelity. Infidelity is non-culpable unless a person actually knows Christianity and rejects it, even if this ignorance is, in Boccaccio's terms, 'of the law' and so culpable.

infants.[78] By contrast, those who came after Christ *are* culpable for their ignorance, and Boccaccio criticizes Dante for putting Ovid, Lucan, Ptolemy, Galen, Avicenna and Averroes, who lived after the preaching of the Gospel, in Limbo (rather than in Hell);[79] he mentions Seneca too, but a little later, on account of his correspondence with Paul, suggests that he might, before death, have benefited from a baptism of desire (*baptisma flaminis*) and so be in Heaven.[80] Boccaccio's attitude to good pagans, though much moulded by Dante, is thus more orthodox, in some respects more accommodating, and altogether less conflicted.

[78] *Esposizioni* II.46; Boccaccio 1965, 274–75.

[79] *Esposizioni* II.49; Boccaccio 1965, 275.

[80] *Esposizioni* I.352–55; Boccaccio 1965, 257–58. Boccaccio makes a very powerful case for why other peoples could not have been expected to follow the Jews and worship their God, showing an awareness, rare in the entire period, of how upbringing and cultural and national feelings guide people's choice of religion (cf. below, pp. 283–84, 293). The Jews, he explains, were a despised people and, in any case, despite an abundance of miracles, the Jews themselves had been reluctant to follow Moses and the law he received from God. Although it is true that beneath the strange customs of the Jews were prefigured the 'highest mysteries of the Incarnation and Resurrection of the Son', how were the other nations to know this? (*Esposizioni* II.30–45, see esp. 30–31; Boccaccio 1965, 271–74, see esp. 271). But, so far as Christianity is concerned, Boccaccio stresses even more than usual that it was universally preached in an unmistakeable fashion (*Esposizioni* II.37–38; Boccaccio 1965, 272–73. This certainty is remarkable because as a young man (in 1341) Boccaccio had translated into Latin an account of the first European expedition to the Canary Islands, and there was nothing at all to suggest that its inhabitants had ever heard of Christianity (ed. in *Monumenta Henricina* 1960, 201–6; cf. Hulme 1994, 179–82).

CHAPTER 11

Langland and Chaucer

WILLIAM LANGLAND AND GEOFFREY CHAUCER, THE TWO GREAT ENGLISH poets writing in the time of Richard II at the end of the fourteenth century, were no less concerned with the Problem of Paganism than Dante had been. For Langland, it is an issue addressed directly, with the focus on the salvation of virtuous pagans. But, despite the explicit doctrinal discussion, Langland is not simply doing the same thing in vernacular verse as the university theologians: the complex form of his poem makes the positions he takes less clearly defined, but allows him to adumbrate daring ideas outside the range of the scholastic discussions. By contrast, Chaucer avoids the theological problems almost entirely; more perhaps than any other medieval writer, he explores the Problem of Paganism by imagining himself within a pagan world, whilst aware, as his readers too would be, that there is an external Christian perspective on it, which is only partly accessible from his viewpoint on the inside.

PIERS PLOWMAN

One of the most dramatic moments in Langland's long, alliterative poem *Piers Plowman* is the brusque entry of Trajan to tell the story of his salvation:[1]

'Ye, bawe for bokes!' quod oen was broken out of helle.
'I, Troianes, a trewe knyht, Y take witnesse of a pope
How Y was ded and dampned to dwellen in helle
For an vncristene creature; Seynt Gregori woet the sothe—
That al the Cristendoem vnder Crist ne myhte me crache fro
        thenne   80

---

[1] Only the two latest and longest recensions of *Piers Plowman*, the 'B text' (from c. 1379) and the 'C text' (c. 1387), contain the Trajan episode and treat the Problem of Paganism. On the background to the poem and its author, see Godden 1990, 1–19 and William Langland 2011, II-1. Rather more than in these presentations, which stress Langland's links with monastic theology, Coleman (1981a, 1981b) makes the case for the influence of university discussions.

Bote onlyche loue and leaute as in my lawes demynge.
Gregori wiste this wel and wilned to my soule
Sauacion for the soethnesse that a sey in my werkes.
And for a wilnede wepynge that Y were ysaued,
God of his goodnesse ysey his grete wille,   85
And withouten mo bedes biddyng his bone was vnderfonge,
And Y saued, as ye may se, withoute syngynge of masses.
Loue withoute lele bileue as my lawe rightful
Saued me, Sarrasyn, soule and body bothe'.[2]

[*woet*—knew; *crache*—snatch; *as in my laws demynge*—shown in ad-
ministering my laws; *soethnesse*—truthfulness; *a sey*—he saw; *And . . .
wille*—And because he willed, weeping, that I was saved, God saw his
great will for goodness; *And withouten . . . vnderfonge*—And without
any more saying of prayers his request was granted]

In the series of dream-visions which make up the poem, the question of
pagan salvation had already been raised. The Dreamer, impatient with a
long speech from Scripture, showed his hostility to the learning she represents by saying that Solomon and Aristotle were two of the wisest men
ever, and yet, he says, 'al Holy Chirche holdeth hem both in helle'.[3] Trajan's interruption itself is to a conversation about how closely salvation
is linked to a person's behaviour. Scripture has cited the Parable of the
Marriage Feast to bring out the moral that few are saved; the Dreamer is
perplexed, but then reassures himself. Christ called all peoples, including
'Sarsens' (a term that includes pagans as well as Muslims), schismatics
and Jews, offering them all a healing remedy for sin ('And bad hem souke
for synne saue at his breste'—'And bid them to suck a salve for sin from
his breast').[4] So far as Christians, at least, are concerned, the Dreamer
reasons, they can all claim entry to Heaven, by Christ's blood, with which
he redeemed them, and by baptism. A Christian cannot deny his religion,
even should he want to do. The most, says the Dreamer, that a Christian
can do is, as it were, to wander away from home. In this case, he will—
unless he has repented and confessed—spend time, even up until the Day

---

[2] C 12.76–89; B 11.140–52. Middle English will be cited in the original, but without any
special Middle English characters. Glosses are provided. *Piers Plowman* is cited from William Langland 2011, and references are to text, passus (the sections into which the poem is
divided) and line numbers. Where B and C are substantially the same, the orthography and
wording of C are cited without further comment.

[3] B 10.385; C 11.221 (this passage is also in an earlier recension A 11.271). In the C text,
these lines are given to a personification called Rechelessnesse, a way of drawing attention
to the fact that they do not express the author's considered or final opinions, but are the
product of an attitude of carelessness; cf. the note to this passage in Langland 1978, 203.

[4] B 11.121; C 12.57.

of Judgement, in Purgatory as a punishment for his *rechelessnesse*. Scripture agrees: there is no sin which is such that mercy cannot put all to right; and, appropriately, Scripture quotes from the Bible (Psalm cxliv, 9): 'his tender mercies are over all his works'. It is to contradict this view that Trajan speaks.

Although Trajan's first remark is to condemn book learning (indeed, the Bible, just cited), a few lines later the poet draws explicit attention to his source, the *Legenda Sanctorum*, that is to say, Jacob of Voragine. In it, Langland would have seen the whole range of ways of shaping and interpreting the story.[5] Yet the version he chooses to give is one missing from the *Golden Legend*. There is no mention of resuscitation, and yet Trajan clearly states, not that merely his punishment has been relieved, but that he has been snatched from Hell and is saved. Gregory's intervention and his own justice during his life are tied closely together in order to explain his salvation. The miracle comes about because of God's response to Gregory's reaction, but Trajan's justice is the precondition for his salvation. Gregory wished for his salvation because of the 'soethnesse' (truth or justice) that he saw in his deeds. In B (XI, lines 151–52), the link is even stronger: 'By loue and by lernyng of my lyuynge in truthe,/Broughte me fro bitter peyne ther no biddyng myghte'.[6]

Modern commentators, often linking this episode with another, later passage in which Trajan is mentioned, have speculated on what theory about the salvation of pagans Langland suggests by his treatment of the story. The special inspiration theory has been mentioned,[7] or by contrast the idea of implicit faith;[8] and his position has been described as 'Pelagian' or 'semi-Pelagian'.[9] But such observations are premature. To bring whatever theory it might be of just pagans to explain Trajan's presence in Heaven is out of place, since it was generally accepted that Trajan died in such a state that he was damned and went to Hell. Langland goes along completely with this view, making Trajan declare that he was (lines 78–79) 'damned to dwell in Hell as an un-Christian creature' (even if, as Langland picturesquely suggests, 'he telde [dwelled] nat depe in helle/That Oure Lord ne hauede hym lihtliche out').[10] There can be no question of his having been saved by a special illumination or by implicit faith, since when he died he was *not* saved. Rather, his soul benefited from Gregory's miraculous intervention. The question is how, within or outside the range of ways the story had been told, Langland chose to put

[5] See chapter 8.
[6] Cf. Minnis 1997, 163.
[7] Dunning 1943.
[8] Whatley 1984a.
[9] For Langland as Pelagian here, see Gradon 1983.
[10] C 14.149–50; B 12.209–10.

it—and, clearly, he broke with precedent to present it in such a way that, without any extraneous apparatus (such as resuscitation), Trajan's soul is saved (and not merely relieved of suffering) because of his justice, which made Gregory's miracle possible. Such a narration certainly suggests a very strong link between good works and salvation, but it does not in itself imply any Pelagian or semi-Pelagian position, because it relates to a miracle. Although Trajan would not have been saved had he not been just, it is God's love (and the good luck that Gregory wept for him) which brings him to Heaven; nothing is implied about what Trajan could do with his natural powers, although Langland would hardly have written as he did if he took an extreme Augustinian position and denied that pagans could perform just acts at all.

Two near contemporary treatments of the Trajan story, one apparently close to his, one very distant, throw his handling of it into sharper relief. In his *On the Church* of 1378–79—almost exactly contemporary with the B text of *Piers Plowman*—John Wyclif gives one of the most theologically unusual explanations of Trajan's salvation.[11] He starts from the idea, common in thirteenth-century scholastic accounts, that the story does not show God, who is immutable, changing his mind: all had been predestined from eternity. But Wyclif then goes on to reject the idea which the rest of the tradition, Langland included, took for granted, that Trajan had indeed been damned. Rather, his time in Hell was merely purgatorial punishment, because he was one of the elect, like Job and Nebuchadnezzar, who were really Christians, although 'because of the particular ceremonies of our religion' we consider them to be outside the faith. The theory about the salvation of those outside Christendom implied by this comment is simply Augustine's: that members of the City of God have belonged to all peoples at every period of history, and these people are only apparently outside Christendom. But the reading of the Trajan story is unparalleled, and it is not surprising that Wyclif has no room for a resuscitation (utterly unnecessary for someone who died in a state of grace). In this respect, Wyclif and Langland are alike, but in this respect only, since Wyclif is using the story to make a point about God's elect, and Langland turns it into an exemplum about the importance of justice.[12]

Equally different, but in another direction, from the Trajan of *Piers Plowman* is the pagan judge who is brought to life by the early English saint, Erkenwald, in the poem named after him and dated to 1385–1410. The story copies that of Gregory and Trajan, except that the Trajan

---

[11] *De ecclesia* 21; John Wyclif 1886, 531, 533–34.

[12] Whatley (1984b, 56–59) presents an excellent discussion of Wyclif's account. I disagree, however, with his view that he is continuing a line of presentation found in Dante and Langland, both of whom—as I suggest in my discussions (here and in chapter 10)—use the story in ways different from each other and sharply different from Wyclif.

counterpart, a just pagan judge, lived long before Christ. None the less, he is damned until Erkenwald, expressing the wish that he could baptize him, utters the words of baptism and happens to let a tear drop on the revived body; the judge having thus been duly, if accidentally, baptized, his soul goes to Heaven.[13] Unlike either Wyclif or Langland, for their different reasons, this poet obviously wants to emphasize the importance of baptism as a sacrament.

It is characteristic of Langland, who rarely allows an issue to be resolved or forgotten, but brings it up again from another perspective, that he does not leave Trajan's own understanding of his story as the final word. First, in the person of Ymagynatif, a semi-authoritative speaker, not bound to an official position, but presenting the poet's own considered, though perhaps not final, views, the question about the ancient wise men is considered again. Ymagynatif's opinion about their fate, unlike that of the 'reckless' Dreamer, is agnostic. No 'scripture' can say whether Porphyry and Plato, Socrates and Solomon, or 'Aristotle the wise' are in Heaven or Hell, but

God is so gode, Y hope that seth he gaf hem wittes
To wissen vs weyes therwith that wenen to be saued
(And the bettere for here bokes), to bidden we ben yholde
That God for his grace gyue here soules reste;
For letrede men were as lewede men yut, ne were the lore of tho
    clerkes.[14]

[*wissen us weyes*—teach us people; *wenen*—hope; *For . . . clerkes*—Because learned men would still be uneducated without the teaching of these scholars]

The Dreamer then brings up the question of whether non-Christians of his own times could be saved. He believes that the Church gives a negative answer. We are told, he says, by priests, following their books, that without baptism neither Jews nor 'Saracens' (Muslims or any sort of pagan) can be saved. Ymagynatif does not agree:

'*Contra!*' quod Ymaginatif tho, and comesed to loure,
And saide, '*Vix saluabitur iustus in die iudicii*;
    Ergo saluabitur!' quod he, and saide no more Latyn.[15]

---

[13] See lines 208–9 (before Christ); lines 318–23 accidental baptism. The best edition is Peterson 1977.
[14] C 14.194–98; B 12.269–73.
[15] C 14.202–4; B 12.277–79.

Ymagynatif begins, as if contributing to a disputation, with the Latin tag *contra*—'against this ‹it may be argued›'. His first argument is from biblical authority. In his first epistle, Peter (iv, 18) asks rhetorically, 'If the just man will scarcely be saved, where will the impious man and the sinner appear?' Although Peter's intention is to stress how difficult salvation is, from the fact that the just man will scarcely be saved it follows (*ergo*) as a matter of logic, as Ymaginatif says, that he will indeed be saved (*saluabitur*). Next, Ymaginatif appeals, as another argument from authority, to Trajan, a pagan who has been saved as 'the boek'—that is to say, the *Golden Legend*—says,

> Troianes was a trewe knyht and toek neuere Cristendoem,
> And he is saef, saith the boek, and his soule in heuene.[16]

These two lines have led many commentators to treat the whole passage as if its purpose were to explain how it is that Trajan (or at least, Trajan in especial) was saved.[17] But Ymagynatif is answering a question about the salvation—by normal means, if any, not in the miraculous manner of Trajan's—of contemporary non-Christians. Trajan, whose story has already been told, is a useful exemplum, because he was a pagan (and, indeed, one who lived in Christian times) whose soul is known, on good authority, to have been saved (Langland chooses not to remember that not all the interpretations set out by Jacob of Voragine hold that he goes to Heaven.) The Dreamer had suggested that the reason why no non-Christians now can be saved is that they lack baptism ('follyng'), and Ymagynatif now tackles this point:

> Ac ther is follyng of font and follyng in bloed schedyng,
> And thorw fuyr is fullyng, and al is ferme bileue:
> *Aduenit ignis divinus, non comburens set illuminans . . .*[18]

[*al is ferme bileue*—'everything that has been said is accepted Christian doctrine'[19]; *Aduenit . . . illuminans* 'There came a divine fire, which did

---

[16] C 14.205–6; B 12.280–81.
[17] Dunning 1943; Whatley 1984a, 10–11; and Schmidt in William Langland 2011, II-2, 623 and most commentators read this passage as a continuation of Trajan's own intervention; Wittig 1972, 256–67 (persuasively) takes the opposite view.
[18] C 14.207–8; B 12.282–83.
[19] Schmidt (William Langland 2011, II-2, 623) suggests a reading like this, but also as an alternative to it 'each of these three modes of baptism constitutes real faith'. But this alternative is strange, because baptism cannot 'constitute faith'. The B text (12.283) reads 'and that is ferme bileue'. This could mean much the same as suggested above for the C text, or it could be an explanation of baptism by fire: baptism because a person believes firmly.

not burn, but illuminated' from a Pentecost antiphon in the Sarum breviary, alluding to the account of Pentecost in Acts, esp. ii, 3][20]

Ymagynatif is here simply pointing to what had always been orthodox doctrine, that in addition to the normal form of baptism ('of font'), there was the baptism of martyrdom ('in bloed schedyng') for those who died for Christ without having been baptized (a classic example are the innocents slaughtered by Herod), and there was also baptism 'of fire': a person (an obvious example would be a catechumen) who already believes all that is necessary for salvation, but dies before normal baptism is possible is none the less considered to be baptized.[21] Lack of baptism is not, therefore, in itself a barrier to contemporary non-Christians being saved. But Ymagynatif still has to explain on what positive basis a non-Christian might be saved, and his language becomes complex and tentative:

> Ac Treuth that trespassed neuere ne trauersed ayens his lawe,
> But lyuede as his lawe tauhte and leueth ther be no bettere,
> (And yf ther were, a wolde), and in such a wille deyeth—
> Ne wolde neuere trewe God but trewe treuthe were alloued.
> And wher it worth or worth nat, the bileue is gret of treuthe,
> And an hope hangeth ay theron to haue that truethe deserueth:
> *Quia super pauca fuisti fidelis . . .*[22]

The sense of this passage is most probably this: Consider a just person who never breaks the law of justice,[23] but has lived in accordance with this law, and who thinks there is no better law and would follow a better law (that is to say, Christianity), if it were presented to him (the B text [12.286] has 'and if ther were, he wolde amende') and who dies with his will in this state. May God, who is just, never wish but that just justice be counted as meritorious![24] And whether it turns out so or not, great trust should be placed in justice, and there is always a hope attached to

[20] See William Langland 2011, II-2, 623.

[21] See above, pp. 14–15, and below, p. 292.

[22] C 14.209–14, B 12.284–89.

[23] An alternative interpretation would be: 'his own law (the law of his religion and country)'—but this is probably more relativistic than Langland would countenance. The law of justice, by contrast, would be a facet of natural law.

[24] Schmidt (William Langland 2011, II-2, 623) gives two readings, one of them this, but the other one in which *Ne wolde* is preterite indicative, and so Langland is stating a position rather than expressing a wish. Most commentators read it in this second way. But the phrase 'Wher it worth or nat worth'—whether it turns out so or not—fits perfectly with a wish, but is strange if it follows a definite statement, since Ymagynatif would thus be stating that something is the case, and then almost immediately adding that it is uncertain whether or not it is the case. For 'alloued' meaning 'be credited to', 'be considered meritorious', cf. Whatley 1984a, 2–3.

it that justice will receive what it deserves. Ymagynatif then quotes from the Parable of the Talents (Matthew xxv, 21/23) 'because thou hast been faithful over a few things, ‹I will place thee over many things: enter thou into the joy of thy lord›'—a story in which a lord's servants are rewarded for acting justly.

Commentators on this passage debate whether Langland is proposing a theory based on *faciens quod in se est* and special inspiration,[25] or rather on implicit faith.[26] Neither solution, though, is satisfactory. Had Langland wanted, boldly, to extend salvation of pagans by implicit faith to Christian times, he would have needed to say so and indicate how the beliefs actually held by the pagans imply faith in Christ. But nothing of the sort is said. Rather, the comments on the virtuous pagan (who is made into a personification of justice [Treuth]) are close to those made by Aquinas and many others about good pagans who act as well as they can, given their beliefs and who then receive special inspiration. This theory, as opposed to that of implicit faith, was usually applied to post-Christian pagans. But Ymagynatif does not say anything about special inspiration. The implication is that, without special inspiration, just pagans might be saved simply because of their justice. Such a theory would be bold indeed, beyond the bounds of what academic theology would allow, since it would allow salvation without faith in Christ. But Ymagynatif does not actually propose the view, so much as adumbrate it. And he finishes by emphasizing that, even on this view, it would not be a matter of simple merit:

> And that is loue and large huyre, yf the lord be trewe,
> And a cortesye more then couenant was, what so clerkes carpe!
> For al worth as God wol'—and therwith he vanschede.[27]

'The lord' mentioned here is, primarily, the lord in the Parable of the Talents. When in the parable the lord is 'true', he gives the servants much more than they deserve—they have been faithful over a few things, but they receive many. In the case of God and the good pagan, too, it is suggested, the justice to which Ymagynatif appealed ('Ne wolde neuere trewe God but trewe treuthe were alloued') would not, in fact, be justice,

---

[25] Dunning 1943.

[26] Whatley 1984a, 6–11, accepted by Schmidt (William Langland 2011, II-2, 623).

[27] C 14.202–17. The parallel passage in B is 12.277–95. There are no significant changes in meaning until line 214 (B 289) which says (still very close) 'And an hope hangynge therinne to haue a mede for his truth'. What follows is different, however (B 12.290–95): 'For *Deus dicitur quasi dans [eternam vitam] suis, hoc est fidelibus. / Et alibi, Si ambulauero in medio vmbre mortis . . . /*The glose graunteth vpon that vers a greet mede to truth. / And wit and wisdom', quod that wye, 'was som tym tresor / To kepe with a commune—no catel was holde better—and much murthe and manhod'—and right myd that he vanysshed'.

but love and generosity ('large huyre'), a matter of gracious favour ('cortesye') rather than sticking to an agreement.[28]

Ymagynatif does not stay to be cross-questioned, but his comments are not Langland's last on the salvation of pagans. The climax, though not the end, of the poem is a vision of the Crucifixion and the harrowing of Hell. Before he leads out of Hell the people 'he loves and who believed in his coming' and binds Satan in chains, Christ has a speech of victory. Here he looks forward to his second coming, on the Day of Judgement, when he will take out of Hell all the human souls which are there and decide whether they should be saved or not. He divides humans into his whole brothers, who are related to him by blood and baptism—that is to say Christians— and his half-brothers, related to him, God-made-man, by blood alone. With regard to the Christians, his whole brothers, Christ says that they will not go back to Hell—a statement that implies that they will all be saved.[29] Although Langland's concern here is mainly with Christians, in the C text he goes on, very clearly, to refer to his half-brothers, the non-Christians. His nature, the fact that he too is a human, will constrain his will

> To be merciable to money of my halue-bretherne.
> For bloed may se bloed bothe afurst and acale,
> Ac bloed may nat se bloed blede, bot hym rewe.[30]

[*afurst*—thirsty; *acale*—suffering from the cold; *rewe*—pity]

Christ, then, promises to save many—though not, it seems, all—of the non-Christians on the Day of Judgement.

Theologically Langland seems to be heterodox here, not so much in the promise of salvation to many non-Christians—although the 'many'

---

[28]This idea should be seen in relation to the Oxford theologians of the 1320s to 1340s, such as Ockham and Holcot, who put great stress on the idea that God acts *according* to the covenant he has made with humans. God was not bound to make such a covenant, but having done so he has bound himself by it (cf. McGrath 2005, 113–15). By emphasizing that Trajan's salvation falls outside any covenant, Langland might be rejecting such thinking (or even showing his ignorance of it). But it is perhaps more probable that he believes this case of salvation—of a pagan after the time of Christ—to lie outside any covenant.

[29]C 20.420. B 18.379 has, even more explicitly: 'Shul noghte be dampned to the deeth that is withouten ende'. In the lines that follow, Christ compares himself to a king who can choose to pardon a man who has been hanged and not died should he be passing by at the time. Similarly, he can choose to pardon those who have already suffered in Hell, even if they were very evil. He adds (C 20.430; B 18.389) that if their sins are 'enythyng abouhte'—if there are any compensating good acts—he can be merciful out of his justice (*rihtwysnesse*).

[30]C 20.436–38. B (18.394–96) has 'bretheren' rather than referring to half-bretheren. But since Christ has already said he will pardon *all* his full bretheren, and his reasons for mercy are here couched in terms of common blood (with no mention of baptism), it is reasonable to suppose that the non-Christians are meant, and that in C he clarifies his thought without changing it.

is very unusual—as in the suggestion that all Christians, even the most wicked, will be saved, and the implication that their purgatorial punishment takes place in Hell and so that many (indeed all Christians) who are sent to Hell will not stay there for ever. But, then, Langland is not a theologian writing a treatise, nor a priest delivering a sermon. Two of the traditions on which *Piers Plowman* draws are that of personification-allegory poetry and, even though he may have known about it only indirectly, that of scholastic disputation. Both traditions allowed, in their different ways, for the presentation of many different perspectives on a problem, but also, usually, for an authorial view to be made clear. In their written-up form, scholastic disputations contained a determination by the presiding Master, on the basis of which arguments against the position he is proposing can be refuted or dissolved. In most (though certainly not all) allegorical poems, the story has a clear shape and the nature and degree of authority of each personification is clear. Much of *Piers Plowman*, however, reads like a disputation carried out in the absence of a Master to control it; and the authority of the personifications who take part in it is constantly being brought into question. The earlier pronouncements about the salvation of pagans, tentative even as they were, are further qualified because they are made by Ymagynatif, whose words have some weight, but not final authority. In the passage here, by contrast, Christ himself, Truth, is speaking. But Langland is giving the account of a vision, and the end of the passus, where he wakes and calls his wife and daughter to come and reverence the cross, underlines its personal character. The statements Langland gives to Christ, though they lack the concern for good works in the earlier discussion, chime with the views expressed there in their generally optimistic view of pagan salvation and in seeing it, ultimately, as the result of God's overwhelming love. What they do, however, is not to state a position, but open a conceptual space.[31]

CHAUCER

In his two great works set in pagan antiquity, the *Knight's Tale* and *Troilus and Criseyde,* Chaucer pointedly refrains from speculation on the destination of his characters' souls in the true Christian universe.[32] Although the *Knight's Tale* was used as part of the *Canterbury Tales,* it was probably written separately, earlier, at about the same time as

[31] On the idea of opening a conceptual space in philosophy, see Marenbon 2010, 37; Langland's space is not, however, opened in the field professional philosophical thinking, but that of theological and, even more, practical moral and spiritual reflection.

[32] At least one further work by Chaucer seriously considers ideas about paganism: the *Franklin's Tale*: see Minnis 1986, 218–37.

Troilus, in the early 1380s. The two works are closely based on poems by Boccaccio—the *Knight's Tale* on his twelve-book epic, the *Teseida*, and *Troilus* on his shorter *Filostrato*. In both, though more pervasively and successfully in the *Teseida*, Boccaccio tried to reconstruct an ancient pagan world, complete with its temples and prayers, with an authenticity unprecedented in the medieval romances of antiquity, the tradition of poems which used ancient settings and stories (such as that of Troy or of Thebes or the *Aeneid*).[33] Chaucer was sensitive to this facet of Boccaccio's compositions, and it may indeed have been why he chose them as his models. Rather than, like Langland, looking in as a theologian from the outside and asking how pagans fit into the Christian scheme of the universe, Chaucer looks out from the inside of the pagan world he imagines, posing questions about it for his Christian readers, but leaving his answers to them uncertain. He was helped to take this inside view by one work in especial, Boethius's *Consolation of Philosophy*, which he had translated into English. The *Consolation* both set a precedent, as a work written by a Christian but working within the framework of pagan philosophy, and provided suitable non-Christian, philosophical material.[34]

The *Knight's Tale* cuts down the *Teseida* to a terse narrative of little more than two thousand lines, yet Chaucer finds room to preserve and even add significant detail, and Boccaccio's pervasive reference back to the epic tradition, in the form of Statius's *Thebaid*, is echoed and amplified.[35] The ancient gods, who play an important part in Boccaccio's story, are kept by Chaucer, but their role is changed. For Boccaccio, they are fictions, with allegorical meanings, as he carefully explains in a set of glosses he wrote for his text.[36] For Chaucer, they are rather ways of speaking about planetary influences, and he arranges his rewriting with

[33] See McGregor 1991 (on how Boccaccio strives for authenticity) and Nolan 1992 for Boccaccio in relation to the tradition of the *roman antique*.

[34] See above, chapter 4, where it is shown that there is little real Christianizing of the *Consolation* by its interpreters. By the late Middle Ages, the *Consolation* was regarded even more clearly as a work by a Christian but written to explore what can be known by reason without revelation. A striking indication of this outlook, from almost exactly the time of *Troilus*, is that in Pierre d'Ailly's *quaestio* commentary (c. 1380) the question which is supposed to relate to all except the final book is 'whether a philosopher through philosophical enquiry can come, by the light of nature, to a true knowledge of human happiness'. See Chappuis 1997. Cf. also Minnis 1982, 10–11.

[35] See Anderson 1988, esp. 192–224. The most detailed comparison of Chaucer's poem with its main source is Boitani 1977.

[36] It is, however, by no means certain that Chaucer knew the poem in a glossed version: see Coleman 2005, 110–14.

exquisite care so as to make his account astrologically precise.[37] By this move, he increases the independence of the pagan world he is creating, since its deities, understood as stars, can be accepted as exercising genuine causal influence.

In telling the story, Chaucer concentrates on the central thread of Boccaccio's plot, a tale which emerges from the fratricidal strife at the centre of the matter of Thebes. Two Theban cousins, Palamon and Arcite, sentenced by Theseus, lord of Athens, to perpetual imprisonment for no fault of their own, both fall in love with his daughter Emily, whom they glimpse from the window of their cell. Eventually, having been released or escaped from prison, they decide to engage in single combat to decide which shall purse Emily, but they are surprised in their battle by Theseus and his court. Theseus decides to organize an elaborate combat, with each cousin supported by a hundred warriors; whichever one wins will marry Emily. For the event, Theseus builds a stadium and temples to Venus, Mars and Diana, the special gods of Palamon, Arcite and Emily respectively. Before the combat, each of the cousins prays, Palamon that, whether or not he is victorious, he will win Emily, Arcite for victory. Each receives a sign that his prayer has been answered, causing contention among the gods of Olympus, since Venus and Mars have each granted their worshipper's apparently incompatible demands. But Saturn intervenes, promising a solution. Arcite's party wins the combat, as Mars had promised him, but immediately afterwards an infernal Fury, sent by Saturn, frightens Arcite's horse: he is thrown off and injured, his wound festers and he dies. Theseus arranges a suitably grand funeral and, some years later, summons Palamon and, as Venus had granted, he is united with Emily.

Despite the happy ending, the world of the *Knight's Tale* is a grim one. The cousins are presented as helpless victims both of Theseus's decisions, and of their own passions: love for Emily and consequent hatred for each other. And various changes of detail contribute to making the setting in which Chaucer's Palamon and Arcite are placed a blacker one than Boccaccio had provided. For example, in the temple of Mars, Chaucer makes his account far more horrific by substituting vivid detail for Boccaccio's generalities: 'Betrayals with their hidden weapons' become 'The smylere with the knyf under the cloke'; 'bloody weapons', 'harsh threats' and 'cruel judgements' are replaced by images of the stable 'brennynge with the blake smoke' and of 'The treson of the mordrynge in the bedde';[38] and

---

[37] See North 1969 and Brooks and Fowler 1970; their conclusions are summarized in Cooper 1996, 83–84.

[38] Compare *Knight's Tale* (*KnT*) 1998–2001 and *Teseida* VII.34–35. *KnT* is quoted from Geoffrey Chaucer 1987; for the *Teseida*, Boccaccio 1965 is used.

he adds the examples of a hunter killed by bears and a baby in a cradle eaten by a pig.[39] Chaucer makes Saturn characterize himself in terms that outdo even Mars's violence:

> Myn is the drenching in the see so wan;
> Myn is the prison in the derke cote;
> Myn is the stranglyng and hangyng by the throte . . . [40]

[*cote*—cell]

Most pointedly, where Boccaccio, though carefully keeping clear of any Christian judgement about its fate, looks back to Cicero's *Dream of Scipio* to give a moment of enlightenment to Arcita's soul after his death, the Knight takes the opportunity to declare his ignorance:

> His spirit changed hous and wente ther,
> As I cam never, I kan nat tellen wher.
> Therefore I stynte; I nam no divinistre . . . [41]

[*stynte* stop; *divinistre* theologian]

The reader, it seems, is guided to take a view about the dark world in which the cousins live and die by the allusions to the *Consolation* and also through the figure of Theseus and the 'Boethian' speech he makes at the end of the poem. There are a number of direct references to Boethius throughout the poem, almost all of which are inappropriate, incomplete or both.[42] For example, Arcite is released from prison but banished from Athens so he can no longer gaze at Emily. He then paraphrases Philosophy in the *Consolation*, explaining that we should not complain about fortune, because often it gives us better than we would choose if left to ourselves; so in his case he was better off in prison than now, in exile.[43] Arcite's use of the idea is inappropriate, since Philosophy's aim is to make Boethius the Prisoner give up the false goods of fortune in search of the unchanging Highest Good, which is God, whereas Arcite's complaint is about his failure to gain the good of fortune which he persists in want-

---

[39]*KnT* 2019–20. There is a careful and illuminating comparison of the whole of the larger section of the *Teseida* (book VII) in which these passages occur and *KnT* in Boitani 1977, 76–102.

[40]*KnT* 2456–58.

[41]*KnT* 2809–11.

[42]For a list, see Coleman 2005, 134–35. Chaucer's primary source for the allusions is his own translation ('*Boece*'), with the Latin text of Boethius in the background: see Coleman 2005, 95.

[43]Compare *KnT* 1251–67 and *Consolation* III.2.4,13 (*Boece*, in Geoffrey Chaucer 1987, 422:22–25, 82–88) and possibly other vaguer allusions: see Coleman 2005, 134–35.

ing. Palamon follows, with a soliloquy which not only misuses Boethian arguments, but presents them in a partial and therefore distorted way:

> . . . o crueel goddes that governe
> This world with byndyng of youre word eterne,
> And writen in the table of atthamaunt
> Youre parlement and youre eterne graunt,
> What is mankynde moore unto you holde
> Than is the sheep that rouketh in the folde?
> For slayn is man right as another beest,
> And dwelleth eek in prison and arreest,
> And hath siknesse and greet adversitee,
> And ofte tymes giltelees, pardee.
> What governance is in this prescience,
> That giltelees tormenteth innocence?[44]

Even without the Boethian context, the argument here is hard to accept, since Palamon complains both that everything is fixed according to divine providence and that the gods have no concern for humans. The two ideas recall two different moments in the *Consolation*. Boethius the Prisoner's initial view is that God has left humans outside his providence, and in the final book, he puts forward an argument which purports to show that humans have no free choices, because of God's prescience. But Philosophy convinces the Prisoner both that God providently rules over humankind, the wicked do not really prosper nor are the good oppressed, and that, although God foresees all things, humans can still act freely. Chaucer seems, therefore, to be setting up the argument and conclusion of the *Consolation* as a standard—of the best thinking available to a pagan—against which to measure and judge the characters in this story, and so the informed reader realizes here that, just as Arcite's concern with the goods of fortune is misdirected, so Palamon's view here is limited and, although understandable given his circumstances, ultimately wrong.

Theseus is often seen, by contrast, as someone who, though a pagan, manages through his virtue and wisdom to steer his own better path through this harsh world.[45] The poem is full of pointers to his virtue. The speech he makes finally to unite Palamon with Emily, based on Boccaccio, but striking a far more philosophical tone, adds, in the opinion of most recent critics, to this picture of a pagan, not merely virtuous but eloquent

[44] Compare *KnT* 1303–14 and *Consolation* I, m. 5, esp. 25–41 (*Boece*, in Geoffrey Chaucer 1987, 404–5, esp. 404:31–405:49), but see my discussion for the first four lines.

[45] See, e.g., Cooper 1996, 79–81; Minnis 1982, 117–31. Minnis 1982, 121 writes that 'Duke Theseus is the most perfect of all Chaucer's good pagans; indeed, he is the closest Chaucer ever got to portraying a hero'.

228 • CHAPTER 11

in Boethian wisdom.[46] Yet there is nothing specifically Boethian in the thought of this speech, although its language may be influenced by the *Consolation*. Referring, not like Boethius to God or the Highest Good, but to the 'First Moevere', Theseus gives, in a vague form, a standard Neoplatonized Aristotelian account of effects deriving from an eternal first cause; it is more personalized in its expression than a real ancient philosopher would have made it, but the deity is envisaged as remoter from his creation than the Christian God. Theseus's point is simply that individuals do not last for ever, but species do, and therefore we must accept death as part of the order of things and 'maken vertu of necessitee' by allowing Palamon to wed Arcite. The 'vertu' here is not the sort of virtue Boethius discusses, nor does the system of values implied, in which the best outcome in terms of enjoying the goods of fortune is achieved, have anything to do with that of the *Consolation*. The speech is indeed sufficiently far from Boethius for it not to be seen as falling short by comparison. Rather, it is a clever reconstruction of how a pagan statesman, with a smattering of Aristotelian philosophy, might tart up a speech which, Chaucer explains explicitly, has a very political purpose: it had been decided at the 'parlement' in Atthenes 'To have with certain contrees alliaunce, / And have fully of Thebans obeisaunce'.[47] Careful readers are generally agreed, despite their (undue) praise for the philosophical qualities of the 'First moevere' speech, that Theseus is presented as falling short, though not by his own fault, of what Christianity would require, and so is in the end no more able to escape his pagan world than the fatalistic Palamon and Arcite.[48] But perhaps Chaucer is not even trying to make a comparison of his pagan world (which turns out to be not so very different from his and his readers' own) with Christian values. His poem may be even more unsettled in its stance, and ultimately cynical, than it appears.

Where the *Knight's Tale* drastically abbreviates the *Teseida*, *Troilus and Criseyde* expands Boccaccio's earlier *Filostrato*, deepening it psychologically and philosophically, although Chaucer translates many lines directly from the Italian. The poem is set in ancient Troy, besieged by the Greeks. Troilus, a prince, falls in love with a young widow, Criseyde, whose father, Calchas, foreseeing the fall of Troy, has gone over to the Greeks. She accepts his courtship and they become lovers, but when Calchas arranges for Criseyde to be swapped for a Trojan prisoner and to

---

[46] *KnT* 2987–3089; cf. *Teseida* XII, 6–19. The Boethian character of the speech is generally accepted. Coleman (2005, 134–35) cites six different passages from the *Consolation*; cf. Minnis 1982, 125–27; Cooper 1996, 70; Nolan 1992, 279.

[47] *KnT* 2973–74.

[48] See, in their different ways, Minnis 1982, 128–31; Nolan 1992, 272–81. Salter 1983 gives a very finely nuanced account of the complex way Theseus is presented.

come to the Greek camp, she quickly transfers her affections to a Greek, Diomede. Troilus, who seeks vengeance on Diomede in particular and the Greeks in general, is finally slain by Achilles.

This simple story is presented with a complexity which derives, not only from Chaucer's own understanding and skill in presenting character, psychological change and interaction, but also from the range of other sources he uses besides the *Filostrato*, and how he handles them. On the one hand, there is the whole gamut of Trojan material, from Joseph of Exeter, to Benoît de Sainte-Maure, to the Latin paraphrase of this work by Guido de Columnis.[49] Chaucer pretends, however, that he is using just one authority, a Latin writer called 'Lollius';[50] the shade of deceptive truth behind this pretence is that, through this multiplicity of sources (and his own imagination), he can appear to give a more fully and broadly historical account of the life and circumstances of Troy surrounding the two lovers than the *Filostrato*.[51] On the other hand, there is, the *Consolation of Philosophy*, never named but used even more pervasively and at greater length than in the *Knight's Tale*.

In the *Filostrato*, Boccaccio tried—though less consistently and successfully than in the *Teseida*—to present a faithful account of ancient customs and religion.[52] Chaucer follows him, 'inventing', as one recent scholar has put it, 'a precise simulacrum of the kind of narrative which, in his view, a secular pagan poet would *have had* to write about Troy and Troilus if he were to be true to his subject'.[53] Chaucer, then, is a Christian producing, though supposedly at one remove, a pagan work, in the way that Bernardus Silvestris did in his *Mathematicus* or (even more closely) John of Salisbury in the material he claimed to have taken from Plutarch.[54] For the two twelfth-century scholars, the move seems to have been intended, in part, to uphold pagan virtues as genuine and pagan wisdom as valuable for Christians and in harmony with their religion. *Troilus* allows no such simple conclusion to be drawn. Indeed, like much of Chaucer's work, the poem seems to be deliberately open: Chaucer does not merely, like Langland, avoid precise doctrinal formulations, but

[49] On the sources, see Windeatt 1992, 37–137.

[50] References to *Troilus* are to the (book and line numbers of the) text in Geoffrey Chaucer 1984. For Lollius, see 1.394, 5.1653. Lollius is not otherwise known as an ancient author, but a misreading of Horace's *Epistle* I.2, lines 1–2 could have led Chaucer to think that he was a great writer on the Trojan War; for a discussion of the problem and bibliography, see Windeatt 1992, 37–40.

[51] See Nolan 1992, 198–243 for a fine account on these lines; for the Trojan sources, see Windeatt 1992, 72–96.

[52] See McGregor 1991.

[53] Nolan 1992, 209 (Nolan has a comma after 'poet', which I have removed, since it must be a typographical error).

[54] See above, chapter 6.

weaves together his material so as to prevent any single position clearly emerging from it. Two features may, however, give some indications, since they mediate between the pagan setting, characters and narration and their Christian author and audience: the way in which Boethius's *Consolation* used, and the ending of the poem, in which Chaucer comes out from behind the veil of Lollius. But both turn out to raise more questions than they resolve.

As in the *Knight's Tale*, the uses of the *Consolation* in *Troilus* are usually either inappropriate or incomplete. For example, when Troilus first falls in love, he refuses at first to tell his great friend and confidant, Pandarus (who is also Criseyde's uncle) the name of the woman. Pandarus is trying to persuade him and says 'ffor who-so list haue helying of his leche [body], /To him byhoueth first vnwre [reveal] his wownde'. The line translates a comment Philosophy makes to the Prisoner shortly after her appearance, but where Troilus's wound is caused by romantic longing and the role of Pandarus, the doctor, will be to enable him to consummate his passion, Philosophy is about to try to cure Boethius's despair in providence, his wound, by showing him that God rules over all things and that the good do not really suffer.[55] Philosophy's high-minded observations are continually applied, in this sort of way, to the progress of the couple's amours.[56] The longest borrowing of all, however, becomes inappropriate by being incomplete. After it has been decided that Criseyde will be sent to her father in the Greek camp, Troilus goes to the temple and makes a long monologue about whether, as he puts the problem, it had been foreseen for ever that he would lose Criseyde, or whether there is no fixed destiny but everyone has free choice. The passage is a direct translation from the *Consolation*.[57] Boethius, the Prisoner, is speaking and he is putting his argument for why, since God foresees what will happen, everything happens of necessity. But Philosophy will go on to refute the Prisoner's argument and show, to his satisfaction, that divine prescience is compatible with the contingency of the future. Troilus, by contrast, does not get beyond the determinist conclusion.

One reaction is to conclude that Chaucer has simply adapted and used the *Consolation* as his purposes required, and that, if he chose the determinist part of the argument from Book V and left out the refutation

<hr />

[55] Compare *Troilus* I.857–58 and *Consolation* I.4.1.

[56] A particularly strikingly inappropriate use of Boethius is when Philosophy's lines about the transitoriness of the goods of fortune are used by Criseyde in response to a made up story (and one she probably has guessed is made up) that Troilus is dying of jealousy because he believes she has turned her attention to another man: compare *Troilus* III.813–15 and *Consolation* II.4.20; *Troilus* III.816–19 and *Consolation* II.4.12 (Boethius 2000, 38:40–42); *Troilus* III.820–33 and *Consolation* II.4.26–27.

[57] Compare *Troilus* IV.974–1079 with *Consolation* V.3.4–17.

which upholds freedom of the will, this is because he wanted to give Troilus the determinist argument, and perhaps he was even convinced by it himself. Another reaction is to suppose that Chaucer intended his readers to have the *Consolation* in their minds and use it as an authoritative standard (whether Christian or pagan is debatable) against which to measure the characters' views and behaviour. But there are also other ways of regarding the presence of the *Consolation*—both what is quoted and what is left out. Chaucer might, for instance, with no disrespect to Boethius's position, be reflecting ruefully on how philosophy can be trivialised when put to use in everyday life. At the end of his long argument on providence and free will, Troilus prays to 'almighty Jupiter' to pity him and relieve him and Criseyde of their sorrow. But, according to the necessitarian view he has just established, such prayer is pointless. Chaucer seems, then, to be showing, not so much that Troilus is wrong to accept determinism, but that a person in grief is unlikely to take intricate logical arguments to heart. More positively, it would be insensitive to take Troilus's blending of cosmic love, as described by Boethius's Philosophy, with his own romantic happiness in the song from the high point of his romance as merely inappropriate, since he has come to a genuine, if incomplete and impermanent, enlightenment through his experience with Criseyde.[58]

The ending of the poem has often been taken to give a firmer guide to interpreting it. There are really two conclusions. The first is a conclusion within the pagan story. Before Troilus's soul is assigned its place fully in accord with the pagan context ('ther as Mercurye sorted him to dwell'),[59] Chaucer uses exactly the two stanzas he leaves out when adapting the *Teseida* for the *Knight's Tale* to give him a few moments of pagan enlightenment:

> And down from thennes faste he gan auyse
> This litel spot of erthe that with the se   1815
> Embraced is, and fully gan despise
> This wrecched world, and held al vanite
> To respect of the pleyn felicite
> That is in heuene aboue; and at the laste,
> Ther he was slayn, his loking down he caste;   1820
>
> And in hym self he lough right at the wo
> Of hem that wepten for his deth so faste,

---

[58] Compare *Troilus* III.1744–71 with *Consolation* II m. 8.
[59] *Troilus* IV.1827: this is taken verbatim from the passage in the *Teseida*; in the *Filostrato* there is no comment.

And dampned al oure werk that foloweth so
The blynde lust, the which that may not laste,
And sholden al our herte on heuen caste.[60]   1825

Chaucer is here translating almost word for word, and yet he makes
a small change which changes everything. Boccaccio has Arcita see 'il
poco / globo terreno, a cui intorno il mare / girava e l'aere e di sopra il
fuoco' ('the little earthly globe, around which the sea goes round and the
air and above fire')—an accurate scientific description of the disposition
of the elements. Chaucer, rather, makes him glimpse down at the earth,
as if from outer space, and describes it with infinite tenderness, the earth
made precious by its littleness and 'embraced' by the sea. This tenderness makes it difficult fully to accept that the 'wrecched world' is entirely
vain, or that the tears of Troilus's family deserve no more than scornful
laughter.

The second conclusion is sometimes described as a palinode, in which
Chaucer finally rejects, as a good Christian, the secular values which have
dominated the narration (or, on a different interpretation, he says openly
what has been ironically implied all along). It is, rather, the one moment
when Chaucer moves outside the pagan frame, so as to reflect, as a Christian, on the story he has told, on 'the forme of olde clerkes speche / In po-
etrie' in which is told 'the fyn and guerdon for travaille / Of Iove, Appollo,
of Mars, of swich rascaille!' But, just as the narrator undercuts Troilus's
pagan enlightenment, so the stanzas which began rejecting the pagan
story turn back on themselves: abandoning what has gone before, but
with all the fondness we feel for 'This world that passeth soone as floures
faire'.[61] It is not, of course, that when he invokes the love of Christ, and
asks God's blessing for his readers, Chaucer is in the least insincere. He
has indeed left behind the pagan world he had so carefully created. But
he refuses to distance himself and his readers from it. Christ may, indeed,
be there to defend him and them 'from visible and invisible foon' [foes],
but they are not—so Chaucer hints—thereby spared from the human
complexities Troilus had faced.

---

[60] *Troilus* V.1814–25; cf. *Teseida* XI.1–3.

[61] *Troilus* V.1841. On the way in which these stanzas turn back on themselves and seem
'to express a deep sadness for a doomed potential', see Donaldson 1970.

PART III

The Continuity of the Problem
of Paganism, 1400–1700

CHAPTER 12

Pagan Knowledge, 1400–1700

THIS CHAPTER OPENS THE THIRD AND FINAL PART OF THE BOOK, WHERE in turn the three aspects of the Problem of Paganism—knowledge, virtue and salvation—will be examined for the period 1400–1700. There was a clear rationale for beginning Part II, the main body of this study, with the Carolingian period, since—despite its self-conscious classicism—there was a definite break between its culture and the late ancient civilization to which Boethius, the last author studied in Part I, belonged. No such break marks out 1400 as the date from which to start Part III. The choice has been made, rather, for negative and editorial reasons. Since one of the aims here is to argue for the idea of a Long Middle Ages, stretching up to 1700, it was important to avoid any division which could be taken to mark off the Middle Ages from the Renaissance or from Modernity. The year 1400 is too early to create any such confusion—or so, at least, it may be hoped. The editorial reason concerns the increase in material on the Problem of Paganism in, very roughly, these three centuries. In order to keep the book to a manageable length, and the lines of the story it tells clear, this period is treated separately in this final part, and handled differently from the preceding three centuries, more rapidly and selectively. There exist fine studies of many of the areas which will be covered: the aim is not to replace or compete with them, but to put them, as has not been done before, into the wider context of the Problem of Paganism in the Long Middle Ages. The present chapter begins by looking at discussions, mainly about ancient Greek and Latin pagans and their writings, in and out of the universities, before going on to see how the problem was complicated and given special relevance, but not fundamentally changed, by contacts, from 1492 onwards, with large groups of contemporary pagans, in America and then in China.

THE VIA ANTIQUA AND THE VIA MODERNA

The many new universities which were founded in German-speaking lands (as in the rest of Europe) from 1400 onwards quickly became involved in a *Wegestreit*—a conflict between the 'ways': the old—the *via antiqua*—and the new—the *via moderna*. Some universities decided to devote themselves exclusively to teaching one way, whilst at others there were separate masters for each way, with their own students housed in distinct residences. Both at the time and in many recent accounts the *via antiqua* is identified with realism over universals, and the *via moderna* with nominalism. In fact, the intellectual origins of this institutional dispute had less to do with logic and metaphysics than with the question of pagan knowledge, in the form of ancient philosophy, and its relation to theology.[1]

The tendency in early fourteenth-century Paris and Oxford, as explained above, had been to abandon the way of unity championed by Aquinas and emphasize the distinctness of theology, with its basis in revelation, from philosophy, which had been developed by pagans. During the later fourteenth century at Paris University, where many of those who would found or mould the new universities were educated, this tendency was followed and developed. For example, two of Buridan's outstanding successors, Nicole Oresme and Albert of Saxony (who became the first rector of the new University of Vienna) followed him in maintaining that according to natural reason and the most plausible interpretation of Aristotle the human soul is mortal; its immortality is a truth to be accepted by faith.[2] The most influential figure at the very end of the fourteenth century, Peter of Ailly, followed this general line and was a decided opponent of Thomism. His pupil and successor as Chancellor, Jean Gerson (d. 1429), a multifaceted and in some ways ambiguous figure, began to turn against this intellectual current, led by his interest in pastoral theology and his impatience with what he considered useless argumentation. He advocated a return to the 'well-worn way'. At the same time, John of Maisonneuve, an arts master, attacked the dominant school in Paris more directly and advocated a return to the teaching of Albert the Great.

The label 'nominalist' is an appropriate one for Buridan and his successors, since they did indeed take this view about universals, as did the other fourteenth-century thinkers, such as William of Ockham, Adam Wodeham and Gregory of Rimini, appealed to by the fifteenth-century followers of the *via moderna*. The position on universals of the great thirteenth-century masters such as Albert the Great and Thomas Aquinas had been, by contrast, realist, and the attraction for the nominalists of putting their differences in terms of an objection to realism was increased because realism, adopted from Wyclif, had been implicated in the alleged heresies of Jerome of Prague and John Hus, burned at the stake in 1415

---

[1] See Hoenen 2004. I have drawn on this article for various information in the following paragraphs. See also Hoenen 2003 and, for important background discussion, Kaluza 1995.

[2] On Buridan's position, see above, pp. 154–55.

and 1416. A summary of the nominalist position in a Cologne document of 1425 brings out this connection as well their underlying position about philosophy and theology. The nominalists complain that beginners (*iuvenes*) are introduced to the works of Aquinas, Albert the Great and other such old masters and 'although the teaching of such doctors is not bad, it is however above the capacity of young beginners'. The result is that these beginners 'not understanding the subtle sayings and high principles of this doctrine, but none the less presuming to speak according to this teaching, fall into pernicious errors or heresies or various controversies. There is the example of the people in Prague [Jerome, Hus and their followers], whose error flowed from such teaching'. By contrast, more recent masters, such as Buridan and Marsilius of Inghen, 'aware of this danger, have brought the teaching of the arts back to a humbler manner, and to other terms and manners of speaking, from which no contagion of error can derive'.[3] As this phrasing suggests, although these fifteenth-century Arts Masters are keeping the spheres of philosophy and theology separate, they can hardly considered, like Buridan and his immediate successors, as champions of a distinctive sphere of reason-based enquiry looking back to the ancient pagans, especially Aristotle. They accept their role as teaching the young in a way suited to their lack of experience; Aristotle's oeuvre is in their view 'outstanding, but extremely obscure', in need of unravelling in order to lead students to the truth.[4] Indeed, one of the accusations made against the followers of this way was that they departed from Aristotle's teachings.[5] There were, moreover, some theologians, as well as Arts Masters, who identified themselves as followers of the *via moderna* and, following Gregory of Rimini, Marsilius of Inghen and Peter of Ailly, were sharply critical of relying too much on Aristotle in developing Christian doctrine. Such a view, coming from within theology, can only be thought of as a downgrading of pagan wisdom, not an assertion of its autonomy.[6] The defenders of pagan wisdom turn out, rather, to be the followers of the *via antiqua*, since defending Aquinas and Albert also meant defending the study of Aristotle and the commentary tradition on him. The idea that the best preparation for biblical study is to work on Aristotle is stressed by Stephan Hoest, speaking to graduates of the *via antiqua* in Heidelberg in 1468.[7] The link is brought out even more strongly, three decades later, by the case of Lambertus de Monte, a

[3] Ehrle 1925, 282.

[4] This is the view which Stephan Hoest, vice-chancellor of Heidelberg, gives to the *moderni* (Stephan Hoest 1971, 176:195–201. Hoest writes separate celebratory speeches (1468 and 1469) for those receiving their degrees following each *via*: see below.

[5] See Hoenen 2003, 10–11, 15–16.

[6] See Hoenen 2004, 142–44.

[7] Stephan Hoest 1971, 150:85–93.

Cologne master whose strong adherence to Thomism led him to write a treatise arguing that Aristotle, whom he portrays as supremely wise and virtuous, is among the blessed in Heaven.[8]

Although the *Wegestreit* itself would disappear amidst the intellectual and religious changes of the sixteenth century, in the mainstream of Catholic university thinking—a powerful force until the end of the seventeenth century and beyond—there is no doubt that the *via antiqua* was victorious. Already by the turn of the sixteenth century, Peter Crockaert had made the innovation of using Aquinas's *Summa Theologiae* rather than the *Sentences* of Peter the Lombard as the textbook for his theology lectures at the University of Paris. The practice was copied by his pupil, Francisco Vitoria, when he became a professor at Salamanca, and was adopted by the Iberian theologians, who dominated the subject in the sixteenth and early seventeenth centuries. Moreover, Aquinas's thought was a shaping force behind the theology of the Council of Trent, called to respond to the challenge of Protestantism.

GOING BEYOND THE WAY OF UNITY: THINKERS OUTSIDE THE UNIVERSITIES, AND THE ANCIENT THEOLOGY

Some fifteenth- and sixteenth-century thinkers did not merely agree with Aquinas and the *via antiqua* that there is a unity between ancient pagan thought and Christianity; they wanted to go further. They were in general scholars working outside the strongly Aristotelian universities, who were deeply involved in the assimilation of the texts by Plato and late ancient Platonists that were now becoming available. These writings suggested to them—as a much smaller selection of them had done, three centuries before, to Abelard—that even in areas which Aquinas considered exclusively the preserve of Christian teaching, there was an underlying unity between ancient thinking and the doctrine of the Church, not merely a shared philosophy but a shared theology.

The first of these thinkers, Nicholas of Cusa (1401–64), however, approached the question from a slightly different perspective, because of his role as a leading churchman, deeply concerned with religious unity in practice as well as theory. He wrote *The Peace of Faith* (*De pace fidei*) in 1453 as a response to the fall of Constantinople to the Turks and the atrocities which followed. He represents himself as praying to God to 'hold back the persecution' which was taking place 'because of the different rites of the religions', and of witnessing an ecstatic dream in which peoples of all faiths are reconciled to a form of Christianity and

---

[8] See below, chapter 14.

everlasting peace is established. No dialogue has a loftier setting—Heaven itself—nor such exalted speakers: God and the Word of God, who turns to Saints Peter and Paul to explain the subtler points of theology. Their interlocutors are the representatives of different peoples and faiths. Nicholas's view, as explained through his divine spokespersons, is that religious wars and persecutions are caused because the followers of each religion believe that they will please God and achieve salvation through them,[9] and that all the different religions have the same underlying faith. Although *The Peace of Faith* is therefore an important document in the history of tolerance, Nicholas is convinced that by rational persuasion, combined with his own distinctive negative theology, a doctrinal consensus can be reached which will contain not only the Trinity but the Incarnation, the idea of faith as necessary for salvation and the sacramental core of Christianity, including baptism. In order not to disturb peace and in view of human weakness, some diversity can be allowed with regard matrimony, priesthood and extreme unction, whilst Nicholas thinks that diversity in forms of worship, dietary laws and ecclesiastical organization might even be a stimulus to devotion.[10]

Whilst Nicholas's main interest is in Islam (he also wrote a somewhat hostile *Sifting* [*Cribratio*] of the Qur'an) and the Jews, representatives of the pagans also appear before God. The first representative is clearly an ancient Greek philosopher, and the second, the 'Italian', a Roman one. They agree, in terms which would have been familiar to Abelard, that as philosophers they are lovers of a wisdom which cannot be other than single. 'None of us hesitates in thinking that there is one wisdom', says the Greek, 'which we all love and through which we are called "philosophers"; many are wise by participation in it, but wisdom remains in itself simple and undivided'.[11] The difficult question of idolatry is left to be brought by the Indian representative; Nicholas must have had in mind the travel accounts which represented Indian religions as idolatrous. The figure of the Tartar is used, by contrast, not to introduce another religion, but rather to present the whole question of religious diversity from an external point of view, and to show that even from this perspective, the underlying unity of the object of every people's worship is evident. The Tartar declares, 'I have heard many things in this place previously unknown to me. The Tartars are many and simple-minded; worshipping the one God as many, they wonder at the variety of the rites of others who worship, along with them, the same God'. He goes on to mention, as matters for their derision, circumcision, facial branding

---

[9] III; Nicholas of Cusa 1959, 10:14–17.
[10] XIX; Nicholas of Cusa 1959, 61:11–62:8.
[11] IV; Nicholas of Cusa 1959, 12:1–4.

and baptism, the diversity of marriage customs (strict monogamy, monogamy with concubinage, polygamy) and the type of sacrifice where the Christians 'offer bread and wine and say that it is the body and blood of Christ—which, after offering the sacrifice, they eat, which seems very abominable: they eat what they worship'.[12] St Paul's answer, which starts from the proposition that the soul is saved not by works but by faith, might seem irrelevant, but Nicholas is in fact using the only plausible argumentative strategy by bringing in faith at this point. He does not in any way wish to consider baptism or the Eucharist as particular rites, which some believers in true religion might follow, others not. Although all peoples may, by reason, recognize God as one, they need to accept faith in Christ, which then opens the way to a religion which might take diverse superficial forms, but has an underlying Christian sacramental structure.

Whereas Nicholas of Cusa saw a universal religion, which remained Christianity, as a prayerful hope for the future, the two leading thinkers in Italy in the later fifteenth century, Marsilio Ficino (1433–99) and Giovanni Pico della Mirandola (1463–94), considered this unity between supposedly pagan thinking and Christian doctrine a historical fact. Ficino developed his views during a career devoted to translating Plato, Plotinus and (significantly) the Hermetic corpus, and to using Platonic themes and arguments as the basis for his own philosophical positions. Ficino, who was ordained as a priest in midlife, conceived this scholarly and philosophical work as being in the service of Christianity, to which he believed Platonism was far closer than Aristotle. In his treatise *On the Christian Religion* (*De Christiana Religione*; Latin version published 1476), he contends that *religio*—respect for and worship of God—is what distinguishes humans from other animals, and he shows, from prophecies, miracles and the testimonies of non-Christians, that Christianity is the right form of it.[13] From the earliest times, however, people made sacrifices to God, the 'highest cause of things', and there were both priests and philosophers, and often the same people filled both functions, as for instance the 'mathematicians and metaphysicians' among the Egyptians, the Brahmans (*bragmanni*) among the Indians, and in Gaul the Druids. In Greece, he names the earliest of these priest-philosophers as Linus and Orpheus.[14] Representatives of this Ancient Theology can be appealed to as witnesses to Christian teaching: for example, Orpheus, Hermes Trismegistus and

[12] XVI; Nicholas of Cusa 1959, 50:14–51:6.
[13] There is a full discussion of this work and Ficino's views in it about the Ancient Theology in Trinkaus 1995, II, 734–53, see esp. 741–42. For a more wide-ranging assessment of Ficino's discussion of religious truth and philosophy, see Hankins 2009.
[14] Proemium; Marsilio Ficino 1500, f. 3r.

Zoroaster taught that God generated a word or son.[15] The explanation for this widespread wisdom lies in divine revelation and, in *On the Christian Religion*, Ficino presents the revelation as being made to the early patriarchs of Genesis and to the Jews and then transmitted by them to other nations,[16] and he mentions, with apparent approval, the identification of Zoroaster with Canaan, son of Noah's son Ham.[17] But in other works, written both before and after this treatise, Ficino also used a different, multilinear model of the Ancient Theology, which allowed for multiple revelations to different peoples.[18] Ficino probably looked to patristic writers, such as Clement of Alexandria, Lactantius, Eusebius and Augustine, and perhaps ancient Jewish ones, such as Josephus, for the idea of the Ancient Theology in its unilinear form. But it was not a Renaissance rediscovery, since from the twelfth century the idea, mainly as suggested by Augustine, had been available. The possibility of direct prophetic inspiration to different, individual pagans—an ancestor, perhaps, of the multilinear theory—was accepted by most theologians and emphasized particularly by Aquinas, although it was introduced usually in connection with the possibility of pagan salvation rather than as a way of explaining pagan knowledge. There was also an important minority tradition of medieval theologians, including Abelard, Roger Bacon, Robert Holcot and Thomas Bradwardine, who come even closer to the idea of an Ancient Theology.

For Ficino's flamboyant younger contemporary, Giovanni Pico della Mirandola (1463–94), the unity of wisdom was not merely a way of authorizing pagan writers, but a guiding principle for his work. Like Ficino, he subscribes to the idea of 'the theologies of most ancient times', and only a few paragraphs into his *Oration on the Dignity of Man* he is appealing to Pythagoras, the Chaldaeans and Zoroaster.[19] He was also responsible for adding another source of Ancient Theology to those considered by Christian thinkers—the Cabala. But incorporating these ancient traditions was only one part of Pico's far broader project of unification. The *Oration*—now his most famous work, but almost unknown in his own time—was written to introduce *900 Conclusions*: theses drawn from

[15] XIII; Marsilio Ficino 1500, f. 22r. For this identification, which Ficino may not have finally accepted, and Ficino's attitude to Zoroaster, see Allen 1998, 31–41, esp. 33.

[16] XXVI; Marsilio Ficino 1500, f. 33r-v.

[17] XXVI; Marsilio Ficino 1500, f. 34r. Ficino gives Zoroaster an important place in his Ancient Theology, under the influence of Gemisthos Plethon, who attributed the Chaldaean Oracles (translated by Ficino) to Zoroaster: see Woodhouse 1986, 47–61.

[18] See Idel 2002. Idel introduces the distinction between a unilinear and a multilinear approach and he suggests (2002, 141) that Plethon was Ficino's source for the 'multilinear' approach.

[19] 103–41; Giovanni Pico della Mirandola 2012, 162–80.

scholastic theologians, classical Greek, Arabic and Jewish philosophers, ancient sources of wisdom (the Cabala included), along with many proposed by Pico himself, as his own views or interpretations of earlier thinkers. Published in 1486, the *Conclusions* were intended to be the subject of a disputation held at Rome, where Pico hoped to show that there was underlying agreement between a variety of apparently discordant, or at least diverse, positions: Plato's and Aristotle's, the scholastic tradition, the Platonic or Platonically-inclined material favoured by Ficino and the Italian humanists and, within scholasticism, between Thomism and Scotism; and also between all of this material and the various sources of the Ancient Theology. Although, then, Pico is indeed, like Ficino, using the Ancient Theology to bring together pagan thought and Christianity, he is aiming for a wider, almost all-embracing syncretism, in which pagan philosophy has only a limited part to play. Moreover, Pico gave first place to the Cabala as a source of ancient wisdom—his one completed, published work was a cabalistic exegesis of the Genesis creation story, the *Heptaplon*. He chose Cabala especially because it derived from within the biblical tradition. Pagan wisdom was relegated to second place.

The direct historical result of Pico's unbounded ambition to unify knowledge was, in fact, the very reverse of the welcoming attitude to pagan wisdom shown by Ficino and in his own *Oration*. Some of the *Conclusions* were found to be heretical, and as a result the oration was never delivered, and the grand disputation never took place. Later in his short life, Pico was reconciled with the Church and became a follower of the ascetic, millenarian preacher, Savonarola, who had a very low estimate of the ancient philosophers' wisdom and a particular dislike for Platonism. In his final work, the *Disputations against Astrology*, Pico accepts the value of what the ancient Greeks discovered by reason, but turns against the idea of the Ancient Theology, declaring that he had been misled by the supposed wisdom of the Egyptians, and mentioning Zoroaster and Hermes Trismegistus in slighting terms.[20] Pico's work was continued by his nephew Gianfrancesco Pico della Mirandola (1469–1533) and taken in the direction which he seems himself to have been following. Gianfrancesco edited his uncle's works and prefaced them with a *Life* which emphasized the devotional turn of his later years.[21] The most important of Gianfrancesco's own writings, finished by 1514, bears the revealing title *Examination of the Emptiness of the Teaching of the Pagans*

---

[20] See Valcke 2005, 303–5.

[21] Copenhaver (2012) points out that Gianfrancesco exercised editorial control over both the letters of his uncle that were printed and the text of his last work, a treatise against astrology. It may be, therefore, that he has deliberately exaggerated the extent of Giovanni's turn to ascetic religion at the end of his life. For Gianfrancesco and his *Examination*, see Schmitt 1967.

and the Truth of Christian Teaching.[22] Giovanni's tendency, even in his earlier writings, to emphasize Judaeo-Christian revelation, becomes in his nephew's work an absolute contrast between Christianity along with the one Ancient Theology which truly foreshadowed it, that of the Hebrews, and pagan teaching, whether ancient or classical Greek and Roman. No less aware than his uncle of the variety of pagan doctrine, Gianfrancesco responds to it by the very reverse of syncretism. Outside the true path of Old and New Testament revelation, he sees the ancient philosophical schools in unending dispute, with none able to establish its doctrines with certainty. He is aided in this task by Sextus Empiricus's *Outlines of Pyrrhonism*, which he read in Greek and was the first Latin writer to use substantially: large parts of books 1, 2 and 3, which consider the schools of ancient philosophy apart from the Aristotelians, translate or follow Sextus closely, and the detailed critique of Aristotle in books 4 and 5 is also indebted to Sextus (as well as to the Jewish philosopher Hasdai Crescas).[23]

Gianfrancesco Pico della Mirandola's extreme answer to the Problem of Paganism—so extreme that there is no longer any problem—has precedents in the medieval ascetic tradition (Peter Damian, for example, or Abelard's great opponent, Bernard of Clairvaux), but it had rarely been anticipated in mainstream scholastic theology. Even Bonaventure is far more nuanced. In the sixteenth century, however, a radically dismissive attitude to pagan philosophy would become common among Protestants, inspired by Luther.[24] It was part of the more general attack on scholasticism, and so it centred especially on Aristotle.

There were, however, writers who followed and developed the syncretistic views of Ficino and Pico's earlier years, the most remarkable of whom was Agostino Steuco, an Augustinian canon and librarian of the Vatican, who used his knowledge of oriental languages and vast reading to compose *On Perennial Philosophy* (published 1540), nearly six hundred closely printed pages devoted to showing the unity of all wisdom.[25] The reason for this unity is that the main source of wisdom was a single one—Adam himself, who was able to converse directly with God. Through their overlapping lives, Steuco explains, Adam himself, Methuselah, Noah and then Abraham preserved and passed on this truly ancient wisdom to the various ancient peoples, who all lived in the East,

---

[22] Pico della Mirandola, Gianfrancesco 1520, title page.

[23] There was in fact a Latin translation of Sextus made in about 1280 (Wittwer 2002), but it seems not to have been used. For details of Gianfrancesco's use of Sextus in books I–III, see Schmitt 1967, 49–52.

[24] On Luther's attitude to pagan philosophy, see Büttgen 2011.

[25] For Steuco's background and influence, and an introduction to his work, see Schmitt 1966.

among whom the Hebrews best preserved it.[26] The Greek philosophers, therefore, owed their wisdom to the barbarians.[27] But this ancient wisdom was transmitted very imperfectly, part forgotten, part turned into fables; and, whilst the study of creation, Steuco accepted, can also teach about of God, it tends to overshadow this primary and better source of knowledge. It is only with Christianity that the original philosophy was revived in even clearer form.[28] Most of *On Perennial Philosophy* is devoted to finding the main Christian doctrines—one God, the persons of the Trinity, the Creation, heavenly reward and punishment in Hell—in a succession of pagan thinkers, stretching back to the Chaldaean Oracles and Hermes Trismegistus, through Plato and Aristotle, up to Simplicius.

The tools of philological and historical criticism ostensibly put an end to the Ancient Theology when, in his *Exercises* (*Exercitationes*) of 1614, Isaac Casaubon mined its foundations by showing that the writings of Hermes Trismegistus were not products of the remotest antiquity but, rather, the late Roman Empire.[29] Yet the Ancient Theology, and even the ancient-ness of Hermes, lived on in some areas, not least the study of China, for more than a century.[30]

The Ancient Theology was a particular, and extreme form of the path of unity, originally championed by Aquinas as his response to the Problem of Paganism. Gianfrancesco Pico and Protestants such as Luther followed the different path of Selective Rejection, which Bonaventure in especial had marked out, though again in an extreme form, so that it became unqualified rejection. The third of the thirteenth-century ways of approaching pagan knowledge, that of limited relativism, also survived in the fifteenth and sixteenth centuries. In many Italian universities, Averroism flourished in the Arts Faculties, although it was usually qualified or adapted.[31] But the outstanding, and most extreme, proponent of limited relativism in this period was not an Averroist in his mature teaching and writing. Pietro Pomponazzi (1462–1525) spent his career teaching Aristotle, mainly to medical students, in Padua, Bologna and other north Italian universities. He applied hylomorphism even more thoroughly than Aristotle himself, revising the accepted Aristotelian model of how understanding takes place in a naturalistic direction which made it more coherent.[32] Besides commentaries on Aristotle, his works on Aristotelian science include a treatise *On Enchantments*, which gives naturalistic

[26] *De perenni philosophia* 1.1; Steuco 1578, ff. 1r–3r.
[27] *De perenni philosophia* 2.2; Steuco 1578, ff. 35r–36r.
[28] *De perenni philosophia* 1.2; Steuco 1578, ff. 3r–3v.
[29] See Grafton 1991, 145–77.
[30] See the epilogue.
[31] See Marenbon 2012b, 231–32 for general survey, with bibliography.
[32] As argued very convincingly in Rubini 2013.

explanations of miracles, though it excludes those of the New Testament, and his most celebrated and controversial treatise, *On the Immortality of the Soul*.[33] Pomponazzi begins from a position none of his contemporaries would have disputed. There are elements in the human soul, he explains, such as the power of growth and sensation, which are intrinsically tied to the body and so are mortal, and other elements, the power of intellectual thought and of volition, which are exercised without bodily instruments and so give grounds to think that the soul is immortal. One way in which the soul might be both mortal and immortal, as these features suggest, is that all humans share an immortal soul but each have their own mortal soul—this is Averroes's view; another way is that each human might have a mortal soul and an immortal one—this is Platonism, as revived by Ficino and his followers. Pomponazzi gives a series of arguments against both these positions, relying mainly on Aquinas in his rejection of Platonic dualism.[34] Since no one would defend the idea that there is one mortal soul and many immortal ones, it must be that humans have just one soul, which is both mortal and immortal; and since it cannot be both mortal and immortal without qualification, which would be a contradiction, either its mortality or its immortality must be qualified (*secundum quid*). Aquinas's position, according to Pomponazzi, is that the soul is immortal without qualification, and mortal in a qualified sense. After setting out Aquinas's views, Pomponazzi proclaims that 'I have no doubt about the truth of this position, since the Bible, which is to be preferred to any human reasoning or experience, since it has been given by God, supports it. But what I do have doubts about is whether these statements go beyond the limits of natural science by presupposing something that is believed or revealed, and whether they are in accord with what Aristotle says, as St Thomas himself claims'.[35] Pomponazzi proceeds to give arguments against Aquinas's position, citing in many of them Aristotle's own statements. Concluding that the position does not seem to agree with Aristotle and is 'very uncertain' (*valde ambiguus*), Pomponazzi proposes the remaining alternative, that the human soul is mortal without qualification and immortal in a qualified way, and he proceeds to argue for it—taking, therefore, the position of Alexander of Aphrodisias, which

[33] Pomponazzi also wrote a long book on predestination, in which he ventures into specifically theological questions. Some modern readers have concluded that Pomponazzi's covert intention was to propound a determinism at odds with Christian doctrine, and with his explicit conclusions, but it is more plausible to take Pomponazzi at his word and see this as a work *not* written from within the sphere of Aristotelian, natural knowledge, but a sincere attempt by Pomponazzi, using his analytical skills, to solve some of the deepest puzzles in Christian doctrine.

[34] *De immortalitate animae* 3–6; Pomponazzi 1990, 12–44.

[35] *De immortalitate animae* 8; Pomponazzi 1990, 52.

Buridan had thought the most convincing on purely rational grounds—
and to bring up and answer repeated objections to it.[36] Pomponazzi ends,
however, by declaring the immortality of the soul a 'neutral problem',
like that of the eternity of the world. There are no demonstrative arguments for a positive or a negative answer. But it would be unfitting and
inexpedient, he accepts, to leave such a question unresolved, and there is
no need to do so, since the teaching of the Bible makes the immortality
of the soul completely clear. It is no wonder that philosophers should
disagree about the immortality of the soul, since it is a question which relates to faith, and it should be handled by the methods appropriate to it:
through revelation and the Bible. Philosophers who debate the question
using philosophical tools are using the wrong tools for the job.[37]

Despite this conclusion, *On the Immortality of the Soul* was fiercely
attacked when it was published. Even with his profession of faith taken
at face value, the treatise goes against the ruling of the Fifth Lateran
Council, made in 1513, that philosophers should find arguments to show
that the soul is immortal and refute the positions contrary to Christian
doctrine; though Pomponazzi was allowed to continue his career unhindered. Many readers, from Renan in the nineteenth century onwards,
have indeed refused to take his professed acceptance of Church teaching
on the soul's immortality.[38] They see him as someone who wished to argue
that our souls are mortal, but needed to protect himself from charges of
heresy by ostensibly rejecting the position. This reading, however, is not
only historically dubious; it also obscures what, from a methodological
point of view, and as a reflection on the Problem of Paganism, is most
interesting about Pomponazzi's treatise. Pomponazzi is using the path set
out by Boethius of Dacia, and followed by the Averroists and, to a great
extent, Buridan, in which natural science is isolated as a sphere in which
the Aristotelian philosopher can work according to reason, so long as the
truth claims of his conclusions are not upheld outside this sphere where
they contradict Christian doctrine. But there is a big difference. Boethius's
natural scientist proudly proclaims the value of his discipline, even as he
denies, as he must within it, the Christian truths (such as the Resurrection), which outside the sphere of his scientific profession he upholds.
Pomponazzi would certainly uphold the value of Aristotelian science in
dealing with most questions about the natural world. But on a question
such as human immortality, which is a matter of faith, he believes that it
is misapplied. There is indeed a justification for discussing such things in
rational, Aristotelian terms, as Pomponazzi does, not in order to establish

[36] On his discussion of some of the moral objections, see chapter 13.
[37] *De immortalitate animae* 15; Pomponazzi 1990, 228–32.
[38] See e.g., Pine 1986.

the truth in any sphere, but (in a somewhat proto-Kantian way) to establish the bounds of human reasoning. Although Aquinas's theory of the intellect is subjected to his remorseless criticism, the limited relativism Pomponazzi ends by defending, based on an awareness of the limitations of human reasoning, has more in common with the treatise *On the Eternity of the World* by Aquinas than with Boethius's of Dacia's.

PAGAN KNOWLEDGE IN THE NEW WORLD

Within roughly four decades from 1492, Europeans came into contact with—and all too rapidly made themselves the rulers of—a vast number of previously unknown pagan peoples, in what was before long recognized to be a new continent in the West, although its first explorer, Columbus, had been trying to find a sea passage to the East and believed that he had discovered outlying islands of Asia. After Columbus's first landing in the Bahamas, the Spaniards rapidly colonized many of the Caribbean islands. Between 1519 and 1521, under Hernán Cortés, they defeated the Aztec Empire (in present-day Mexico) and in 1533, under Francisco Pizarro, the Inca Empire (in present-day Peru). Reports about these newly discovered peoples soon circulated. Peter Martyr (d'Anghiera), chaplain at the royal court of Spain, never visited the New World, but began to write letters about the discoveries apparently as early as 1493 and collected his observation into 'decades' which, published progressively in 1504, 1511, 1516 and 1530, were widely read and translated.[39] Meanwhile, there was what one recent historian has called the 'tabloid journalism' of Amerigo Vespucci (from whom, by an irony of history, the new continent took its name): eyewitness reports based, in fact, on information from others, his sense of what his readers wanted as well as some first-hand experience—he did make the journey to the New World, though not the repeated voyages he described.[40] Far more thoughtful and carefully informed accounts were written in the next century, of which the most important are those by Las Casas and Acosta.[41] Bartolomé de las Casas had gone to settle in Santo Domingo (now Haiti) in 1502, but it was only ten years later that he began to devote himself to the cause of the Native Americans, joining the Dominicans in 1522 and spending the rest of his long life trying, with some limited success, to rouse the moral

---

[39] See Brennan 1996–97, 229–35.

[40] Abulafia 2008, 241–61.

[41] There are many other notable accounts of different aspects of the conquest and peoples of the New World, but of less importance for this book. They include Oviédo's *General and Natural History of the Indies* (published, though not in its entirety, in 1535) as well as accounts of the conquests of Mexico and Peru.

indignation of the Spanish monarchy against the cruelties practised by its subjects in the New World. His literary contribution to this campaign, *A Short Account of the Destruction of the Indies*, published in 1555, was very widely read and translated, but his two lengthy and sophisticated studies of the Indians, their history, way of life, geographical setting and religion—the *History of the Indies* (written between 1527 and 1561) and the *Apologetic History of the Indies* (after 1551 in the main)—were not published in his lifetime. Seventeenth-century readers who wanted a detailed picture of America, its geography, vegetation, animals and, above all, its diverse inhabitants would turn, rather, to the *Natural and Moral History of the Indies*, published in 1590, by the Jesuit José de Acosta, a less passionate man than Las Casas, who kept a greater intellectual distance from the people he wrote about and knew well, having spent fifteen years (from 1571) in America, mostly in Peru.

The Indians' religious beliefs, or lack of them, were always among the topics which most interested the writers.[42] Both Peter Martyr and Vespucci suggested—wrongly, as observers in the next century would see—that they were without religion altogether: 'We found no evidence that these people followed any law. They cannot be called Moors or Jews, and they are worse than gentiles, because we did not see them making any sacrifices, nor even did they say prayers. I judge their way of life to be Epicurean'.[43] The Aztecs and the Incas had, by contrast, obvious and highly developed religious systems, along with priests, magnificent temples and ceremonies which shocked Christians because they included human sacrifice. Both Las Casas and Acosta describe all these elements in detail, comparing them to the simpler religious practices of the less urbanized and sophisticated tribes and trying to analyse and explain the various 'idolatries', as they called them. Although it is not wrong to recognize them as pioneers of religious anthropology, they were both continuing, although developing, a long tradition among Christian writers who describe strange peoples, going back to John of Piano Carpini and Adam of Bremen.[44] Even the analytic side of their treatment of pagan worship had been anticipated in the *Book* of Mandeville (a work studied intently by Columbus) and Acosta's comparisons between biblical, Chinese and Japanese and American paganisms had a simpler precedent in Roger Bacon's parallels between Mongolian practices and those he read about in the Old Testament.[45]

---

[42] The term 'Indians' will in general be used for the indigenous peoples of America, since this was the word used at the time and adopted by the people themselves—for example, de la Vega describes himself as an *indios*.

[43] Vespucci, *Lettera* I, 14; Pozzi 1993, 144.

[44] See above, chapters 4 (Adam) and 7 (John).

[45] See above, chapter 7 (for Mandeville) and chapter 8, p. 130, for Bacon.

The sixteenth-century interest in the Indians' paganism was given an edge by more immediate concerns. The special grounds on which Spain claimed dominion over the newly discovered lands were a series of bulls issued by Pope Alexander VI in 1493, granting them to the Spanish king and queen in order to bring the inhabitants to the Christian faith.[46] Columbus himself, whose expedition preceded these bulls, was inspired in part by zeal to convert the heathen,[47] and both Las Casas and Acosta were missionary priests. Las Casas, as will become clear, had special reasons to study American paganisms, and some of the missionaries, such as Bernardino de Sahagún (d. 1590), developed a strong interest in indigenous beliefs as cultural history worth preserving for its own sake. But even Acosta, who had nothing but scorn for these 'superstitions', believed that Christians must study them and discussed them at length.

Each of the three main aspects of the Problem of Paganism was touched by the new perspectives opened up by this new source of information, interest and perplexity. Although the missionaries aimed to answer problems about the Indians' salvation by converting them to Christianity, the prima facie conclusion from the discovery of America was that, contrary to the widespread belief before, there were large parts of the world where the Gospel had never been preached. This realization would eventually change thinking about what was required for salvation, although—as will be explained in chapter 14—in a less obvious and clear-cut way than might have been expected. Ideas about virtue could be challenged—as chapter 13 will discuss—by the apparently strange values of various Indians. With regard to the subject of the present chapter, pagan knowledge, the beliefs of the Indians posed the same general problem as other forms of paganism: to what extent did they show, or derive from, a knowledge of the true God, gained from revelation or reached by reason? It might be expected that, beyond this general theme, there would be little relation between treatments of these paganisms and those of the ancient Greeks and Romans, whose literature and philosophy were even more obviously central to European intellectual life in the two centuries after Columbus than they had been in the previous millennium. But in fact, these two areas of discourse became strongly connected, in part because of Las Casas's determination to refute the reasoning used by some to justify the Spaniards in taking the Indians' land and, in practice if not theory, using them as forced labour.

[46] As made especially clear in the bull *Inter caetera* of 4 May 1493: Davenport 1917, 72–75.

[47] Columbus was also very keen to find gold, although this was in part to finance the recovery of Jerusalem for Christendom: see Todorov 1982, 11–23.

One of the two main reasons these Spaniards gave to justify their behaviour was that the Indians were 'natural slaves'. The term 'natural slave' goes back to Aristotle's *Politics*, where he identifies a class of people whose excellence consists in their bodies and who are so intellectually weak that they cannot use reason, although, unlike other animals, they know that such a faculty exists. Such people, Aristotle says, are natural slaves, made by nature with sturdy bodies to perform work and who should belong to and serve those fully endowed with reason and able to take part in civic life.[48] It seems to have been John Major, a highly influential Scottish theologian who was professor at Paris, who first, by 1510, had the idea of linking this theory with the newly discovered peoples and labelling the Indians as natural slaves.[49] He implied that the Indians' supposed lack of natural ability to rule themselves was a justification for a Christian ruler taking their land and making them his subjects, and some Spanish writers followed this line to justify Spanish rule.[50] The defender of the natural slave theory who has become notorious was Juan Ginés de Sepúlveda, who had been educated in Italy in the rhetorically based, humanistic fashion (though he says he also studied under Pomponazzi).[51] His *Democrates Secundus* (written c. 1544) is an extended defence of the Spanish right to wage war on and subjugate the Indians. In fact, although it does use the idea of natural slavery (which Sepúlveda considers a specifically philosophical notion, as opposed to the legal concept of slavery), it is only one argument among many.[52] He emphasizes more the idea that the Spaniards' conquest of the Indians is deserved punishment for their violations of natural law in practising idolatry and human sacrifice.[53] But it is the manner of the book, rather than its argument, which is most striking. He talks with contempt about

[48] *Politics* I.5, 1254a–b.

[49] Commentary on *Sentences* II, dist. 44, q. 3; Major 1510, f. xcvi ra.

[50] For example, in chapter 2 of his *Libellus de insulanis oceanis* (written between 1512 and 1516) Palacios Rubios (Palacios Rubios 1954, esp. 25–26) uses the idea of natural slavery in a tentative way (cf. Pagden 1982, 54–56). A half century later, Juan de Matienzo can still be found using the idea in his *Gobierno del Perú* (1567)—see Pagden 1982, 42. But it is evident that, from its first use by John Major onwards, the idea of natural slavery is not in fact employed to justify the enslavement of the Indians, but simply their subjugation to Spanish rule. Legally, in the eyes of the Spaniards, they were not slaves, but free men and women, subject to the Spanish crown. In reality, though, as Las Casas and other critics would protest, the *encomendiera* system, which put Indians into the power of their Spanish employers, was no better than slavery.

[51] On Sepúlveda's background and his rhetorical approach, see Pagden 1982, 109–18.

[52] *Democrates secundus* I.5; Sepúlveda 1997, 53–56.

[53] *Democrates secundus* I.11; Sepúlveda 1997, 67–72. Vitoria (*Relectio de indis* I.2.21–22; Vitoria 1967, 67–72) rejects, as the fifth of the illegitimate claims he lists, the idea that the sins of the Indians against natural law provide a justification for the Spanish conquest.

the Indians, portraying them as subhuman: '. . . those lesser human beings (*homunculi*), in whom you may find hardly a trace of humanity, who not only have no learning, but neither know nor use writing. . . . If you ask about their virtues, seeking for temperance or gentleness, what can be hoped from these people, given over to every sort of intemperance and wicked indulgence, many of whom eat human flesh . . . ?'[54] The type of approach Sepúlveda takes had already been powerfully rejected by the leading Spanish theologian and legal theorist of the day, Francisco Vitoria. His special lecture (*relectio*) *On the Indies*, written in 1539, is a powerful attack on most aspects of Spanish behaviour in America. Although he stops short of openly condemning the entire colonial venture, he allows only a few ways in which the Spaniards might have justly come to rule in America, and does not accept that they have in fact gained the lands in these ways. Among the grounds he dismisses is the argument that they have broken natural law—even if they have, it would not justify the Spaniard's dispossession of them. The idea that the Indians are slaves by nature is brought up as the main argument to support the view, which Vitoria rejects, that the Indians lack any property rights.[55] Vitoria explains that Aristotle did not intend his remarks on natural slaves to provide reasons to enslave people or deprive them of their property.[56] He does allow as a possible argument, which he neither accepts nor rejects, that the Indians come close to lacking the use of reason, and so they need to be governed by others, as if they were children—but such rule would have to be according to the Indians' best interests.[57] In any case, Vitoria accepts that the Indians are in fact rational. They 'have the use of reason in their own way' as their way of life, which includes marriage, laws and even 'the appearance of religion' indicates. The appearance of stupidity comes, he suggests, from their bad education, just as in the case of rustics in his own country.[58]

Given Vitoria's great prestige and influence, it is not surprising that Sepúlveda's book was refused permission to be published. Las Casas was particularly angered by it, and the result of his outrage, and Sepúlveda's own indignation at the banning of his book was a disputation between the two men at Valladolid in 1550, arranged by some of the leading theologians of the time, such as Melchior Cano and Domingo de Soto.[59] Las Casas's contribution to the debate is contained in his *Apology*, which

[54] *Democrates secundus* I.10.1; Sepúlveda 1997, 65–66.
[55] *Relectio de indis* I.1.1; Vitoria 1967, 13:1–14:26.
[56] *De indis* I.1.16; Vitoria 1967, 30:10–31:33.
[57] *De indis* I.3.17; Vitoria 1967, 97:1–98:47; and cf. Pagden 1982, 65–95, for an illuminating discussion of the *relectio* and natural slavery.
[58] *De indis* I.1.15; Vitoria 1967, 29:4–30:20.
[59] See Pagden 1982, 109–11.

concentrates mainly on rejecting the claim that the Spanish have the right to punish the Indians for aspects of their paganism. But the debate also led him to write, at leisure and incorporating earlier material, an *Apologetic History*. In it Las Casas aims to refute the claim at the basis of the natural slave theory, as applied to America and re-rehearsed by Sepúlveda, that the Indians lack 'the good reason to govern themselves, to constitute a political society and an ordered republic'.[60] To do so, he examines the six classes which, according to Aristotle's *Politics*, are found in all political societies, showing that they are found among the Indians too and comparing Indian with other societies. One of these classes consists of priests, and Las Casas enters into a very lengthy comparison of all aspects of Indian paganisms (not just their priests, but their gods, temples and ways of worship and sacrifice) with those of other paganisms, especially ancient Greek and Roman religion. Sepúlveda has nothing but praise for the Greeks and Romans. Las Casas wants to show, by contrast, that the Indians' paganism was superior, as paganisms go, to that of classical antiquity. He also aims to reply to the second main argument used to justify the dispossession of the Indians: that they had broken natural law. Las Casas will show that, on the contrary, the Indians acted in accord with natural law.

In his treatment of idolatry, sacrifices and the pagan gods, Las Casas manages to combine a relativistic evaluation of practices of devotion according to how they are conceived and intended with a Christian understanding of the universe, in which God alone should be worshipped. He begins from the premise, generally accepted in antiquity and through the Long Middle Ages, and which he supports with Cicero's authority, that humans have an innate knowledge that there is something divine: God or gods.[61] God has put into each human soul a light, along with the impetus or appetite to search for God and worship him. The light (which is what philosophers and theologians, he explains, call the 'agent intellect') tells each soul that God exists, and the impetus makes it seek him as its happiness. But the knowledge of God normally obtained by natural reason is confused and is not usually sufficient to show whether there is one God or many.[62] Moreover, because of ignorance and Original Sin ('the corruption of human nature with which we are all born'), people transfer the worship which is due to God to created things. There are, therefore, Las Casas explains, two sorts of worship: *latria*, which is directed to the true God, and *idolatria*, directed towards creatures.

---

[60] *Apologética historia*, Argumento; Las Casas 1967, I, 3.
[61] *Apologética historia* III.72; Las Casas 1967, I, 372–75. There is an illuminating analysis of Las Casas's treatment of idolatry in Bernand and Gruzinski 1988, 41–121.
[62] *Apologética historia* III.71; Las Casas 1967, I, 370.

One effect of this division is to present idolatry in entirely negative terms. It is 'the perverting and abuse of the reverence and sacrifice' which is naturally directed towards God to 'that which is not God'; and Las Casas, like most of his contemporaries, gives a role to the devil in fostering this false worship.[63] The origins of idolatry do not go back to the beginning of the world. Originally the one true God was worshipped, and it was only after Babel, when different peoples could no longer communicate, that the worship of false gods and idolatry took root.[64] Nor are polytheism and idolatry inevitable for non-Christian peoples. Through a lengthy process of philosophizing, Las Casas explains, Aristotle was able to show that there is one first cause of all things, the supreme good,[65] and he also believes that the Chinese (*seres*) 'do not adore or have any idol . . . and they worship only him whom they believe rules the sky, who is true God' and they 'keep natural law perfectly'—and similarly the Brahmans in India.[66]

Las Casas's division between *latria* and *idolatria* also, however, has the very opposite effect. Although the two are, in one sense, opposites, Las Casas sees them as species of the same genus, since both are ways—though idolatry is a misguided way—of worshipping the divine. He brings out this idea by the way in which he describes how, if we are without grace or teaching, we enter into idolatry. We give the obedience and service which should go to God to 'things in which some sign or appearance of goodness or excellence is known, which we call idols, or to the things which the idols represent, because whatever goodness or loftiness or nobility that creatures hold or show are nothing but footprints and signs of the divine elevation, excellence and majesty'.[67] Las Casas goes on to explain that it is also natural to humans to make sacrifices to what they hold to be God, and so ever since humans began to multiply there have always been sacrifices, whether to the true God or to false ones; no one can live without a God, false or true.[68]

The combination of these two perspectives allows Las Casas to condemn idolatry entirely from the absolute point of view of Christian truth, and yet also see it relativistically as an expression of genuine piety. Las Casas does not, however, relativize to the customs of each people and so accept every people's idolatry as equally pious. Rather, he relates them to the positive ideal he finds in the (admittedly perverse) activity of idolatry—the fact that it is directed towards the 'footprints' of God. The

[63] *Apologética historia* III.74; Las Casas 1967, I, 387.
[64] *Apologética historia* III.74; Las Casas 1967, I, 383.
[65] *Apologética historia* III.71; Las Casas 1967, I, 371.
[66] *Apologética historia* III.99; Las Casas 1967, I, 631.
[67] *Apologética historia* III.73; Las Casas 1967, I, 378.
[68] *Apologética historia* III.73; Las Casas 1967, I, 379–80.

nearer that the gods whom the idolaters worship come to God himself, the more rational and worthy is the idolatry: 'It is a common and natural concept of all people who reach knowledge that there is God, that God is the greatest among all the things that can be imagined. So the nation which chooses virtuous men for God or gods has a better conception and estimation of God and in that more worthy than that people which chooses and accepts for God or gods men known for vicious deeds . . .'.[69] Using this measure, Las Casas is able to argue that, in general, the idolatry of the American Indians is worthier and more rational than that of the ancient Romans and Greeks. Worst of all are the Egyptians, who worshipped vile animals.

When he comes to discuss the practices of pagan worship, Las Casas leans far more to the relativistic side of his position, asserting that 'there is no difference between the obligation to offers sacrifices to the true God or to a false one if he is held and received as the true one. This is because an erroneous conscience, so long as it is not given up, obliges equally as much as a true (buena) one'.[70] He also considers that all people know through natural reason that God deserves our greatest service and we should sacrifice to him whatever is most precious. The degree of reason and understanding in a people can therefore be seen by looking at the value of what they sacrifice, even to false gods. These principles allow Las Casas to address the most serious charge of unnaturalness and unreasonable cruelty made against the Indians by Sepúlveda and others, their practice of human sacrifice. From his principles, it follows that the more precious and dignified what is sacrificed, the worthier is a people's conception of God's excellence. It therefore shows more understanding to sacrifice animals than herbs, incense or foods (Las Casas refers contemptuously to 'fritters and dumplings'), the more the nobler the animal, whilst human sacrifice is the best of all, because we are offering what we consider most precious and is naturally most loved by all.[71] Not surprisingly, the detailed comparison with pagan worship in classical antiquity finds very much in the Indians' favour.[72] Las Casas has not only managed to produce counterarguments to Sepúlveda's contention that the Greeks and Romans were obviously more rational than the Indians, but also, in providing the context which allowed for this comparison, to develop a way in which pagan wisdom can be seen, not in a philosophical grasp of the one God, but in the very practices of polytheism and idolatry which, on the surface, seem signs of ignorance and folly.

[69] Apologética historia III.127; Las Casas 1967, I, 666.
[70] Apologética historia III.183; Las Casas 1967, II, 242.
[71] Apologética historia III.143, 183; Las Casas 1967, II, 43, 242–44. The theory is also expounded in the Apologia 35–36; Las Casas 1988, 43–48.
[72] Apologética historia III.186–93; Las Casas 1967, II, 258–93.

Las Casas's naturalism and relativism rest on a theological basis, the God-given rational light in each human being. But there was a different theological basis also available, which was used by some other writers of the time, who like him thought highly of the Indians, to ground their claim to knowledge of God non-relatively. The first explorers who encountered the Indians assumed, naturally enough, that they had never heard of Christ, and their view was accepted by most theologians who interested themselves in the question. As a result, the theologians had to face the problem of explaining why so many people had been left for so many centuries without the Gospel.[73] But there was a way of avoiding this problem—by supposing that the Gospel had indeed reached the Indians of America long ago. This strange view was also encouraged by three special factors.[74] There were aspects of religious imagery in America, such as the use of crosses, which many sixteenth-century Christians took as reliable indications that Christianity had once been preached. There was also the long-accepted story of St Thomas preaching in India, and the initial identification of America as India. Although by the mid-sixteenth century no one thought the American Indians lived on the fringes of Asia, this earlier confusion seemed to make it more plausible that Thomas may also have preached there. Finally, there were a number of similarities which allowed the figure of Thomas the Apostle to be rooted more firmly to America by identifying him with the god Quetzalcóatl, or to 'Pope' Topiltzin, the human, historical form of the god, on some accounts a figure of outstanding virtue. The most important exponent of this view was a Dominican, Diego Durán (c. 1537–88), in his *History of the Indians of New Spain*, who—himself probably a converted Jew—added the idea that the Indians were originally descended from the Hebrews.[75] The legend of St Thomas-Quetzalcóatl, with its implication that the Indians had been evangelized centuries before the Spanish arrived, appealed to the patriotism of the creoles, Mexican-born Spaniards, who wanted to give their country a long and independent Christian history. Further developed in the mid-seventeenth century by the Augustinian, Antonio de la Calancha, and in 1675 by the Jesuit Manuel Duarte, who collected a dossier of material on the question, the legend and its nationalistic power survived until the early nineteenth century.

Rather than claim knowledge for the Indians by the thesis of pre-evangelization, it was also open to argue for their wisdom about the true God in more genuinely pagan terms, by seeing their religion as a sort of

[73] See chapter 14.

[74] Lafaye 1974, 202–78. The following account is based on Lafaye's beautiful presentation.

[75] On the seventeenth-century debate over the origins of the Indians, see Gliozzi 1977.

philosophical monotheism, touched by divine revelation. This was the path followed by Garcilaso de la Vega (d. 1616), known as 'the Inca', because he was descended, on his mother's side, from the Incan nobility, though he spent most of his adult life in Spain. In the first book of his *Royal Commentaries* (published 1609), he tells the history of Peru before the Spanish conquest, its society and religion. He begins with an account of Peruvian paganism which concentrates on the worship of many gods, including vile animals, and on human sacrifice conducted with shocking cruelty.[76] But, he emphasizes, this description applies only to the period before Inca rule. Not only did the Incas put an end to human sacrifice, they also abandoned polytheism: so de la Vega insists, despite claims to the contrary by Spanish historians who have failed to distinguish between pre-Incan and Incan times and also been misled through their ignorance of the Incan language.[77] According to de la Vega, externally Inca monotheism appears to be directed towards the Sun, which is the only object of their worship. But in fact the Inca kings and their wise men (*amautas*) or 'philosophers' believed in the one true God, creator of Heaven and Earth. They called him Pachacámac, 'animator of the universe', and they worshipped him as the unknown God, not with outward ceremonies, but inwardly in their hearts, hardly daring even to utter his name.[78] De la Vega strengthens the idea that the Incas enjoyed a genuine revelation of God by explaining how they kept a cross in one of their holy places,[79] and he says that they held both the immortality of the soul and the resurrection of the body.[80] He does, however, add that they did not conceive this resurrection as one to glory or punishment, but simply to the present earthly life, above which 'they did not lift their understandings', and he does see the devil as implicated even in Incan worship.[81] Whilst, then, to a large extent de la Vega treats the Incan attitude to God in the same general way as a whole line of thinkers, from Abelard (and even in some respects Augustine) onwards, had envisaged that of Plato and other ancient Greek philosophers, he—'a Christian, Catholic Indian', as he calls himself[82]— still prefers to keep a certain distance from the religion of his ancestors.

It would be wrong, however, to leave the impression that the theme of pagan knowledge was generally treated in a way favourable to the Indians. The very opposite view was forcefully put by the widely read,

[76] *Comentarios reales* I.9–11; de la Vega 1976, I, 26–31. On de la Vega, see Bernand and Gruzinski 1988, 124–33.

[77] *Comentarios reales* II.1, 4–5, 8; de la Vega 1976, I, 59–61, 66–72, 77–78.

[78] *Comentarios reales* II.2; de la Vega 1976, I, 61–64.

[79] *Comentarios reales* II.3; de la Vega 1976, I, 64–66.

[80] *Comentarios reales* II.7; de la Vega 1976, I, 75–76.

[81] *Comentarios reales* II.9; de la Vega 1976, I, 78.

[82] *Comentarios reales* II.2; de la Vega 1976, I, 63.

officially appointed historian of the Indies, Acosta. Where Las Casas gives the devil a subsidiary role, as an encourager of idolatry, for Acosta every aspect of the Indians' religion is a diabolical contrivance. The treatment of American religion begins with a disquisition on the devil's pride and how he makes idolaters deny God and worship what is lower than themselves. Satan is never far away in the following chapters as the causal agent behind every type of idolatry.[83] Acosta treats these varieties in a more systematic and self-disciplined manner than Las Casas. Types of idolatry are divided by their objects. There are two main divisions, according to whether what is worshipped is a natural thing or the result of human imagination or artifice. Natural things are further divided into those worshipped in particular (this or that river or tree) and things worshipped in general; and non-natural things into artefacts, such as statues, and things which really existed but are not as the idolaters imagine them to be, such as the dead.[84] This division may well lead to a more finely grained analysis than Las Casas provides, but, as developed by Acosta, it leaves no room for an evaluative distinction between different paganisms. All polytheistic, idolatrous worship is seen as the work of the devil and duly condemned, though Acosta reserves a special outrage for human sacrifice, which he describes in gory detail.[85] Acosta notices that there are various features in Indian worship and religious life which are reminiscent of Christian practices, such as monasticism, communion, anointing and confession. But he does not see them as evidence for the early evangelization of America, despite the fact that he used a manuscript based on Durán's work as his source for information in Mexican religion. Predictably, he chooses to explain them too through his general thesis of diabolic causation: the devil mimics the sacraments of the Church. Acosta does not entirely exclude the idea of pagan wisdom from his view of things. But he follows the traditional path of finding it in a supposed element of monotheism within pagan beliefs. He says that the Peruvians and Mexicans do have the idea of a supreme deity, and he makes the comparison with Plato, Aristotle and Hermes Trismegistus (and also the Chinese), but they have the idea only dimly, so that there is no word in the Indian languages, he says, for God.[86] There is no trace of Las Casas's relativism.

The devil's agency appears prominently in another widely read account of America, Jean de Léry's *Story of a Journey Made to the Land of Brazil*. De Léry tells the story of the time he spent in 1557–58, twenty years before, when he and his Protestant companions had to flee the

---

[83] *Historia natural* V.1; Acosta 1962, 217–18.
[84] *Historia natural* V.2; Acosta 1962, 218–19.
[85] *Historia natural* V.19–21; Acosta 1962, 248–54.
[86] *Historia natural* V.3; Acosta 1962, 219–20.

short-lived settlement made by the French in what they called 'la France antarctique'. De Léry's first-hand knowledge of the Tupí, a warrior people who ate their captured enemies in an elaborate ritual, makes his book probably the most vivid of all the early accounts, and he suggests, in the manner of his description, a remarkably favourable moral judgement on them, which Montaigne would develop.[87] This side of his work will be examined in the next chapter. The other, ill-matched side sees the devil, not simply as the cause for quasi-religious phenomena, but a destructive force, directly attacking the Indians through his demons. This picture, which owed much to de Léry's belief that he and his fellow Protestants were a small band of the elect in a wicked world, was grounded by his use of the theme of pagan knowledge, but in a way entirely adverse to the Indians he is describing. At one point, he seems to deny that the theme has any application, saying that Tupí are an exception to Cicero's well-known observation that there is no people so brutal, barbarous and savage as to lack the notion that there is a divinity. Not only do they not believe in the true God. They do not even seem to reverence any gods, and they have no forms or places of worship.[88] But this is not de Léry's final view. He is persuaded, by their belief in a life after death, by their fear of thunder and the credence given by them to sorcerers, that they do have traces of knowledge of God.[89] He even entertains the idea—though in a far vaguer way than those who supported the story of St Thomas-Quetzalcoatl— that one of the Apostles may have come and preached to them.[90] These traces of knowledge are not, however, seen by de Léry as being to their benefit: on the contrary, they make them inexcusable, because they cannot claim that they are simply ignorant of God.[91] Indeed, de Léry considers that the Tupí provide a vivid example of an accursed people (he traces their ancestry back to Noah's cursed son, Ham), abandoned to the devil and daily suffering from the encroachments of his demons.[92]

MATTEO RICCI AND THE INVENTION OF CONFUCIAN MONOTHEISM

Europe did not have to discover China for itself, as it did America. The 'land of silk' was known in the ancient world, and medieval readers could have learned about it from Marco Polo's first-hand accounts. There was

[87] See chapter 13.
[88] *Histoire d'un voyage* 16; de Léry 1994, 377–79.
[89] *Histoire d'un voyage* 16; de Léry 1994, esp. 384–85.
[90] *Histoire d'un voyage* 16; de Léry 1994, 414–16.
[91] *Histoire d'un voyage* 16; de Léry 1994, 395.
[92] *Histoire d'un voyage* 16; de Léry 1994, 385–89, 419–23.

even a bishopric in Beijing in the fourteenth century.[93] Yet with regard to intellectual life, and especially thinking about pagans, China was as important a discovery in the seventeenth century as America had been in the sixteenth. Unlike the European incursion into America, with its vast human, political and economic consequences, the encounter with China was almost exclusively intellectual. There was no question of defeating or occupying China, but the Jesuits hoped they might convert it. It was the Jesuits' policy for their missionaries to learn the language and absorb the culture of the peoples they wished to convert. Michele Ruggieri, the first Jesuit to reside in mainland China (from 1580), thought it appropriate to dress himself as a Buddhist priest, even though he was strongly critical of Buddhism. His companion and successor, Matteo Ricci, chose rather, once he had gained some knowledge of Chinese society, to dress as one of the literati: the mandarins who had been educated and rigorously examined in the Confucian classics and who, under the emperor, governed this vast, highly populated and, to European eyes, impressively well-ordered land.[94] Ricci's identification with Confucianism went far beyond dress. He sought out the society and conversation of the literati and targeted them, with some success, for conversion. His strategy was to master not just the Chinese language, but the classic texts of Confucianism, and then to develop a version of Confucianism completely compatible with Christianity, so that the Chinese literati could become Christians while fully retaining their cultural identity. This project turned on the central of the problem of pagan knowledge: to what extent do pagans, or some of them, know the one true God?

As Ricci and other European visitors knew, in China there were, besides a few Jews, some Muslims and the traces of Nestorian Christianity, three main sects (*setti*): Confucians, Buddhists and Daoists. Ricci is consistently hostile to Daoism, and to Buddhism too, although he recognizes some features it has in common with Christianity and, indeed, believes that it was influenced by Greek philosophy.[95] He seems to have taken the strategic decision to side with Confucianism, around which official culture and the examination system were based, although the three sects were less exclusive of each other for the Chinese than Ricci conceptualizes them as being—and indeed he himself recognizes and deprecates the view, which he describes as 'the most common among those who believe themselves wiser', that the three sects are really just one, so that they can

[93] See chapter 7.

[94] On Ricci's decision about dress and its background, see Spence 1985, 114–16. On the wider background to Ricci, the Jesuits in China, and their attitude to (and shaping of) Confucianism, see Rule 1986; Jensen 1997; and Po-Chia Hsia 2010 (a biography of Ricci).

[95] [*Diaries*] I.10, nn. 182–99; Ricci 1942, 121–32.

all be followed together.[96] Another reason for choosing Confucianism is that Ricci could argue that it was free from the vice found in most sorts of paganism, and strongly present, he thought, in Buddhism: idolatry. Although the Confucians had temples, to Confucius and to various protector spirits, Ricci presents them as places not of worship, but rather of instruction and assembly. He records the solemn ceremony among the literati of offering each year food, perfume and silk to their dead ancestors. It sounds exactly like the sort of pagan rite which had been practised by some early Christians, but Ricci explains that it is not idolatry of any sort. The dead ancestors are neither thought to need the offerings, nor to be any sort of divinities, nor is anything asked of them. The ceremony is a way of expressing love and gratitude and, according to some, intended more for the living than the dead, to impress on the ignorant the importance of serving their living parents, when such honour is given even to dead ancestors.[97]

Ricci was also, however, all too well aware that the Confucianism followed by the literati of his time, strongly based on the interpretations of the classics made over five hundred years before during the Song dynasty, was anything but compatible with Christian teaching. They denied the immortality of the soul and favoured a sort of pantheism, according to which everything, including God, is part of the same substance.[98] But Ricci claimed that, in holding these beliefs, the literati of his own day had diverged from the original tradition of Confucius. Ricci has a great deal of respect for what he considers to be that original tradition, not because he sees Confucius as the beneficiary of revelation, but as someone who follows natural reason: 'in what he says and in his good way of living in conformity with nature, he is not inferior to our ancient philosophers, but exceeds them by many things'.[99] And, despite their false—and he would consider rationally confutable—beliefs about God and immortality, Ricci is happy about the way the Confucians of his own time do not so much constitute 'a fully-formed law', but rather 'an academy, instituted to govern the state well', since it means that they can continue to be Confucians and yet become Christians.[100] Confucianism is not a rival religion.

The literary monument to Ricci's missionary policy of what came to be called 'accommodation', and the view of Chinese paganism which supported it, is a treatise he wrote in Chinese and published in 1603–4, *The True Meaning of 'Lord of Heaven'* (*Tianzhu shiyi*). It takes the form of

---

[96][*Diaries*] I.10, nn. 199; Ricci 1942, 132; *Tianzhu shiyi* VII.508–20; Ricci 2013, 221–24.

[97][*Diaries*] I.10, nn. 177–80; Ricci 1942, I, 117–20.

[98][*Diaries*] I.10, nn. 176; Ricci 1942, I, 115–16.

[99][*Diaries*] I.5, n. 55; Ricci 1942, I, 39.

[100][*Diaries*] I.10, n. 181; Ricci 1942, I, 120.

a dialogue between a literatus from the West, Ricci himself, and a Chinese literatus, an open-minded, highly educated Confucian. Ricci sets out, successfully, to persuade his interlocutor that there is a supreme God, creator of Heaven and Earth, and that our souls are immortal and will be rewarded in Heaven or punished in Hell. His argumentative weapons are philosophical reasoning—he employs, for instance, somewhat crude versions of some of Aquinas's Five Ways, along with moral arguments, to show the existence and unicity of God[101]—and authoritative texts. But the authorities are not those of the Christian tradition, but the Confucian classics. Ricci wants to show that, interpreted correctly, these ancient texts teach the fundamental truths he is urging. Only in the case of Hell, for which he knows he can find no support in the Confucian tradition, does Ricci resort to the argument that the absence of mention of something in the canonical books does not mean that it does not exist—any more than the fact that the Bible does not name the most ancient emperors of China implies their non-existence.[102] The two main targets he attacks are, characteristically, Buddhism and the Neo-Confucianism widespread at the time, which denied the existence of a transcendent deity and the immortality of the soul. Ricci is hasty to reject any parallels the Chinese literatus suggests between Christianity and Buddhism and, by analysing the position of the Neo-Confucians according to the substance-accident metaphysics of Aristotelianism, he shows to his own satisfaction that their position is logically incoherent.[103] Only at the end of the work does Ricci talk about more specifically Christian doctrine and, although his interlocutor requests baptism, he takes his leave finally to think over what he has learned. As a missionary, Ricci wished no doubt to win souls. But in his writing he places all his emphasis on showing that there exists the precondition which, he believes, will allow them easily to be won in China: an almost perfect coincidence between natural law and the ancient Chinese literary and philosophical tradition.

The True Meaning reached a wide Chinese, and also Japanese, audience, but was unknown in the West.[104] Ricci's ideas, in briefer form, influenced the European debate through his diaries which, though edited in their original Italian only in the twentieth century, were translated into Latin (with alterations, but not so many as to obscure the main lines of his thinking) and published by a fellow Jesuit, Nicholas Trigault, in 1615.[105] But Ricci's main influence was through the succession of Jesuits in the seventeenth century who went to China and wrote about it for

---

[101] *Tianzhu shiyi* I.29–50; Ricci 2013, 11–23.
[102] *Tianzhu shiyi* VI.394; Ricci 2013, 174–75.
[103] *Tianzhu shiyi* II.98; Ricci 2013, 43.
[104] Ricci 2013, lviii–lix.
[105] See Mungello 1985, 46–48.

European readers. Although his policy of accommodation was rejected by some, such as his successor in China, Niccolò Langobardo, most of his confreres adopted it.[106] *Confucius the Philosopher of the Chinese*, which was published in 1687 under the general editorship of Philippe Couplet, shows how Ricci's approach stretched late into the century.[107] It contains translations of three of the classic Confucian texts, the result of a group effort stretching back for decades, to which Ricci himself had contributed, along with a life of Confucius and a hundred-page introduction. Here Couplet explicitly defends and restates Ricci's view of an original monotheistic Confucianism pushed aside by the atheistic misinterpretation of the Neo-Confucians, although the root of this approach is now traced to one of the classic texts, the ancient *Book of Changes*, and the Neo-Confucian interpretation is recognized as not entirely atheistic.[108] Another new theme is the placing of China's beginnings shortly after the Flood and the suggestion that the earliest Chinese kingdoms benefited for many years from a revealed knowledge of the one God.[109] This turn from Ricci's emphasis on natural reason to seeking in ancient China a belief in God based on revelation, on the model of the already outdated idea of the Ancient Theology, would prove surprisingly influential.[110]

---

[106] See Mungello 1985, 74–299.
[107] Couplet 1687; see Mungello 1985, 247–99 and Kern 1998, 262–67.
[108] For a discussion of the *Book of Changes*, see Couplet 1687, xxxviii–lxiv.
[109] Couplet 1687, lxxiv–lxxvii.
[110] See below, the epilogue.

CHAPTER 13

Pagan Virtue, 1400–1700

THE DOMINANT VIEW AMONG SCHOLASTIC THEOLOGIANS IN THE LATE thirteenth and fourteenth centuries was that pagans could be genuinely virtuous, although their virtues were not of the sort which could merit salvation. It was developed in dialogue with the leading opponent of this view, Augustine, whose texts (especially those from his late *Against Julianus*) were quoted and, since his authority had to be respected, interpreted charitably to accord with the position he wanted to reject. In the period after 1400, mainstream Catholic theologians in the scholastic tradition tended to take the same broad view as their predecessors, drawing especially from Aquinas's work, but reformulating it to take account of new opponents. By contrast, and surprisingly, writers more influenced by humanism, such as Valla and More, were often more sceptical about pagan virtue, although they presented their doubts in sophisticated literary forms which admit of various readings. From 1500, the newly discovered pagans of America presented another side to the problem of pagan virtue, overlooked by most mainstream writers on them, but noticed by Jean de Léry and probed by Montaigne. This chapter looks at each of these approaches in turn.

PAGAN VIRTUE IN THE LATE SCHOLASTIC TRADITION

In the fifteenth and sixteenth centuries, ideas about pagan virtue going back mainly to Aquinas were developed in a fresh dialogue with Augustinianism: not with Augustine himself, but with theologians who presented his views more systematically and rigidly than he himself had done—and with whom it was permitted openly to disagree. The first, and in many ways most influential of these neo-Augustinians, Gregory of Rimini, lived a little earlier, in the mid-fourteenth century. But he had Catholic successors, such Michael de Bey (Baius; d. 1589) and Cornelius Jansen (1585–1638), and, although there were differences of emphasis and degree, Protestants tended to take a similar but more extreme view, that even with grace all humans sin.[1] Gregory of Rimini had posed a challenge to any attempt to uphold a human good apart from the Christian life, arguing with remorseless logic that any action not for the sake of God was not in accord with right reason and so morally evil.[2] De Bey rejected Aquinas's idea that, as he put it, 'because virtues refer to some true particular good, they can be referred to universal good'. He thought that no such reference could be made if the agent was not acting for the universal good (that is, God), and might even hold it in contempt.[3] He therefore insisted that, when Augustine described the pagans' supposed virtues as vices, he did not mean merely that they did not lead to salvation.[4] He bases his position on the view that human free will is powerless, without God's aid, to do good or to resist any temptation.[5] Jansen followed and developed de Bey's views. In his view the deeds of pagans are 'evils and sins' and so 'not true virtues, but vices hidden by the name and appearance of virtues'.[6]

The process of meeting these new challenges by recasting weapons Aquinas had once used had already begun shortly after 1400, when John Cabrol ('Capreolus'; 1380–1444) wrote his *Defences of the Theology of Thomas Aquinas*, in which the whole range of problems in contemporary philosophy were answered by reference to Aquinas's texts. Capreolus modelled his answer closely on the materials left by Aquinas, especially the idea that, for an act where a person is not bound by divine law, it is enough for it to be directed to some proximate good end; though, he adds, this end must be one that is itself referable to the final end.[7] Thomas de Vio (Cardinal Cajetan, 1468–1534) extended this line of thought. The universe, he says, is *in fact* ordered with God as its end. He is then able to argue that, although it is necessary to love God as the final end in order to act well, this requirement does not prevent non-Christians from being able to perform good acts: 'To love God in this way [as the final end] happens in two ways, implicitly and explicitly: explicitly when someone directs his intention to it; implicitly when someone's inclinations are to things as they are. For, from the fact that things are rightly ordered, and are ordered to God, with the universe as intermediary, an inclination

[1] This is how Suárez (*De gratia Dei* I.3; Suárez 1857 369–74) describes the views of Luther, Calvin and Melanchthon. He distinguishes their position from that of Baius, who held that everyone without sanctifying grace cannot avoid sinning (I.4; Suárez 1857, 375).

[2] See above, pp. 186–87.

[3] *De virtutibus impiorum* II.4; Baius 1565, 42v.

[4] *De virtutibus impiorum* II.5; Baius 1565, 43r–44v.

[5] *De virtutibus impiorum* II.8–9; Baius 1565, 46v–49v.

[6] *Augustinus* II.4.17; Jansenius 1640, II, 627.

[7] *Defensiones* II, d. 41, q. 1, a.3; John Cabrol 1967, 470–74, esp. 470.

which tends to things as they are set up in their gradations tends to them implicitly as they exist for the sake of everything, and ultimately for the sake of God'.[8] Pagans can, he believes, know that God is the end of all things through philosophy, but 'if they were not to know this, it is enough for avoiding sin in many of their actions to love and set their intentions on God implicitly, by always inclining to things as they are, although this is not sufficient for eternal salvation, nor to avoid all sins'. Similarly, Cajetan explains that, in the case of someone who explicitly desires to know philosophy without any other intention, he is implicitly desiring it for the sake of the universe and God, because his inclination is tending towards the thing as it is. In effect, Cajetan uses the way the universe is in fact—created by and centred around the Christian God—to make pagans Christian-like despite their own, he would say defective, understanding of why they are acting. Vitoria, commenting on Aquinas's *Summa Theologiae* a little after Cajetan (in 1534–37 for this part), may have seen that this approach is problematic, since it is too externalist to be credited: it drives too thick a wedge between the way it describes acts and how the agents themselves envisage them. He does not reject his predecessor's solution out of hand, but he prefers to stick with the idea that an act can be good without being performed for the sake of the final good, God.[9]

The most thoroughgoing, bold yet careful development of this position is due to Francisco Suárez (1548–1617), the greatest of all the sixteenth- and seventeenth-century philosophers who worked, broadly, in the scholastic tradition. Suárez's central point is that the moral value of an act can be judged without reference to any end beyond the action itself. If the act's object is right, then a free will can be moved by it, as the intrinsic end of its deed, and such an act is itself right and an example of moral virtue. Although we are commanded to love God above all things, we are not obliged to be doing so always: there is no injunction given by God that *every* act should be referred to a higher end.[10] On this view, even an idolater or an atheist can perform morally good acts. The fact that such a person's unbelief is part of the context (one of the 'circumstances') of the act need not undermine its goodness, so long as the agent acts for the sake of rightness not for that of his unbelief; even an idolater might not perform every act for the sake of his idol.[11] Suárez does, however,

[8] Commentary (section 2) on Aquinas *Summa Theologiae*, IIaIIe, q.10, a.4; Thomas Aquinas 1882–, VIII, 83.

[9] Commentary on Aquinas *Summa Theologiae*, IIaIIe, q. 10, a.4—section 10; Vitoria 1932, 178–79.

[10] *De gratia Dei* I.6.15; Suárez 1857, 390–91.

[11] *De gratia Dei* I.6.13–14; Suárez 1857, 389–90.

set a limit to the ability of fallen humans to act well without the special assistance of grace, since we can neither always resist strong temptation, nor succeed in observing natural law entirely.[12]

PAGAN VIRTUES OUTSIDE THE UNIVERSITIES

Lorenzo Valla was one of the outstanding fifteenth-century exponents of humanism, a movement which prized study of the ancient literary classics above everything. He cast his *On Pleasure* (first published 1431)[13] in the form of a Ciceronian dialogue among a group of humanists. Yet the purpose of the work, he claims, is to attack the idea that there were virtuous pagans, such as the philosophers, who lived almost irreproachable lives.[14] Valla insists, by contrast, on the harshly Augustinian position that the pagans 'did nothing rightly and nothing with virtue'. Unlike Gregory of Rimini, and the theologians who, in the following two centuries, would defend this position, Valla establishes it through a purely philosophical argument, which emerges from the juxtaposition of views he presents. The first two books pit Catone, a defender of Stoicism against Vegio, an Epicurean. Catone praises the virtues, as shown in the lives of great ancient heroes such as Regulus and Fabritius and philosophers and poets, such as Socrates, Plato, Aristotle, Homer and Euripides.[15] The good, according to him, is 'righteousness' (*honestas*), which consists in having the virtues and which is sought for its own sake.[16] Vegio's Epicureanism is based on the usual medieval sources (Valla does not seem to have been influenced by Poggio's discovery in 1417 of Lucretius's *On the Nature of Things*).[17] His central doctrine is the authentically Epicurean view that the good is pleasure (*voluptas*), which includes bodily pleasures but also mental ones. Yet, unlike earlier accounts which sought to rehabilitate Epicurus (such as Abelard's or John of Salisbury's), Vegio does not emphasize the simple, ascetic aspect of Epicurus's ideal of tranquillity, but gives plenty of room to sensual pleasures such as wine drinking. He goes further, indeed, advocating adultery, except for the dangers involved if it

[12] *De gratia Dei* I.24, 8, 20; I.26; Suárez 1857, 492, 495–96, 507–11.

[13] He revised the work substantially (changing the names of the interlocutors) in 1433, and again in 1444–49. The title he finally chose for it was *On the True and False Good* (*De vero falsoque bono*). For an account of the different versions of the dialogue, see (the introduction to) Lorenzo Valla 1970, xxx–lvii. Lorenzo Valla 1977, to which references are made, reprints the text and apparatus of this critical edition and gives a parallel English translation.

[14] Bk. 1, Proem. 4; Lorenzo Valla 1977, 48–50.

[15] Bk. 1, II.3; Lorenzo Valla 1977, 56.

[16] Bk. 1, XV.2; Lorenzo Valla 1977, 88.

[17] See above, chapter 5, note 40 on medieval knowledge of Epicureanism.

is detected, and deprecating virginity.[18] And, though the virtues too have a place, as means to gaining pleasure (they are servants and pleasure is their mistress and not, as usually presented, 'the whore among good-living married women'), they turn out to be rather different from what their names traditionally describe: for instance, prudence consists simply in knowing how to gain what is advantageous for oneself and avoid the disadvantageous, continence means giving up one pleasure so as to gain more and greater pleasures and justice is 'that by which you can gain goodwill, thanks and advantages from people', as when a leader divides the spoils with his soldiers after a victory, because otherwise they will desert or even kill him.[19]

Vegio, then, denies that there are distinctively moral values. *Honestas*, he claims, is 'an empty and useless word, which serves no purpose, proves nothing and on account of which nothing should be done'.[20] Vegio is, in contemporary terms, a moral non-realist, who also has the belief that each human pursues what seems to be his or her own greatest pleasure. He sees this as the disposition of (a very un-Epicurean) providentially conceived Nature, so that in following pleasure as an end humans are living in the way they have been constructed to live.

The final main speaker, Antonio, puts forward the Christian view. In doing so, however, he bases himself on the contrast that has just been developed between the two philosophical views, Stoicism and Epicure-anism. Antonio reproaches Catone for having spoken as if he were not a Christian, though he is one.[21] Antonio's own position—exactly that which Valla puts in his own voice in the Proemium—is uncompromis-ingly Augustinian: all that the ancients, other than the Jews, did was not only not worthy of reward, but deserved punishment.[22] Yet Antonio finds common ground, not with the upright Stoic, Catone, but rather with Vegio, the Epicurean. Partly this is because he considers that Vegio has not been speaking seriously, but as a feigner, whereas Catone meant what he said literally.[23] But there is a serious core to Vegio's feigning, which Antonio (and by implication Valla himself) accepts. Although he does not consider Vegio's libertine Epicureanism even as a seriously meant recom-mendation for Christians on how to live, he accepts his Epicurean analy-sis which makes pleasure the end for which humans do and should act. Humans are constructed so as to be pleasure seekers, he believes, and it is right for them to make pleasure their end. Christians, therefore, Antonio

[18] Bk. 1, XXVIII.1–XLV.12; Lorenzo Valla 1977, 112–28.
[19] Bk. 1, XXXIII.2; Lorenzo Valla 1977, 114.
[20] Bk. 2, XV.2; Lorenzo Valla 1977, 170.
[21] Bk. 3, VII.7; Lorenzo Valla 1977, 260.
[22] Bk. 3, XI.2; Lorenzo Valla 1977, 268.
[23] Bk. 3, VII.5–6; Lorenzo Valla 1977, 260.

argues, should indeed seek pleasure, but the pleasure of the world to come. He insists that, whilst God is the object of Christians' love, they do not love him for his own sake, but for the sake of the pleasure (identical to the loving of him) that God gives: God is to be loved as an efficient, rather than a final cause.[24] As for pagans, Vegio's Epicureanism, in which moral values disappear, is the only way in which pagans can think honestly, since the knowledge that the only reliable and permanent source of such pleasure is the Christian God is denied to all who live outside the aegis of revelation. That is why Antonio says about *all* the Greeks and Romans that 'since they did not worship God, it is necessary that they were won over and compelled by Epicurean arguments and should accept that debauched sex, adultery, crimes and almost every sort of wickedness are not to be condemned but numbered among the goods'.[25]

Reluctant to see an admiring connoisseur of ancient civilization take so harsh a view of its heroes, in the past some historians tried to find an authorial view in *On Pleasure* different from Antonio's.[26] Deeper knowledge of Valla's background and aspirations, and the fact that he repeats similar views in a later non-dialogue-form work, have made such interpretations implausible. Nearly a century later, in 1515, another humanist, Thomas More, wrote a dialogue, also treating of pagan virtue, which offers no similar interpretative near certainty. The longer part of it is a report by a certain Raphael Hythlodaeus, supposedly a companion of Vespucci's, of an island which reveals its imaginary status by its very name: Utopia ('No Place'). Utopia is organized according to strict laws, which enforce common ownership of property, work for all and communal meals. Although the Utopians, having heard about Christianity from Hythlodaeus and his companions, have been won over to it in large numbers, More chooses to make them, when discovered, pagans. But does he make them *virtuous* pagans?

It would be easy to conclude that he does, since Utopia is often considered to have been intended as an ideal society, a reading supported by the fact that the description of Utopia is preceded by an account, added later, of the ills in European society, which Utopian arrangements avoid. Many contemporaries, and some modern scholars, read the book in this way; Guillaume Budé, who contributed a prefatory letter, calls Utopia 'Hagnopolis', a holy city, where 'a celestial life, below heaven but above

[24] Bk. 3, XIII.2–3; Lorenzo Valla 1977, 274.
[25] Bk. 3, XI.2; Lorenzo Valla 1977, 268.
[26] See Fois 1969; rounded interpretations of Valla as a Christian thinker are given by Lorch 1985 and Trinkaus 1995, 103–70. Valla returned to the same ideas (though with some important new developments) in his *Repastinatio dialectice et philosophie* (first version 1439, subsequently revised; often referred to as *Dialectical disputations*): I.10; Lorenzo Valla 1982, 3–98; see the excellent discussion in Nauta 2009, 152–90.

the draff of the known world' is lived.[27] Recent readers, however, have not been content with so simple a reading. Some scholars point to certain Utopian customs, notably euthanasia, which the author is unlikely to have endorsed, whilst some go further and suggest that Utopia, with its lack of freedom and aggressive behaviour if brought into war, is a most un-ideal state.[28] Moreover, after Hythlodaeus's description, the narrator, More himself, briskly dismisses as 'absurd' most of the striking and unusual aspects of Utopia, especially its communism.[29] But then this dismissal is so abrupt, and seems so completely to miss the point both of Hythlodaeus's arguments and the way Utopia answers problems raised in book 1, that perhaps 'More' should not be taken as the author's voice— and some interpreters, indeed, have seen the book as aiming to provoke thought rather than to put forward any one view.[30]

Since no secure overall interpretation from which to read More's attitude to paganism is available, it is best to begin with the details given about the Utopians' pagan thought. Like Valla, whose *On Pleasure* certainly influenced him, More turns to Epicureanism when he presents the Utopians' philosophy.[31] They consider that pleasure (*voluptas*) is the measure of human happiness, and that the only good reason for making a less pleasant choice is that it will lead to greater pleasure in the long run. But this teaching is qualified in two important ways. First, although *voluptas* is commonly used to mean bodily pleasure, it is quickly made clear that it is not every sort of pleasure that leads to happiness, but only 'good and upright' pleasure.[32] It turns out, indeed, that bodily pleasures of any kind are ranked very low, since they are usually simply the relief of some pain (eating, for example, relieves the pain of hunger), although health is valued highly. But the pleasures which are ranked most highly are mental pleasures, and among these they think 'the foremost comes from the exercise of the virtues and the conscience of a good life'.[33] Although virtues are not, as for the Stoics, valued for themselves, they turn out to be the best way to the pleasantest life. The second qualification

[27] More 1965, 12:5–9. For a modern reading in this vein, see J .H. Hexter in his part of the introduction to More 1965, esp. lxxvii.

[28] See, e.g., Hanan 2010.

[29] More 1965, 244:13–21.

[30] Baker-Smith 1991, 225: 'the function of the book is not to establish a preferred viewpoint but to convey through its literary form a complex interplay of ideas which lie at the very roots of Western political discussion'.

[31] More 1965, 160:13–178:15. This, and all the references to *Utopia* which follow, are to book 2; unfortunately there are no chapter divisions. More's sources are accounts of the Epicurean position (as given especially by Cicero) but also Plato's *Philebus*. For a detailed discussion, see Logan 1983, 144–81.

[32] More 1965, 162:16.

[33] More 1965, 174:30–31.

departs radically from the Epicurean model. Whereas Epicurus denied that our souls survive after death, in Utopia the discussion of happiness in terms of pleasure is always coupled, we are told, with principles taken from Utopian religion: that the soul is immortal and people will be rewarded or punished in the afterlife for their good deeds or crimes.[34] The Utopians say that, were it not for these beliefs, it would be foolish for anyone not to seek to maximize pleasure by whatever means. Anyone who denies immortality, they consider, will try to break the laws and is therefore not entrusted with any duties and is generally scorned.[35] There is a rather obvious conflict between the two qualifications, since if the highest pleasure consists in being virtuous, then no one will ever maximize pleasure by acting viciously. It is easy, though, on one level to find a charitable interpretation of this rather loose presentation of a philosophical position by an observer, Hythlodaeus, who may be supposed not fully to grasp it. Presumably, even in so well-educated and egalitarian society as Utopia, there are many who do not realize that practising virtue gives more pleasure than more obviously pleasure-bringing activities; and so these people will be restrained from pursuing anti-social pleasures on earth by the belief that they will receive heavenly reward or punishment. On a deeper level, however, More introduces a note of tension by suggesting that the rational consideration which leads the Utopians to accept the religious principle of post-mortem reward and punishment is precisely the fact that they are needed to act as restraints in this way.[36] True, they regard deniers of human immortality as subhuman—people who have lowered 'the sublime nature of their soul to the vileness of a beast's little body'[37]—but More does not supply the Utopians with any rational argument for immortality.

[34] More 1965, 160:26–162:2.
[35] More 1965, 220:20–222:14.
[36] The account makes clear that the idea of post-mortem reward and punishment belongs to religion, which is a different source of principles from philosophy 'which uses reasoning' (*quae rationibus utitur*) (More 1965, 160:28–29). Reason itself is regarded as being 'insufficient and weak' (160:30) without these religious principles. When, then, a few lines later, Hythlodaeus says that 'although these principles belong to religion, they judge that they are led by reason to believing and conceding them' (162:4–5), the reason which leads them cannot be a rational argument for their truth (since they are not truths of reason), but rather, as the syntax indeed indicates, the conclusion they reach without hesitation that 'when these principles are removed, no one would be so stupid as not to feel that he should seek pleasure whether through acting well or wickedly' (162:6–7). Skinner (1987, 149) notices the problem in putting together these ideas, but considers that they point to an admission by the Utopians that their religious outlook 'may not be altogether satisfactory'.
[37] More 1965, 220:26–27. More too believed that it was a 'brutish beastly perswasion' to believe that human souls are mortal, but accepted that many pagan philosophers held this view: see texts cited in More 1965, 524–25.

Such tensions show that the treatment of paganism in *Utopia* is two-sided. One side might be called 'humanist', since it shows More's tendency, as an admirer of the Greek and Latin classics, to emphasize the achievements of a pagan civilization like theirs; or even more fittingly 'Abelardian', since without knowing Abelard's works, More comes very close at times to the way Abelard sets up political institutions in a pagan society as an ideal to be emulated by Christians—indeed, his ideal cities are also, like Utopia, communistic.[38] Abelard may, moreover, offer a suggestion as to why More chose to base Utopian philosophy on Epicureanism. When Abelard created an imaginary philosopher, in order to explore what could be known by human reason, without revelation, he deliberately avoided making him a Platonist or even an Aristotelian, because he thought that those philosophies had been influenced by revelation. Perhaps the same train of thought led More to choose a blend of Epicureanism and Stoicism (similar to that of Abelard's Philosopher) for the philosophy of a civilization that he has deliberately cut off from revelation. Just as Abelard shows how close to Christianity pure reasoning about pleasure, virtue and happiness has brought his Philosopher, so More presents the Utopians with a way of thinking that makes them easy and willing converts. Yet he adds more shadows than Abelard.

The other side of More's thinking about pagans might be called 'Augustinian'. But it is Augustinian in a complex way. When Augustine criticizes Roman civilization, his major charge against its best representatives is that they sought glory, as exemplified both in their military conduct, or became proud, as the Stoics did by pursuing virtue for its own sake. More has carefully designed his Utopian pagan civilization to avoid, and indeed go against, these two defects. A large part of the description is given over to a critique, by reference to Utopian practices, of the concern for military glory normal among More's European contemporaries, whilst Utopian philosophy carefully avoids any valuing of virtue for itself, even while making the virtuous life the best one. More is thus superficially anti-Augustinian, suggesting that the particular Roman vices most excoriated by Augustine are not endemic to every pagan civilization. But, underlying his use of Utopia to criticize the social arrangements of European societies is a deeper Augustinianism. Augustine did not contrast the Roman Empire with a Christian state, but with the City of God, people from all countries and all ages living their earthly lives usually unknown to each other and brought together in a fellowship virtual on earth, because it would be realized only in Heaven. Christian states might be better than pagan ones, but both are on the same level as societies of fallen, sinful humans. From this Augustinian point of view, it makes very good

[38] See above, p. 86.

sense to investigate how best to organize human society by pursuing a rational best commonwealth exercise and setting revelation aside, since the problems of social organization confronted by Christians in a fallen world are the same as those faced by pagans. More's optimistic view that in principle a pagan society might avoid the vices of the Roman Empire is balanced by a pessimism, seen in the rebarbative aspects of Utopian arrangements which have disconcerted some of its readers.[39] Utopia, although pagan, is an ideal society, but it is a practical, worldly ideal, which the Christian states of More's Europe *could* attain. The underlying irony is that they are so far from doing so.

When, in *On the Immortality of the Soul*, Pomponazzi has answered the direct objections to the view that, except in a relative sense, the human soul is mortal, he turns to answer a type of indirect objection which corresponds exactly to the Utopians' view about deniers of human immortality: on such a view, it is objected, no one would ever give up his life for the good of the commonwealth, even if avoiding death meant acting disgracefully.[40] Pomponazzi answers by putting forward the Stoic view (though he supports it by reference to Aristotle and Plato) that virtue is the most precious and happy thing for humans, and so that we should choose it for itself, even should it lead to our death.[41] The rewards or punishments after death which his opponents believe are needed to make people willing to sacrifice themselves would be merely accidental, as opposed to the essential reward of virtue itself and the punishment of guilt. And, he adds, those who act from hope of an (accidental) reward are less virtuous than those who act for the sake of virtue itself.[42] Altogether he considers that 'Those who assert the mortality of the soul seem better to be able to uphold the definition of virtue than those who assert its immortality. For hope of reward and fear of punishment seem to imply a certain servility, which does not fit with the definition of virtue'.[43] Pomponazzi does, however, go on to add an important qualification. He explains that most people are not so well constituted by God that they will pursue virtue for its own sake. Rewards and punishments are necessary to make them virtuous, and for some, so fierce and perverse that even these will not influence them, the statesman—says Pomponazzi—needed

[39]The point is well made in the introduction to More 1995: 'Despite its abundant wit, *Utopia* is in fact a rather melancholy book. More evidently shared with St Augustine . . . the conviction that no human society could be wholly attractive'.

[40]Chap. 13; Pomponazzi 1990, 156. He also raises (162–64) and dismisses (chap. 14; Pomponazzi 1990, 220) the accusation (which corresponds to the Utopians' opinion) that deniers of immortality have been the most impious and wicked of people.

[41]Chap. 14; Pomponazzi 1990, 186–90.

[42]Chap. 14; Pomponazzi 1990, 192–94.

[43]Chap. 14; Pomponazzi 1990, 224.

to promise reward and punishment after death, especially the latter, because 'the greater part of humans, if they do good, act more from fear of eternal harm than from hope of eternal good'. In doing so, the statesman did not mind about truth, but acted like a good doctor, in order to cure citizens of their moral ills. Pomponazzi therefore shares Valla's and the Utopians' views about moral motivation so far as most people are concerned, but not about the real nature of moral values. He implicitly concedes that the ideas of reward and, especially, punishment after death serve a socially valuable purpose, but points out that this concession does not provide grounds for accepting their truth, since they will have their valuable effects if people are made to believe in them, even by rulers who do not themselves share the belief. Although this line of argument could be read as undercutting Christian belief, it need not be. Pomponazzi's point—directly contrary to Valla's—is simply that some exceptional people can lead fully upright moral lives without Christian (or indeed any other) religious belief. This view does not exclude Christians from moral uprightness (though it does prevent them from attaining the highest level of it),[44] and it implies that most people, who are not motivated by virtue for its own sake, will lead more virtuous lives if they are Christians than if they have no belief about divine reward and punishment. Pomponazzi's view is also compatible with holding that there are non-moral excellences of behaviour open to Christians alone.

The question of whether a paganism without rewards and punishment in the afterlife is compatible with morality was taken up by other writers in the following century and a half. Pomponazzi's upright pagans who denied the soul's immortality are ancient Greeks and Romans, such as Hippocrates, Galen, Alexander of Aphrodisias and Seneca, along with more recent Arabic philosophers (al-Fârâbî, Ibn Tufayl, Ibn Bâjja).[45] Matteo Ricci faced more immediate proponents of the same view. In a section of his dialogue *The True Meaning of 'Lord of Heaven'* which is closely based on conversations he had with a Confucian scholar, Zhang Huang, the Chinese literatus is made to put to Ricci the view that the Confucian sages do not consider consequences, but merely the beauty of virtue itself.[46] Ricci answers by saying that, while Christians accept the intention to act well in order to gain eternal rewards is good, the intention simply to obey God's will is even better. He illustrates the point with the story of an early Franciscan who, even when told that he is destined for Hell, is all

---

[44]Chap. 14; Pomponazzi 1990, 194: when a good is accidentally rewarded (as by happiness in Heaven), then 'it seems that the essential good is diminished and does not remain in its perfection'.

[45]Chap. 14; Pomponazzi 1990, 220.

[46]*Tianzhu shiyi* VI.341; Ricci 2013, 153.

the more eager to serve God while he can, on earth.[47] This line of thinking would provide a way of rebutting Pomponazzi's suggestion that the hope of a heavenly reward makes the virtue of a Christian less than that of a pagan who can be motivated only by virtue as an end in itself.

Valla, More's Utopians (and presumably More himself), Pomponazzi and Ricci, despite their deep differences, share the somewhat pessimistic view that, for the majority of people, the prospect of pleasure or pain after death is an essential factor in making them lead good lives. In *Various Thoughts on the Comet* (1682), Pierre Bayle rejects this position, because his view of human nature is even more pessimistic. He points out that people are often believing and even pious Christians, yet they regularly perform all sorts of actions forbidden by God and punished by him. It is not general principles, he considers, which guide people's particular actions, but rather their passions.[48] Bayle uses this principle in an extended comparison between the behaviour of two groups of, ostensibly, pagans: atheists and idolaters. By 'atheists' Bayle means, in accord with the usage of his time, those who reject the existence of a providential God who rewards and punishes people in an afterlife. Although atheism, in this sense, is often thought of as a specifically modern, seventeenth-century concern, Bayle's atheists have their forebears in earlier centuries: Dante's Epicureans, Pomponazzi's deniers of immortality, Ricci's contemporary Chinese literati. Since the promise of otherworldly reward or punishment is ineffective, Bayle contends that a society of atheists 'would practise civil and moral actions as well as other societies, provided that it punished crimes severely and attached honour or infamy to certain things'.[49] Like Pomponazzi, he insists that the known atheists of antiquity led virtuous lives, and he goes on to portray Epicurus as someone who not only led an upright life, but worshipped the gods who, he believed, have no concern for us, simply because he judged them worthy of worship: 'And so it is true that reason discovered, without the help of religion, the idea of that piety so boasted about by the Church Fathers, which brings it about that a person loves God and obeys his laws solely because of his infinite perfection'.[50]

The idolaters, with whom Bayle compares the atheists, are officially the followers of polytheistic pagan religions of antiquity. But most of

[47] *Tianzhu shiyi* VI.366–71; Ricci 2013, 163–65.

[48] See esp. *Pensées diverses* 136; Bayle 1727, 87–88; Prévot 2004, 976–77. (References are to the collected edition of Bayle, published early in the eighteenth century, and also to Prévot's collection, which reprints the text of 1683, a somewhat enlarged version of the text he had originally published the year before.)

[49] *Pensées diverses* 172; Bayle 1727, 109; Prévot 2004, 1035.

[50] *Pensées diverses* 174, 178; Bayle 1727, 110–12, 114–15; Prévot 2004, 1038–42, 1047–49.

Bayle's examples of the inefficacy of religious belief to bring about virtuous behaviour concern Christians of his own times. The context of Bayle
and his *Various Thoughts* suggest why there is this disparity, and what it
means. Bayle was a Calvinist, forced to flee his native France and live in
the Netherlands. *Various Thoughts* appeared anonymously and, in order
to facilitate publication and perhaps also because of the particular ironies
Bayle intended, it is supposedly written by a Catholic. What this invented
Catholic author identifies as the idolatry of the ancient pagans is made,
by his own all too acute, almost undisguisedly Baylian, analyses of contemporary social behaviour, to apply by implication to the idolatrous
religion of contemporary Christians: Catholics especially, but the point
being made is not narrowly sectarian. Bayle takes a view of virtue that is
deeply Augustinian, although it differs from him verbally. He is willing to
talk about the virtuous acts of pagans (both idolaters and atheists), but
not only are they not meritorious—as most theologians, Protestant and
Catholic, would agree—they neither derive from a good principle nor are
directed towards a good end. Mere belief in God, or even in the Christian
God, is not enough to enable someone to act virtuously for the right end
and so meritoriously; what is required is sanctifying grace.[51] The reader
acute to Bayle's Calvinist subtext will gather that very few people, even
in the Christian (and mostly Catholic) Europe of the seventeenth century,
benefit from this grace. Virtue, as normally found, in Bayle's own day as
much as in antiquity, is not merely pagan, but atheistic, in the sense that
belief in gods, or even in the true God, adds nothing to it.[52]

BEING VIRTUOUS DIFFERENTLY

Although it might make no sense to talk of virtues with contents utterly different from those we recognize, it is certainly possible—as the
practice of both anthropologists and some moral philosophers today
illustrates—to envisage sharply different understanding of what is virtuous or morally good from one culture to another. In all the discussions of
virtue so far, however, it has been taken for granted that the content of
virtue is roughly the same, either superficially or deeply, between Christians and pagans, ancient or contemporary. With regard to the pagans of
ancient Greece and Rome, Christian thinkers took over their very classi-
fications of virtue (as Abelard pointed out)[53] from the philosophers. Even

---

[51] *Pensées diverses* 146; Bayle 1727, 94; Prévot 2004, 993–94.
[52] Bayle has been taken by many, since his own day, to have been aiming to undermine
Christian belief entirely. The improbability of such an interpretation emerges when he is put
into his Protestant context: see Labrousse 1964, 1985.
[53] *TChr* (Peter Abelard 1969) II.27.

Augustine admitted that the pagans grasped correctly what the virtues are superficially, although they did not understand correctly the deep structure of true virtues, according to which all good actions are done for the sake of God. Although Ricci and his successors could not have been more aware of the vast differences between the culture they strove to assimilate and their own, they urged the case for the moral excellence of the Chinese in terms of their following the one, natural law followed by virtuous pagans everywhere (and when Ricci wanted to compose a book of moral advice and comfort for his literati friends, he simply translated— with a few additions and changes—from Epictetus, a virtuous pagan of ancient Greece).[54] Sepúlveda and Acosta condemn American Indian practices by reference to this same, single natural law. Las Casas may seem to be an exception. He argues that the human sacrifices which some of them practised, regarded in Christian culture as abhorrent, should be seen, on the contrary, as showing their devotion to God and the superiority of their paganism to paganisms where less precious things were sacrificed. But Las Casas makes these assertions on the basis of what he takes to be a principle applicable to all humans that we should sacrifice to God what is most precious; Christians do not make such sacrifices because they are instructed to do otherwise by revelation. His relativism in this respect is thus real, but superficial.

There is, however, one writer, at least, who brings a deeper relativism to the content of virtue in his discussion of distant but contemporary pagans, in one of the best known texts in the whole area. In his essay *On Cannibals*, Montaigne states near the beginning that we call barbarism 'what is not our custom' and he goes on, 'Indeed, we have no criterion of truth or reason other than the example and idea of the opinions and practices of the land where we are. Perfect religion, perfect government, the perfect and right use of all things is always *there*'.[55] This has been taken to indicate, especially when coupled to the shocking expectations raised by the essay's title, Montaigne's relativistic intentions. But in order to be assessed and placed in relation to the Problem of Paganism his essay needs to be seen in relation to other writings which, like it, told a European audience about the anthropophagous Tupí Indians of Brazil. Montaigne insists that he has his information from oral sources, especially a servant who had spent ten or twelve years there.[56] But almost all the details in his account seem to have been taken from

[54]The work was his *Ershiwu yan* of 1605; cf. Po-Chia Hsia 2010, 259.
[55]*Des cannibales* is essay 30 of bk. 1; Montaigne 2007, 208–21; this reference, Montaigne 2007, 211.
[56]Montaigne 2007, 208.

two published works, André Thevet's *Singularities of Antarctic France* (1557) and Jean de Léry's *Story of a Journey Made to the Land of Brazil*.

Thevet, an unwilling Franciscan, spent only a few weeks in Brazil, and his work, based on the first-hand accounts of interpreters, is more a compilation than an original composition. But it is rich in information, and it describes in detail the cannibalistic ceremony which would give Montaigne his title. When, in the constant tribal wars undertaken just out of desire for revenge, a warrior is taken prisoner, he is treated as an honoured guest, provided with a woman (perhaps his captor's daughter) and fattened up on the best food. All this, though, as he knows, is just a prelude to the day when he will be slaughtered in front of his enemies, dismembered, cooked and eaten. Yet he does not try to escape. Rather, he boasts that he himself has eaten the relations of his captors, promises that his people will avenge him and is full of joy when the preparations to kill him are being made.[57]

De Léry's descriptions are often close to Thevet's, but usually far more lively, both because of his extensive first-hand experience and his ability to convey it. His view of the Tupí Indians as people lost to the devil (shared by Thevet, despite the confessional divide) was discussed in the last chapter.[58] But this pessimistic, Calvinist assessment is only one side of his book. De Léry also felt great affection for the 'savages' as he calls them, who offered genuine unstinting hospitality and, unlike many of his fellow Christians, were undissimulating, so that he admits, writing twenty years later, that he is often sorry not to be among them.[59] At times, he portrays them using the language of the Golden Age which Columbus and the earliest writers on the New World had employed to describe the Indians they encountered: not only do the Tupí live extraordinarily long and healthy lives, they are free from want, greed, ambition and envy.[60] In one remarkable passage, he eavesdrops on his hosts' dance ceremony, described by him with great precision; despite his Calvinist disapproval of dancing, he is enchanted, and even twenty years later, writing his account, the sound of their singing rings in his ears.[61]

---

[57] *Les Singularités de la France Antarctique* 40; Thevet 1997, 160–62.

[58] For Thevet on the diabolical possession of the Indians, see chaps. 35–36, Thevet 1997, 142–44.

[59] *Histoire d'un voyage* 21; de Léry 1994, 508. For the hospitality, see chap. 18 (de Léry 1994, 449–67).

[60] *Histoire d'un voyage* 8; de Léry 1994, 211–12; cf. Lestringant 2005, 90–94; on the Golden Age picture in the earliest accounts, see Abulafia 2008, 110–14.

[61] *Histoire d'un voyage* 16; de Léry 1994, 399–406; see the penetrating study in Lestringant 2005, 147–70.

De Léry's description of the ceremonious killing and eating of prisoners is, like almost everything in his book, more vivid than Thevet's, especially the victim's defiant joy and his taunts to those about to kill him. Both writers comment explicitly on the cruelty of the practice, although de Léry saves his main explicit condemnation for 'the end of this strange tragedy' when the captive's child, if he has fathered one, is also eaten.[62] Both also contextualize what they have described, to make it less strange and less exceptionally evil than it may seem. Thevet comments briefly that it is not strange if the Indians 'who walk in darkness' should seek and carry out vengeance, when Christians do the same, even though they are expressly forbidden.[63] De Léry tells—adding more and more detail in later editions of his book, until it formed a separate chapter—of equally horrific cruelty and cannibalism metaphorical and real in Europe and, indeed, France.[64] Even in Thevet's laconic description, the unyieldingness of the victim brings a comment: 'they take no account of death, even less than it is possible to think'.[65] De Léry goes further, comparing the prisoner's defiance to that of Regulus, a Roman whom even Augustine found it hard fault.[66]

Montaigne's trick is to recount the act of cannibalism in a single sentence. He accepts that there is 'barbaric horror' in it, but immediately qualifies the point by his famous comparison with the horrors perpetrated in his times in the Wars of Religion: 'it is more barbarous to eat a living human being, than a dead one'.[67] His attention, however, is on the meaning of the practice, as an ultimate expression of revenge—something which Thevet and de Léry clearly recognized, but did not make central in the same way. For Montaigne, it is a key to understanding what is recognizably a 'moral science' (the irony here is directed less against Tupí simplicity than European pretention to wisdom), but one that 'contains just two articles: resolution for war, and love for their wives'.[68] De Léry had explained how their wars were not for the sake of conquest or booty, but simply from the wish for vengeance. He links the 'barbarian cruelty' of these irreconcilable enmities to the behaviour of another group also in the clutches of the devil: Machiavelli and his followers.[69] By contrast,

[62] *Histoire d'un voyage* 15; de Léry 1994, 369–70.

[63] *Les Singularités de la France Antarctique* 41; Thevet 1997, 165.

[64] *Histoire d'un voyage* 15; de Léry 1994, 375–77 and chap. 15bis, 571–95; cf. Lestringant 1997, 68–80.

[65] *Les Singularités de la France Antarctique* 40; Thevet 1997, 161.

[66] *Histoire d'un voyage* 15; de Léry 1994, 357.

[67] Montaigne 2007, 216. The condensed account of the act of cannibalism is found on the page before: 'they roast him, together they eat him and send little pieces of him to those of their friends who are absent'.

[68] Montaigne 2007, 214.

[69] *Histoire d'un voyage* 14; de Léry 1994, 336–37.

Montaigne presents the same behaviour in terms of a type of moral excellence. Such war is 'entirely noble and generous' and 'it has no basis among them but a seeking for virtue (*jalousie de la vertu*)'.[70] With this noble warfare Montaigne connects the element of the cannibalistic ceremony on which alone he focuses: the victim's 'grandeur of invincible courage', which—like de Léry, but far more emphatically—he elevates with a series of classical comparisons.[71] Montaigne's praise is not limited to the military side of Tupí life. What Montaigne calls their 'love for their wives' was manifested in a polygamous society, where the best warrior would have the most wives. These arrangements had led Thevet to moralize on how, even though creatures may be endowed with reason, they continue to live like brutes, unless God gives illumination.[72] Léry explains, rather, that the wives are not jealous of each other, but then goes on to doubt whether such harmony is possible, citing the biblical story of Rachel and Leah: even a single wife is bad enough, he adds, probably thinking of his own unhappy marital experience.[73] Montaigne, however, singles out Tupí marriage, and this feature in especial, for aesthetic and moral praise: it is 'a striking beauty' of their marriages that each wife wants her husband to have as many wives as possible, because that is a sign of his excellence (*vertu*)—such a desire is 'matrimonial virtue at the highest level', and Montaigne points to the story of Rachel and Leah, taking it very differently from de Léry, to illustrate the point.[74]

The comparison with his two sources shows very clearly how Montaigne insists on a certain relativism with regard to the content of virtue, quite foreign to Thevet, and discernible in de Léry only by the gap between his judgement of the Tupí, as the Calvinist minister he had become, and his open, sympathetic reaction to them at the time. Yet Montaigne wisely does not try to make the relativism absolute. He makes the barbarian virtues more familiar through Greek parallels, though he also keeps a certain distance: when he says that he wishes Plato and Lycurgus, the Spartan legislator, had known about these people, it is not because they bear out their conceptions of an ideal society, but that they surpass anything which philosophy could conceive or even desire: they '*could not imagine*', says Montaigne, the simple, pure childlikeness 'as we see it by experience'.[75] He also realizes that his attempt to see Tupí behaviour in its own terms and his admiration for it as such does not prevent him from also remaining a moral observer within his own society and on the basis

[70] Montaigne 2007, 216.
[71] Montaigne 2007, 217–19.
[72] *Les Singularités de la France Antarctique* 42; Thevet 1997, 167.
[73] *Histoire d'un voyage* 17; de Léry 1994, 427–28; cf. Lestringant 2004, 106–8.
[74] Montaigne 2007, 219–20; cf. Lestringant in de Léry 1994, 427n2.
[75] Montaigne 2007, 212.

of his own values. In the middle of praising their warlikeness, he slips in a qualification from this other standpoint: 'Their war is entirely noble and generous, and has as much justification and beauty as this human infirmity can admit'.[76] It may well be, indeed, that *On Cannibals* both shows how a moral system based on courage in war, cruelty and the desire for vengeance can be beautiful and, in a way, admirable, and at the same time criticizes similar values, as manifested in the Wars of Religion, in his own countrymen.[77]

Comparison with the two earlier accounts also reveals another feature of *On Cannibals*. Although he is writing about pagans, Montaigne does not confront the Problem of Paganism. Both the other writers base their understanding (conflicted, admittedly, in de Léry) of the Tupí on the fact that they are pagans. They discuss their religious beliefs carefully and see them as in the devil's grasp. Montaigne says nothing of the devil and records their belief in the immortality of the soul in a fleeting sentence.[78] He is simply not interested in the Tupís' chances of salvation or their knowledge of the true God, nor in the relationship between their virtues and Christian sin or merit. And it may be that it is just because he stands outside the framework of thinking provided by the Problem of Paganism that he is able, unlike any of those who worked within it, to propose a certain, though not complete, relativism about the content of virtue.[79]

---

[76] Montaigne 2007, 216.

[77] See, for instance, the interpretation given in Quint 1990. Todorov's critique (1989, 51–62) of Montaigne's relativism for inconsistency is instructive, but does not see that relativism by its very nature involves taking different, inconsistent standpoints, and that relativism and universalism are not the contraries they might appear.

[78] Montaigne 2007, 214.

[79] I touched on Montaigne's distance from the Problem of Paganism in Marenbon 2009b, 165.

CHAPTER 14

The Salvation of Pagans, 1400–1700

THE DISCOVERY AT THE END OF THE FIFTEENTH CENTURY OF AMERICA and other lands where, to all appearances, Christianity had never been preached, raised a new theological challenge. Although previously theologians had discussed the case of virtuous pagans, living after the preaching of the Gospel, who had no chance of hearing about Christianity (labelled here as 'invincibly ignorant pagans'), it was assumed that there were in reality few, if any. Now the evidence suggested that there were many millions of them. The main, central part of this chapter will examine how sixteenth- and seventeenth-century theologians faced this problem. But the opening section, on some fifteenth-century treatments of pagan salvation, and the final one, on seventeenth-century treatments of illustrious ancient pagans, will show that this new challenge was not entirely new, and that the older lines of discussion were continued, though in a modern format.

THREE FIFTEENTH-CENTURY VIEWS: AN ARISTOTELIAN AND TWO HUMANISTS

Lambertus de Monte probably wrote his *quaestio* Aristotle's salvation shortly before his death in 1499.[1] Lambertus is certain that Aristotle is in Heaven, and his theological explanation is based on Aquinas's theory of implicit faith, in which the philosophers were not required to have the explicit faith of the *maiores* among the Jews; although he also, in the same breath, quotes from Nicholas of Lyra, who followed Aquinas but made implicit faith not vicarious but generalized belief.[2] This closeness to Aquinas is not at all surprising, since Lambert was a dedicated exponent of the 'way of Aquinas', and indeed it is his adherence to this *via antiqua* that lies behind his wish not just to praise Aristotle, but to show the

---

[1] There is a fine discussion of this work and its place in von Moos 2013a, an earlier version of which is presented more briefly in French in von Moos 2013b.

[2] *De salvatione Aristotelis* III.2; ed. Roelli in von Moos 2013a, 175:336–178:424.

closeness between his thinking and Christian doctrine, crowned officially by his place, alongside Aquinas, among the saints in Heaven.[3]

Lambert, however, is more pessimistic than Aquinas about the salvation of pagans after Christianity has been preached. He believes that the Gospel very quickly reached the whole world and he quotes Jerome's view 'that no people remains which does not know the name of Jesus and, even if they have not had a preacher, they cannot however be unaware of the faith from neighbouring peoples'.[4] Aquinas too thought that Christianity had reached most—though not all—of the world, but he left open the possibility of special inspiration for a person (the boy brought up among wolves) who, in Christian times, remained genuinely ignorant of it, and his theory about the first act when a person comes to the age of reason also suggested an openness to the possibility of salvation for contemporary pagans. Lambert does not raise the idea of special inspiration, and he uses the theory about the age of reason to back up the conclusion that the spreading of Christianity through fame (if not for every nation by a preacher) is sufficient 'so that all humans are obliged to follow those things which are the means for acquiring the grace of Christ'.[5] When someone comes to the age of reason, he should be in a position, so Lambert goes on to argue, to order himself to his due end by following Christianity, of which he will certainly have heard.[6] Lambert's confidence that the Gospel had been preached everywhere may seem ironic, since he was writing at the time of Columbus's voyages.[7] But a contemporary of Lambert's, Galeotto Marzio, shows that, even before these discoveries, it was possible to take the imaginative step of seeing that Christianity was not known everywhere, and that it was practically inaccessible to many people even in places where it was known.

The fact that Galeotto Marzio di Narnia (d. 1492) has such different views from Lambert's can be explained in part because of the very different cultural and intellectual world he inhabited. A medical expert and humanist, he taught poetry and rhetoric at Bologna University (1463–65, 1472–77) and spent many years at the court of Matthias Corvinus, the Renaissance culture-loving king of Hungary.[8] He developed his views

---

[3] On the *Wegestreit*, see above, chapter 12. Negri 2011 looks more closely at *De salvatione Aristotelis* itself within the context of the Cologne Thomists' project; and see also Senger 1982 and Hoenen 2012.

[4] *De salvatione Aristotelis* IV.2; ed. Roelli in von Moos 2013a, 225:136–38, quoting Jerome, Commentary on Matthew; Jerome 1969, sec. 4, lines 432–34.

[5] *De salvatione Aristotelis* IV.2; ed. Roelli in von Moos 2013a, 221:46–48.

[6] *De salvatione Aristotelis* IV.2; ed. Roelli in von Moos 2013a, 225:139–47.

[7] Cf. von Moos 2013a, where he includes (115–24) a 'Nachwort: "Um so schlimmer für die Tatsachen"—zur Weltlage um 1500'.

[8] See Briggs 1974 and, for a wider discussion of *De incognitis vulgo*, Vasoli 1980.

about the salvation of pagans in a work aptly titled *What Is Unknown to the Crowd* (*De incognitis vulgo*), which was condemned by the Inquisition in 1477, shortly after it was written, and led to Marzio's imprisonment, until Pope Sixtus IV and Lorenzo de Medici intervened and procured him a retrial.[9] Marzio was not, however, an anti-religious anticipator of the Enlightenment. God, he believes, will not save those who are without faith. And, so far from being a rationalist, Marzio finds the necessity for faith in the fact that only someone who, without arguments, accepts God's word is 'captive' to God's commandments. 'He who does not believe and is moved only by reason does not seem to acquiesce in God's word'.[10] This view is of a piece with his narrow definition of what counts as faith. Faith can only be in what is heard.[11] Faith is trust in aural testimony. Someone who forms a belief because of witnessing a miracle does not, he explains, form it on the basis of faith.[12] If something believed by faith accords with what philosophers and learned people hold, it is really faith only if it is believed *because* it is said by God.[13]

From his theory of faith, Marzio derives a sort of relativism, not about the ultimate truths which can be the object of faith, but about the value of the act of faith. It is in the nature of testimony accepted on trust that it might be deceptive. God, Marzio thinks, values the act of placing trust in him, whether or not the testimony about him is in fact correct, since there is no way in which people can check the veracity of such testimony. Marzio also thinks that it is a characteristic of holding beliefs based on faith in God to think badly of people who hold different beliefs on this basis— those, that is to say, who belong to a different religion—because if people consider that their beliefs are pleasing to God, they will judge that a different set of beliefs is displeasing.[14] Roman religion, therefore, including its hatred of Christianity, is an acceptable faith from God's perspective, and Marzio dismisses with contempt the suggestion that the Romans ought to have adopted the religion of the Jews, whom they despised.[15] As evidence for this position, Marzio makes the most idiosyncratic use of the Gregory-Trajan story in the whole long history of this exemplum. Trajan not only was not a Christian: he was a cruel persecutor of Christians,

---

[9] See Marzio 1948, 105–7 for testimonies about his trial and punishment. *De incognitis vulgo* has never been printed in its entirety, but some chapters, including a long discussion about faith and the salvation of pagans, are printed by Frezzi (Marzio 1948, 67–96), along with an Italian translation.

[10] *De incognitis vulgo* 5.17–18; Marzio 1948, 82.

[11] *De incognitis vulgo* 5.2; Marzio 1948, 70–71.

[12] *De incognitis vulgo* 5.9; Marzio 1948, 74.

[13] *De incognitis vulgo* 5.10; Marzio 1948, 76.

[14] *De incognitis vulgo* 5.5; Marzio 1948, 72.

[15] *De incognitis vulgo* 5.14; Marzio 1948, 80.

who made them sacrifice to idols or killed them. Yet, and it is a Christian who says it, 'his soul was taken to heaven because of his highest justice and the integrity of his life'. His salvation shows that his persecution of Christians did not displease God, because he carried it out for God's sake, judging his own religion, which had been passed down from his parents, to be the true one.[16]

Is Marzio able to prevent his relativism about faith from undermining the truth claims of Christianity? It may seem not, when he writes that, if Christians consider that the virtuous ancient Romans are damned because they did not understand what they could in no way have understood, then they should fear for their own damnation, since they themselves are simply placing their faith in the testimony of their histories and the Gospel.[17] But there is no reason to think that Marzio does not himself have complete faith in the Christian testimonies—otherwise, by his own lights, he would fail to please God. He needs to be able to move between this unreflective level and that of reflectively comparing different religions. Such moves are always problematic for relativisms, but they by no means obviously lead to incoherence.

Despite his special concern, characteristic of a humanist, with the ancient Romans, Marzio argues for the salvation of contemporary pagans too. No one, he thinks, can be blamed or damned by God for having a false faith, except after they have seen that it is false. Those who accept Christianity and then leave it, from negligence or through perversity, are therefore in his view to be condemned.[18] This attitude leaves by implication room for peoples to follow their own religion in good faith, even after they have heard of Christianity, if they are not convinced to follow it (indeed, the case of Trajan exemplifies this point).

But Marzio prefers to concentrate on the existence of peoples who have not heard of Christianity. He speaks of people born 'at the end of the world', who have not heard of Christ and, even if they did, would not understand it. If they live sincerely according to their faith, and always worship God 'as they think', which judge, asks Marzio, would be so perverse as to damn them?[19] As someone who thinks that the Antipodes exist, Marzio denies that Christ's word went to all the world. Whereas everyone everywhere agrees on the basic teachings of natural law, such as cherishing parents, children and one's country, and not doing to others what we would not have done to us, no one accepts Christ's commands about the beginning of faith and with regard to ceremonies unless

[16] *De incognitis vulgo* 5.8; Marzio 1948, 73–74.
[17] *De incognitis vulgo* 5.13; Marzio 1948, 79–80.
[18] *De incognitis vulgo* 5.15–16; Marzio 1948, 81.
[19] *De incognitis vulgo* 5.16; Marzio 1948, 81–82.

they have been told about them. But the antipodeans have never been taught about Christianity, he observes, nor the *acephali*, nor the *blenni*—citing two of the monstrous races, familiar from the tradition of Plinian geography.

It would be wrong, however, to think that humanism normally went along with a particularly optimistic view of the chances of pagans to be saved. Humanists were often pessimists in this respect, just as they frequently denied pagan virtuousness.[20] Marsilio Ficino did not interest himself in the fate of contemporary pagans, but in one of his letters he discusses what happens to the great ancient philosophers—he names Pythagoras, Socrates and Plato—the man he so revered; Aristotle is not mentioned. Ficino does manage to place them in Heaven, but only with difficulty. As worshippers of the one God, he believes that they avoided condemnation to Hell. But he does not simply conclude, as many medieval theologians would have done, that they went to Heaven. Rather, they were sent to Limbo, and there, he explains, either through the prophets (because the Old Testament prophets were detained there until Christ's harrowing of Hell) or through angels, they learned of Christ and so were saved.[21]

THE NEW DISCOVERIES AND PAGAN SALVATION

The discovery of America and other lands where, from all appearances, Christianity had never been preached (or, as some would hold, the traces of it had all but disappeared)[22] did not transform discussions about the salvation of pagans, but it changed them. A problem previously addressed only on the sidelines, or by rare thinkers such as Marzio, now became central, and the old positions were re-used and developed in new ways. Despite appearances to the contrary, the official pronouncements of the Church left theologians with a fairly free hand, since even the often-repeated statement that 'there is no salvation outside the Church' was open to interpretation.[23] The difficulties were rather produced by biblical passages and the theological tradition.

There were four main approaches. Some favoured a compromise solution, according to which invincibly ignorant pagans are neither damned nor go to Heaven. Some continued to use the theory of special inspiration, which had been the usual way in the preceding centuries, to explain

---

[20] See above, chapter 13.
[21] Bk. 5, letter 48 to Antonio Ivani of Sarzana; Marsilio Ficino 1988, 64.
[22] See chapter 12.
[23] See Sullivan 2002, 66–67, 83–84; Sesboüé 2004, 82–104, 125–26.

the salvation of what were then thought to be the very few good pagans who remained invincibly ignorant after the Gospel had been disseminated. Another approach was to extend salvation by implicit faith into Christian times, whilst an uncommon fourth way looks, as Marzio had done, at the beliefs of non-Christians from their own point of view.

The post-mortem fate of invincibly ignorant pagans presented many thinkers of the time with a dilemma, if they accepted that there are strong biblical grounds to say that they cannot be saved without explicit faith in Christ, but thought it outrageous for them to be sent to Hell. The compromise solution was attractive because it avoided both the clash with scriptural authority and that with ordinary moral intuitions. Moreover, the doctrine confirmed by Pope Innocent III in 1201 in connection with unbaptized babies seemed to support it: the punishment for Original Sin is simply deprivation of the beatific vision, whereas the fires of Hell are punishment for actual sin.[24] It is not, then, surprising that perhaps the earliest theologian to react to Columbus's discovery—he was writing less than ten years after the first voyage—took this path. Baptistus of Mantua explained that the indications in the New Testament that the Gospel had been preached everywhere did not apply to the islands discovered by the king of Spain 'in our days' in the Indian, Ethiopian and Atlantic Oceans, about which the ancient geographers, such as Strabo, Pliny, Pomponeus Mela and Ptolemy knew nothing. He says that if the people there lived justly according to inward natural law, even if they sinned sometimes and repented, they will, in accord with God's 'justice and clemency', 'have some sort of happiness after death and will be assigned to some place where they will live better or at least less badly' than those who had vicious lives.[25] Johannes Trithemius (d. 1516) took up a similar position about the newly found peoples: 'If there are those among the peoples without knowledge of Christ who lived according to the law of nature, calling on the one God, even if they sinned sometimes, but repented before their death, they have been or will be damned less seriously than those who either heard about Christ and scorned him, or in either case lived badly or shamefully'.[26] Trithemius then explains that without faith in Christ and baptism no one can escape, as a punishment for Original Sin, being deprived of blessedness in Heaven. Those who have sinned mortally merit also punishment by the fires of Hell—and they include the Jews and Muslims who scorn the Christian faith, but Trithemius can see no reason why those who have never heard of Christ should suffer this

[24] Denzinger 1976, no. 780 (410). There was also a precedent in one of the ways of glossing the legend of Trajan (see above, p. 181), in Dante (see above, pp. 208–9) and in Ficino (see above, p. 285), although none of these examples was adduced.

[25] *De penitencia* III.11; Baptistus of Mantua 1501, n.p.

[26] Trithemius 1621, 15. The whole discussion of pagan salvation is q. 2, pp. 8–16.

punishment 'of the senses', although they will be for ever deprived of the beatific vision.

A more developed, and more generous, theory, but on very similar lines, was proposed by Claude Seyssel in *On Divine Providence* (published 1518).[27] While leaving open the opportunity for the very best invincibly ignorant pagans to gain faith by special inspiration and so be saved, Seyssel suggests that for ordinarily good pagans there will be an intermediary place, where they will be happy but will not see God. He cites explicitly the non-damnation of unbaptized infants as a precedent for his theory.[28] A somewhat different compromise view was proposed in the seventeenth century by Collius, a professor at Milan, who considers a pagan who reaches the age of reason, does not sin mortally and then dies. His tortuous discussion ends by suggesting that this pagan's condition is like that of unbaptized infants, and so he should go to Limbo.[29]

For all their attractiveness, most sophisticated theologians tended to reject these compromise views. The leading Parisian master of theology at the time of the new discoveries, John Major, writing soon after him, dismissed Baptistus's position as not even probable. Instead, he used a hybrid theory. The context of his discussion is whether circumcision has been replaced as a sacrament by baptism. Major insists that this is the case only where the requirement for baptism has been publicized, and no such publication had taken place in the islands recently discovered by Spain, including Madagascar and those in the Atlantic, where the inhabitants had never heard of any law but followed natural reason. If there were Jews living on such an island, Major says, then circumcision would continue to serve as a sacrament against Original Sin and enable them to be saved. Pagans living there could, in the same way, be saved through the sacraments of natural law (sacrifices and prayers to God). But, he adds, 'if there should be any adults to whom the news of the Gospel has not come and they do not have any sacrament against Original Sin, if they do what is in them, God will illumine them and baptize them with the baptism of desire (*baptisma flaminis*), and there is the same judgement about them as about the Athenian philosophers, of whom some lived well according to what reason suggested to them, and they were saved'.[30] On the one hand, then, Major seems to have returned to the way of thinking found in some of the earliest twelfth-century discussions, before a theory about implicit faith was developed, where the emphasis fell on the sacraments—which

[27] *De divina providentia* Tr. 2, a. 3; Seyssel 1543, ff. 71v–82v, esp. ff. 73r–v.

[28] *De divina providentia* Tr. 2, a. 3; Seyssel 1543, f. 73r.

[29] Pt. 1, bk. 1, chap. 13 (the next chapter too is marked '13' in this edition); Collius 1738, 31–35.

[30] The discussion is in d. 3, qu, unic., of bk. IV of his *Sentences* commentary, written before 1509; Major 1509, ff. 19r–v (the quotation is on f. 19va).

might be circumcision or simply the sacrifices dictated by natural law—to make salvation possible. On the other hand, if the sacraments are absent, he turns to the well-worn special inspiration theory (which he would also use to explain the salvation of the virtuous ancient philosophers).

Only this second side of his account seems to have been followed. Palacios Rubios, a Spanish official writer on the new discoveries, used Major explicitly within a few years to discuss the salvation of the American Indians. He quotes him at some length, and accepts the idea that, in principle, some Indians might have been saved by special inspiration, but tends rather to turn the special inspiration theory against them (rather as Holcot had done, thinking about ancient pagans), suggesting that the fact that they had not been informed in some way about the Gospel indicates that they did not do what was in them to find and serve God.[31] Vitoria, who had studied under Major, assumes a remarkably similar position in his *Lecture on the Indies* (1539). It comes out most clearly through an implication of one of his arguments. Defending the view that the Indians are rational, Vitoria says that, were they not, they would have, without any guilt, been outside the state of salvation for many thousands of years, since they would have been born in sin and not had baptism nor the use of reason to seek for what is necessary for salvation.[32] The implication is that beings endowed with reason can at any time use it to seek and in principle gain what is necessary for salvation—just as Major proposed; and also, in line with Rubios, that in fact the Indians did not use their reason in this way. Unlike Major, Rubios and Vitoria were quite well informed about the lives and beliefs of the Indians. When the special inspiration theory was brought up against the real practices of a contemporary pagan community, where it did not seem that anybody in fact had been given knowledge of the faith internally or externally, it became ineffective as a way of explaining how any of them might in fact have been saved.[33]

The best theoretical option, then, for allowing the salvation of invincibly ignorant pagans was to extend the theory of implicit faith to Christian times. But the biblical requirements for explicit faith after the preaching of the Gospel, accepted unanimously by the scholastic tradition, made

---

[31] *De insulis* I; Palacios Rubios 1954, 6–25, esp. 23–24.

[32] *Relectio de Indis* I.1.15; Vitoria 1967, 30:14–17.

[33] Matteo Ricci uses this theory when he puts forward the hope that the ancient Chinese who 'never believed about the King of Heaven and the other spirits, his servants, the sort of obscene things which our Romans and Greeks, the Egyptians and other foreign nations did' were saved by natural law 'with that special help which God is accustomed to offer to those who do as much as they can on their part to receive him'. [*Diaries*] 10, n. 170; Ricci 1942, 109. He does, indeed, want to argue for the real salvation of many Chinese people, but only the ancient ones, since he believes that the later Chinese literati are atheists (see chapter 12).

this apparently simple move a very hard one. A number of attempts to reason along these lines proved incomplete or abortive.

Melchior Cano (d. 1560) elaborated a theory which went halfway towards allowing invincibly ignorant pagans to be saved by implicit faith. He based himself on the thinking about a youth's first act on coming to the age of reason which Cajetan and Vitoria, his own teacher, had developed on the basis of Aquinas. Neither of these thinkers was proposing a theory about salvation, but they both wanted to insist that even a pagan, on coming to the age of reason, could perform a morally good act by choosing to turn to God, and they were willing to interpret this choice in a broad and psychologically plausible way.[34] As Vitoria puts it, 'when someone first thinks and deliberates about life, it is necessary that he has a purpose for the good, either in general, or also fitting to knowledge of God'.[35] Cano's own view about the first act is in fact stricter than Vitoria's, since he thinks such an act is impossible for someone who has 'no religion or knowledge of the divine name'.[36] But he starts to link the first act directly to the salvation of pagans, by saying that it can justify someone—that is to say, purge a person of the guilt of Original Sin, so long as it involves an implicit knowledge of God (though he prefers the solution in which a person making such an act is given an explicit knowledge of God's existence, in the same sort of way in which we can all grasp the principle of the excluded middle).[37] Cano, however, separates justification from salvation, and insists that such a pagan, though justified, is not thereby saved.[38] Although this final move was doctrinally dubious and rejected by most theologians, it is not surprising that Cano should have made it, since in the preceding discussion he has strictly held the line that implicit faith—by which he, and all those of his period, mean (in the manner of Nicholas of Lyra) unspecific or indistinct faith[39]—is not enough for salvation in Christian times. Those invincibly ignorant of Christianity will not be punished for positive lack of faith, but this does not mean that, without faith in Christ, they can attain eternal life.[40]

[34] See Cajetan, Commentary on IaIIe 89.6; Thomas Aquinas 1882–, VII, 146–48; Vitoria *Relectio de eo ad quod tenetur homo cum primum venit ad usum rationis* (1535).

[35] *Relectio de eo ad quod tenetur . . .* III.14; Vitoria 1960, 1373.

[36] *Relectio de sacramentis*, pt. 2; Cano 1580, f. 12v.

[37] *Relectio de sacramentis*, pt. 2; Cano 1580, f. 20v.

[38] *Relectio de sacramentis*, pt. 2; Cano 1580, f. 12r.

[39] *Relectio de sacramentis*, pt. 2; Cano 1580, f. 7v: 'someone who in times past believed that God, the procurer of human salvation, would through some means bring mortals back to eternal life has implicit faith'. For Nicholas of Lyra, see above, p. 172.

[40] *Relectio de sacramentis*, pt. 2; Cano 1580, f. 11r. Cano also rejects recourse to special inspiration: at the time of natural law, he says, God was indeed ready to reveal what was necessary for salvation to those who did what was in them, but now 'the light of the Gospel shines out and whoever does not have it remains in darkness' (f. 11v).

The upshot of Cano's discussion is, then, a version of the compromise position.

In the first, 1547 edition of his treatise *On Nature and Grace*, the Dominican Dominicus Soto put forward a very bold position about natural knowledge of God. The light of reason alone, he said, allowed people to know of the existence of God and that he is a rewarder (the Pauline minimum), and in this there is implicit a confused cognition of Christ. Since at the time of natural law there was no more detailed revelation, nothing more than this naturally available knowledge was needed for salvation, although there was also the need for supernatural aid to raise up people's inclinations. Soto is not talking here about pagans of his own or recent times, but his discussion suggests that they too could be saved. But in the second edition of his treatise, just two years later, he retracts this view.[41] He does, however, go on specifically to discuss invincibly ignorant pagans in his own time.[42] Soto considers that there are two possibilities, between which he does not decide. The one is that there are genuinely invincibly ignorant pagans, and in that case, he suggests, they can be saved without explicit faith (and he suggests ways of interpreting the biblical passages apparently incompatible with this position). The other position is that there are no such invincibly ignorant virtuous pagans, because, he explains (giving the special inspiration theory its often-used negative turn), had they been virtuous, they would have been illuminated with the truths they required.

Andreas Vega (d. c. 1560), a Franciscan, rejected this negative use of the special inspiration theory, which is contradicted, he points out, by Paul's comment (Romans x, 14) that people cannot hear (of the Gospel) without someone to preach it. In any case, 'we are not asking what God might do miraculously, but what he does according to the common way of things (*secundum legem communem*)'.[43] Vega argues vigorously that, for those living under natural law, those in the earliest times of the Church 'and finally for all whom the promulgation of the Gospel has not yet reached', explicit faith in Christ is not necessary for salvation.[44] Yet, at the end of the discussion, he says that in fact he does not know of any sect or nation (and not even any individual), after the preaching of the Gospel in the world, which, without sin against 'the natural light' did not believe in Christ or quickly turn to that belief. While, then, he rejects the statement that no one can be saved without explicit faith in Christ, since no law

---

[41] *De natura et gratia* II.12; De Soto 1549, f. 143r–v, where he presents the original view 'which I sometimes defended in the schools and judged to be the most probable in the first impression of this book in Venice' along with his critique of it.

[42] *De natura et gratia* II.12; De Soto 1549, f. 148r–49r.

[43] *De iustificatione* VI.20; Vega 1621, 107.

[44] *De iustificatione* VI.22 (cf. also 19–21); Vega 1621, 108–9 (cf. 105–8).

would be broken if it happens, he accepts it if it is understood to mean that it probably never happens that anyone is saved without such faith.

Suárez, by contrast, proposed a theory in which invincibly ignorant pagans could definitely and in practice be saved. Whilst he completely rejects Cano's idea that such pagans might be justified but not saved,[45] he aims to hold both that explicit faith in Christ is needed for salvation in Christian times, and that salvation then is possible through implicit faith alone.[46] He negotiates this apparent paradox through the idea that the requisite explicit faith need not be actual, but merely in promise (*in voto*).[47] Following the tradition of Cajetan, Vitoria and Cano, he uses the first act of someone reaching the age of reason to provide the privileged perspective from which to think about the subject. Against those who demand explicit faith in actuality, rather than implicit faith, he combines the case of the boy growing up in the forest with this idea. Suppose the boy does what is in him and turns to God, he will be illuminated and gain faith in God, but he cannot gain explicit faith in Christ, because that requires preaching. Indeed, as Suárez remarks, he is in the same position as those before the coming of Christ. Given that his ignorance of Christ is invincible, he is not guilty of positive infidelity, and so he will be cleansed of Original Sin (and so, should he die then, he will be destined for Heaven, given Suárez's rejection of Cano's position), but without explicit faith in Christ. Suárez is not convinced by the standard riposte that, in such a case, the boy would receive special illumination about the mysteries of the Trinity and the Incarnation. If explicit faith in Christ is necessary for salvation, he argues, then 'this is simply a result of God's ordaining that it is so and positive divine law'. (He is entitled to make this point, because his opponents agree that people can in principle be saved without such explicit knowledge, since until the time of the Gospel they were saved in that way.) But, Suárez says, 'in those things which are necessary only from divine commandment and positive law, God is not accustomed, even in the case of necessity, to provide extraordinary providential help so that they are fulfilled and take place in actuality (*in re ipsa*), but the desire or promise (*desiderium aut votum*) for them usually suffices, as is clear for confession and baptism'.[48]

---

[45] Commentary on IIaIIae, tract 1, disp. 12, sec. 4.15; Suárez 1858, 356a.

[46] Suárez (Commentary on IIaIIae, tract 1, disp. 12, sec. 4.10; Suárez 1858, 353a) considers that a number of theologians already held that they could be saved by implicit faith. He mentions Soto, Vega, Medina, Corduba and Maldonatus as supporters of the view. But neither Soto nor Vega (nor Medina: cf. Capéran 1934, 257) supports this as a practical possibility. It may be that Suárez wanted to make his bold move seem more widely accepted than it was.

[47] Commentary on IIaIIae, tract 1, disp. 12, sec. 4.18; Suárez 1858, 357a.

[48] Commentary on IIaIIae, tract 1, disp. 12, sec. 4.11; Suárez 1858, 353a–54b.

It is this contrast between something in actuality and in promise, and the parallel he draws here and will go on to emphasize, with baptism and confession, which allow Suárez to say that, in some sense, explicit faith in Christ is indeed required after the preaching of the Gospel. It is required precisely as something laid down by God, and so it can fulfilled by being a mere intention, desire or promise. The case with baptism was already very well established. Baptism is required for salvation, but everyone agreed that it was enough to intend to be baptized. As Suárez points out, if a catechumen dies before he is baptized, it is accepted that he is not thereby excluded from going to Heaven—no one would argue that, if God intended to save him he would miraculously preserve his life until he could be baptized. He then suggests an invented scenario, but one which he insists might really take place: a catechumen has not yet reached the level of instruction to have an explicit belief in Christ and he becomes terminally ill and loses the use of his reason: such a person could be baptized, and it would be right to baptize him, and if he died straight away, he would go to Heaven, since his sins were washed away by baptism. But he would not have had explicit faith in Christ. Not only does this case show that the case of someone being saved now without actual explicit faith in Christ cannot be excluded. It also brings out the parallel between baptism *in voto*—in the case of the catechumen who dies believing in Christ explicitly but unbaptized—and explicit faith *in voto*—in the case of the catechumen who dies baptized but without explicit knowledge of Christ.[49] This promise or intention, Suárez explains, is that of 'wishing to fulfil all that is necessary'.[50]

The fourth approach, which follows the same line of thought pursued by Marzio (though not as a result of direct influence, since his book did not circulate), had only one obvious champion, the sixteenth-century theologian Albert Pighi (d. 1542).[51] Like a number of thinkers at the time, Pighi thought that the traditional chronological scheme of the Old and New Law needed to be modified to take account of the recently discovered peoples to whom the Gospel had only just been announced. Such people, he says, are in the same position as Cornelius, before he was taught by Peter—by which he implies that they please God by their mer-

[49] Commentary on IIaIIae, tract 1, disp. 12, sec. 4.16–17, 19–20; Suárez 1858, 356a–57a; 357b–58a.

[50] Commentary on IIaIIae, tract 1, disp. 12, sec. 4.19; Suárez 1858, 357b.

[51] Sullivan 2002, 94–99, followed by Sesboüé 2004, 133–34, presents the Jesuit, Juan de Lugo (1583–1660), as a thinker who followed Pighi's approach, but he bases himself on passing comments. De Lugo's main concern in this area (disp. XII.3; de Lugo 1686, 255 [no. 13]—272 [no. 81]) is to reject the views of his fellow Jesuit, Juan de Ripalda. On Ripalda's views and the controversy, see Capéran 1934, 332–51.

its and may be saved.[52] But where he is remarkable is in his appreciation of how cultural factors can make belief in explicit Christian doctrines a practical impossibility. He puts his point with regard to those born among the Muslims and taught Islam from birth by their parents, but the same thinking would apply to some pagans, as his own discussion of it makes clear. Suppose, he says, that such people know and revere God as the cause of all things and the repayer of good and evil (the Pauline minimum), follow the law of nature written in their hearts and submit themselves to the will of God. Do they have the same position as Cornelius? He imagines himself in dialogue with someone who denies it. His opponent says that the position is different, because now the Gospel of Christ has been sufficiently promulgated. But Pighi replies that the facts contradict this position, since 'still every day' nations are being found who have not—or at least their fathers had not—heard any trace about the Gospel. These are in a far less good position to know about Christ than Cornelius, who lived among the Jews. Then he continues (it is unclear whether he is thinking of the people in Islam or those in the newly discovered nations; perhaps both),

> But let it be that they have heard the name of Christ, they however have been so instructed that they think our faith false and erroneous and the faith they have imbibed true, and that God commands that they should believe this (so indeed they are taught by their parents and the *maiores* to whom natural reason rightly subjects the lesser ones and children, unless and until divine illumination should teach something else). Nor is it allowed to doubt such things, but rather they will be damnable if they doubt them. Therefore they believe in that by which they might please God, and so as not to be damned. Nor do they know anything of divine revelations. They have seen no miracles to tell them of God against ‹their belief›, nor heard anything told ‹about Christian belief› which would deserve their credence (*nec audierunt quidem ita, vt merito tenerentur ea narrantibus credere*).

Pighi goes on to argue that someone is not damned just because his or her faith is not entirely correct—the example of Cornelius is cited once again to show that it is enough to believe the Pauline minimum.[53]

The preceding paragraphs may have given the impression that sixteenth- and seventeenth-century theologians were all searching, in their different ways, to find explanations for the salvation of wider groups of pagans. In fact, the most striking development of the time, already discussed in

---

[52] *De libero hominis arbitrio* X; Pighius 1542, f. 180v–81r.
[53] *De libero hominis arbitrio* X; Pighius 1542, f. 181r–v.

connection with pagan knowledge, was the reemergence of a very powerful, strict Augustinian position on all matters to do with salvation: its chief
proponents among Catholics were de Bey, Jansen and Antoine Arnauld.
Arnauld sets out the case with great clarity: implicit faith is 'chimerical
and imaginary', because it is not really faith in Christ, and the special
inspiration theory cannot be accepted since we are not given grace according to our natural merits, which are insufficient to follow natural law.[54]
Among the Protestants, the Augustinian position was all but universal.[55]

These characteristic Protestant positions are passed over here much
more quickly than their historical importance would merit, because their
usual refusal to allow that even pre-Christians were saved or that there
was any reason why they should have been tends simply to unproblema-
tize the Problem of Paganism. There are some exceptions, however, to the
Protestants' hard line. Luther's early view of the salvation of pre-Christian
pagans was very indulgent. By acting humbly towards God or the highest being, whom they knew, pagans could be freed of Original Sin. They
were not bound to know Gospel and Christ 'expressly'.[56] But he quickly
adopted the very different view that there can be no justification without
explicit knowledge of Christ.[57] Zwingli, however, adhered to a generous
view about the salvation of ancient pagans. In a famous, and much criticized, passage from his *Brief and Clear Exposition of the Christian Faith*,
he envisages in Heaven, along with Adam, Abraham, the Old Testament
patriarchs and the disciples, a band of ancient heroes and philosophers,
including Hercules and Theseus, as well as Socrates.[58] Zwingli did not,
however, go against the fundamental Augustinian view that salvation is
through Christ alone and good works depend on faith: he simply considered that God had extended his grace to the ancient world.[59]

THE PAGAN PHILOSOPHERS IN THE SEVENTEENTH CENTURY

Despite the special intellectual challenge posed by the invincibly ignorant
pagans of their own times, the great pagans of antiquity and their fate

[54] *De la nécessité de la foi en Jésus Christ pour être sauvé*; Arnauld 1777, 65–377. This
book was in part a response to le Vayer's *De la vertu des païens*, discussed below. For implicit faith, see I.7; for special inspiration, see III.3.
[55] Some seventeenth-century Anglicans, such as those associated with 'Cambridge Platonism', are, of course, exceptions, but they were hardly Protestants doctrinally, although
they rejected the pope.
[56] See Blöchle 1995, 46–47, and Luther's commentary on Romans ii, 12 and 14.
[57] See Blöchle 1995, 47–51. The new view is found even in the same commentary on
Romans, to iii, 19.
[58] *Christianae fidei brevis et clara expositio*; Zwingli 1841, 44–67, at 65.
[59] See Stephens 1986, 124–27.

in the afterlife continued to fascinate some seventeenth-century scholars. Where in earlier centuries writers had been content to list, without justification, names of those outstanding pagans who were saved, or else looked just at the case of Aristotle, concentrating on his philosophical views and their compatibility with Christianity, now they used the tools of historical scholarship to investigate the whole range of the problem. In his two volumes (1622, 1623) *On the Souls of Pagans*, after a theoretical discussion, Collius scrupulously examines the lives of classical and biblical pagans one by one, in order to see if their lives were such that they may have been saved. He is not at all interested in contemporary pagans. He does indeed examine in detail Seneca and Epictetus, two philosophers living in Christian times. He is full of praise for their lives and their thought and accepts its closeness to Christianity (he also accepts the correspondence between Paul and Seneca as genuine). None the less, in both cases he points out that the philosophers did not in fact become Christians, and that is enough, in his view, to make it certain that they are damned.[60] With regard to pagans of pre-Christian times, Collius accepts that they could act virtuously, but not that they would ever, from their natural powers, have been able to live entire lives of the sort which would lead to their salvation.[61] For that, supernatural grace is required, and Collius believes that it was made available in all sorts of miraculous ways.[62] He relies, then, on the special inspiration theory to save pagans. This theory leads him to expect a high degree of concord between the pagans' views and Christian doctrine and so, as often when it was applied, leads to a pessimistic conclusion about who is actually saved. Collius ends by declaring Hermes Trismegistus, Socrates, Plato, Aristotle and all the figures from the classical tradition he examines to be in the torments of Hell. Even Trajan falls victim to historical scholarship: the story of Gregory's intervention is declared false (as Bellarmine had already found it to be). Only biblical pagans, such as Melchisedech and Job, along with the Sibyls, are found to have been saved.[63]

Less than twenty years later, François de La Mothe le Vayer published a book which seems mainly concerned, like Collius's work, with the salvation or damnation of illustrious figures of the ancient world, though its

---

[60] On Seneca's fate, see pt. 2, bk. 1, chap. 11 (Collius 1633, 28–30). The discussion of Epictetus (pt. 2, bk. 1, chaps. 17–22) is so praising that Capéran (1934, 287) mistakenly believes that Collius says he is saved: see pt. 2, bk. 1, chap. 21 (Collius 1633, 50) for a clear statement that he is not.

[61] Pt. 1, bk. 1, chaps. 13–14, 21.

[62] These are the subject of pt. 1, bk. 2.

[63] For Trajan, see pt. 2, bk. 2, chaps. 14–24; Collius 1633, 104–33. The examination of the different figures from the Old Testament and of the philosophers is conducted in roughly chronological order in pt. 1, bks. 3–5, and pt. 2, bk. 1.

title—*On the Virtues of Pagans*, and not *On the Salvation of Pagans*—turns out in the end to fit better that it may at first seem.[64] Le Vayer believes that the salvation (aided by supernatural grace) of those who lived virtuously under natural law is straightforward, and he considers—rightly, so far as mainstream Catholic theology is concerned—that it is generally accepted. Indeed, he takes the view, which had been diffused since the early Middle Ages through unrecognized Pelagian writings, that the many of the patriarchs immediately following Adam were exceptionally virtuous.[65] He explains salvation of pagans at the time of the Old Law through implicit faith,[66] but he also uses the special inspiration theory ('God never refuses his grace to those who do all they can to make themselves worthy of it') in a general way, as an argument that good pagans must have been saved. The position for those living at the time of the New Law, he recognizes, is more difficult. But here, more trenchantly than most professional theologians, le Vayer argues that it is now clear from Japan and America that there are many peoples who heard nothing of the Gospel until centuries after the time of Christ. Since this geographically occasioned ignorance is in no way different from the ignorance of those who lived chronologically before the time of Christ, how, asks le Vayer, can the effects be different? 'How then can one imagine that a poor American, who, two hundred years ago, had never heard the true religion spoken of, could not therefore in any way avoid eternal punishment, even though he lived well morally and resembled the good pagans of whom we have spoken [those of antiquity] who allowed themselves to be guided by the natural light of our reason, worshipped a single God, creator of all things, and lived without idolatry . . . ?'[67] Yet he also suggests that for God to save a pagan after the time of Christ, even one who has turned to him begging for illumination and preferring to die than to do anything which would offend him, would be an instance of the divine freedom to act against the usual order of things.[68] This is perhaps why his general position is so qualified: 'I maintain merely that it is very probable that those among the non-idolatrous pagans who possessed so perfect a use of reason and the natural light that, for this reason, St Justin called them Christians, were sometimes granted extraordinary grace, and that they

[64]The work was first published in 1641; in 1647 a second edition appeared, with an important additional section of 'Proofs', answering objections. Prévot's edition, used here, is based on the 1647 text.

[65]I; Prévot 2004, 14; for the Pelagian view in the early Middle Ages, see above, p. 64–65. There was also a tendency to think of the early days of creation as a Golden Age in exponents of *prisca theologia*, especially in Agostino Steuco; see above, pp. 243–44.

[66]I; Prévot 2004, 16–17.

[67]I; Prévot 2004, 28–29.

[68]I; Prévot 2004, 30.

had the implicit faith which the Angelic Doctor and all the schoolmen attribute to them'.[69] It is the requirement for *extraordinary* grace which makes this position so weak. Grace, of course, is required for salvation, whether of a pagan or a Christian, as le Vayer himself observes. But here he seems to concede that no pagan is saved without extraordinary grace, though perhaps he is thinking specially about post-Christian pagans. Vega and Suárez had seen it as their goal to explain how even after the preaching of the Gospel, good pagans could be saved without extraordinary intervention, and Suárez had succeeded in doing so. Le Vayer is far more timid, although perhaps, writing in the vernacular for a general audience, he could not convey the fine theological distinctions that Suárez needed in order to avoid heresy.

Most of the book is devoted to looking at individual cases, in which le Vayer is often dissenting from, but also in many respects following, Collius; Leibniz mentions the two books in the same breath.[70] Collius condemned all the figures he discussed from the non-biblical tradition. Le Vayer (who does not discuss biblical figures) suggests that a few pre-Christian ancient philosophers, such as Socrates, Plato and Pythagoras may have been saved, and even, perhaps, the post-Christian Seneca— not because of the correspondence with St Paul, which he (along with the scholars of his time) rejects as obviously inauthentic, but just on the condition that he did not know anything of Christianity. The one figure he considers who is not from the Graeco-Roman world comes from the same, pre-Christian period: Confucius, who is represented—on the basis of Ricci's account, as published by Trigault—as a worshipper of the one God and follower of natural law.[71] Le Vayer holds out no hope, however, for Epicurus, Diogenes and the Sceptics, and he is even very doubtful about the salvation of Aristotle. He puts his views about those who may have been saved very tentatively, concluding, for instance, about Socrates that 'although we say nothing definite about [his] salvation, the knowledge of which God seems to have wished to keep to himself, we believe that one can have a very good opinion of it and that, at the least, no one should fail to speak of him with the respect that a man of such rare virtue merits'.[72] This final phrase gives the clue to what seems le Vayer's main aim (which explains why the book's title is, after all, appropriate): to establish that, whatever the case about their salvation, these great pagans were remarkably virtuous people—something on which le Vayer insists in

[69] Preuves; Prévot 2004, 203.

[70] The debt to Collius is pointed out in Capéran 1934, 317 and 323. See Leibniz, *Nouveaux essais sur l'entendement humain* IV.18; Leibniz 1990b, 396.

[71] II; Prévot 2004, 132–38. Le Vayer does not discuss the present day Chinese literati, nor mention their atheism.

[72] II; Prévot 2004, 47.

every case. He even includes a chapter on Julian the Apostate, although he admits from the start that he was damned, so as to try to restore a balance in the assessment of someone whose character and actions were so severely condemned by Christian writers. Taken on its own, against the background of earlier and contemporary treatments of pagan salvation, *On the Virtues of Pagans* seems to be the response by someone with moderate, somewhat traditional theological views, who admires ancient philosophy and its proponents, to the extreme Augustinian position of Jansen and his French followers.

Le Vayer, however, is usually considered to be among the *libertins*—the group of French seventeenth-century writers who, often covertly, disbelieved in central aspects of Christian teaching. Although some specialists accept the orthodoxy of *On the Virtues of Pagans*, most find that the stance of the work needs explanation.[73] Either it is hypocrisy, an attempt to please Cardinal Richelieu, to whom the work is dedicated;[74] or else it is merely apparent, and the text has a hidden, subversive dimension.[75] In its most subtle form, this reading suggests that le Vayer's book at once provides, at it claims to do, the orthodox, yet liberally minded rebuttal of the extreme Augustinian position, but also includes more than this ostensible project would require and, through passages deliberately ambiguous or from which a reader could draw heterodox implications, casts doubt on orthodoxy for those receptive to such cues.[76] Once the decision is taken to read the text in this sophisticated way, a powerful case can be made for such an interpretation. Whether it should be accepted depends on the judgement made about le Vayer's whole position and the Christian scepticism which he, at least ostensibly, espouses. It has been argued that le Vayer places the ancient sceptic Pyrrho in Hell for a scepticism which is like his own.[77] But, as le Vayer himself makes clear in his dialogue *About the Divinity*, the Christian sceptic, like the ancient ones, suspends judgement on all philosophical and scientific questions, but simply accepts Christian doctrine as a matter of faith.[78] St Paul, he comments, did not teach us to know, but to believe.[79] That dialogue,

[73] See, for an instance of a critic who accepts Le Vayer's basic orthodoxy, Prévot's introductory notice (2004, 1445–57).

[74] Cf. Pintard 1943, 520–22.

[75] In addition to Moriarty's view (see the next note), see Paganini 2008, esp. 520–22 (she judges (520) that le Vayer puts forward a 'doctrine, en fin de compte, passablement subversive'), and see Moriarty 2011, 177 for a fuller bibliography on interpretations of le Vayer and *La vertu des païens*.

[76] See Moriarty 2011, 175–209. He makes a subtle and powerful case, which needs to be studied as a whole.

[77] Paganini 2008, 88–94.

[78] La Mothe le Vayer 1716, esp. 339–44.

[79] La Mothe le Vayer 1716, 413.

which was published pseudonymously, can be, and often is, read as a work designed to undermine Christian belief, but there is nothing there to prevent it from being read according to the sceptical, fideist view it advocates. With regard to interpretation of *On the Virtues of Pagans*, perhaps the wisest course—not inappropriately for the work of a sceptic—is to suspend judgement.

The first author after antiquity studied here in detail was Peter Abelard. The final one—and he is very probably the last major philosopher who can be usefully considered within the framework of the Problem of Paganism—is Leibniz. The pairing of these two figures is more than accidental, since their interest in the Problem of Paganism is related to an outlook which they share. Although Leibniz, who knew (probably at second-hand) some of Abelard's work refused to acknowledge the affinity, both saw God as being bound to follow an absolute standard of goodness.[80] As a result, neither could tolerate the idea that the chance to be saved, to act virtuously, or to know about God should be offered to some but not others, since God would thereby be acting wilfully and not in accord with rightness and justice. Abelard developed his own idiosyncratic doctrine which allowed for the salvation of many just pagans, and Leibniz, looking back on the complicated but uncertain theology of salvation which had developed by his day, followed the same aim. Although a Lutheran, he was struck by the injustice and cruelty attributed to God by those, including most Protestants, who took a strict Augustinian view of salvation. Those who are willing, he says, to follow Augustine's view that unbaptized infants are condemned to the flames of Hell 'care even less about adults' and, he continues pointedly, 'it might be said that they have become hardened from thinking about seeing people suffering'.[81] Among the others, he commends the Catholics who 'go further than the Protestants and do not absolutely damn all those who are outside their communion, and even outside Christianity, when measured by explicit faith alone'.[82] He cites the *facientibus quod in se est* maxim and calls it 'an eternal truth', and he mentions Aquinas and Bradwardine as authors who look to it. He does not enter into theological details, however, except to say that even if today (after the preaching of the Gospel) an explicit knowledge of Christ is necessary, it can still be said that God will give it to all those who do what they can as humans, although it might require a miracle. Just as babies receive a sort of faith in baptism, although they can remember nothing of it afterwards, so it is possible that God could give 'something similar, or even more explicit' to those at the point of

[80] See Marenbon 2013a, 140–44.
[81] *Essais de Théodicée* 1.95; Leibniz 1960–61, VI, 155.
[82] *Essais de Théodicée* 1.96; Leibniz 1960–61, VI, 156.

death (at which stage it is impossible for anyone to question them about it). There are, Leibniz concludes, 'an infinity of ways open to God which give him the means to satisfy both his justice and his goodness'.[83] This, from him, is more than a rhetorical flourish. Leibniz argued that God chose from the infinite number of possible world histories which he could bring into being the very best possible one.

[83] *Essais de Théodicée* 1.98; Leibniz 1960–61, VI, 157.

EPILOGUE

LEIBNIZ AND CHINA

THE VIRTUOUS PAGANS WHO LOOMED SO LARGE FOR ABELARD WERE THE philosophers of ancient Greece and Rome. Leibniz's preferred virtuous pagans were also ancient philosophers, but those of China. Leibniz showed an interest in China from the mid-1670s and, from 1689, roughly in the middle of his career, he began to conduct a correspondence with a number of the Jesuit missionaries to China, seeking information about Chinese writings, thought and language, as well as current news about political and religious developments.[1] In 1697 he edited and wrote a preface for *The Latest News from China*, a collection of material mainly about the progress of Christianity there. Shortly afterwards, he began his most philosophically interesting exchange of letters on China, with the Jesuit Joachim Bouvet. Although, to his intense frustration, Leibniz received no further letters from Bouvet after 1702, his intense interest in China and his voracious reading of all he could find out about it continued, and his fullest thoughts about Chinese religion are expressed in one of his last works, a letter *On the Natural Theology of the Chinese*, written in 1716, the year of his death.

Leibniz initially viewed China in the context of the missions, world politics, Chinese inventions and the Chinese language—he shared with a number of scholars the belief that there was an underlying logical structure to Chinese characters and a key could be found to them which would dispense with the tedious business of learning them one by one.[2] Contact with Bouvet, in especial, deepened his interest in the Chinese knowledge of God. Like most of the Jesuits, Bouvet followed Ricci's strategy of accommodation, and he accepted the contrast he had made between ancient Confucianism, which was compatible with Christianity, and the materialism and atheism espoused by the Confucian scholars of more recent times. Bouvet's main Chinese audience, however, no longer consisted of

---

[1]The letters are collected in Leibniz 1990b. On Leibniz and China, see Mungello 1977; Perkins 2004 and the useful collection of translations (with introduction and notes); Ching and Oxtoby 1992.

[2]See Perkins 2004, 108–14; on the search for a key to Chinese, see Mungello 1985.

the literati but the Kangxi Emperor himself, an intelligent and cultivated man, who took a great personal interest in the Jesuits, especially but not only as teachers of science and mathematics.[3] Moreover, Bouvet completed, following Couplet, the move away from Ricci's use of natural reason to explain the knowledge of God enjoyed by the ancient Chinese. He founded an approach to early Chinese history and literature known as figurism, a variant of the Ancient Theology, which holds that the Chinese share with the Europeans a common descent from Noah and that, at the very earliest stage of their history, the Chinese had from this source a near complete knowledge of revealed truth—shared, says Bouvet, by Moses and the Jews, and 'the divine Plato'—which was subsequently lost, distorted or put into mythical form.[4] Fuxi, the legendary first Chinese ruler, was considered by Bouvet as identical with one or another of the great originators in the Ancient Theology, Hermes Trismegistus (about Casaubon's unveiling of whom he was apparently ignorant) or Zoroaster, 'or even Enoch'.[5] Bouvet accepted the traditional attribution of the *Book of Changes* to Fuxi, but, where Couplet had traced the corruption of Confucianism back to it, he saw it, the most ancient of all books, as containing in coded form the complete knowledge of revelation, which was grasped only dimly even by Confucius himself.[6] When Leibniz told him about his binary system of arithmetic, Bouvet pointed out that a famous diagram in the *Book of Changes*, built up from continuous and broken lines, showed 'the same thing'.[7] Leibniz enthusiastically accepted the idea that his binary arithmetic could be used to 'decode' the ancient Chinese diagram.[8]

Since Leibniz tended to link together the binary system, God's creation of a perfect universe from chaos and his quest for a 'Universal Characteristic' which would yield the whole of scientific knowledge, there was a congruity between his thinking and Bouvet's claims about the lost complete knowledge of the ancient Chinese.[9] The binary arithmetic of the *Book of Changes* is the subject of the final, uncompleted section of what he described as his 'discourse on the natural philosophy of the

[3] See Mungello 1985, 300–307.
[4] On figurism, see Collani 1981; Mungello 1985, 307–11; Rule 1986, 150–82; on Plato and Moses, see Bouvet, Letter to Le Gobien, for Leibniz; Leibniz 1990b, 125 (no. 39).
[5] Letter to Leibniz, 4 November 1701; Leibniz 1990b, 154 (no. 44).
[6] His most detailed letter to Leibniz about it is dated 4 November 1701: Leibniz 1990b, 147–63 (no. 44).
[7] Letter to Leibniz, 4 November 1701: Leibniz 1990b, 149–56 (no. 44).
[8] See Letter to Bouvet, 18 May 1703: Leibniz 1990b, 181–87 (no. 49); 'Explication de l'arithmétique binaire' (1703): Leibniz 1863, 223–27, at 226–27.
[9] See Mungello 1977, 60–68. The linking of these themes is brought out well in a letter he wrote to Duke Rudolph August in 1697 (just before his attention was drawn by Bouvet to the *Book of Changes*): Leibniz 1838, 401–7 (translated with useful commentary in Ching and Oxtoby 1992, 71–80).

Chinese'.[10] The rest of the work, however, as its title indicates, keeps a certain distance from Bouvet's claims about a primitive revelation and defends, rather, Ricci's view that the ancient Chinese had a natural theology, through which they knew of God and the immortality of the soul. The stimulus for the treatise was the receipt from a friend of two books written by opponents of Ricci's views (Longobardi and a Franciscan, Antoine de Sainte-Marie). By carefully interpreting the very translations with which these two tried to prove that the ancient Chinese lacked a conception of God and immortality, Leibniz aims to show the opposite, and he even claims that they may have had a notion of Hell or Purgatory.[11] But, by the time Leibniz, now a rather isolated figure, left behind in Hanover when his employer went to take up the British throne, wrote this treatise, the pope had already decided against the Jesuits' missionary strategy of accommodation, so closely linked to the views he was championing.[12] In the context of the early eighteenth century, the *Discourse*, Leibniz's last work, reads like a remnant from a past, and in many ways more hopeful, age.

[10] In a letter to Rémond (27 January 1716), for whom the *Discourse* was written: Leibniz 1960–61, III, 670; cf. Mungello 1977, 162n8.

[11] Leibniz 1987, 137.

[12] There is a vast literature on the so-called Chinese rites controversy. A useful summary is in Rule 1986, 124–49; detailed papers in Mungello 1994.

General Conclusion

THE INTRODUCTION PROMISED THAT THIS BOOK WOULD REACH NO FIRST-order general conclusions about the Problem of Paganism. Unlike an enquiry in the natural sciences, it has, and should have, no results. But it is worth mentioning two striking negative points that it has, silently, established. The Middle Ages in Western Europe are frequently associated with narrowness and religious bigotry, and the Renaissance and seventeenth century with the beginnings of the Enlightenment. It would be natural, therefore, to expect that attitudes to pagans would progress from medieval severity, according to which pagans lacked knowledge and virtue and were heading for eternal punishment, to Early Modern toleration, in which pagan goodness, wisdom and salvation were widely accepted. But there was no such progression. No sixteenth- or seventeenth-century writer pleaded the pagan case more fervently than Abelard in the twelfth century. No early medieval ascetic (nor even Augustine himself) so willingly accepted the wickedness of pagans as many seventeenth-century Protestants and Jansenists. Was the movement then in the reverse direction, with a hardening of attitudes to pagans, like that towards groups such as Jews, homosexuals and lepers in the later Middle Ages?[1] This view is equally contradicted by the (very different) ideas of, for instance, Pomponazzi, Las Casas, Suárez and Leibniz. The full gamut of reactions was available to thinkers throughout the period, because the Problem of Paganism did not admit of any solution which allowed them (with rare exceptions) to retain all their doctrinal commitments. Similarly, it might be expected that the European discovery of America, and the new contacts with India, and then Japan and China, would transform thought about paganism. But there was no transformation, just a gradual change without a shift in fundamental principles.

Such unchangingness is remarkable, because according to almost every historical account, the three centuries involved were a time of epochal change, of the transition to what is called 'modernity', and the most emblematic event of the new era, Columbus's voyages, had a direct bearing on the Problem of Paganism. Of course, it would be wrong to generalize on the basis of one theme, even an important one. But the preceding

---

[1] I put forward this view in Marenbon 2012d, 52–53 (which was written far earlier than the publication date would suggest).

pages should at least raise a query over the traditional account of modern times and their origins. One reaction might be to place the beginning of modernity much later than is customary, around 1700, rather than two centuries earlier, as the very notion of the Long Middle Ages, used throughout this study, may be thought to imply. But this reaction would be too simple and superficial. The idea of the Long Middle Ages is intended merely to be a heuristic device, which prevents historians from taking for granted that there is a fundamental division of periods around 1500 *or at any other time*. The most appropriate reaction to the negative conclusion reached here is rather to regard deep epochal divisions, such as that which supposedly distinguishes modernity from the Middle Ages, with scepticism, as attempts to find meaning and order where there is none.

Meaning and order dwell, not in the movement of history, but in the fleeting movements of individual minds. This book has tried to recover some of them and, in doing so, it suggests a method: a way of approaching philosophy, in the broad sense, from the Long Middle Ages (though it could also be applied more widely to any period of past philosophy). It might be called 'Historical Synthesis'. It differs from Historical Analysis, where investigators start from a problem or area of problems in contemporary philosophy in order to find what, in the medieval texts, is still of interest and will yield to philosophical understanding.[2] They then place the discussions they analyse back into their context, explaining how the questions involved are different from those present-day ones which they resemble. Historical Analysis favours technical, abstract discussions—logic, metaphysics, metaethics—since it is here that an interest based in contemporary philosophy will find apparent common ground with earlier philosophy. In Historical Synthesis, investigators choose a problem, such as the Problem of Paganism, which does not belong to the contemporary world, but is deeply rooted in the intellectual life of the Long Middle Ages and, because it reveals a fundamental tension there, is addressed in writing of many sorts—philosophy and theology, but also poetry, chronicles, essays, even (as here) travel literature. The vital connection with our interests today comes from an analogy with problems we now face—as the Problem of Paganism resembles in form, though it is different from, contemporary questions about relativism, about religious difference and atheism. Historical Synthesis, as the name suggests, proceeds not just by analysing arguments but also by reading texts carefully and synthesizing material, to show how thinkers in the past tried to treat problems which were ultimately intractable for them. By engaging with

---

[2]'Historical Analysis' is my own term (introduced in Marenbon 1987). I discuss and justify this approach there and, most recently, in Marenbon 2011b and 2011c.

thicker philosophical issues, closer to the concerns of everyday life, than Historical Analysis usually handles, the understanding it promises may be more appealing for historians. But it also, even more than Historical Analysis, offers philosophers the chance to examine not only what their subject was once, but what it is, or might be, now.

Bibliography

Abulafia, David (2008) *The Discovery of Mankind: Atlantic Encounters in the Age of Columbus*, New Haven: Yale University Press.

Acampora-Michel, Elsbeth (ed.) (2001) *Liber de Pomo. Buch vom Apfel*, Frankfurt: Klostermann.

Acosta, José de (1962) *Historia natural y moral de las Indias*, 2nd edn., ed. Edmundo O'Gorman, Mexico: Fondo de Cultura Económica.

Adam of Bremen (2002) *The History of the Archbishops of Hamburg-Bremen*, trans. Francis J. Tschan, with new introduction by Timothy Reuter, New York: Columbia University Press.

Aertsen, Jan A., Kent Emery Jr. and Andreas Speer (eds.) (2001) *Nach der Verurteilung von 1277: Philosophie und Theologie an der Universität von Paris im letzten Viertel des 13. Jahrhunderts. Studien und Texte* (Miscellanea Mediaevalia 28), Berlin: de Gruyter.

Aertsen, Jan A. and Andreas Speer (eds.) (1998) *Was ist Philosophie im Mittelalter?* (Miscellanea Mediaevalia 26), Berlin: de Gruyter.

Aethicus Ister (2011) *The Cosmography of Aethicus Ister*, ed. and trans. Michael W. Herren (Publications of the Journal of Medieval Latin 8), Turnhout: Brepols.

Akbari, Suzanne C. (2009) *Idols in the East. European Representations of Islam and the Orient, 1100–1450*, Ithaca, N.Y.: Cornell University Press.

Albert the Great (1890–99) *Opera omnia*, ed. Auguste Borgnet, Paris: Vivès.

———. (1987) *Super Ethica* VI–X, ed. Wilhelm Kübel (Alberti Magni opera omnia 14.2), Münster: Aschendorff.

Alcuin (1863) *Opera* in *PL* 101.

(Alexander of Hales) (1924–48) *Summa Theologica*, ed. Bernhard Klumper, Quaracchi: Collegium S.Bonaventurae.

Allen, Don C. (1970) *Mysteriously Meant. The Rediscovery of Pagan Symbolism and Allegorical Interpretation in the Renaissance*, Baltimore: Johns Hopkins University Press.

Allen, Michael J. B. (1998) *Synoptic Art. Marsilio Ficino on the History of Platonic Interpretation* (Istituto Nazionale di Studi sul Rinascimento. Studi e testi 40), Florence: Olschki.

Anderson, David (1988) *Before the Knight's Tale. Imitation of Classical Epic in Boccaccio's* Teseida, Philadelphia: University of Pennsylvania Press.

Anzulewicz, Henryk (2012) 'Albertus Magnus über die *philosopi theologizantes* und die natürlichen Voraussetzungen postmortaler Glückseligkeit: Versuch einer Bestandsaufnahme' in Steel, Marenbon and Verbeke 2012, 55–83.

Arnauld, Antoine (1777) *Oeuvres* X, Paris: Sigismond d'Arnay.

Athanassiadi, Polymnia and Michael Frede (eds.) (1999) *Pagan Monotheism in Late Antiquity*, Oxford: Oxford University Press.

Augustine (1992) *Confessions*, introduction, text and commentary by James J. O'Donnell, Oxford: Oxford University Press.

———. (1996) *Vingt-six sermons au peuple d'Afrique*, ed. François Dolbeau (Collection des études augustiniennes. Série antiquité 147), Paris: Institut d'études augustiniennes.

Averroes (1953) *Commentarium magnum in Aristotelis de anima libros,* ed. Francis S. Crawford (Corpus commentariorum Averrois in Aristotelem, versionum latinarum 6,1), Cambridge, Mass.: Mediaeval Academy of America.

———. (2011) *Long Commentary on the De Anima of Aristotle* I, trans. with commentary by Richard C. Taylor, New Haven: Yale University Press.

Baius, Michael (1565) *De meritis . . . De primi hominis iusticia et de virtutibus impiorum*, Louvain: Ioannes Bogardus.

Bak, János M. (2011) 'Christian Identity in the Chronicle of the Czechs by Cosmas of Prague' in Garipzanov 2011b, 167–82.

Baker-Smith, Dominic (1991) *More's* Utopia, London: HarperCollins.

Baranski, Zygmunt (2006) '*Alquanto tenea della oppinione degli Epicuri.* The *Auctoritas* of Boccaccio's Cavalcanti (and Dante)' in *Mittelalterliche Novellistik im europäischen Kontext. Kulturwissenschaftliche Perspektiven*, ed. Mark Chinca, Timo Reuvekamp-Felber and Christopher Young (Beihefte zur Zeitschrift für Deutsche Philologie 13), Berlin: Schmidt, 280–325.

———. (2008) 'Guido Cavalcanti tra le *cruces* di *Inferno* IX–XI, ovvero Dante e la storia della ragione' in *Versi controversi. Letture dantesche*, ed. Zygmunt Baranski, Domenico Cofano and Sebastiano Valerio (Letterature e interpretazione 3), Foggia: Rosone, 39–112.

———. (2013) '(Un)orthodox Dante' in *Reviewing Dante's Theology*, Bern: Peter Lang, 253–320.

Barlow, Claude W. (ed.) (1938) *Epistolae Senecae ad Paulum et Pauli ad Senecam ‹quae vocantur›* (Papers and Monographs of the American Academy in Rome 10), Horn: American Academy in Rome.

Bayle, Pierre (1727) *Ouvres diverses* III, The Hague: P. Husson.

Bejczy, István P. (2003) 'Deeds without Value: Exploring a Weak Spot in Abelard's Ethics', *Recherches de théologie ancienne et médiévale* 70: 1–21.

———. (2005) 'The Problem of Natural Virtue' in Bejczy and Newhauser 2005, 133–54.

———. (2011) *The Cardinal Virtues in the Middle Ages. A Study in Moral Thought from the Fourth to the Fourteenth Century* (Brill's Studies in Intellectual History 202), Leiden: Brill.

Bejczy, István P. and Richard G. Newhauser (eds.) (2005) *Virtue and Ethics in the Twelfth Century* (Brill's Studies in Intellectual History 130), Leiden: Brill.

Berend, Nora (2001) *At the Gate of Christendom. Jews, Muslims and 'Pagans' in Medieval Hungary, c. 1000–1300* (Cambridge Studies in Medieval Life and Thought, 4th series, 50), Cambridge: Cambridge University Press.

Bernand, Carmen and Serge Gruzinski (1988) *De l'idolâtrie. Une archéologie des sciences religieuses*, Paris: Seuil.

Bernardus Silvestris (1978) *Cosmographia*, ed. Peter Dronke, Leiden: Brill.

———. (1996) 'Bernardus Silvestris, *Mathematicus*. Edition and translation, Deirdre M. Stone', *Archives d'histoire doctrinale et littéraire du moyen âge* 63: 209–83.

Bettetini, Maria and Francesco D. Paparella (eds.) (2005) *Le felicità nel medioevo* (FIDEM. Textes et études du Moyen âge 31), Louvain-la-neuve: Fédération internationale des instituts d'études médiévales.

Bezzola, Gian A. (1974) *Die Mongolen in Abendländischer Sicht (1220–1270). Ein beitrag zur Frage der Völkerbegegnungen*, Bern: Francke.

Bianchi, Luca (1984) *L'errore di Aristotele. La polemica contro l'eternità del mondo nel XIII secolo* (Publicazioni della facoltà di lettere e filosofia dell'Università di Milano 104. Sezione a cura del dipartimento di filosofia 2), Florence: la nuova Italia.

———. (1987) 'La felicità intelletuale come professione nella Parigi del Duecento', *Rivista di filosofia* 78: 181–99.

———. (1998) '1277: A Turning Point in Medieval Philosophy?' in Aertsen and Speer 1998, 90–121.

———. (1999) *Censure et liberté intellectuelle à l'université de Paris (XIIIe–XIVe siècles)*, Paris: les Belles Lettres.

———. (2003) 'New Perspectives on the Condemnation of 1277 and Its Aftermath', *Recherches de théologie et philosophie médiévales* 70: 206–29.

———. (2005) 'Felicità intelettuale, "ascetismo" e "arabismo". Nota sul "De summo bono" di Boezio di Dacia' in Bettetini and Paparella 2005, 13–34.

———. (2009) 'Students, Masters, and "Heterodox" Doctrines at the Parisian Faculty of Arts in the 1270s', *Recherches de théologie et philosophie médiévales* 76: 75–109.

———. (ed.) (2011) *Christian Readings of Aristotle from the Middle Ages to the Renaissance* (Studia Artistarum 29), Turnhout: Brepols.

Biard, Joël (2001) 'La place de la félicité intellectuelle dans l'Éthique buridanienne' in Aertsen, Emery and Speer 2001, 977–83.

Bibliorum sacrorum (1603) *Bibliorum sacrorum cum glossa ordinaria . . . cum postilla Nicolai Lyrani . . .*, Venice: Junta.

Bliemetzrieder, Franz (1919) *Anselms von Laon systematische Sentenzen* (Beiträge zur Geschichte der Philosophie des Mittelalters 18), Münster: Aschendorff.

Blöchle, Herbert (1995) *Luthers Stellung zum Heidentum im Spannungsfeld von Tradition, Humanismus und Reformation* (Europäische Hochschulschriften ser. 13, 531), Frankfurt: Peter Lang.

Boccaccio, Giovanni (1965) *Tutte le opera* VI: *Esposizioni sopra la comedia di Dante*, ed. G. Padoan, Verona: Mondadori.

Boethius (2009) *The Old English Boethius. An Edition of the Old English Versions of Boethius's 'De Consolatione Philosophiae'*, ed. Malcolm Godden and Susan Irvine, Oxford: Oxford University Press.

Boethius of Dacia (1976) *Opuscula*, ed. Neils J. Green-Pedersen (Corpus Philosophorum Danicorum Medii Aevi 6.2), Copenhagen: Gad.

———. (2003) *Sull'eternità del mondo*, ed. Luca Bianchi, Milan: UNICOPLI.

Boethius, Anicius Manlius Severinus (1925) *De consolatione Philosophiae*, ed. Adrianus A Forti Scuto (*anglice* Fortescue), London: Burns Oates and Washbourne.

Boethius, Anicius Manlius Severinus (2000) *De consolatione Philosophiae. Opuscula theologica*, ed. C. Moreschini, Munich: Teubner.

Boitani, Piero (1977) *Chaucer and Boccaccio* (Medium Aevum Monographs, n.s. 8), Oxford: SSMLL.

Bonaventure (1882–1902) *Opera Omnia*, ed. Patres Collegii S. Bonaventurae, Quaracchi: Collegium S. Bonaventurae.

Boutet, Dominique (1996) *Le Cycle de Guillaume d'Orange. Anthologie*, Paris: livre de poche.

Brady, Ignatius (1972) 'The Questions of Master William of Baglione, O.F.M., *De aeternitate mundi* (Paris, 1266–1267)', *Antonianum* 47: 362–71, 576–616.

Brenet, Jean-Baptiste (2003) *Transferts du sujet. La noétique d'Averroes selon Jean de Jandun*, Paris: Vrin.

————. (2006) 'Théorie de l'intellect et organisation politique chez Dante et Averroes', *Rivista di filosofia neo-scolastica* 98: 467–87.

Brennan, Michael (1996–97) 'The Texts of Peter Martyr's *De orbe novo decades* (1504–1628): a response to Andrew Hadfield', *Connotations* 6: 227–45.

Briggs, E. R. (1974) 'Un pionnier de la pensée libre au XVe siècle: Galeotto Marzio da Narni (1427?–1497?)' in *Aspects du libertinisme au XVIe siècle*, ed. Marcel Bataillon et al, Paris: Vrin, 75–84.

Brooks, Douglas and Alastair Fowler (1970) 'The Meaning of Chaucer's "Knight's Tale"', *Medium Aevum* 39: 123–46.

Brunhölzl, Franz (1965) 'Der Bildungsauftrage der Hofschule' in *Karl der Grosse. Lebenswerk und Nachleben* II *Das geistige Leben*, ed. B. Bischoff, Dusseldorf: Schwann, 28–41.

Buchner, Rudolf and Werner Trillmich (1961) *Quellen des 9. und 11. Jahrhunderts zur Geschichte der hamburgischen Kirche und des Reiches* (Ausgewählte Quellen zur deutschen Geschichte des Mittelalters 11), Darmstadt: Wissenschaftliche Buchgesellschaft.

Bullet, Gabriel (1958) *Vertus morales infuses et vertus morales acquises selon Saint Thomas d'Aquin* (Studia friburgensia, n.s. 23), Fribourg: éditions universitaires.

Burnett, Charles S. F. (1977) 'What Is the *Experimentarius* of Bernardus Silvestris? A Preliminary Survey of the Material', *Archives d'histoire doctrinale et littéraire du moyen âge* 44: 79–125.

Büttgen, Philippe (2011) *Luther et la philosophie. Études d'histoire*, Paris: Vrin and Éditions de l'École des hautes études en sciences sociales.

C. de Bridia (1967), *Hystoria tartarorum*, ed. Alf Önnerfors (Kleine Texte für Vorlesungen und Übungen 186), Berlin: de Gruyter.

Caiazzo, Irène (2002) *Lectures médiévales de Macrobe. Les Glose Colonienses super Macrobium* (Études de philosophie médiévale 83), Paris: Vrin.

Calma, Dragos (2011) 'Du bon usage des grecs et des arabes. Reflexions sur la censure de 1277' in Bianchi 2011, 115–84.

Cameron, Alan (2011) *The Last Pagans of Rome*, New York: Oxford University Press.

Cano, Melchior (1580) *Relectiones duae*, Milan: Pacificus Pontius.

Capéran, Louis (1934) *Le problème du salut des infidèles. Essai historique*, revised edn., Toulouse: Grand séminaire.

Carron, Delphine (2006) 'Sénèque, exemplarité ambigüe et ambiguïté exemplaire (IVe–XIVe siècle)' in Ricklin 2006a, 307–33.

———. (2010) *Le héros de la liberté. Les aventures de Caton au Moyen Âge latin, de Pierre Diacre à Dante*, doctoral thesis, Universities of Paris IV and Neuchâtel.

Cary, George A. (1954) 'A Note on the Medieval History of the Collatio Alexandri cum Dindimo', *Classica et mediaevalia* 15: 124–29.

———. (1956) *The Medieval Alexander*, ed. D.J.A. Ross, Cambridge: Cambridge University Press.

Casagrande, Carla (2006) 'Le philosophe dans la tempête. Apathie et contrôle des passions dans les *exempla*' in Ricklin 2006a, 21–34.

Cerutti, M. V. (2010) '"Pagan Monotheism"? Towards a historical typology' in *Monotheism between Pagans and Christians in Late Antiquity*, ed. Stephen Mitchell and Peter Van Nuffelen, Louvain: Peeters, 15–32.

Chadwick, Henry (1981) *Boethius: the Consolations of Music, Logic, Theology and Philosophy*, Oxford: Oxford University Press.

Chappuis, Marguerite (1997) 'Le traite de Pierre d'Ailly sur la Consolation de Boece, question 2. Etude preliminaire' in *Boethius in the Middle Ages: Latin and vernacular traditions of the Consolatio philosophiae*, ed. Maarten J.F.M. Hoenen and Lodi Nauta (Studien und Texte zur Geistesgeschichte des Mittelalters 58), Leiden: Brill, 69–86.

Chenu, Marie-Dominique (1948) 'Les "Quaestiones" de Thomas de Buckingham' in *Studia mediaevalia in honorem admodum reverendi patris Raymundi Josephi Martin*, Bruges: De Tempel, 229–41.

Chibnall, Marjorie (1975) 'Pliny's *Natural History* and the Middle Ages' in *Empire and Aftermath. Silver Latin II*, ed. T. A. Dorey, London: Routledge & Kegan Paul, 57–78.

Ching, Julia and Willard G. Oxtoby (eds.) (1992) *Moral Enlightenment. Leibniz and Wolff on China* (Monumenta serica monograph series 26), Nettetal: Steyer.

Christiansen, Eric (1980) *The Northern Crusades. The Baltic and the Catholic Frontier, 1100–1525*, London: Macmillan.

Chroust, Anton-Hermann (1945) 'A Contribution to the Medieval Discussion: utrum Aristoteles sit salvatus'. *Journal of the History of Ideas* 6: 231–38.

Clanchy, Michael (1997) *Abelard. A Medieval Life*, London: Blackwell.

Coleman, Janet (1981a) *English Literature in History, 1350–1400: Medieval Readers and Writers*, London: Hutchinson.

———. (1981b) *Piers Plowman and the Moderni*, Rome: Edizioni di storia e letteratura.

Coleman, William E. (2005) 'The Knights' Tale' in *Sources and Analogues of the Canterbury Tales* II, ed. Robert M. Correale with Mary Hamel, Woodbridge: Brewer, 87–247.

Colgrave, Bertram (1985) *The Earliest Life of Gregory the Great by an Anonymous Monk of Whitby: text, translation and notes*, Cambridge: Cambridge

University Press (originally published Lawrence: University of Kansas Press, 1968).

Colish, Marcia (1996) 'The Virtuous Pagan: Dante and the Christian Tradition' in *The Unbounded Community: Papers in Christian Ecumenism in Honor of Jaroslav Pelikan*, ed. William Caferro and Duncan G. Fisher, New York: Garland, 5–40.

Collani, Claudia von (1981) *Die Figuristen in der Chinamission* (Würzburger Sino-Japonica 8), Frankfurt: Lang.

Collius, Franciscus (1633) *De animabus paganorum*, vol. 2, Milan: Ambrosiana.

———. (1738) *De animabus paganorum*, vol. 1, Milan: Malatetta.

Cooper, Helen (1996) *Oxford Guides to Chaucer: The Canterbury Tales*, 2nd edn., Oxford: Oxford University Press.

Copenhaver, Brian (2012) 'Giovanni Pico della Mirandola' in *The Stanford Encyclopedia of Philosophy*, Summer 2012 edn., ed. Edward N. Zalta, http://plato .stanford.edu/archives/sum2012/entries/pico-della-mirandola/.

Corbett, George (2013) *Dante and Epicurus. A Dualistic Vision of Secular and Spiritual Fulfilment* (Italian Perspectives 25), Oxford: Legenda.

Cosmas of Prague (1923) *Die Chronik der Bohmen des Cosmas von Prag*, ed. Bertold Bretholz (Monumenta Germaniae historica. Scriptores rerum Germanicarum. Nova series 2), Berlin: Weidmann.

Corti, Maria (1982) *Dante a un nuovo crocevia* (Società Dantesca Italiana, Quaderno 1), Florence: Sansoni.

Couplet, Philippe (1687) *Confucius sinarum philosophus siue scientia sinensis latine exposita*, Paris: Horthemels.

Courcelle, Pierre (1964) *Histoire littéraire des grandes invasions germaniques*, 3rd edn., Paris: Études augustiniennes.

———. (1967) *La Consolation de Philosophie dans la tradition littéraire*, Paris: Études Augustiniennes.

———. (1968) *Recherches sur les Confessions de Saint Augustin*, 2nd edn., Paris: de Boccard.

Cross, Richard (1999) *Duns Scotus*, New York: Oxford University Press.

Cuttini, Elisa (2010) 'Pomponazzi e Aristotele: il problema del fine dell'uomo' in *Pietro Pomponazzi. Tradizione e dissenso*, ed. Marco Sgarbi, Florence: Olschki, 261–70.

Dales, Richard C. (1984) 'The Origin of the Doctrine of the Double Truth', *Viator* 15: 169–79.

———. (1990) *Medieval Discussions of the Eternity of the World* (Brill's Studies in Intellectual History 18), Leiden: Brill.

Dales, Richard C. and Omar Argerami (1991) *Medieval Latin Texts on the Eternity of the World* (Brill's Studies in Intellectual History 23), Leiden: Brill.

Daniel, Norman (1984) *Heroes and Saracens. An Interpretation of the* Chansons de geste, Edinburgh: Edinburgh University Press.

———. ([1960] 1993) *Islam and the West. The Making of an Image*, rev. edn., Oxford: Oneworld.

Dante Alighieri (1966–67) *La Commedia secondo l'antico volgare*, ed. Giorgio Petrocchi, Milan: Mondadori.

———. (1988) *Convivio*, ed. with commentary Cesare Vasoli and Domenico De Robertis (*Opere minori* 1.2—*La letteratura italiana. Storia e testi* 5), 2 vols., Milan: Ricciardi.

———. (1989) *Monarchia*, ed. with commentary by Ruedi Imbach and Christoph Flüeler, Stuttgart: Reclam.

———. (1991–94) *Commedia, con il commento di Anna Maria Chiavacci Leonardi*, Milan: Mondadori.

———. (1995) *Convivio*, ed. Franca Ageno (Le opere di Dante, edizione nazionale 3), 3 vols., Florence: le Lettere.

———. ([1979] 1996) *Opere minori* III.1 *De vulgari eloquentia. Monarchia*, ed. Piero V. Mengaldo and Bruno Nardi, Milan: Ricciardi.

———. (1996–2004) *Das Gastmahl (Convivio)*, trans. Thomas Ricklin; commentary by Francis Cheneval (books I and III), Thomas Ricklin (book II), Ruedi Imbach (book IV) (Philosophische Bibliothek 466a-d), 4 vols., Hamburg: Felix Meiner.

———. (2009) *Monarchia*, ed. Prue Shaw (Le opere di Dante, edizione nazionale 5), Florence: le Lettere.

Davenport, Francis G. (1917) *European Treaties Bearing on the History of the Unites States and Its Dependencies to 1648*, I, Washington, D.C.: Carnegie Institution.

Davidson, Herbert A. (1992) *Alfarabi, Avicenna, and Averroes, on Intellect: Their Cosmologies, Theories of the Active Intellect, and Theories of Human Intellect*, New York: Oxford University Press.

Davis, Charles T. (1957) *Dante and the Idea of Rome*, Oxford: Oxford University Press.

Dawson, C. (ed.) (1955) *The Mongol Mission*, New York: Sheed and Ward.

De la Vega, Garcilaso (1976) *Comentarios reales de los Incas*, ed. Aurelio M. Quesada (Biblioteca Ayacucho 5–6), Caracas: Biblioteca Ayacucho.

De Léry, Jean (1994) *Histoire d'un voyage faict en la terre du Brésil*, ed. Frank Lestringant, Paris: Livre de Poche.

De Lugo, Ioannes (1686) *Disputatio scholastica de virtute fidei divini*, Lyons: Borde and Arnaud.

Deluz, Christiane (1988) *Le livre de Jehan de Mandeville. Une «Géographie» au XIVè siècle* (Publications de l'Institut d'Études Médiévales. Textes, études, congrès 8), Louvain-la-neuve: Université catholique de Louvain.

De Soto, Domingo (1549) *De natura et gratia*, Paris: Foucher.

De Vogel, Cornelia (1972) 'Boethiana II', *Vivarium* 10: 1–40.

Demougeot, E. (1951) *De l'unité à la division de l'Empire Romain 395–410. Essai sur le gouvernement impérial*, Paris: Adrien–Maisonneuve.

Denifle, Heinrich and Émile Châtelain (1889) *Chartularium Universitatis Parisiensis* I, Paris: Delalain.

Denzinger, Heinrich (1976) *Enchiridion symbolorum, definitionum et declarationum de rebus fidei et morum*, revised Adolf Schönmetzer, Barcelona: Herder. (online edition, up to 1957, at http://catho.org/9.php?d=g1).

Detlev, Jasper (ed.) (1988) *Fälschungen im Mittelalter: internationaler Kongress der Monumenta Germaniae Historica, München, 16.–19. September 1986* I (Schriften der Monumenta Germaniae Historica 33,1), Hannover: Hahn.

Dobell, Brian (2009) *Augustine's Intellectual Conversion. The Journey from Platonism to Christianity*, Cambridge: Cambridge University Press.

Donaldson, E. Talbot ([1963] 1970) 'The Ending of Troilus' in his *Speaking of Chaucer*, London: Athlone Press, 84–101.

Dörrie, Heinrich (1956) 'Drei Texte zur Geschichte der Ungarn und Mongolen', *Nachrichten der Akademie der Wissenschaften in Göttingen*, phil.-hist. Klasse, 125–202.

———. (1971) 'Was ist spätantiker Platonismus? Überlegungen zur Grenzziehung zwischen Platonismus und Christentum', *Theologische Rundschau* 36: 285–302.

Dronke, Peter (1974) *Fabula. Explorations into the Uses of Myth in Medieval Platonism* (Mittellateinische Studien und Texte 9), Leiden: Brill.

———. (1986) *Dante and Medieval Latin Traditions*, Cambridge: Cambridge University Press.

———. (1990) *Hermes and the Sibyls: Continuations and Creations*. Cambridge: Cambridge University Press, reprinted in Dronke 1992, 219–44.

———. (1992) *Intellectuals and Poets in Medieval Europe* (Storia e letteratura 183), Rome: edizioni di storia e letteratura.

———. (2008) *The Spell of Calcidius. Platonic Concepts and Images in the Medieval West*, Florence: SISMEL, Edizioni del Galluzzo.

Dronke, Peter and Ursula Dronke (1977) 'The Prologue of the Prose *Edda*: Explorations of a Latin Background' in *Sjötíu Ritgerthir helgathar Jakobi Benediktssyni* I, Reykjavik, 153–76, reprinted in Dronke 1992, 81–102.

Dronke, Ursula (1997) *The Poetic Edda.* II *The Mythological Poems*, Oxford: Oxford University Press.

Dublanchy, E. (1923) 'Charité' in *Dictionnaire de théologie catholique* II, 2217–66, Paris: Letouzay et Ané.

Dümmler, Ernst (ed.) (1881) *Poetae latini aevi carolini* 1 (Monumenta Germaniae Historica—poetae latini medii aevi 1), Berlin: Weidmann.

Dunn, J.D.G. (1998) *The Theology of Paul the Apostle*, Edinburgh: Clark.

Dunning, T. P. (1943) 'Langland and the Salvation of the Heathen', *Medium Aevum* 12: 45–54.

Durandus of St Pourçain (1571) *In Sententias commentaria*, Venice: Guerraea.

Ebbesen, Sten (1990) 'Boethius as an Aristotelian Commentator' in *Aristotle Transformed. The Ancient Commentators and Their Influence*, ed. Richard Sorabji, London: Duckworth, 373–91.

———. (2009) 'The Aristotelian Commentator' in Marenbon 2009a, 34–55.

Edwards, M. (2004) 'Pagan and Christian Monotheism in the Ages of Constantine' in *Approaching Late Antiquity. The Transformation from Early to Late Empire*, ed. M. Edwards and M. Swain, Oxford: Oxford University Press, 211–34.

———. (2009) 'Justin's Logos and the Word of God', *Journal of Early Christian Studies* 3: 261–80.

———. (2010) *Culture and Philosophy in the Age of Plotinus*, London: Duckworth.

Ehrle, Franz (1925) *Der Sentenzkommentar Peters von Candia des Pisaner Papstes Alexanders V: ein Beitrag zur Scheidung der Schulen in der Scholastik des vierzehnten Jahrhunderts und zur Geschichte des Wegestreites* (Franziskanische Studien, Beiheft 9), Münster: Aschendorff.

Fioravanti, Gianfranco (2005) 'La felicità intellectuale: storiografia e precisazioni' in Bettetini and Paparella 2005, 1–12.

Flint, Valerie (1976) 'The "School of Laon": a reconsideration', *Recherches de théologie ancienne et mediévalé* 43: 89–110.

Fois, Mario (1969) *Il Pensiero Cristiano di Lorenzo Valla nel quadro storicocultrale del suo ambiente* (Analecta Gregoriana 174), Rome: Libreria editrice dell'Università Gregoriana.

Foster, Kenelm (1977) *The Two Dantes, and Other Studies*, London: Darton, Longman and Todd.

Frede, M. (2010) 'The Case for Pagan Monotheism in Greek and Graeco-Roman Antiquity' in Mitchell and Van Nuffelen 2010, 53–81.

Frezza, Mario (1962) *Il problema della salvezza dei pagani (da Abelardo al Seicento)*, Naples: Fiorentino.

Friedman, Russell (2012) 'Latin Philosophy, 1200–1350' in *The Oxford Handbook of Medieval Philosophy*, ed. John Marenbon, New York: Oxford University Press, 192–219.

Friedman, Russell L. and Lauge O. Nielsen (2003) *The Medieval Heritage in Early Modern Metaphysics and Modal Theory, 1400–1700* (The New Synthese Historical Library 53), Dordrecht: Kluwer.

Fürst, Alfons, et al. (2006) *Der apokryphe Briefwechsel zwischen Seneca und Paulus*, Tübingen: Mohr Siebeck.

Gagliardi, Antonio (1999) *Giovanni Boccaccio: poeta, filosofo, averroista*, Catanzaro: Rubettino.

Galonnier, Alain (1997) *'Anecdoton Holderi' ou 'Ordo Generis Cassiodororum'. Éléments pour une étude de l'authenticité boécienne des 'Opuscula sacra'* (Philosophes Médiévaux 35), Louvain-la-Neuve: Éditions de l'Institut supérieur de philosophie and Peeters.

———. (2007) *Boèce. Opuscula sacra. I. Capita dogmatica (Traités II, III, IV) . . . Introduction, traduction et commentaire* (Philosophes Médiévaux 47), Louvain-la-Neuve: Éditions de l'Institut supérieur de philosophie and Peeters.

Garipzanov, Ildar H. (2011a) 'Christianity and Paganism in Adam of Bremen's Narrative' in Garipzanov 2011b, 13–29.

———. (ed.) (2011b) *Historical Narratives and Christian Identity on a European Periphery. Early History Writing in Northern, East-Central, and Eastern Europe (c. 1070–1200)* (Medieval Texts and Cultures of Northern Europe 26), Turnhout: Brepols.

Gauthier, R. A. (1984) 'Notes sur Siger de Brabant II. Siger en 1272–1275; Aubry de Reims et la scission des Normands', *Revue des sciences philosophiques et théologiques* 68: 3–50.

———. (1993) *Introduction à Saint Thomas d'Aquin*, Somme contre les Gentils, Paris: éditions universitaires.

Geerlings, W. (1997) '*De civitate dei* XIX als Buch der Augustinischen Friedenslehre' in Horn 1997, 211–33.

Geoffrey Chaucer (1984) *Troilus and Criseyde. A new edition of 'The Book of Troilus'*, ed. Barry A. Windeatt, London: Longman.

———. (1987) *The Riverside Chaucer*, ed. Larry D. Benson, Boston: Houghton Mifflin.

Gersh, Stephen (1978) *From Iamblichus to Eriugena: An Investigation of the Prehistory and Evolution of the Pseudo-Dionysian Tradition* (Studien zur Problemgeschichte der antiken und mittelalterlichen Philosophie 8), Leiden: Brill.

Gerson, L. P. (1990) *God and Greek Philosophy. Studies in the Early History of Natural Theology*, London: Routledge.

Giovanni Pico della Mirandola (2012) *Oration on the Dignity of Man. A New Translation and Commentary* (with Latin text), ed. Francesco Borghesi, Michael Papio and Massimo Riva, New York: Cambridge University Press.

Gliozzi, Giuliano (1977) *Adamo e il nuovo mondo: la nascita dell'antropologia come ideologia coloniale: dalle genealogie bibliche alle teorie razziali (1500–1700)* (Pubblicazioni del Centro di studi del pensiero filosofico del Cinquecento e del Seicento. . . . Serie I, 7), Florence: la nuova Italia.

Godden, Malcolm (1990) *The Making of Piers Plowman*, London: Longman.

Godman, Peter (1990) 'Ambiguity in the "Mathematicus" of Bernardus Silvestris', *Studi medievali* 31.2: 583–648.

Gradon, Pamela (1983) '*Trajanus Redivivus:* Another Look at Trajan in *Piers Plowman*' in *Middle English Studies Presented to Norman Davis in Honour of His Seventieth Birthday*, ed. Douglas Gray and E. G. Stanley, Oxford: Oxford University Press, 93–114.

Grady, Frank (2005) *Representing Righteous Heathens in Late Medieval England*, New York: Palgrave Macmillan.

Grafton, Anthony (1991) *Defenders of the Text. The Traditions of Scholarship in an Age of Science, 1450–1800*, Cambridge, Mass.: Harvard University Press.

Greenblatt, Stephen (1991) *Marvelous Possessions. The Wonder of the New World*, Chicago: University of Chicago Press.

Gregory of Rimini (1980) *Lectura super primum et secundum Sententiarum* VI, ed. Damasius Trapp, Berlin: de Gruyter.

Gregory the Great (1849) *Opera omnia* I in *PL* 75.

Gregory, Tullio (1955) *Anima Mundi. La filosofia di Guglielmo di Conches e la scuola di Chartres* (Pubblicazioni dell'Istituo di Filosofia dell'Università di Roma 3), Florence: Sansoni.

———. (1974) 'Abélard et Platon' in *Peter Abelard*, ed. Eligius M. Buytaert, Leuven: Leuven University Press, 38–64.

Grellard, Christophe (2007) 'Jean de Salisbury. Un cas médiéval de scepticisme', *Freiburger Zeitschrift für Philosophie und Theologie* 54: 16–40.

———. (2008) 'Le socratisme de Jean de Salisbury' in *Réceptions philosophique de la figure de Socrate* (= *Revue diagonale* 2), ed. Souzel Mayer, Lyons: Université Jean Moulin Lyon 3, 35–59.

———. (2013) *Jean de Salisbury et la renaissance médiévale du scepticisme*, Paris: Les Belles Lettres.

———. (2014) *De la certitude volontaire. Débats nominalistes sur la foi à la fin du moyen âge* (La philosophie à l'œuvre 7), Paris: Publications de la Sorbonne.

Grignaschi, Mario (1990) 'Lo pseudo Walter Burley e il Liber de vita et moribus philosophorum', *Medioevo* 16: 131–90.

Gruber, Joachim (2006) *Kommentar zu Boethius, De Consolatione Philosophiae. Texte und Kommentare 9.* 2nd, enlarged edn., Berlin: de Gruyter, 2006.

Hackett, Jeremiah (2005) 'Roger Bacon and the Reception of Aristotle in the Thirteenth Century: An Introduction to His Criticism of Aristotle' in *Albertus Magnus und die Anfänge der Aristoteles-Rezeption im lateinischen Mittelalter: von Richardus Rufus bis zu Franciscus de Mayronis*, ed. Ludger Honnefelder, Rega Wood, Mechthild Dreyer and Marc-Aeilko Aris (Subsidia Albertina 1), Münster: Aschendorff, 219–47.

Hadot, P. (1960) 'Citations de Porphyre chez Augustine (à propos d'un ouvrage récent)', *Revue des études augustiniennes* 6: 205–44 ; 'Comment of Prof. O'Meara', 245–47.

Hahn, Thomas G. (1974) *God's Friends: The Virtuous Heathens in Later Medieval Thought and English Literature*, PhD dissertation, University of California, Los Angeles.

———. (1978) 'The Indian Tradition in Western Medieval Intellectual History', *Viator* 9: 213–34.

Halm, Karl (1863) *Rhetores latini minores*, Leipzig: Teubner.

Hamesse, Jacqueline (1990) 'Le dossier Aristote dans l'oeuvre de Vincent de Beauvais. À propos de l'*Éthique*' in Paulmier-Foucart et al. 1990, 197–217.

Hanan, Yoran (2010) *Between Utopia and Dystopia: Erasmus, Thomas More, and the Humanist Republic of Letters*, Lanham, Md.: Lexington Books.

Hankins, James (2009) 'Marsilio Ficino and the Religion of the Philosophers', *Rinascimento* n.s. 48: 101–29.

Harding, B. (2008) *Augustine and Roman Virtue*, London: Continuum.

Harent, Stéphane (1922) 'Infidèles, Salut des', *Dictionnaire de théologie catholique* VII, Paris: Letouzay et Ané, col. 1726–1930.

Heather, P. J. (1991) *Goths and Romans, 332–489*, Oxford; Oxford University Press.

Helmold of Bosau (1963) *Slawenchronik [Chronica slavorum]*, ed. Heinz Stoob (using the text of Berhard Schmeidler) (Ausgewählte Quellen zur deutschen Geschichte des Mittelalters 19), Berlin: Rütten and Loening.

Henry of Ghent (1985) *Quodlibet XIII*, ed. Jos Decorte (Ancient and Medieval Philosophy. Series 2), Leuven: Leuven University Press.

Herbord (1974) *Dialogus de vita S. Ottonis*, ed. Jan Wikarjak and Kazimierz Liman (Monumenta Poloniae Historica series nova, 7.3), Warsaw: Państwowe Wydawnictwo Naukowe.

Herdt, Jennifer A. (2008) *Putting on Virtue: The Legacy of the Splendid Vices*, Chicago: University of Chicago Press.

Higgins, Iain M. (1997) *Writing East. The "Travels" of Sir John Mandeville*, Philadelphia: University of Pennsylvania Press.

Hilduin (1851) *Passio Sancti Dionysii* in PL 106, 13–24.

Hilka, Alfons (ed.) (1977) *Historia Alexandri Magni (Historia de Preliis). Rezension J2 (Orosius-Rezension)*, II (Beiträge zur Klassische Philologie 89), Meisenheim am Glan: Hain.

Hissette, R. (1977) *Enquête sur les 219 articles condamnés à Paris le 7 mars 1277* (Philosophes médiévaux 22), Louvain: publications universitaires.

———. (1990) 'Note sur le syllabus "antirationnaliste" du 7 mars 1277', *Recherches de théologie ancienne et médiévale* 88: 404–16.

Hoenen, Maarten J.F.M. (2003) '*Via antiqua* and *via moderna* in the Fifteenth Century: doctrinal, institutional, and church political factors in the *Wegestreit*' in Friedman and Nielsen 2003, 9–36.

———. (2004) 'Zurück zu Autorität und Tradition. Geistesgeschichtliche Hintergründe des Traditionalismus an den spätmittelalterlichen Universitäten' in *Herbst des Mittelalters'? Fragen zur Bewertung des 14. und 15. Jahrhunderts*, ed. Jan A. Aertsen and Martin Pickavé (Miscellanea Mediaevalia 31), Berlin: de Gruyter, 133–46.

———. (2012) 'How the Thomists in Cologne Saved Aristotle: The Debate Over the Eternity of the World in the Late-Medieval Period' in *Philosophy and Theology in the 'Studia' of the Religious Orders and at Papal and Royal Courts*, ed. William J. Courtenay and Stephen M. Metzger (Rencontres de Philosophie Médiévale 15), Turnhout: Brepols, 181–217.

Horn, Christoph (ed.) (1997) *Augustinus. De civitate dei* (Klassiker Auslegen 11), Berlin: Akademie Verlag.

Hulme, Peter (1994) 'Tales of Distinction: European Ethnography and the Caribbean' in Schwartz 1994, 157–97.

Huygens, R. B. C. (ed.) (1954) 'Mittelalterliche Kommentare zum *O qui perpetua . . .*', *Sacris Erudiri* 6: 373–427.

Hyde, John K. (1991) *Literacy and Its Uses: Studies on Late Medieval Italy*, ed. Daniel Waley, Manchester: Manchester University Press.

Idel, Moshe (2002) 'Prisca Theologia in Marsilio Ficino and in Some Jewish Treatments' in *Marsilio Ficino: His Theology, His Philosophy, His Legacy*, ed. Michael J. B. Allen, Valery Rees and Martin Davies (Brill's Studies in Intellectual History 108), Leiden: Brill, 137–58.

Imbach, Ruedi (1991) 'L'Averroïsme latin du XIII siècle' in *Gli studi di filosofia medievale fra otto e novecento. Contributo a un bilancio storiografico*, ed. Ruedi Imbach and Alfonso Maierù, Rome: Edizioni di storia e letteratura, 191–208.

———. (1992) 'Die politische Dimension der menschlichen Vernunft vei Dante' in *Der Mensch—ein politisches Tier? Essays zur politischen Anthropologie*, ed. Otfried Höffe, Stuttgart: Reclam, 26–42 (reprinted in Ruedi Imbach, *Quodlibeta. Ausgewählte Artikel/ Articles choisis*, ed. Francis Cheneval et al., Freiburg, Switzerland: Universitätsverlag, 1996, 385–97).

———. (1994) 'Aristoteles in der Hölle. Eine anonyme *quaestio*, Utrum Aristotiles sit salvatus' im Cod. Vat. Lat. 1012 (127ra-127va) zum Jenseitsschicksal des Stagiriten' in *Peregrina Curiositas. Eine Reise durch den orbis antiquus: zu Ehren von Dirk van Damme*, ed. Andreas Kessler, Thomas Ricklin and Gregor Wurst, Freiburg, Switzerland: Universitatsverlag and Vandenhoeck and Ruprecht, 297–318.

———. (1996) *Dante, la philosophie et les laïcs* (Vestigia 21), Paris: Cerf and Éditions Universitaires de Fribourg.

Irwin, Terence (2007) *The Development of Ethics. A Historical and Critical Study* I, Oxford: Oxford University Press.

Jacob of Voragine (1890) *Legenda Aurea, vulgo Historia Lombardica dicta*, 3rd edn., ed. Theodor Graesse, Bratislava: Koebner.

Jaeger, W. (1947) *The Theology of the Early Greek Philosophers*, Oxford; Oxford University Press.

Jansenius, Cornelius (1640) *Augustinus*, Louvain: Zeger.

Janson, Henrik (2000) 'Adam of Bremen and the Conversion of Scandinavia' in *Christianizing Peoples and Converting Individuals*, ed. Guyda Armstrong and Ian N. Wood, 83–88 (International Medieval Research 7), Turnhout: Brepols.

Jean le Long (2010) *Le voyage en Asie d'Odoric de Pordenone traduit par Jean le Long OSB*, ed. Alvise Andreose and Philippe Ménard, Geneva: Droz.

Jeauneau, Edouard (1957) 'L'usage de la notion d'*integumentum* à travers les gloses de Guillaume de Conches', *Archives d'histoire doctrinale et littéraire du Moyen Âge* 24: 35–100 (reprinted in his « *Lectio philosophorum* ». *Recherches sur l'École de Chartres*, Amsterdam: Hakkert, 1973, 127–92).

———. (2011) 'Quand un médecin commente Juvenal' in Obrist and Caiazzo 2011, 111–21.

Jefferson, Bernard L. (1917) *Chaucer and the 'Consolation of Philosophy' of Boethius*, Princeton: Princeton University Press.

Jensen, Lionel M. (1997) *Manufacturing Confucianism. Chinese Traditions and Universal Civilization*, Durham, N.C.: Duke University Press.

Jerome (1969) *Commentarii in euangelium Matthaei*, ed. D. Hurst and M. Adriaen (Corpus Christianorum series latina 77), Turnhout: Brepols.

John Cabrol ([1900–1908] 1967) *Defensiones Theologiae Divi Thomae, IV*, ed. C. Paban and T. Pègues, Frankfurt: Minerva.

John Duns Scotus (1950–) *Opera omnia* 1, ed. Carolus Balić et al., Vatican City: Typis (Polyglottis) Vaticanis.

John Mandeville (2000) *Le livre des merveilles du monde*, ed. C. Deluz (Sources d'histoire médiévale 31), Paris: CNRS.

———. (2011) *The Book of John Mandeville with Related Texts*, ed. and trans. Iain M. Higgins, Indianapolis: Hackett.

John of Piano Carpini (1930), *Geschichte der Mongolen und Reisebericht 1245–1247*, ed. Friedrich Risch (Veröffentlichungen des Forschungsinstituts für vergleichende Religionsgeschichte an der Universität Leipzig 2 reihe, 2), Leipzig: Pfeiffer.

———. (1965) *Histoire des Mongols*, trans. Jean Becquet and Louis Hambis, Paris: Maisonneuve.

———. (1989) *Storia dei Mongoli*, ed. E. Menestò et al. (Biblioteca del 'Centro per il collegamento degli studi medievali e umanistici nell'università di Perugia' 1), Spoleto: Centro italiano di studi sull'alto medioevo.

John of Salisbury (1909) *Policraticus*, ed. Clement C. I. Webb, Oxford: Oxford University Press.

———. (1987) *Entheticus Maior and Minor*, ed. Jan van Laarhoven (Studien und Texte zur Geistesgeschichte des Mittelalters 17), Leiden: Brill.

John of Wales (1511) *De regimine vite humane seu Margarita doctorum ad omne propositum* . . . , Lyons.

John Wyclif (1886) *Tractatus De ecclesia*, ed. Johann Loserth, London: Trübner for the Wyclif Society.

Jolivet, Jean (1963) 'Abélard et le Philosophe (Occident et Islam au XIIe siècle)', *Revue de l'histoire des religions* 164: 181–89.

———. (1980) 'Doctrines et figures de philosophes chez Abélard' in *Petrus Abaelardus (1079–1142): Person, Werk und Wirkung*, Trier: Paulinus, 103–20.

Julius Valerius (1888) *Res gestae Alexandri Macedonis*, ed. Bernard Kuebler, Leipzig: Teubner.

Justin (2006) *Apologie pour les chrétiens*, ed. C. Munier (Sources chrétiennes 507), Paris: éditions du Cerf.

Kaluza, Zénon (1995) 'Les débuts de l'albertisme tardif (Paris et Cologne)' in *Albertus Magnus und der Albertismus. Deutsche philosophische Kultur des Mittelalters*, ed. Maarten J.F.M. Hoenen and Alain de Libera (Studien und Texte zur Geistesgeschichte des Mittelalters 48), Leiden: Brill, 207–95.

Kaylor, Noel H. and Philip E. Philips (eds.) (2012) *A Companion to Boethius in the Middle Ages* (Brill's Companions to the Christian Tradition 30), Leiden: Brill.

Kent, Bonnie (2002) 'Habits and Virtues (IaIIae, qq. 49–70)' in *The Ethics of Aquinas*, ed. Stephen J. Pope, Washington, D.C.: Georgetown University Press, 116–30.

Kern, Iso (1998) 'Die Vermittliung chinesischer Philosophie in Europa' in *Die Philosophie des 17. Jahrhunderts* I, ed. Jean-Pierre Schobinger (Grundriss der Geschichte der Philosophie), Basel: Schwabe, 225–95.

Kerner, Max (1988) 'Die Institutio Traiani—spätantike Lehrschrift oder hochmittelalterliche Fiktion' in Detlev 1988, 715–38.

King, Peter (1999) 'Ockham's Ethical Theory' in *The Cambridge Companion to Ockham*, ed. Paul V. Spade, Cambridge: Cambridge University Press, 227–44.

———. (2012) 'Body and Soul' in Marenbon 2012c, 505–24.

Kirk, G. S., J. E. Raven and M. Schofield (eds.) (1983) *The Presocratic Philosophers. A Critical History with a Selection of Texts*, Cambridge: Cambridge University Press.

Klingner, Friedrich ([1921] 1966) *De Boethii Consolatione Philosophiae* (Philologische Unterschungen 27), Zurich: Weidmann.

Klopprogge, Axel (1993) *Ursprung und Ausprägung des abendländischen Mongolenbildes im 13. Jahrhundert:ein Versuch zur Ideengeschichte des Mittelalters* (Asiatische Forschungen 122), Wiesbaden: Harrassowitz.

Klutstein, Ilana (1988) *Marsilio Ficino et la théologie ancienne. Oracles chaldaïques—hymnes orphiques—hymnes de Proclus* (Istituto nazionale di studi sul rinascimento, quaderni 5), Florence: Olschki.

Knowles, David (1951) 'The Censured Opinions of Uthred of Boldon', *Proceedings of the British Academy* 37: 305–42.

Kuksiewicz, Zdzisław (1965) *Averroisme bolonais au XIVe siècle*, Wroclaw: Ossolineum.

Labrousse, Elisabeth (1985, 1964) *Pierre Bayle* (Archives internationales d'histoire des idées 1 and 6). Dordrecht: Lancaster (vol. 1, 2nd edn.); the Hague: Nijhoff (vol. 2).

Lafaye, Jacques (1974) *Quetzalcóatl et Guadalupe. La formation de la conscience nationale au Mexique (1531–1813)*, Paris: Gallimard.

La Mothe le Vayer, François de (1716) *Cinq dialogues faits à l'imitation des Anciens* (par Oratius Tubero), Frankfurt: Savius.

Landgraf, Artur M. (1952–56) *Dogmengeschichte der Frühscholastik*, Regensburg: Pustet.

Langland, William (1978) *Piers Plowman. An Edition of the C-Text*, ed. Derek Pearsall, London: Arnold.

Las Casas, Bartolomé (1967) *Apologética historia sumaria*, ed. Edmundo O'Gorman (Serie de historiadores y cronistas de Indias 1), Mexico: Universidad Nacional Autónoma de México.

———. (1988) *Apologia*, ed. Angel Losada (Obras completes 9), Madrid: Alianza.

Le Goff, Jacques (1957) *Les intellectuels au moyen âge*, Paris: Seuil.

Lee, G. W. (2011) 'Republics and Their Loves: Rereading *City of God* 19', *Modern Theology* 27: 553–81.

Leff, Gordon (1961) *Gregory of Rimini. Tradition and Innovation in Fourteenth Century Thought*, Manchester: Manchester University Press.

Leibniz, Gottfried F. W. (1838) *Deutsche Schriften,* I, ed. G. E. Guhrauer, Berlin: Beit.

———. (1863) *Mathematische Schriften*, ed. C. J. Gerhardt, 2–3 (VII), Halle.

———. ([1875–90] 1960–61) *Die philosophischen Schriften*, ed. C. J. Gerhardt, Hildesheim: Olms.

———. (1987) *Discours sur la théologie naturelle des chinois, plus quelques écrits sur la question religieuse de Chine*, ed. Christiane Frémont, Paris: l'Herne.

———. (1990a) *Leibniz korrespondiert mit China. Der Briefwechsel mit den Jesuitenmissionaren (1689–1714)*, ed. Rita Widmaier (Veröffentlichungen des Leibniz-Archivs 11), Frankfurt: Klostermann.

———. (1990b) *Nouveaux essais sur l'entendement humain*, ed. Jacques Brusnchwig, Paris: Flammarion.

Lestringant, Frank (1997) *Cannibals. The Discovery and Representation of the Cannibal from Columbus to Jules Verne*, trans. Rosemary Morris (The New Historicism 37), Berkeley: University of California Press.

———. (2004) *Le Huguenot et le sauvage. L'Amérique et la controverse coloniale, en France, au temps des guerres de Religion (1555–1589)*, 3rd edn., Geneva: Droz.

———. (2005) *Jean de Léry ou l'invention du sauvage. Essai sur l'«Histoire d'un voyage faict en la terre du Bresil»*, Paris: Champion.

Libera, Alain de (1991) *Penser au moyen âge*, Paris: Seuil.

———. (1998) 'Philosophie et censure. Remarques sur la crise universitaire parisienne de 1270–1277' in Aertsen and Speer 1998, 71–89.

———. (2003) *Raison et foi, archéologie d'une crise d'Albert le Grand à Jean-Paul II*, Paris: Seuil.

———. (2004) *L'Unité de l'intellect. Commentaire du 'De unitate intellectus contra averroistas' de Thomas d'Aquin*, Paris: Vrin.

———. (2005) *Métaphysique et noétique: Albert le Grand*, Paris: Vrin.

Liebeschütz, Hans (1950) *Mediaeval Humanism in the Life and Writings of John of Salisbury* (Studies of the Warburg Institute 17), London: Warburg Institute.

Liebeschuetz, J. H. W. G. (1979) *Continuity and Change in Greek Religion*, Oxford: Oxford University Press.

Limone, Oronzo (1978) 'La Vita di Gregorio Magno dell'Anonimo di Whitby', *Studi medievali* 19: 37–68.

Lofmark, Carl (1972) *Rennwart in Wolfram's 'Willehalm'. A Study of Wolfram von Eschenbach and His Sources*, Cambridge: Cambridge University Press.

Logan, George M. (1983) *The Meaning of More's 'Utopia'*, Princeton: Princeton University Press.

Lorch, Maristella de Panizza (1985) *A Defense of Life: Lorenzo Valla's Theory of Pleasure* (Humanistische Bibliothek, Reihe 1, Abhandlungen 36). Munich: Fink.

Lorenzo Valla (1970) *De vero falsoque bono*, ed. Maristella de Panizza Lorch, Bari: Adriatica.

———. (1977) *On Pleasure. De voluptate*, trans. A. Kent Hieatt and Maristella de Panizza Lorch, New York: Abaris.

———. (1982) *Repastinatio dialectice et philosophie* I, ed. Gianni Zippel (Thesaurus Mundi 21–22), Padua: Antenore.

Lottin, Odin (1949, 1954, 1959) *Psychologie et morale aux XIIe et XIIIe siècles*, vols. 3, 4 and 5, Louvain: Abbaye du Mont César and Duculot.

———. (1953) 'Les vertus morales acquises sont-elles de vraies vertus?', *Recherches de théologie ancienne et médiévale* 20: 13–39.

———. (1961) *Études de morale, histoire et doctrine*, Gembloux: Duculot.

Love, Rosalind C. (2012) 'The Latin Commentaries on Boethius's *De Consolatione Philosophiae* from the 9th to the 11th Centuries' in Kaylor and Phillips 2012, 75–133.

Lucentini, Paolo (2007) *Platonismo, ermetismo, eresia nel medioevo* (Textes et études du moyen âge 41), Louvain-la-Neuve: Fédération internationale des instituts d'études médiévales.

Lusignan, Serge and Monique Paulmier-Foucart (eds.) (1997) *Lector et compilator, Vincent de Beauvais, frère prêcheur: un intellectuel et son milieu au XIIIe siècle* (with Marie-Christine Duchenne) (Memoria del tempo 35), Grâne: Créaphis.

Macrobius (1970) *Commentarii in Somnium Scipionis*, ed. James Willis, Leipzig: Teubner.

Madec, Goulven (1962) 'Connaissance de Dieu et action de grâces. Essai sur les citations de l'*Ép. Aux Romains* I, 18–25 dans l'oeuvre de saint Augustin', *Recherches Augustiniennes* 2: 273–309.

———. (1981) 'Si Plato viveret (Augustine *De vera religione*, 3,3)' in *Néoplatonisme, Mélanges offerts à Jean Trouillard* (Les cahiers de Fontenay, 19, 20, 21, 22), Fontenay aux roses: E.N.S., 231–47.

———. (1994) 'La *De ciuitate Dei* comme *De uera religione*' in *Sant'Agostino: Confessioni. Volume III (Libri VII–IX)*, ed. G. Madec and L. F. Pizzolato, Verona: Fondazione Lorenzo Valla/Mondadori, 189–213.

Mähl, Sibylle (1969) *Quadriga virtutum. Die Kardinaltugenden in der Geistesgeschichte der Karolingerzeit* (Beihefte zum Archiv für Kulturgeschichte 9), Cologne: Böhlau.

Maier, Franz G. (1955) *Augustin und das antike Rom* (Tübinger Beiträge zur Altertumswissenschaft 39), Stuttgart: Kohlhammer.

Major, John (1509) *In quartum sententiarum*, Paris: Pigouchet.

———. (1510) *In secundum sententiarum*, Paris: Ioannes Parvus and Jodocus Badius Ascensius.

Mandouze, André (1958) *Saint Augustin et la religion romaine*, Paris: Études Augustiniennes.

Mantuanus, Baptistus (1501) *De penitencia*, Deventer: Pafraet.

Marenbon, John (1987) *Later Medieval Philosophy (1150–1350): An Introduction*, London: Routledge.

———. (1988) *Early Medieval Philosophy (480–1150): An Introduction*, 2nd edn., London: Routledge.

———. (1990) 'Symposium on the Theoretical and Practical Autonomy of Philosophy in the Middle Ages: Latin Philosophy, 1250–1350' in *Knowledge and the Sciences in Medieval Philosophy*, ed. Monika Asztalos, John E. Murdoch and Ilka Niiniluoto (Acta Philosophica Fennica 48), Helsinki: Yliopistopaino, 262–74.

———. (1992) 'Abelard's Concept of Natural Law' in *Mensch und Natur im Mittelalter*, ed. Albert Zimmermann (Miscellanea Mediaevalia 21,2), Berlin: de Gruyter, 609–21.

———. (1994) 'Carolingian Thought' in McKitterick 1994, 171–92.

———. (1997a) *The Philosophy of Peter Abelard*, Cambridge: Cambridge University Press.

———. (1997b) 'The Platonisms of Peter Abelard' in *Néoplatonisme et philosophie médiévale*, ed. Linos Benakis (Rencontres de philosophie médiévale 6), Turnhout, 109–29, reprinted in Marenbon 2000a.

———. (2000a) *Aristotelian Logic, Platonism and the Context of Early Medieval Philosophy in the West* (Variorum Collected Studies Series 696), Aldershot, Ashgate.

———. (2000b) 'Humanism, Scholasticism and the School of Chartres': review article on R. W. Southern, *Scholastic Humanism and the Unification of Europe I. Foundations*, *International Journal of the Classical Tradition* 6: 569–77.

———. (2000c) 'Twelfth-Century Platonism: Old Paths and New Directions' in Marenbon 2000a, item XV.

———. (2001a) 'Dante's Averroism' in Marenbon 2001b, 349–74.

———. (ed.) (2001b) *Poetry and Philosophy in the Middle Ages. A Festschrift for Peter Dronke* (Mittellateinische Studien und Texte 29), Leiden: Brill.

———. (2003) *Boethius*, New York: Oxford University Press.

———. (2004a) 'Abelard's Intellectual Contexts' in *The Cambridge Companion to Abelard*, ed. Jeffrey Brower and Kevin Guilfoy, Cambridge: Cambridge University Press, 13–44.

———. (2004b) 'Boethius and the Problem of Paganism', *American Catholic Philosophical Quarterly* 78: 329–48.

———. (2005) 'Robert Holcot and the Pagan Philosophers' in *Britannia Latina. Latin in the Culture of Great Britain from the Middle Ages to the Twentieth Century*, ed. Charles Burnett and Nicholas Mann (Warburg Institute Colloquia 8), London: Warburg Institute and Nino Aragno, 55–67.

———. (2006) 'Les exemples de philosophes et les philosophes comme exemples' in Ricklin 2006a, 119–33.

Marenbon, John (2007a) 'Latin Averroism' in *Islamic Crosspollinations. Interactions in the Medieval Middle East*, ed. Anna Akasoy, James E. Montgomery and Peter Pormann, London: Gibb Memorial Trust, 135–47.

———. (2007b) *Medieval Philosophy: An Historical and Philosophical Introduction*, London: Routledge.

———. (2007c) 'Peter Abelard and Platonic Politics' in *The Political Identity of the West*, ed. Marcel van Ackeren and Orrin F. Summerell, Frankfurt: Peter Lang, 133–50.

———. (ed.) (2009a) *The Cambridge Companion to Boethius*, Cambridge: Cambridge University Press.

———. (2009b) 'Imaginary Pagans: From the Middle Ages to the Renaissance' in *Continuities and Disruption between the Middle Ages and the Renaissance*, ed. Charles S. F. Burnett, Jacqueline Hamesse and José Meirinhos (Textes et études du moyen âge 48), Louvain-la-neuve: FIDEM, 151–65.

———. (2010) 'The Emergence of Medieval Latin Philosophy' in *The Cambridge History of Medieval Philosophy*, ed. Robert Pasnau, Cambridge: Cambridge University Press, 26–38.

———. (2011a) 'Peter Abelard's Theory of Virtues and Its Context' in *Knowledge, Discipline and Power in the Middle Ages. Essays in Honour of David Luscombe*, ed. Joseph Canning, Edmund King and Martial Staub (Studien und Texte zur Geistesgeschichte des Mittelalters 106), Leiden: Brill, 231–42.

———. (2011b) 'When Was Medieval Philosophy?', inaugural lecture, University of Cambridge, http://www.dspace.cam.ac.uk/handle/1810/240658.

———. (2011c) 'Why Study Medieval Philosophy' in *Warum noch Philosophie? Historische, systematische und gesellschaftliche Positionen*, edited by Marcel van Ackeren, Theo Kobusch and Jörn Müller, Berlin: de Gruyter, 65–78.

———. (2012a) *The Hellenistic Schools and Thinking about Pagan Philosophy in the Middle Ages. A Study of Second-Order Influence* (Freiburger mediävistische Vorträge 3), Basel: Schwabe.

———. (2012b) 'Latin Philosophy, 1350–1550' in Marenbon 2012c, 220–44.

———. (ed.) (2012c) *The Oxford Handbook of Medieval Philosophy*, New York: Oxford University Press.

———. (2012d) 'A Problem of Paganism' in Steel, Marenbon and Verbeke 2012, 39–54.

———. (2012e) 'Theology and Philosophy' in *European Transformations. The Long Twelfth Century*, ed. Thomas F. X. Noble and John Van Engen, Notre Dame, Ind.: University of Notre Dame Press, 403–425.

———. (2013a) *Abelard in Four Dimensions. A Twelfth-Century Philosopher in His Context and Ours*, Notre Dame, Ind.: University of Notre Dame Press.

———. (2013b) 'Divine Prescience and Contingency in Boethius's *Consolation of Philosophy*', *Rivista di storia della filosofia* 2013: 9–21.

Markus, R. A. (1970) *Saeculum: History and Society in the Theology of Augustine*, Cambridge: Cambridge University Press.

Marsilio Ficino (1500) *De christiana religione*, Venice: Ottinus Papiensis.

———. (1988) *The Letters IV*, London: Shepheard-Walwayn.

Marzio, Galeotto (1948) *Quel che i più non sanno (De incognitis vulgo)*, ed. Mario Frezza, Naples: Pironti e Figli.

Matthew of Aquasparta (1903) *Quaestiones disputatae selectae* I (Bibliotheca franciscana scholastica medii aevii 1), Quaracchi: Collegium S. Bonaventurae.

Matthew Paris (1872–83) *Chronica Majora* (Rolls Series, no. 57), ed. Henry R. Luard, London: Longman.

Matthews, J. (1975) *Western Aristocracies and Imperial Court, A. D. 364–425*, Oxford: Oxford University Press.

Matuzova, Vera I. (2001) 'Mental Frontiers: Prussians as Seen by Peter von Dusburg' in *Crusade and Conversion on the Baltic Frontier, 1150–1500*, ed. Alan V. Murray, Aldershot: Ashgate, 253–59.

McFarland, Timothy (2002) 'Giburc's Dilemma: Parents and Children, Baptism and Salvation' in *Wolfram's 'Willehalm'. Fifteen Essays*, ed. Martin H. Jones and Timothy McFarland, Rochester, N.Y.: Camden House, 121–42.

McGrath, Alister E. (2005) *Iustitia Dei. A History of the Christian Doctrine of Justification*, 3rd edn, Cambridge: Cambridge University Press.

McGregor, James H. (1991) *The Image of Antiquity in Boccaccio's* Filocolo, Filostrato *and* Teseida (Studies in Italian Culture. Literature in History 1), New York: Peter Lang.

McKitterick, Rosamond (ed.) (1994) *Carolingian Culture: Emulation and Innovation*, Cambridge: Cambridge University Press.

Mercken, H. Paul F. (1973) *The Greek Commentaries on the Nicomachean Ethics of Aristotle in the Latin Translation of Robert Grosseteste, Bishop of Lincoln (d. 1253)*, I (Corpus latinum commentariorum in Aristotelem Graecorum 6.1), Leiden: Brill.

Michon, Cyrille (2004) *Thomas d'Aquin et la controverse sur* L'Éternité du monde, Paris: Flammarion.

Minio-Paluello, Laurenzio (1955) 'Tre note alla Monarchia' in *Medioevo e rinascimento: studi in onore di B. Nardi* (Pubblicazioni dell'Istituto di filosofia dell'Università di Roma 1–2), Florence: Sansoni, 503–11.

Minnis, Alistair J. (1982) *Chaucer and Pagan Antiquity* (Chaucer Studies 8), Woodbridge: Boydell and Brewer.

———. (1986) 'From Medieval to Renaissance? Chaucer's Position on Past Gentility', *Proceedings of the British Academy* 72: 205–46.

———. (1997) 'Looking for a Sign: The Quest for Nominalism in Chaucer and Langland' in *Essays on Ricardian Literature: In Honour of John Burrow*, ed. Alistair J. Minnis, Charlotte C. Morse and Thorlac Turville-Petre, Oxford: Oxford University Press, 142–78.

Mitchell, S. and P. Van Nuffelen (eds.) (2010) *One God. Pagan Monotheism in the Roman Empire*, Cambridge: Cambridge University Press.

Momigliano, Arnaldo (1955) 'Cassiodorus and the Italian Culture of His Time', *Proceedings of the British Academy* 41: 207–45.

Montaigne, Michel (2007) *Les Essais*, ed. Jean Balsamo, Michel Magnien and Catherine Magnien-Simonin, Paris: Gallimard.

Monumenta Henricina I (1960) Coimbra: Comissão Executiva das Comemorações do V Centenário da Morte do Infante D. Henrique.

Moorhead, John (1992) *Theoderic in Italy*, Oxford: Oxford University Press.
———. (2009) 'Boethius's Life and Late Antique Philosophy' in Marenbon 2009a, 13–33.
More, Thomas (1965) *The Complete Works*, IV, ed. Edward Surtz and J. H. Hexter (*Utopia*), New Haven: Yale University Press.
———. (1995) *Utopia. Latin Text and English Translation*, ed. George M. Logan, Robert M. Adams and Clarence H. Miller, Cambridge: Cambridge University Press.
Moriarty, Michael (2011) *Disguised Vices: Theories of Virtue in Early Modern French Thought*, Oxford: Oxford University Press.
Morton, Catherine (1982) 'Marinus of Avenches, the "Excerpta Valesiana", and the Death of Boethius', *Traditio* 38: 107–36.
Mungello, David E. (1977) *Leibniz and Confucianism. The Search for Accord*, Honolulu: University Press of Hawaii.
———. (1985) *Curious Land: Jesuit Accommodation and the Origins of Sinology* (Studia Leibnitiana supplementa 25), Stuttgart: Steiner.
———. (ed.) (1994) *The Chinese Rites Controversy. Its History and Meaning* (Monumenta serica monograph series 33), Nettetal: Steyer.
Nardi, Bruno (1930) *Saggi di filosofia dantesca* (Biblioteca Pedagogica antica e moderna italiana e straniera 57), Milan: Società anonima editrice Dante Alighieri.
———. (1945) *Sigieri di Brabante nel pensiero del Rinascimento italiano*, Rome: edizioni italiane.
———. (1960) *Dal «Convivio» alla «Commedia». (Sei saggi danteschi)* (Istituto storico italiano per il medio evo, studi storici fasc. 35–39), Rome: Istituto storico italiano per il medio evo.
Nauta, Lodi (2009) *In Defense of Common Sense. Lorenzo Valla's Critique of Scholastic Philosophy*, Cambridge, Mass.: Harvard University Press.
Nederman, Cary J. (2000) *Worlds of Difference. European Discourses of Toleration, c. 1100–1550*, University Park: Pennsylvania State University Press.
Negri, Silvia (2011) 'La *Quaestio* "De salvatione Aristotelis" del tomista Lamberto di Monte' in Palazzo 2011, 413–40.
Nicholas of Cusa (1959) *De pace fidei*, ed. Raymund Klibansky and Hildebrand Bascour (Nicolai de Cusa opera Omnia 7), Hamburg: Meiner.
Niewöhner, Friedrich and Loris Sturlese (eds.) (1994) *Averroismus im Mittelalter und in der Renaissance*, Zurich: Spur.
Nifo, Agostino (2011) *De intellectu*, ed. Leen Spruit (Brill's Studies in Intellectual History 201), Leiden: Brill.
Nolan, Barbara (1992) *Chaucer and the Tradition of the 'Roman Antique'* (Cambridge Studies in Medieval Literature 15), Cambridge: Cambridge University Press.
North, John D. (1969) 'Kalenderes enlumyned ben they. Some Astronomical Themes in Chaucer', *Review of English Studies* n.s. 20: 129–54.
Oberman, Heiko A. (1963) *The Harvest of Medieval Theology. Gabriel Biel and Late Medieval Nominalism*, Cambridge, Mass.: Harvard University Press.

Obrist, Barbara and Irène Caiazzo (eds.) (2011) *Guillaume de Conches: philosophie et science au XIIe siècle* (Micrologus Library 42), Florence: SISMEL—Edizioni dell Galluzzo.

O'Connell, R. J. (1984) *Saint Augustine's Platonism*, Villanova, Pa.: Villanova University Press.

O'Daly, G. (1999) *Augustine's 'City of God'. A Reader's Guide*, Oxford: Oxford University Press.

O'Meara, John J. (1959) *Porphyry's Philosophy from Oracles in Augustine*, Paris: Études Augustiniennes.

Orchard, Andy (2003) *A Critical Companion to Beowulf*, Rochester: Brewer.

Padoan, Giorgio (1977) *Il pio Enea, l'empio Ulisse: tradizione classica e intendimento medievale in Dante* (L'Interprete 5), Ravenna: Longo.

Paganini, Gianni (2008) *Skepsis. Le débat des modernes sur le scepticisme: Montaigne, Le Vayer, Campanella, Hobbes, Descartes, Bayle* (De Pétrarque à Descartes 78), Paris: Vrin.

Pagden, Anthony (1982) *The Fall of Natural Man. The American Indian and the Origins of Comparative Ethnology*, Cambridge: Cambridge University Press.

Pagnoni, M. R. (1974) 'Prime note sulla tradizione medievale ed umanistica di Epicuro', *Annali della Scuola Normale Superiore di Pisa, Classe di lettere e filosofia*, ser. 3, 4: 1443–77.

Palacios Rubios, Juan López de (1954) *De las Islas del mar Océano* (with Matías de Paz, *De domino de los Reyes de España sobre los indios*) (Biblioteca americana (Mexico). Serie de cronistas de Indias 25), ed. Silvio Zavala, trans. Agustin M. Carlo, Méxíco: Fondo de Cultura Económica.

Palazzo, Alessandro (ed.) (2011) *L'antichità classica nel pensiero medievale* (Texte et études du Moyen Âge 61), Porto: FIDEM and Gabinete de Filosofia Medieval/Faculdade de Letras da Universidade do Porto.

Papio, Michael (2012) 'Boccaccio: Mythographer, Philosopher, Theologian' in *Boccaccio in America*, ed. Elsa Filosa and Michael Papio, Ravenna: Longo, 124–42.

Pasnau, Robert (ed.) (2010) *The Cambridge History of Medieval Philosophy*, Cambridge: Cambridge University Press.

Paulmier-Foucart, Monique (ed.) (2004) *Vincent de Beauvais et le Grand Miroir du Monde* (with Marie-Christine Duchenne), Turnhout: Brepols.

Paulmier-Foucart, Monique, Serge Lusignan and Alain Nadeau (eds.) (1990) *Vincent de Beauvais: intentions et réceptions d'une oeuvre encyclopédique au Moyen Âge* (Cahiers d'études médiévales. Cahier spécial 4), Saint-Laurent: Bellarmin and Vrin, 1990.

Perkins, Franklin (2004) *Leibniz and China. A Commerce of Light*, Cambridge: Cambridge University Press.

Pertz, Georg H. (1835) *Monumenta Germaniae Historica* III—Legum I, Hannover: Hahn.

Peter Abelard (1969) *Opera theologica* II, ed. Eligius M. Buytaert (Corpus Christianorum continuatio mediaeualis 12), Turnhout: Brepols.

———. (1970) *Dialectica*, ed. Lambertus M. De Rijk, 2nd edn., Assen: Van Gorcum.

Peter Abelard (1971) *Ethics*, ed. and trans. David E. Luscombe, Oxford: Oxford University Press.

———. (1984) 'Peter Abelard "Soliloquium". A critical edition', ed. Charles Burnett, *Studi medievali* 25: 857–94.

———. (1987) *Opera theologica* III, ed. Eligius M. Buytaert and Constant J. Mews (Corpus Christianorum continuatio mediaeualis 13), Turnhout: Brepols.

———. (2001) *Collationes*, ed. and trans. John Marenbon and Giovanni Orlandi, Oxford: Oxford University Press.

———. (2006) *Petri Abaelardi opera theologica* 6, ed. D. Luscombe and C. J. Mews (Corpus Christianorum continuatio mediaeualis 14), Turnhout: Brepols.

Peter of Dusburg (2012) *Cronaca della terra di Prussia. L'Ordine Teutonico dalla fondazione al 1326*, ed. Piero Bugiani (Biblioteca del 'Centro per il collegamento degli studi medievali e umanistici in Umbria' 23), Spoleto: Centro Italiano di studi sull'alto medioevo.

Peter the Lombard (1971–81) *Sententiarum libri iv* (Spicilegium Bonaventurianum 4–5), Grottaferrata: Editiones Collegii S. Bonaventurae ad Claras Aquas.

Peterson, Clifford (1977) *Saint Erkenwald*, Philadelphia: University of Pennsylvania Press.

Pfister, Friedrich (1941) 'Das Nachleben der Überlieferung von Alexander und den Brahmanen', *Hermes* 76: 143–69, reprinted in Pfister, *Kleine Schriften zum Alexanderroman* (Beiträge zur klassischen Philologie 61), Meisenheim am Glan: Hain, 1975, 52–79.

Philip the Chancellor (1985) *Summa de bono*, ed. Nikolaus Wick (Opera philosophica Mediae Aetatis selecta 2), 2 vols., Bern: Franke.

Piaia, Gregorio (1983) *"Vestigia philosophorum": il Medioevo e la storiografia filosofica*, Rimini: Maggioli.

Piché, David (1999) *La condemnation parisienne de 1277: nouvelle édition du texte latin*, Paris: Vrin.

Pico della Mirandola, Gianfrancesco (1520) *Examen vanitatis doctrinae gentium et veritatis Christianae disciplinae*, Mirandola: Ioannes Mazochius.

Pighius, Albertus (1542) *De libero hominis arbitrio et diuina gratia*, Cologne: Melchior Novesianus.

Pinborg, Jan (1974) 'Zur Philosophie des Boethius de Dacia. Ein Überblick', *Studia Mediewistyczne* 15: 165–85, reprinted in Jan Pinborg, *Medieval Semantics. Selected Studies on Medieval Logic and Grammar*, ed. Sten Ebbesen, London: Variorum, 1984.

Pine, Martin L. (1986) *Pietro Pomponazzi: radical philosopher of the Renaissance* (Centro per la storia della tradizione aristotelica nel Veneto, Saggi e testi 21), Padua: Antenore.

Pintard, René (1943) *Le libertinage érudit dans la première moitié du XVIIe siècle*, Paris: Boivin.

Plezia, Marianus (ed.) (1960) *Aristotelis qui ferebatur liber de pomo versio latina Manfredi* (Auctorum graecorum et latinorum opuscula selecta 2), Warsaw: Państwowe wydawnictwo naukowe.

Plummer, Charles (1896) *Venerabilis Baedae historia ecclesiastica*, II— Commentarium, Oxford: Oxford University Press.

Po-Chia Hsia, Ronnie (2010) *A Jesuit in the Forbidden City: Matteo Ricci 1552–1610*, Oxford: Oxford University Press.

Poirel, Dominique (2002) *Livre de la nature et débat trinitaire au XIIe siècle. Le De tribus diebus de Hugues de Saint Victor* (Bibliotheca Victorina 14), Turnhout: Brepols.

Pomponazzi, Pietro (1990) *Abhandlung über die Unsterblichkeit der Seele*, ed. Burkhard Mojsisch (Lateinisch-Deutsch), Hamburg: Felix Meiner.

Porro, Pasquale (2001) 'Lo statuto della *philosophia* in Enrico di Gand' in Aertsen, Emery and Speer 2001, 497–504.

Power, Amanda (2013) *Roger Bacon and the Defence of Christendom* (Cambridge Studies in Medieval Life and Thought, 4th series, 84), Cambridge: Cambridge University Press.

Pozzi, Mario (ed.) (1993) *Il Mondo nuovo di Amerigo Vespucci: scritti vespucciani e paravespucciani*, Alessandria: edizioni dell'Orso.

Prévot, Jacques (ed.) (2004) *Libertins du XVIIe siècle* II, Paris: Gallimard.

Putallaz, François-Xavier and Ruedi Imbach (1997) *Profession: Philosophe. Siger de Brabant*, Paris: éditions du Cerf.

Quint, David (1990) 'A Reconsideration of Montaigne "Des cannibales"', *Modern Language Quarterly* 51: 459–89.

Raucheisen, Alfred (1997) *Orient und Abendland. Ethisch-moralische Aspekte in Wolframs Epen* Parzival *und* Willehalm (Bremer Beiträge zur Literatur- und Ideengeschichte 17), Frankfurt: Peter Lang.

Relihan, Joel C. (1993) *Ancient Menippean Satire*, Baltimore: Johns Hopkins University Press.

———. (2007) *The Prisoner's Philosophy. Life and Death in Boethius's* Consolation, Notre Dame, Ind.: University of Notre Dame Press.

Rémy, Gérard (1979) *Le Christ médiateur dans l'oeuvre de Saint Augustin*, Lille: Atelier Reproduction des Thèses.

Ricci, Matteo (1942) *Fonti Ricciane* I, ed. Pasquale M. d'Elia, Rome: Libreria dello Stato.

———. (2013) *Le sens réel de « Seigneur du Ciel »*, ed. Thierry Meynard, Paris: les Belles Lettres.

Richard of Middleton (1591) *Super quatuor libros Sententiarium*, III, Brescia.

Ricklin, Thomas (2002) 'Théologie et philosophie du *Convivio* de Dante Alighieri' in Solère and Kaluza 2002, 129–50.

———. (2005) 'La mémoire des philosophes. Les débuts de l'historiographie de la philosophie au moyen âge' in *La mémoire du temps au Moyen Âge*, ed. Agostino Paravicini Bagliani (Micrologus Library 12), Florence: SISMEL, Edizioni del Galluzzo.

———. (ed.) (2006a) *Exempla docent. Les exemples des philosophes de l'Antiquité à la Renaissance* (Études de philosophie médiévale 92), Paris: Vrin.

———. (2006b) 'Jean de Galles, les *Vitae* de Saint François et l'exhortation des philosophes dans le *Compendiloquium de vita et dictis illustrium philosophorum*' in Ricklin 2006a, 203–23.

———. (2011) 'Il "Nobile Castello" dantesco e le riappropriazioni delle tradizioni filosofiche antiche' in Palazzo 2011, 279–306.

Ridings, D. (1995) *The Attic Moses. The Dependency Theme in Some Early Christian Writers* (Studia graeca et latina gothoburgensia 59), Göteborg: Acta universitatis Gothoburgensis.

Robert, Aurélien (2013) 'Épicure et les Épicuriens au Moyen Âge' in *Micrologus* 21 (The Medieval Legends of Philosophers and Scholars), Florence: edizioni del Galluzzo, 3–45.

Robert Grosseteste (1982) *Hexaëmeron*, ed. Richard C. Dales and Servus Gieben (Auctores Britannici Medii Aevi 6), London: British Academy.

Robert Holcot (1489) *Super Sapientiam Salomonis*, [Basel?].

———. (1518) *In quatuor libros Sententiarum questions argutissime . . .*, Lyons: Clein.

Robinson, Fred C. (1991) 'Beowulf' in *The Cambridge Companion to Old English Literature*, ed. Malcom Godden and Michael Lapidge, Cambridge: Cambridge University Press, 142–59.

Roger Bacon (1900) *Opus maius* I, ed. John H. Bridges, London: Williams and Norgate.

———. (1920) *Secretum secretorum cum glossis et notulis . . . fratris Rogeri*, ed. Robert Steele (Opera hactenus inedita Rogeri Baconi 5), Oxford: Oxford University Press.

———. (1953) *Moralis philosophia*, ed. Eugenio Massa, Turin: Thesaurus Mundi.

———. (1988) *Compendium of the Study of Theology. Edition and Translation with Introduction and Notes*, ed. Thomas S. Maloney (Studien und Texte zur Geistesgeschichte des Mittelalters 20), Leiden: Brill.

Ross, David A. (1988) *Alexander Historiatus. A Guide to Medieval Illustrated Alexander Literature*, 2nd edn. (Beiträge zur klassischen Philologie 186), Frankfurt: Athenaeum.

Rousseau, Mary F. (1968) *The Apple or Aristotle's Death. (De pomo sive de morte Aristotilis)*, Milwaukee: Marquette University Press.

Rowell, Stephen C. (1994) *Lithuania Ascending. A Pagan Empire within East-Central Europe, 1295–1345*, Cambridge: Cambridge University Press.

Rubini, Paolo (2013) *Pietro Pomponazzis Erkenntnisauffassung. Naturalisierung des menschlichen Geistes im Spätaristotelismus*, PhD thesis, Humboldt University, Berlin.

Rule, Paul A. (1986) *K'ung-tzu or Confucius? The Jesuit Interpretation of Confucianism*, Sydney: Allen and Unwin.

Ruokanen, Miikka (1993) *Theology of Social Life in Augustine's* De civitate Dei (Forschungen zur Kirchen- und Dogmengeschichte 53), Göttingen: Vandenhoeck and Ruprecht.

Salter, Elizabeth (1983) 'Chaucer and Boccaccio: *The Knight's Tale*' in her *Fourteenth-Century English Poetry. Contexts and Readings*, Oxford: Oxford University Press, 141–81.

Saxo Grammaticus (1931) *Gesta danorum*, I, ed. J. Olrik and H. Raeder, Copenhagen: Bagge.

Schmitt, Charles B. (1966) 'Perennial Philosophy: From Agostino Steuco to Leibniz', *Journal of the History of Ideas* 27: 505–22.

———. (1967) *Gianfrancesco Pico della Mirandola (1469–1533) and His Critique of Aristotle* (Archives internationales d'histoire des idées 23), The Hague: Martinus Nijhoff.

Schmitt, Charles B. and Dilwyn Knox (1985) *Pseudo-Arisoteles Latinus. A Guide to Latin Works Falsely Attributed to Aristotle before 1500* (Warburg Institute Surveys and Texts 12), London: Warburg Institute.

Schwartz, Stuart B. (ed.) (1994) *Implicit Understandings. Observing, Reporting, and Reflecting on the Encounters between Europeans and Other Peoples in the Early Modern Era*, Cambridge: Cambridge University Press.

Scott, John A. (1996) *Dante's Political Purgatory*, Philadelphia: University of Pennsylvania Press.

Senger, Hans G. (1982) 'Was geht Lambert von Heerenberg die Seligkeit des Aristoteles an?' in *Studien zur mittelalterlichen Geistesgeschichte und ihren Quellen*, ed. Albert Zimmermann (Miscellanea Mediaevalia 15), Berlin: de Gruyter, 293–311.

Sepúlveda, Juan Ginés de (1997) *Obras completas* III, ed. J. Brufau Prats, A. Coroleu Lletget, A. Moreno Hernández and Á. Losada, Salamanca: Ayuntamiento de Pozoblanco.

Sesböüé, Bernard (2004) *"Hors de l'Église pas de salut". Histoire d'une formule et problèmes d'interprétation*, Paris: Desclée de Brouwer.

Seyssel, Claude (1543) *De divina providentia*, Paris.

Shanzer, Danuta (2009a) '*Haec quibus uteris verba:* the Bible and Boethius' Christianity' in *The Power of Religion in Late Antiquity*, ed. Andrew Cane and Noel Lenski, Farnham: Ashgate, 57–78.

———. (2009b) 'Interpreting the *Consolation*' in Marenbon 2009a, 228–54.

Sharples, Robert (2009) 'Fate, Prescience and Free Will' in Marenbon 2009a, 207–27.

Siger of Brabant (1972) *Quaestiones in tertium de anima; De anima intellectiva; De aeternitate mundi*, ed. Bernardo Bazán (Philosophes Médiévaux 13), Louvain: Publications universitaires and Béatrice-Nauwelaerts.

———. (1974) *Écrits de logique, de morale et de physique*, ed. Bernardo Bazán (Philosophes médiévaux 14), Louvain: publications universitaires and Béatrice-Nauwelaerts.

Silagi, Gabriel (ed.) (1991) *Die 'Gesta Hungarorum' des anonymen Notars. Die älteste Dartsellung der ungarischen Geschichte* (Ungarns Geschichtsschreiber 4), Sigmaringen: Thorbecke.

Silk, Edmund T. (1935) *Saeculi noni auctoris in Boetii consolationem Philosophiae commentarius* (Papers and Monographs of the American Academy in Rome 9), Rome: American Academy in Rome.

Simon of Saint-Quentin (1965) *Histoire des tartares*, ed. J. Richard (Documents relatifs à l'histoire des croisades publiés par l'Académie des inscriptions et belles lettres 8), Paris: Geuthner.

Skinner, Quentin (1987) 'Sir Thomas More's *Utopia* and the Language of Renaissance Humanism' in *The Languages of Political Theory in Early-Modern Europe*, ed. Anthony Pagden, Cambridge: Cambridge University Press, 123–57.

Smalley, Beryl (1960) *English Friars and Antiquity in the Early Fourteenth Century*, Oxford: Blackwell.

Smits, E. R. (1986) 'Vincent of Beauvais: A Note on the Background of the "Speculum"', in *Vincent of Beauvais and Alexander the Great. Studies on the 'Speculum Maius' and Its Translations into Medieval Vernaculars*, ed. W. J. Aerts, E. R. Smits and J. B. Voorbij, J.B (Mediaevalia Groningana 7), Groningen: Forsten, 1–9.

Solère, Jean-Luc and Zénon Kaluza (eds.) (2002) *La servante et la consolatrice. La philosophie dans ses rapports avec la théologie au Moyen Âge* (Textes et traditions 3), Paris: Vrin.

Somfai, Anna (1998) *The Transmission and Reception of Plato's 'Timaeus' and Calcidius's Commentary during the Carolingian Renaissance*, PhD dissertation, University of Cambridge.

———. (2002) 'The Eleventh-Century Shift in the Reception of Plato's *Timaeus* and Calcidius's *Commentary*', *Journal of the Warburg and Courtauld Institutes* 65: 1–21.

Southern, Richard W. (1962) *Western Views of Islam in the Middle Ages*, Cambridge, Mass.: Harvard University Press.

———. (2001) *Scholastic Humanism and the Unification of Europe* II. *The Heroic Age*, Oxford: Blackwell.

Spence, Jonathan D. ([1984] 1985) *The Memory Palace of Matteo Ricci*, New York: Penguin.

Stang, Charles M. (2012) *Apophasis and Pseudonymity in Dionysius the Areopagite. 'No longer I'*, Oxford: Oxford University Press.

Steel, Carlos, John Marenbon and Werner Verbeke (2012) *Paganism in the Middle Ages. Threat and Fascination* (Mediaevalia lovaniensia. Series 1/Studia 43), Leuven: Leuven University Press.

Steffens, Karl (ed.) (1975) *Die Historia de preliis Alexandri Magni Rezension J3* (Beiträge zur Klassische Philologie 73), Meisenheim am Glan: Hain.

Stephan Hoest (1971) *Reden und Briefe. Quelle zur Geschichte der Scholastik und des Humanismus im 15. Jahrhundert*, ed. and trans. Frank Baron (Humanistische Bibliothek. Abhandlungen und Texte II, 3), Munich: Wilhelm Fink.

Stephens, W. P. (1986) *The Theology of Huldrych Zwingli*, Oxford: Oxford University Press.

Steuco, Agostino (1578) *De perenni philosophia . . .* , Paris: Sonnius.

Stewart, H. F. (1916) 'A Commentary by Remigius Autissiodorensis on the *De Consolatione Philosophiae* of Boethius', *Journal of Theological Studies* 17: 22–42.

Stoneman, Richard (1995) 'Naked Philosophers: The Brahmans in the Alexander Historians and the Alexander Romance', *Journal of Hellenic Studies* 115: 99–114.

———. (2008) *Alexander the Great. A Life in Legend*, New Haven: Yale University Press.

———. ([1994] 2012) *Legends of Alexander the Great*, London: Tauris.

Stover, Justin A. (2011) *Reading Plato in the Twelfth Century: A Study on the Varieties of Plato's Reception in the Latin West before 1215*, PhD dissertation, Harvard University.

Sturlese, Loris (1993) *Die deutsche Philosophie im Mittelalter. Von Bonifatius bis zu Albert dem Grossen (748–1280)*, Munich: Beck.

Suárez, Francisco (1857, 1858) *Opera omnia* VII, XII, ed. Charles Berton, Paris: Vivès.

Sullivan, Francis A. (2002) *Salvation Outside the Church. Tracing the History of the Catholic Response*, Eugene, Ore.: Wipf and Stock.

Swanson, Jenny (1989) *John of Wales. A Study of the Works and Ideas of a Thirteenth-Century Friar* (Cambridge Studies in Medieval life and Thought, 4th series, 10), Cambridge: Cambridge University Press.

Sylla, Edith (2001) '"Ideo quasi mendicare oportet intellectum humanum": The Role of Theology in John Buridan's Natural Philosophy' in *The Metaphysics and Natural Philosophy of John Buridan*, ed. J.M.M.H. Thijssen and Jack Zupko (History of Science and Medicine Library. Medieval and Early Modern Science 2), Leiden: Brill, 221–45.

Tardieu, Michel (2010) 'Le pluralisme religieux' in *La pluralité interprétative. Fondements historiques et cognitifs de la notion de point de vue*, ed. Alain Berthoz, Carlo Ossola and Brian Stock, Paris: OpenEdition Books, http://books.openedition.org/cdf/1421.

Thevet, André (1997) *Le Brésil d'André Thevet. Les Singularités de la France Antarctique (1557)*, ed. Frank Lestringant, Paris: Chandaigne.

Thierry of Chartres (1971) *Commentaries on Boethius by Thierry of Chartres and His School*, ed. Nikolaus M. Häring (Studies and Texts 20), Toronto: Pontifical Institute of Mediaeval Studies.

Thomas Aquinas (1882–) *Opera omnia iussu impensaque Leonis XIII P. M. edita*, Rome: Typographia Polyglotta.

———. (1997) *L'Unité de l'intellect contre les Averroïstes*, trans. Alain de Libera, 2nd edn., Paris: Flammarion.

Thomas Bradwardine (1618) *De causa dei contra Pelagianos*, ed. Henry Savile, London: Billius.

Thomas of Cantimpré (1973) *Liber de natura rerum: editio princeps secundum codices manuscriptos*, I, ed. Helmut Boese, Berlin: de Gruyter.

Todorov, Tzvetan (1982) *La conquête de l'Amérique. La question de l'autre*, Paris: Seuil.

———. (1989) *Nous et les autres. La réflexion francaise sur la diversité humaine*, Paris: Seuil.

Tolan, John V. (2002) *Saracens. Islam in the Medieval European Imagination*, New York: Columbia University Press.

Torrell, Jean-Pierre (1993) *Initiation à saint Thomas d'Aquin. Sa personne et son œuvre* (Vestigia 13), Fribourg: éditions du Cerf and éditions universitaires de Fribourg.

———. (2006) 'Saint Thomas et les non-chrétiens', *Revue Thomiste* 106: 17–49.

Trinkaus, Charles E. ([1970] 1995) *In Our Image and Likeness: Humanity and Divinity in Italian Humanist Thought* I, Notre Dame, Ind.: University of Notre Dame Press.

Trithemius, Johannes (1621) *Curiositas regia. Octo quaestiones a Maximiliano J. Caesari Joanni Trithemio propositae et ab eodem pie et solide solutae*, Douai: Bellerus.

Troncarelli, Fabio (1981) *Tradizioni perdute. La 'Consolatio Philosophiae' nell'alto medioevo*, Padua: Antenore.

———. (1987) 'Boezio nel circolo d'Alcuino: le più antiche glosse carolinge alla *Consolatio Philosophiae*', *Recherches Augustiniennes* 22: 223–41.

———. (2000) '*Mentis cogitatio*. Un prologo di Boezio in un prologo a Boezio?' in *Les prologues médiévaux*, ed. J. Hamesse (Textes et études du moyen âge 15), Turnhout: Brepols, 39–86.

———. (2005) *Cogitatio mentis. L'eredità di Boezio nell'Alto Medioevo* (Storie e testi 16), Naples: D'Auria.

Trumbower, Jeffrey A. (2001) *Rescue for the Dead: The Posthumous Salvation of Non-Christians in Early Christianity*, New York: Oxford University Press.

Tzanaki, Rosemary (2003) *Mandeville's Medieval Audiences. A Study on the Reception of the Book of Sir John Mandeville (1371–1550)*, Aldershot: Ashgate.

Usener, Hermann (1877) *Anecdoton Holderi. Ein Beitrag zur Geschichte Roms in ostgothischer Zeit*, Leipzig: Teubner.

Valcke, Louis (2005) *Pic de la Mirandole. Un itinéraire philosophique*, Paris: les Belles Lettres.

Valente, Luisa (2011) «Exhortatio» e «recta vivendi ratio». Filosofi antichi e filosofia come forma di vita in Pietro Abelardo', in Palazzo 2011, 39–66.

———. (2013) 'Philosophers and Other Kinds of Human Beings According to Peter Abelard and John of Salisbury' in *Logic and Language in the Middle Ages: A Volume in Honour of Sten Ebbesen*, ed. Jakob L. Fink, Heine Hansen and Ana María Mora-Márquez (Investigating Medieval Philosophy 4), Leiden: Brill, 105–23.

Van Nuffelen, P. (2010) 'Pagan Monotheism as a Religious Phenomenon' in Mitchell and Van Nuffelen 2010, 16–33.

Vasoli, Cesare (1980) 'Note su Galeotto Marzio' in his *La cultura delle corti*, Bologna: Capelli, 38–63, reprinting *Acta Litteraria Academiae Scientiarium Hungaricae* 19 (1977): 51–69.

Vega, Andreas (1621) *De iustificatione*, Aschaffeburg: Miraesius.

Veszprémy, László (2011) '"More Paganismo": reflections on the pagan and Christian past in the *Gesta Hungarorum* of the Hungarian anonymous notary' in Garipzanov 2011b, 183–201.

Vincent of Beauvais (1624) *Speculum maius*, Douai: Bellerus.

Vitoria, Francisco de (1932) *Comentarios a la Secunda secundae de Santo Tomás*, I, ed. Vicente Beltrán de Heredia (Biblioteca de Teólogis Españoles 2), Salamanca: Apartado 17.

———. (1960) *Obras de Francisco de Vitoria. Relecciones teologicas*, ed. Teofilo Urdanoz (Biblioteca de autores cristianos: sección 2. Teología y canones 198), Madrid: Biblioteca de autores cristianos.

———. (1967) *Relectio de Indis o libertad de los Indios*, ed. L. Pereña and J. M. Perez Prendes (Corpus Hispanorum de pace 5), Madrid: Consejo superior de investigaciones cientificas.

———. (1991) *Political Writings*, ed. Anthony Pagden and Jeremy Lawrence, Cambridge: Cambridge University Press.

Vitto, Cindy L. (1989) *The Virtuous Pagan in Middle English Literature* (Transactions of the American Philosophical Society 79, 5), Philadelphia: American Philosophical Society.

von Moos, Peter (1988a) 'Eine theoriegeschichtliche Miniatur am Rande der Institutio Traiani' in Detlev 1988, 739–80.

———. (1988b) *Geschichte als Topik. Das rhetorische Exemplum von der Antike zur Neuzeit und die* historiae *im* 'Policraticus' *Johanns von Salisbury* (Ordo. Studien zur Literatur und Gesellschaft des Mittelalters und der frühen Neuzeit 2), Hildesheim: Olms.

———. (2005) 'Die *Collationes* Abaelards und die Lage der Juden im 12. Jahrhundert' in *Abaelard und Heloise. Gesammelte Studien zum Mittelalter* 1, ed. Gert Melville (Geschichte: Forschung und Wissenschaft 14), Münster: LIT, 327–71.

———. (2012) 'Du miroir des princes au Cortegiano. Engelbert d'Admont (1250–1331) sur les agréments de la convivialité et de la conversation' in *Formes dialoguées dans la littérature exemplaire du Moyen Âge*, ed. Marie-Anne Polo de Beaulieu (Colloques, congrès et conférences sur le Moyen Âge 14.), Paris: Champion, 103–62.

———. (2013a) *Heiden im Himmel? Geschichte einer Aporie zwischen Mittelalter und Früher Neuzeit, mit kritischer Edition der* Quaestio de salvatione Aristotelis *des Lambertus de Monte von Philipp Roelli* (Philosophisch-historische Klasse der Heidelberger Akademie der Wissenschaften 54), Heidelberg: Winter.

———. (2013b) 'Païens et païens. La *Quaestio* de Lambert du Mont sur le salut éternel d'Aristote' in *Religiosità e civiltà. Conoscenze, confronti, influssi reciproci tra religioni (secoli X–XIV)*, ed. Giancarlo Andenna, Milan: Vita e Pensiero, 67–118.

Voorbij, J. B. [Hans] (1991) *Het 'Speculum Historiale' van Vincent van Beauvais: een studie van zijn ontstaansgeschiedenis*, Groningen; Universiteitsdrukkerij.

Walker, D. P. (1972) *The Ancient Theology. Studies in Christian Platonism from the Fifteenth to the Eighteenth Century*, London: Duckworth.

Walter Burley (1886) *De vita et moribus philosophorum*, ed. Hermann Knust (Bibliothek des litterarischen Vereins in Stuttgart 177), Tübingen: litterarischen Verein in Stuttgart.

Wang, Tch'ang-tche (1938) *Saint Augustin et les vertus des paiens*, Paris: Beauchesne.

Watson, Nicholas (1997) 'Visions of Inclusion: universal salvation and vernacular theology in pre-reformation England', *Journal of Medieval and Early Modern Studies* 27: 145–87.

Weinberg, Bernard (1968) 'Montaigne's Reading for *Des Cannibales*' in *Renaissance and Other Studies in Honor of William Leon Wiley*, ed. George B. Daniel, Jr., Chapel Hill: University of North Carolina Press, 261–79.

Whatley, Gordon (1984a) '"Piers Plowman" B 12.277–94: Notes on Language, Text, and Theology', *Modern Philology* 82: 1–12.

———. (1984b) 'The Uses of Hagiography: The Legend of Pope Gregory and the Emperor Trajan in the Middle Ages', *Viator* 15: 25–65.

White [Peden], Alison M. (1981) *Glosses Composed before the Twelfth Century in Manuscripts of Macrobius's Commentary on Cicero's 'Somnium Scipionis'*, PhD thesis, University of Oxford.

Wilks, Michael (ed.) (1984) *The World of John of Salisbury* (Studies in Church History. Subsidia 3), Oxford: Blackwell for the Ecclesiastical History Society.

William Langland (2011) *Piers Plowman. A Parallel-Text Version of the A,B,C and Z Versions*, ed. A. V. C. Schmidt, Kalamazoo, rev. edn., Mich.: Medieval Institute Publications.

William of Auvergne (1674) *Opera omnia*, Paris: Dionysius Thierry.

William of Auxerre (1980–87) *Summa Aurea*, ed. Jean Ribaillier (Spicilegium Bonaventurianum 16–20), Paris: éditions du CNRS and Collegium S. Bonaventurae.

William of Conches (1980) *Philosophia mundi: Ausgabe des. 1. Buchs von Wilhelm von Conches' Philosophia mit Anhang, Übersetzung und Anmerkungen*, Pretoria: University of South Africa.

———. (1997) *Dragmaticon philosophiae*, ed. Italo Ronca (with *Summa de philosophia in vulgari*, ed. Lola Badia and Jaime Pujol) (Guillelmi de Conchis opera omnia 1; Corpus Christianorum continuatio mediaeualis 152), Turnhout: Brepols.

———. (1999) *Glosae super Boetium*, ed. Lodi Nauta (Guillelmi de Conchis opera omnia 2; Corpus Christianorum continuatio mediaeualis 158), Turnhout: Brepols.

———. (2006) *Glossae super Platonem*, ed. Edouard A. Jeauneau (Guillelmi de Conchis opera omnia 3; Corpus Christianorum continuatio mediaeualis 203), Turnhout: Brepols.

William of Ockham (1984) *Quaestiones variae*, ed. Girard J. Etzkorn, Francis E. Kelley and Joseph C. Wey (*Opera Theologica* 8), St. Bonaventure: Franciscan Institute.

William of Rubruk (1990) *The Mission of Friar William of Rubruk. His Journey to the Court of the Great Khan Möngke, 1253–1255*, trans. Peter Jackson, notes and introduction by Peter Jackson and David Morgan (The Hakluyt Society, 2nd series 173), London: Hakluyt Society.

William of St Thierry (2007) *Opera omnia*, V, ed. P. Verdeyen (Corpus Christianorum continuatio mediaeualis 89A), Turnhout: Brepols.

Williams, Steven J. (2003) *The Secret of Secrets. The Scholarly Career of a Pseudo-Aristotelian Text in the Latin Middle Ages*, Ann Arbor: University of Michigan Press.

Wilson, Gordon A. (ed.) (2010) *A Companion to Henry of Ghent* (Brill's Companions to the Christian Tradition 23), Leiden: Brill.

Windeatt, Barry (1992) *Troilus and Criseyde (Oxford Guides to Chaucer)*, Oxford: Oxford University Press.

Wittig, Joseph S. (1972) '"Piers Plowman" B, Passus IX–XII: Elements in the Design of the Inward Journey', *Traditio* 28: 211–80.

Wittwer, Rudolf (2002) 'Zur lateinischen Überlieferung von Sextus Empiricus ΠΥΡΡΩΝΕΙΟΙ ΥΠΟΤΥΠΩΣΕΙΣ', *Rheinisches Museum für Philologie* n.f. 145: 366–73.

Wolfram von Eschenbach (1984) *Willehalm*, trans. Marion Gibbs and Sidney M. Johnson, Harmondsworth: Penguin.

———. (1991) *Willehalm, nach der Handschrift 857 der Stiftsbibliothek St. Gallen*, ed. and trans. Joachim Heinzle (Bibliothek des Mittelalters 9), Frankfurt: deutscher klassiker Verlag.

Woodhouse, C. M. (1986) *George Gemistos Plethon. The Last of the Hellenes*, Oxford: Oxford University Press.

Wyngaert, Anastasius van den (ed.) (1929) *Sinica Franciscana* I. *Itinera et relationes fratrum minorum saeculi xiii et xiv*, Quaracchi: Collegium S. Bonaventurae.

Yule, Sir Henry (1913) *Cathay and the Way Thither: Being a Collection of Medieval Notices of China* (Hakluyt Society 2nd series, 33), London: Hakluyt Society.

Zwingli, Huldrich (1841) *Opera* IV, ed. Melchior Schuler and Johannes Schulthess, Turin: Schulthess.

Index

Medieval writers up to c. 1400 are usually listed under their Christian names, and those from late under the surnames. But exceptions are made when an earlier author is usually known by a surname (e.g. Geoffrey Chaucer, listed under 'Chaucer').

faith, 2, 13, 15, 20–21, 36–37, 44, 47, 50,
61–63, 65–66, 69, 88, 90, 100–101, 107,
125–26, 134, 136–39, 142, 145–47, 153–
54, 156, 158, 160–62, 164n20, 170, 179,
190–91, 194, 199n34, 202–203, 207–208,
217, 219n19, 238–40, 246, 283–84, 287,
293, 298; in Christ (explicit), 32, 87–88,
90–91, 93, 168–69, 170–72, 185, 286–92,
294, 299; in Christ (implicit), 66, 125,
168–73, 175, 177–78, 185, 193, 199n35,
207, 212, 216, 281, 286–92, 294, 296–97;
in Christ (shrouded in mystery) 87, 168;
in promise (in voto) 291–92; the same
before and after Christ, 32, 169; seeking
understanding (fides quaerens intellectum), 139. See also justification, by faith
Fall, the, 37, 64, 111, 266, 271–72
Farinata, 211
fate, 59, 99–100
Faustus the Manichee, 28
fear, 130, 150, 272–73
Ficino, Marsilio, 130–31, 240–43, 245;
translations, 240; De christiana religione,
240–41; Letters, 285
Flood, the, 64, 262
Florence, 193, 211–12
Flüeller, Christoph, 206n57
Forms. See Ideas, Platonic
Fortescue, Adrian, 48n21
fortune, 51, 227, 230n56
Franciscans, 114–20, 129, 177, 273–74,
277; anonymous Franciscan author of
quaestio on Aristotle's salvation, 180;
studia of, 127n1
Franks, 67
friendship, 51
Frisia, 67
Fuxi, legendary King of China, 302

Galen, 190, 213, 273
Galonnier, Alain, 48m18
Gassendi, Pierre, 6n
Gauthier, R.-A., 138n32
Gemisthos Plethon, 7
Genghis (Chinggis) Khan, 113
Geoffrey Chaucer. See Chaucer, Geoffrey
Geoffrey of Monmouth, 70
Gerson, Jean, 236
Gilbert of Poitiers, 161
Giles of Rome, 151n74
Gilson,Étienne, 207n60
Giordano da Pisa, 193
Giovanni Boccaccio. See Boccaccio,
Giovanni

Giraldus Cambrensis, 70
glory, 39, 212; desire for, 34, 38
glosses: character of early medieval, 59n6
God, 70, 99, 121, 162, 176, 183, 185, 217,
232, 238–39, 245, 249, 253–54, 258, 260,
264, 272–76, 283–84, 287, 289, 293;
ability to act beyond the ordinary course
of nature, 196; acts of necessity, 150,
155–56; all people have a conception of,
252, 258; attributes of, 102; cannot make
us believe something false, 137; Cato is
worthiest to signify, 199; clear vision of,
186; contemplating in this life, 134–35;
contempt for, 93; the end to which the
universe is ordered, 264–65; eternity of,
26, 46; as final cause alone, 46; footprints
of, 253; freedom of, 21, 296; goodness
of, 4, 26, 51, 79, 89, 215, 265, 299–300;
incorporeity of, 26; immateriality of, 5;
injustice of, 21; infinite perfection of, 274;
justice of 3, 9, 14, 37, 51, 182, 220, 299–
300; his love, 223; mind of, 202; as object
of rightly-directed love, 35; personal, 11;
Plotinus's, 26; power of, 79; predestination by, 33, 58, 217, 245n33; prescience
of, 46, 50–51, 227, 230–31; providence
of 9, 25, 46, 51–52, 102, 138, 172, 178,
191, 210, 227, 330; as repayer of good
and evil, 66, 168, 172, 290, 2939; does
not know singulars, 150; Stoic view of, 8;
takes no care of humans, 46; as voluntary
agent, 11–12; union with, 148, 155; unity
of, 11, 74, 115, 118, 239–40, 244, 252,
256, 259, 261–62, 285, 296; unknowability of, 19, 124, 256; will of, 196,
293; wisdom of, 5, 78–79, 95; 'no word
in (Amer)Indian languages for', 257. See
also beatific vision; Christ; City of God;
existence of God; knowledge of God;
Incarnation; love, of God; monotheism;
Son of God; Trinity; Word of God
gods: of dog-headed people, 122; of European pagans in Middle Ages, 68, 70, 72;
of American Indians, 252, 256
gods of Graeco-Roman antiquity, 9, 23–24,
26, 28–29, 35, 99–100, 104, 201, 224–27,
274; compared with those of Americna
Indians, 252; are good, 29–30; as parts of
the world, 30
Golden Age, 69–70, 124–25, 199n34, 277,
296n65
good, 36, 40, 116, 148, 164–65, 168, 174–
75, 186, 230, 264, 289; common, 39; the
highest, 36, 46, 49, 51, 82, 84, 89, 103,

Nicene Creed, 115
Nicholas of Cusa, 238–40; *Cribratio Alkorani,* 239; *De pace fidei,* 238–39
Nicholas of Lyra, *Postilla super totam bibliam,* 172, 281, 289
Nicole Oresme. *See* Oresme, Nicole
Nietzsche, Friedrich, 9
Nifo, Agostino, *De intellectu,* 148
Noah, 64, 112, 131, 158, 241, 243, 258
nominalism, 236
Norway, 70
nous. See intellect
Novissima sinica, 301
Odin, 70–71

Odoacer, 42
Odoric of Pordenone, *Itinerarium,* 119–23
One, the, 26, 136
order, 40
Oresme, Nicole, 236
Origen, 6, 22
Original Sin, 12–14, 35, 65, 90, 164, 176, 191n9, 208n64, 252, 286–89, 291, 294
Orosius, 106, 191n11
Orpheus, 97, 130, 240
overwriting, 120
Ovid, 45, 190, 213
Oviédo (y Valdés), Gonzalo Fernández de, *Historia general y natural de las Indias,* 247n41

Pachacámac, 256
Padoan, Giorgio, 193
paganism: 'para-spiritual' tradition of thinking about, 1n1. *See also* Problem of Paganism; virtue, pagan
pagans: definition of, 5; imaginary, 4
pagan setting: Christian authors imagining themselves into, 68, 70–72, 99, 104–5, 214, 224
Palacios Rubios, Juan López de, *De insulis,* 288
pantheism, 260
papacy, 69
Paris. *See* University of Paris
Passion of Christ, 80, 78, 80–81
passions, 38, 86
paths of approach to problem of pagan knowledge: path of selective rejection, 137–42, 151, 244; path of unity, 137–43, 151, 236, 241, 244. *See also (for path of limited relativism),* relativism, limited
patience, 36

patriarchs of early chapters of Genesis, 64–65, 90, 131, 157, 176, 183, 192, 241, 296
Patricida, 99
Paul (the Apostle), 19–21, 30–32, 43, 65–66, 77, 91, 158, 183, 240, 298. *See also* Seneca, supposed correspondence with St Paul
Paul the Deacon, *Historia Lombardorum,* 67
Pauline minimum, 66, 87, 92, 162, 168–69, 172, 290, 293
peace, 36, 38–39, 84, 134, 167, 204, 206, 238–39
Pecham (Peckham). *See* John Pecham
Pelagianism, 216–17
Pelagius, 12, 33, 37, 64–65, 296; Letter to *Demetriades,* 65
Pentecost, 220
perception by the senses, 26, 136
Peripatetics. *See* Aristotelianism
person, 44
Peru, 247–48, 256–57
Peter, Saint, 175, 182–83, 292
Peter Abelard, 1n1, 7, 20n4, 73–97, 158, 160–61, 168, 172–73, 178, 191, 238, 241, 243, 256, 266, 271, 299, 304; teacher of John of Salisbury, 100, 102; *Collationes,* 10, 73–74, 81–85, 88n51, 89n56; Commentary on Romans, 94n; *Problemata Heloissae,* 92–93, 172; *Scito teipsum,* 73n1, 93–94, 175; *Sententie,* 73n1, 74n4, 88n52, 94n; *Soliloquium,* 78; *Theologia Christiana,* 70n49, 73–82, 85–91, 96–97, 105, 124–25, 275; *Theologia Scholarium,* 73–80, 82, 87–88, 90, 96–97, 124–25; *Theologia Summi Boni,* 73–80, 82, 88, 96–97. *See also* (works reflecting his views), *Commentarius Cantabrigiensis, Quaestiones in epistolas Pauli*
Peter Damian, 243
Peter Martyr d'Anghiera, 247–48
Peter of Dusburg, *Chronica terrae prussiae,* 68–69, 116n30
Peter of Ailly, 237
Peter the Lombard, *Sentences,* 134, 162, 169–70, 175, 238. *For commentaries on* Sentences, *see* Albert the Great, Bonaventure, Durandus of St Pourçain, John Major, Richard of Middleton, Thomas Aquinas
Peter the Venerable, 110
Philip the Chancellor, 140n36; *Summa de bono,* 181
Philo Judaeus, 21n7

Thomas, Saint, of India, 255, 258
Thomas Aquinas, 3, 133, 137, 140,
144–45, 151, 154, 160, 163, 167, 172,
183, 191n9, 193, 198, 201n43, 202–3,
206n56, 207, 209, 212, 221, 236–37,
241, 244–45, 263–64, 281–82, 297, 299;
commentaries on Aristotle, 139; almost
condemned, 151n74; Commentary on
Boethius *De trinitate*, 137–38; Commentary on Romans, 174; Commentary
on *Sentences*, 140, 143, 163, 170–71,
174–75, 178, 180n83, 181; *De aeternitate mundi*, 140–41, 247; *De unitate
intellectus*, 143–44; *De veritate*, 170–71,
174, 178; *De virtutibus*, 163; *Summa
contra Gentiles*, 138, 140, 143; *Summa
Theologiae*, 11n, 14n14, 140, 143,
163–65, 170, 174, 184, 238, 265. For
commentaries on *Summa Theologiae*, see
Cajetan, Cardinal; Suárez, Francisco; and
Vitoria, Francisco de
Thomas Bradwardine, *De causa Dei*, 158–
59, 178, 184–87, 241, 299
Thomas of Cantimpré, *De natura rerum*,
124
Thomas de Vio. *See* Cajetan
Thoth, 75
thought experiments, 82
time, 46, 139–41
Todorov, Tzvetan, *Nous et les autres*, 280
Tolan, John, 110n4
toleration, 23, 239
Topiltzin, 255
Torrell, Jean-Pierre, 174n56
translation: by Boethius, 44; of Boethius's
Consolation, 42; of Platonist books into
Latin, 26
Trajan, 104; story of Pope Gregory and, 10,
13n13, 63–64, 91–92, 103–4, 180–82,
195–97, 214–19, 283–84
Trent, Council of, 15n16, 238
Trigault, Nicholas, 261
Trinity, 28, 43–44, 58, 99, 131, 140, 150,
156, 209, 239, 291; appropriation of
terms to person of, 95; counter-Trinity
of Mahumet, Tervagan and Apollin, 110,
113; known by pagan philosophers,
73–80, 88–90, 96, 124, 179; not known
by pagan philosophers, 137; Trithemius,
Johannes, *Curiositas regia*, 286–87
Troncarelli, Fabio, 48n21, 59n6
Troy, 190, 224, 228–29
truth, 44, 52, 61–62, 103, 132–33, 140,
145, 149, 154, 156, 180, 201, 205;

eternal, 299; of reason in contradiction
with truth of faith, 150–51; supernatural,
203; truth-value, 146
Tupí. *See* Indians of America, Tupí
Turks, 238
Tyre, 93

unbelief, 5, 93, 164, 265; culpable and non-
culpable, 212n77; negative and positive,
14, 172–73, 291
universe: beginning of. *See* beginning, the
universe has no
universals, 102, 136, 143–44, 171, 236
universities, 235–36, 238; Italian, 244
University of Bologna, 244, 282
University of Cambridge, 158
University of Cologne, 237–38, 282n3
University of Heidelberg, 237
University of Oxford, 127–29, 158, 222n26,
236
University of Padua, 244
University of Paris, 127–29, 133, 236, 250,
287. *See also* Arts Faculty of Paris
University of Salamanca, 238
University of Vienna, 236
Uppsala, 68
Uthred of Bodon, 185–86
Utopia, 268–72

Valentinian, Emperor, 91–92
Valerius Maximus, *Factorum ac dictorum
memorabilium libri IX*, 85–87
Valla, Lorenzo, 7, 263–68, 273–74; *De vero
falsoque bono*, 266n13; *De voluptate*,
266–69; *Repastinatio dialectice et phi-
losophie*, 268n26
Valladolid, Disputation at, 251–52
Vandals, 67
Varro, 25, 36
Vega, Andreas, 291n46, 297; *De iustifica-
tione*, 290–91
Venantius Fortunatus, 57
Vernani, Guido. *See* Guido Vernani
Vespucci, Amerigo, 247–48, 268
Veszprémy, László, 70n51
via antiqua/ via moderna, 157, 235–38,
281–82
vices, 36, 38, 114, 167n31, 182, 272
Vincent of Beauvais, 7; *Speculum historiale*,
105–107, 118–19, 124
Virgil: as character in Dante's *Commedia
divina* 2–3, 188–93, 198–99, 208–210;
Aeneid, 192, 196–97, 209, 224; *Eclogues*,
75, 77, 194

Printed in Great Britain
by Amazon

62285642R00211